"Gregory Charles is dangerous. Not only is he a good thinker, he is a good writer."

Dr. Hunter S. Thompson, Journalist and Author "Fear and Loathing in Las Vegas"

~~~

"Going Down Under will inspire you and leave you begging for more. Gregory Charles is a must read for anyone seeking a roadmap to navigate these challenging times. He turns the Mahatma Gandhi philosophy--to change the world you first have to change yourself--into a new way of living. How can you blame everyone else when you realize you create your own reality? Gregory loved the activism of the 1960s as I did. Now he takes you on a new journey to discover the 'inside job' of the next great frontier. If you feel ready to organize a personal prison break out of the limitations of the human condition, Gregory Charles is passing out keys to anyone who reads this book."

Rennie Davis, Foundation for Humanity and Chicago 7 Member

~~~

"Gregory Charles has plumbed the depths of the human experience to a level few souls have dared to go. He brings wisdom and a rare authenticity to his work as a spiritual teacher, with a message of profound significance for the times in which we live."

Swami Brahmananda, (In The Lineage Of Swami Muktananda)

~~~

"Gregory has spoken at the university on a variety of topics. His knowledge and insight gives his perspective and opinions a power that opens up new ways of seeing the world. He always leaves everyone engaged, alive, and seeing with greater clarity the world and their lives and place in it. He uses humor, directness, wisdom, gentle support, and encouragement to guide participants toward their declared goals."

Glenda D. Walden, PH.D., Instructor in Sociology, UC Boulder

~~~

"Life is becoming more twisted and surreal every day. Into this maelstrom appears the wizard Gregory Charles. He is a dreamer and visionary of high order, an urban shaman, mystical yet rational. His gift to 'see' how your genius can express is uncanny. His insights provide guidance you'll need during these weird times."

Bobby Richards, Hi-Tech Entrepreneur

~~~

"I was Head of Development for the Bank of Ireland and am now a self employed International Consultant. I want to thank you for your considerable input to where I am today. You gave me a new perspective on life and I haven't looked back since. People who know me well tell me I've become a new person. As well as work I have become much more open in relationships. I genuinely believe that you can add value for just about anyone in any situation."

Niall Croty, International Consultant

~~~

Going Down under

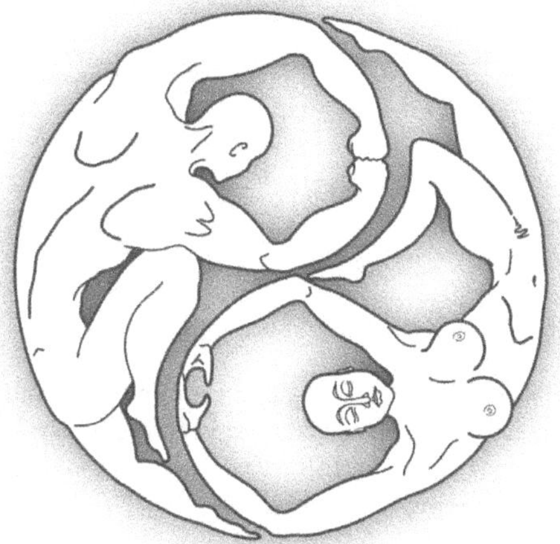

The transcript of an extraordinary 10 day seminar exploring relationships, sexuality & aliveness

LED BY

GREGORY CHARLES

THE AUSSIE RELATIONSHIP GURU

Going Down Under

The transcript of an extraordinary 10 day Seminar on relationships, sexuality and aliveness.

Led by Gregory Charles, The Aussie Relationship Guru

ISBN 978-0-9849401-0-3

The original Yin-Yang cover design by Luke Seer. It is owned and ™ by Look At It llc, Denver, CO

To my son Luke,

the future and the

health of humanity.

Foreword

I imagine him standing at the front of the room, eyes shining. An impish professor, he delivers brilliant guidance, offering imaginative metaphors to help explain ground-breaking ideas. The crowd groans and giggles in response to his many puns. Colorful gesticulations and waves of laughter enliven his words. People smile with one another as he drops a double entendre, they are moved to tears as he brings them through emotional obstacles, they breathe deeply after experiencing a challenging process. Magic is happening here. Reading Going Down Under has the capacity to bring you on a similar journey.

Welcome to the transcript of an Australian Sex and Relationships Seminar led by Gregory Charles. In choosing to read this book, you have given yourself an experience that will bring clarity to some of the most important aspects of human sexuality. Along with the book itself, the accompanying videos and suggested processes provide a framework with which you can delve into yourself, let go of judgement, uncover desires, and develop a connection with your truth that will inform and brighten every facet of your life.

Although I was not physically present for this particular one, I have attended several of Gregory's seminars and have experienced the rewards firsthand. I have dissolved menstrual cramps, unburdened relationships with my family, freed myself from the repetition of unhealthy romances, unleashed mind-blowing orgasms I did not know were possible, let go of physical trauma, healed body image issues, brightened my complexion, and released the weight of so many unhealthy social expectations. The list continues, and I am only one person. Thousands have been touched in profound ways by the awareness gained during Gregory's seminars.

Who am I to be singing the praises of this work? My name is Katrina Pratt and I grew up in a small town in New Hampshire. When I was eighteen I moved to Colorado where, after a weak attempt at University life, I began my own search for meaning. Struggling with an eating disorder and the general dissatisfaction with the society in which I was expected to participate, I left school to heal myself.

Traveling through Western Europe, making my way to Australia and probing the world of psychology, I gave myself an introduction to broader social awareness. I enrolled in massage school, and studied various approaches to natural medicine and energetic healing. I became interested in Gestalt psychology, Eastern philosophy, herbology and Anais Niin. Eventually I returned to school for a more formal educational experience, focusing on medical anthropology and dance for my degree. During that time I also taught preschool, researching child psychology and the socialization process along the way. I spent summers in Peru, working at a water birthing clinic and writing about the political colonization of traditional medicine.

Now, at the age of 27, after years of critical analysis both in and out of the academic realm, I am proud to be working with Gregory as we travel the world. I am his assistant and student. In all my explorations, I find he has answers to my endless flow of questions. Even after six years of friendship, employment and apprenticeship, I am still regularly astounded at his levels of insight. His expertise in alternative healing, personal growth, and the betterment of relationships, restores balance to individual lives and bring humanness back to the social organism.

Gregory's approach to personal growth is a fusion of Western psychology, Eastern philosophy, astrology, metaphysics and his extensive life experiences. His genius is reminiscent of ideas posed by great minds such as Wilhelm Reich, Carl Jung, and Mahatma Ghandi. While his work bears resemblance to that of others, the similarities in his ideas and those that came before him are unintended consequences of a lifelong search for truth and understanding. Through broad travel, the exploration of philosophy and religion, deep feeling release, extensive research into alternative medicine and an unwavering commitment to personal growth and excellence, Gregory has created a phenomenal body of knowledge and healing techniques.

His is the brilliant missing piece to academic theory. Gregory's wisdom is presented in such a way that the journey to personal freedom ceases to be a fantastical idea and becomes rooted in a process available to anyone committed to healing themselves. Likewise, this book is not just a summation of that which is presented during a Sex and Relationship Seminar, it is the actual transcript, an invitation for you to see the processes in action. Here is an opportunity to not only observe a ten-day metamorphosis, but to participate in one.

What does this mean? In short, Gregory suggests that it is through braving fear and pain, blocks and resistance, that we begin to reclaim the parts of ourselves hidden behind the limitations of social conditioning and upbringing. Unless we do so, we remain pale versions of the beauty and greatness of which we are all inherently capable. In his words, we stay 'bonsai people,' appearing normal, yet in reality stunted for a lack of nutrient-rich soil.

Reading Going Down Under is a way of cultivating that soil. The experiences shared in the pages that follow are precious and relevant to anyone who seeks to heal sexually and explore new ways of engaging in relationships. While the focus of the book is on human connection, the journey is inward. As Gregory often says, "You can't have a better relationship with someone else than you have with yourself."

Being Australian and speaking to a group of mostly Australian participants, Gregory often uses Australianisms with which the average American might be unfamiliar. For this reason, as well as a growing legacy of overused new age self-help terms, a glossary has been included to help clarify nomenclature that has either fallen victim to a dilution of meaning or may be culturally misunderstood. The fact remains, however, that within this context, much of the material is presented in a way that is culturally different. The social ethos in which The Sex and Relationships Seminar is conducted varies both subtly and explicitly from that of the political correctness often expected in a similar environment, were one to exist in the United States. Part of the inherent genius of this book arises out of the creation of a space where honesty and fantasy can live without being limited by the 'correctness' of language.

Here people had the opportunity to share the parts of themselves that would be shunned in a group heavily concerned with tiptoeing around social taboo. It is this very dance that keeps so many of us stuck in fear about what we will find if we dig too deep. The glossary will hopefully help to ameliorate confusion about specific terms or phrases, but is in no way an attempt at softening the language. The allowance, indeed the welcoming of language and ideas considered inappropriate, is often the very thing that opens us to release destructive belief systems.

Especially if you have not previously read a transcript, you may have to adjust to this format. Be assured, you will quickly fall into the rhythm of the book. Going Down Under is more than a self-help narrative. It is an experience. I have read it several times and with each re-acquaintance, I am rocked with revelations and intensified self-awareness.

As a documented conversation, there are times when transitions from one topic to another may seem abrupt. During these moments it is possible that the group took a break, that someone was experiencing (non-verbally) an emotional release, or simply that within the framework of a conversation, the energetic exchange is not fully communicated through words. These places are marked with ***.

Congratulations. You are now privy to an extraordinary dialogue. Gregory articulates wisdom that has the potential to magnify your understanding of sex, relationships and how to create what you want in life.

Enjoy the ride!

Katrina Pratt, Emerald Beach, Australia

Contents

Foreword	vii
Author's note	1
Day 1	5
Day 2	37
Day 3	69
Day 4	103
Day 5	155
Day 6	189
Day 7	247
Day 8	275
Day 9	305
Day 10	353
Glossary	383
Acknowledgements	387
About Gregory Charles	391

Author's note

It was a beautiful sunny summer in the coastal hills of Australia. In a large modern farmhouse, surrounded by acres of rolling green paddocks overlooking the Pacific Ocean, I ran my residential 10-day Sex and Relationships Seminar.

People from all over the world - Australia, England, and other parts of Europe - came together (okay, bad pun) to participate. It was a diverse crowd including married, single, gay, straight, older, younger men and women. The prerequisite for doing the Sex and Relationship Seminar, as well as a common denominator, was that everyone had already completed my 3-day The Living Game Seminar with me.

Everyone agreed for me to record the seminar on audio tape and have it transcribed and eventually published. The agreement was that I promised to maintain their confidentiality. I had already delivered many similar Sex and Relationship Seminars in Australia. Everyone involved agreed that "the next time" it needed to be taped: all that transpired, all that was shared within the group, and the obvious value to the participants should be shared with others too. Thus, the idea of this book grew. It was during the seminar that the name for this book came to me. I immediately shared it with the group and it was met with laughter, hilarity and approval.

The tapes of the seminar were transcribed and edited to remove chit chat and some of the less relevant titillating details as well as some processes not easily communicated in written form. The book became an underground sensation in Sydney at the time.

For most of the last 20 years I have been living and traveling in the United States of America. During that time I have resided in many regions and cities, visited over half the states, and driven hundreds of thousands of miles on road trips. I have lectured at two American universities and made multiple media appearances both local and national. I have lived among the rich and the poor, the abled and disabled, religious fanatics and atheists. I have read countless books and had innumerable conversations with a wide range of people throughout the country - from the mega-rich in Aspen to teen gang-bangers in San Francisco to good old boys at hunting camp in West Virginia.

Sadly, I have come to the conclusion that America is a waning empire, slowly dying from the seeds of destruction it has sown over the last 50 years. After having spent so much time in the country, I feel at home here. I realize that something must change if we want to preserve the visionary capability of the United States. Unless we have a real revolution in thought, belief, value and action, it is surely doomed. Recently, the cultural imbalances I have observed and commented on for decades, have produced an economic and political meltdown. We have also had the astonishing election of Barack Obama to the Presidency - a dramatic example of the nation's ability to regenerate itself and a major reason why I feel ready to release this book in America.

In my years here, I have attempted to untangle and understand the many sources of dysfunction in America. I have looked at issues like race, money, religion, and Puritanism and have come to a firm conclusion. What we really need is a sexual revolution.

We need to have a sexual revolution that frees our passion and pleasure for life, that opens us to our glory as human beings. Until we have that collective breakthrough, we will continue blocking, suppressing, and judging all of our inherently wonderful human energy. Instead, it will continue to be funneled into destructive paths like war and vengeance, hate and suppression, torture and oppression.

It is time to complete the sexual revolution that began in the 60's, that said, "Make love, not war." The self-evident phrase that emerged publicly during the same era, "Fighting for Peace is like Fucking for Virginity," is an important reminder.

The more time I spend in America, the more I see the vast differences in how Australians approach sex and relationships. It is clear to me that Aussies really took the sexual revolution to heart, while in America, the combined reactionary forces of religion, puritanism and government have done everything possible to stifle and dismantle the openings that occurred in the 1960's.

Perhaps this comes from core cultural conditioning: whereas the first white Americans were Puritans - uptight, controlling god freaks - Australia's first whites were convicts (both male and female) and their guards. The first night they landed on Sydney's shores after a grueling six month boat trip from England, they celebrated with a wild drunken orgy on the beach of what is now Circular Quay, next to the Sydney Opera House. America was baptized in prayer, penitence and punishment, and Australia was baptized in song, semen and alcohol!

Unfortunately, many Americans are completely ignorant about the fundamental cultural beliefs that keep their country stuck in guilt, fear and righteousness. There are so many examples of the propaganda that exists here to convince Americans that America is "the best country in the world." It is a daily drumbeat that blocks out almost all comparisons to other countries with actual better conditions.

The struggle for women's rights in America is a perfect example. For 20 years in America I have regularly been told that Aussie men are misogynistic. The truth is that Australia was one of the first countries in the world where women got the vote (effortlessly). It was many decades before women in America formed the Suffragette movement and were jailed, beaten, raped and even killed just for participating in protests demanding the right to vote. Another example: 40 years ago all women got equal pay for equal work in Australia where in America today they still average only 70% of men's pay.

Power struggles like this reflect core relationship issues in America. I was shocked by the underlying beliefs about, and almost universal dynamic of power and control games between men and women including the suspicion, anger, ridicule and even violence of both genders toward one another. I had to ask friends what "pussy-whipped" meant when I came here, having never heard the term nor seen it in action anywhere else I had traveled in the world. I learned about the whore-john dynamic in American relationships - a common situation where women try to look beautiful to get a rich man and men believe that the more money they earn the prettier the woman they will get. In fact, a survey in early 2009 had 75% of women in America saying they would marry for money (Prince and Associates). I heard the constant refrain that men are bastards, brutes, not to be trusted, afraid to commit, among other put-downs and ridicule. Men told me that women are sexually withholding, mean, money grubbing, make no sense, etc. Although I heard it often from individuals, this litany of mutual rage is obvious when listening to the wild applause given to stand-up comedians when they are exploiting such perspectives.

Americans would ask me how it was different in Australia and I would reply, "Well, for starters, men and women like each other. Every man I know has close female friends and every woman I know has close male friends." They would look at me like I was from another planet. "I am," I tell them, "I am an Austr-alien."

It is said that the truth is the first casualty of war. No, it is not. The first casualty is love. We kill love and then we kill truth.

After reflecting on the relationship struggles within this country, on both individual and national levels, it became clear that it is time to get this book out there again, only this time in America. I offer it not as the answer, but as a part of the conversation that we people need to be having.

I hope you enjoy it!

Gregory Charles

Day 1

"It's not until you do something different that you start to see what you have been doing."

ENERGY RELEASE - BELIEFS AND CONDITIONING - INITIATING - BREAKING PATTERNS - GROWING COMMITMENTS - HANDLING RESPONSES - POWER GAMES

(Note from Gregory: "Dynamic Meditation was created for Westerners as an acknowledgement that they need movement and action. In is in four parts, up to 10 minutes each, with eyes closed. First is Catharsis, where people stand and yell and scream and make all the noise they can. Next is Who - where people bounce gently (or not) on their feet saying the word "Who?" with each bounce. Then comes Freeze where participants do just that, not moving a muscle, and ends with Natural Dance, with free-form movement. We began each day of the seminar with a 40 minute Dynamic Meditation to get people to loosen up, get their energy flowing, and to get everyone Present in the seminar.")

Participant: ...Sweat drops are a real challenge for me. When I started doing the Dynamic, it would drive me crazy when they were running down my nose and now I really enjoy that. This morning in the Freeze section of Dynamic there was this real mother of a sweat drop I could feel, it was blissful but it was tickling me, and then it just sat there. It was incredible, and what I realized was that I can't stand frustration. It was like "DO something will you, and keep doing it. Don't sit there, do something!" I finally wiped it off. Then I immediately started beating myself up, like "Oh you've got no patience" etc. So finally I made a commitment: "that the next sweat drop, I'll absolutely stay with it, whatever it takes, if it drives me out of my head." It was amazing, the sweat drops kept moving. Not one of them would sit still.

Participant: ...That part of the process is about being still, and the fundamental thing is just my inability to be still, or more my resistance to being TOTALLY still. There's a level where for me survival is called keep moving, keep doing something.

Participant: ...One of the things that happens for me sometimes in the Who, is that suddenly I'm in it and what's happening is that instead of my body kicking me up, and then being on the downstroke, the Who kicks me up and I'm a yo-yo and the Who is the hand that is making my body rise again. It's strange, it's like anti-gravity, like my natural space is to be up and the Who takes me up and then when I end the Who my body comes back but it's not meant to be down there. I don't know whether that makes sense but it's reversed. It's great. The energy takes over.

Gregory: A story I've shared with a few people that really astounded them about the sort of energy we have in our bodies and that we lock in our bodies: When I did Primal Feeling Release work, I finally hit total rage in a session. I was 27 and I'd been totally shut off from my anger. I used to weigh 17 stone (240 pounds), and I was a "nice" Libra who never got angry. It took me many feeling release sessions to feel anger and when I finally did I became Rage. I was lying on my back in the session room that was not quite as big as this room. As I dropped into anger my whole body, from lying on my back, propelled itself like that (makes a sweeping hand gesture) across the room, a good ten, twelve feet. My body hit the floor and went straight back to where it had started. There was absolutely no muscle effort involved, it was just bang bang, my whole body just propelled through the air and I hit and there was absolutely no pain, no bruises, nothing. It was just voom VOOM. I stopped for a second and looked at the facilitator and she said "it's safe go with it". I shut my eyes and my body took off again, and for 5 minutes I bounced around the room and I was literally hitting walls and the floor full-on and just bouncing back. My hands were beside me for the whole time and I was just bouncing around the room. It was like flying. It was extraordinary. In the following 3 weeks I lost 3 stone (42 pounds). Because all that anger was gone, I didn't need to hang on to all the weight to protect me, like a car bumper bar.

Participant: ...In the Catharsis section I found out how much pain I have inside me.

Participant: ...I was switching from crying to laughing.

Gregory: That's called laughing release. They're associated by the way. I'll often have people laugh where I can't see their face and I can't tell whether they're laughing or crying. What passes for laughter is often camouflage crying. That's why so many jokes are painful. The only form of non-violent humor is a pun. All other jokes are about pain, or put downs. Think about it.

Participant: ...I had several sensations all the way through and in the Who I felt nauseated.

Participant: ...With the free dancing I felt parts of me pre-empting what I was doing. It was like trying to reach for the sky, and I couldn't reach far enough, like I was trying to pull myself apart, go sideways and up. Then later on in that same session I felt weaker and weaker and I couldn't even hold my arms up.

Gregory: Sometimes weakness is a reaction. We've learnt to hold our energy down and keep ourselves disempowered on every level. So as you start to do things like Dynamic and your energy starts to open and lift out, then the old controller that learnt or was taught that it's only safe if your energy is kept low, can come back in and go ZAP and shoot your energy back down. That's where you feel really weak, that's one possibility. It's simply a matter of acknowledging to yourself "yes my energy is coming up and it's safe." And then as you do it more your body gets the message, "hey, I'm doing this stuff that I've believed isn't safe and the sky hasn't fallen in." In other words, it is safe.

We carry many beliefs about what is and what is not safe, and about what we should and should not like, and we are not even aware of them, or that they are programmed in us. While we stay unaware of them they run us on automatic pilot.

It's not until you do something different that you start to see what you have been doing unconsciously as a result of your conditioning.

While you're doing everything the same as you always have, the conditioning is invisible. When you start doing things, life itself, differently, the beliefs and voices or reactions start going, that's when you get to see how they work and see what they are. If you want to keep doing the new thing, the more you do it then the more you're giving that old conditioning the new message. You're re-conditioning yourself. You're creating a new program that says it's now safe to do this, whereas the old program has said that it's not safe to do this.

We've learnt to be really scared of new sensations.

I know that I'm going to feel a hell of a lot better if I do the Dynamic than if I don't. But the sensations I have when I don't do the Dynamic are more familiar and therefore they feel safer. I'm still attached to safe sensations at times. When I do it, I have a new sensation and it's like testing the water. The more I let myself have them the safer it gets.

When you acknowledge stuff you can change it. It's that simple. With this body stuff you get a whole new level of what acknowledgement is about. The three fundamentals of The Living Game Seminar are acknowledgement, choice and sharing (action). Just to acknowledge something immediately begins to change it. Because the moment you acknowledge it you're already making a more conscious choice about it.

What we're good at is not acknowledging that because the fear is if I see how hurt and lonely we've been then not only do we have it, but we'll see that we are stuck with it. So the belief is that if we block it out, we might be hurt and lonely but at least it's not painful. So we anesthetized the pain and thus ourselves. But by seeing it you can do something about it. During the Catharsis, with everyone yelling and screaming, what occurred to me was that the whole planet hurts this much. Billions of people on the planet could walk into a room like this and access that sort of hurt and sadness and anger and rage and pain. Now instead of putting energy into avoiding how hurt and lonely you feel you can put the same amount of energy into doing something about it. It's great.

***

Participant: ...I feel the need to touch, almost too much ...

Gregory: The only thing to do with temptation is to give in to it. One of the things that will happen through touching others a lot is that you'll also touch yourself a lot more deeply. The more fully you touch yourself the less you need to touch and you simply do it because it's so enjoyable. Need is a funny word, because need can mean needy, as in dependent and needy. We all have a need to touch, just as we have a need to eat or breathe. We've had that need shut off, so what results is we get needy about it. So have it, fill it up.

The creative spark occurs when people work in groups and combine energies. It is very powerful. And here we are in a society that supports you in staying isolated. It's crazy.

So what's the problem with sex?

Participants: (various) …It's dirty …hard to get …the rules say it has to be one person at a time …it's uncovering …it's not safe to let go …too many damn rules …there's no manual.

Gregory: No you can have it manual - it's called a hand job!

Participants: …(group) Groan!

Participants: (various) …Giving is a problem …so is receiving …the confusion between sex and relationships …mind games, that's another version …expectations …all the strings that are attached.

Gregory: Do you notice that people never sweat in your fantasies, and they never get up to go to the bathroom. And they don't ever fart while you're having a 69.

I have a Virgo friend who's been resisting doing this seminar and she said, "I'd do it, but it's all those bodily juices I'd have to deal with." Virgo's idea of perfect sex is no juices or sweat involved.

Participants: …Sex is physically confronting …paranoia about my body …why is Virgo categorized?

Gregory: Virgos have got a thing about purity and cleanliness. The generalization about them as a group is that they like everything ordered. You can always pick who has lots of Virgo energy at work: they're the one who picks all the fluff off the carpet. So what else doesn't work about sex?

Participants: …Not letting people close …fear of judgement, is it big enough? …am I good enough, my body.

Gregory: So performance judgements.

Participant: …Guilt.

Gregory: Right. Like, "God will get me."

Participant: ...Being a female and the way I've been brought up, the male has the power. He has the car, he's got the power and I just sit there. I felt it was the same with sex, until I started experimenting and found that doing it for me made a whole lot of difference, and it's still hard.

Gregory: What did you do differently that made a lot of difference?

Participant: ...I set up a relationship and approached somebody, which I've never done before. Then I felt that I was in control. Instead of thinking "is it right, will he think I'm too aggressive?" I allowed my feelings to flow. That was great.

Gregory: It's fascinating what women believe about men: they own the car so you feel like they've got the power. People spend a lot of their life to get rich enough to have someone drive them around. One of the greatest status symbols in our society is to have a chauffeur.

The point I'm making is that it's not just what you do it's how you view what you do. Women have also exacerbated their perceived role by having a picture that they're powerless, ineffective and weak. You can be picked up and dropped off and feel weak and passive or you can be picked up and dropped off and know how powerful you are to create a chauffeur!

Participant: ...In our society, the men are expected to make an approach. I don't agree with that. We're expected to make all the bloody rules and it's a pain in the butt, rather than having an equal partnership where you both feel free to make any moves, sexual or otherwise. It's always "unless I get off my butt and do something" nothing happens.

Gregory: This is a huge issue and there's so many parts to it, but one of the things is to take responsibility for the responses you generate. If you are approaching men, and getting negative responses, then they're reflecting your judgement that you shouldn't be strong, aggressive and forward. Then you go back into agreement with that judgement.

What I'm hearing is: let's say 60% of you is traditional role playing, and 40% of you is saying, "Screw that. I want to do it differently." So the 40% of you acts and you walk up to a man and say, "I really want to do it with you', i.e. you make the move. You probably choose the men whose response is, "AAAAAH," to reflect the 60% of you that is saying, "AAAAH! What the hell am I doing?" Then the adventurous 40% of you yells: "AAAAAH

...What the hell am I doing?" So you go into the agreement with the 60% and it gets to win: you retreat back to the old pattern.

So take responsibility for that. So many women fall into this trap. In The Living Game Seminar it comes up again and again. I'll start talking about doing things differently, doing new things, having new experiences. I'll say, "So, women, why not go out and put the hard word on a man," and I know when I say it at least 2 or 3 if not half the women in the room are going to say, "I tried that once. And got a rejection response." Of course you did, so you can give up, or you can take responsibility for it and look for men who like that approach.

Many men acknowledge that they like women making the first approach to them. I love it, and got to a point a couple of years ago where I made a commitment to myself not to proposition any women, not to make any advances. I was so tired of that game. I made a commitment that I would only go to bed with women who propositioned me. It was a scary commitment to make because I realized that I may be waiting a long time!

It took three or four weeks and then I was deluged with women I've known for ages, saying, "I was thinking about you the other night and I'd really like to go to bed with you." When I was willing to change inside then things changed outside. Now it's about 50-50. It's not an issue anymore. If I like someone I might say, "Hey I'd really like to go to bed with you," and sometimes I get "yes" and sometimes it's "no," and sometimes women say to me, "Hey I'd really like to go bed with you." And sometimes my response is "yes" and sometimes it's "no." The balance happens.

Participant: ...Getting back to control. I realized over the last 3 or 4 years that subconsciously I might have been putting out vibes, so certain people show up in my life, but I have no idea how to handle attracting a man who realizes that I would like to have sex with him. So, what I'm saying is I would like to be more in control.

Gregory: The way it's been, is that the man appears to be in control. That's the traditional relationship. That's the story that we've bought; that men have controlled women and they've controlled relationships. What hasn't been acknowledged is the women controlling the men who think they're in control.

Control is more than it appears to be. An example from my nursing days; there are people who appear to be totally powerless, they are grossly retarded - "vegetables" - zero IQ. They can't talk, or walk, they can't feed themselves. They appear to be the most un-controlling human beings on the planet. They can't even control their bowels.

Yet have a look at the control they have. They have the Government and the community spending a fortune on them, something like $55,000 a year each. They are so controlling that they sit there and get fed, washed, bathed, dressed and carried. That's like living your life as an Eastern Potentate. Phenomenal control from a totally passive posture.

What has existed is a structure in relationships where men and women have simply played different control games. Men have had the overt control and women control by less obvious methods.

In your questionnaires for this seminar a lot of you had either a fear or a desire to lose control. You either fear losing control, or you want to learn to lose control. We've come from a Judeo - Christian cultural background where Man(kind) dominates the Earth, and look what we've done with nature. We live in the incredibly arrogant belief that we can dominate nature, and we're learning the folly of that belief.

In relationships we control and dominate other people. Now the trap for women is to say, "Well I'm sick of these suckers dominating me so I'll do it to them!" A good example of where women fall into that is in business, where many women think that to be successful in business is to be more like men than men, and just play men's games better. What you end up with is men without dicks.

Now the joke is that at the same time men are getting sick of playing those old games in business. They're looking for a better way. So as they're stepping into new possibilities women are taking up their role. Men have already spent 3000 years finding out it doesn't work.

Participant: ...Is that really happening though?

Gregory: In segments of society it's happening. In business I have been having a lot of interaction with many successful, wealthy and powerful business people, specifically men. These guys are just sitting there saying,

"I don't want to do business like this. I've done it, I've made it, there's got to be more to life than this shit."

At the moment I've got a 100% success rate in enrolling the heads of successful companies into The Living Game Seminar. That's the degree to which successful men in business are looking for new ways. But if women in business don't wake up fast they'll step into the old roles thinking that that's how you win. The men are already learning that that's not how you really win.

The opportunity for women is to be powerful in their own right just as a lot of men are becoming powerful men in their own right, letting go of the old roles. But while you have any relationship based on unconscious control, then you have a power game. You see the old type of relationship where the man was nominally in control and the woman nominally felt hard-done-by or passive or weak or out of control. Whenever that situation arises she has to do something to re-establish control in order to feel safe.

Participants: ...What? ...I didn't hear it ...went blank.

Gregory: You and a lot of others. I'll say it again. Take it off relationships. In any situation where you feel like someone else is in control of you and you feel little, weak and powerless, you have to find a way to re-establish some control so that you feel safe. It might be to mess them up. It might be to sabotage them. It might be to rebel against them. It might be to leave the situation.

When some unconscious control exists, something has to balance it. That is happening in the context of a power game. In a relationship that is based on struggling for who is going to be on top, you're in a power game and you're putting your energy into winning and beating.

Participant: ...I don't like being passive or accommodating. Yet I don't want to be aggressive and controlled so I just back off.

Participant: ...It should be mutual, shouldn't it?

Gregory: I'm not saying it should be, all I'm saying is we've done relationships on the basis of a power game. Therefore, if you don't feel like you're in control then one urge is to be on top, to be in control. But that doesn't solve it. That just keeps you stuck in the power game. You may feel in control but you won't feel safe, because even if you get to be in control, then you're scared you'll lose it. So you must go into heavier control to reassure your fears. This is why dictators become more and more repressive. I don't know how to have an enjoyable, satisfying and fulfilling relationship on that basis.

Take it off close personal relationship, and have a look at how you organized breakfast this morning. Who was in control?

Participant: ...Each of us.

Gregory: Yes, and did someone set up as a leader to guide things or did leadership move around?

Participant: ...Yes, the latter.

Gregory: O.K. What usually happens in a situation like that, is that everyone is in control and there is a designated leader, or leadership moves from person to person. There are suggestions, guidance and coaching such as "Where's this?" "It's over there." "Don't forget to wash your plate," etc. ...There is interchange with everyone as equal, valid and valuable individuals.

Now that is a relationship you are having. That's called a group relationship. There is no control game and no power game and everyone acknowledges everyone else's right to get what they want their way within the context and the purpose of the relationship, which is called, "Let's have breakfast."

Get the difference? Now can you just spend a moment and see if you can visualize running your personal sexual relationships like you ran breakfast. Did anyone think, "Oh I'd like to sit with them and have breakfast" and you went and sat down? Did anyone do that? Great. Did anyone have the experience of someone sitting near you and you didn't want them to and you moved away. Great. How would it work if you ran your sexuality like that? Gee I'd like to do it with you. Gee that would be good. Can I come and sit over there and we'll make out? You know what I mean?

It's just a different position to come from. It has nothing to do with roles, control, and winning. It has nothing to do with possessiveness. It has nothing to do with pay-back. It is to do with you getting what you want, with everyone around you getting what they want, simply and honestly. No ego, so no-thing to prove or fight over.

You all get what you want together. One of the most powerful sexual relationships I have ever had is with a friend of mine, a woman. I've never had sex with her. It's just never been there but one of the things we do is share in great depth what our sexual relationships are like and it's fantastic. We may or may not ever get around to having sex together, but that is not the point.

Participant: ...Gregory, when I did The Living Game Seminar you said that was my biggest issue. After that major changes happened, like I had sex again.

Gregory: Can I tell them something about that? She was in the middle of The Living Game Seminar and she yelled, "I'm wet, I'm wet!" We suddenly realized what she was talking about and all laughed.

Participant: ...Then I was having sex selfishly, and I approached it to please myself. Now it's completely satisfying and easier.

Participant: ...How do you move that into the work situation? There's not a lot of people who work like that.

Gregory: Your experience is that the places you have worked in are control situations: you work there and get pissed off and don't think it can be any other way, even though you want it to be.

The minute that I'm not willing to work under certain conditions, even if it means being unemployed for the rest of my life, then I get clear finding what I want. So it's "ask and you shall receive." The Universe will give you whatever you are committed to, and you must be willing to take a risk.

I was bored with the game of approaching women and initiating things. I wanted to have it the other way. So first I made a commitment to stop doing it the way I didn't want to do it. Then other, different things can happen. But while ever I hold on to the old pattern, I don't have a 100% commitment to have the new and I'm compromising mySelf. The minute I have an absolute commitment to something the Universe provides it. In other words, my commitment manifests out there. While I'm playing it small, that's what I get. You get what you go for.

Participant: ...An example of that, over the past 6 months I was doing seminars with you, I knew that my work was not working for me. I was shit scared to leave. For the last four months I've been working with you, having made the commitment to do what I really wanted. This is the only relationship I have had with my boss and my partner and I haven't had any ugly confrontations. Breaking the pattern was the thing. I didn't think that I could do it or I didn't think there was another way.

Gregory: Your example is great. He was running his own advertising agency, running himself ragged. That's how people in the advertising world think life is. You run yourself ragged, get ulcers and die young ... rich, but young.

In the meantime you compromise every value you've ever had and you let clients decide when you shit. When he did Turning Fear Into Power, I really put it on him to do The Living Game Seminar. He said "I don't have time" to which I replied "you don't have time to not do it'. He came and did the next weekend and realized he had to clear up his relationship with his partner, then did Fast Forward and realized he had to get out of the business. Then did the Leadership Day and saw he had to get out of advertising.

He made that commitment to himself not knowing what was going to happen, then decided he wanted to work with me. We had a meeting two days later and he said, "I want to work with you, tell me what job is available. I will wash the floors, I'll clean the toilets, I'll make coffee, whatever the job is I want to work with you." How could I refuse???

You can't refuse someone who is that committed. Even if previously I thought he was a prick, which I didn't, someone who comes from that degree of commitment is unstoppable. So I said "be my Sales and Marketing Manager, and I can't pay you". He said O.K.

The joke from his end was, he was terrified of leaving the advertising agency, terrified of the change it would mean. He works on a commission with me, so he does freelance advertising two days a week and he is making more money in advertising than he has ever made in twenty years! See, that is how the universe rewards you for the risks you take.

He felt that the risk was so big it was as if he was facing death. When you take risks that big your commitment is that big so that is the result. Instead of working nine days a week and struggling he is working two days a week. He is making more money than he ever had. He hasn't had to look for a job, he's had people ring him up saying, "Will you work, will you work, will you work." He is knocking work back left, right and centre. In fact he is now training someone else because there is so much work available.

Joe did the same thing last year after he did the last Sex and Relationships Seminar. He was working in architecture, had a nice safe job that bored him and didn't open up his creativity. He made the decision to leave and create his own graphics business. You were crapping your pants, weren't you? He was breathless with fear at times. He rented the front office from me, moved in and the phone didn't stop ringing! It was instant, work pouring in the door. It doesn't matter what it is; sex, money, work, whatever ...while you are willing to have less than you want, you will get less than you want.

To come back to what it may take to turn that other 60% around; it might take putting the hard word on 543 men. And the 544th man will say, "I love it." It might be that that is the process you need to go through to grow the 40% to be 100% and to reduce the 60% to 0%. Each time you go for it, and get a no, you ask yourself, "Am I going to agree with the old me or the new me?"

That is the process, and sometimes it feels like you are not getting anywhere. The word "seminar" literally means seed, it comes from the word seminal which is semen, which becomes seminar. When a woman gets pregnant, you don't see anything for up to 5 months, it doesn't seem like anything is happening, but there is a lot happening. It's the same thing - you might do it 543 times and it seems like you're getting nowhere. But every time you take that risk and go for it, you develop your ability and you diminish your resistance.

Sometimes it is a gradual progression where you see a small benefit step by step till you get there. Sometimes it seems like nothing has changed for months and then suddenly it is all there. Sometimes it's immediate. While I keep going for it, I will get it.

Participant: ...With that process last night, saying "I want to fuck you." I have never asked anybody that before, so it was really hard for me. Once I did it, it felt like all the terror had gone. And also the terror was that I wouldn't get asked at all, and I got asked a few times.

Gregory: Terror can be highly motivating.

Participant: ...With my experience of fear, I'm almost being blasé about it.

Gregory: That is the other side of fear. It's called taking a walk. The fear is losing it's power.

Participant: ...When I woke up this morning, I really felt like part of me was just saying, "maybe it will over the next few days."

Gregory: I was at least 27 before I knew that I even had fear, or anger, or sadness for that matter. I was cut off. I just didn't have those problems, thank you. This guy I used to work with once said to me, "Gee, you are an angry man." I was enraged! "How dare you say I'm angry, I'm not angry. I'M NOT ANGRY!"

One of the ways we deal with our fear is to take a walk on ourselves. When we're really scared of our fear, or scared of feeling fear, we just step out. The extreme version of that is Space Cadets. We space out. We get out of our space. We leave our bodies on Earth to get on with our life and "we" float out in space.

***

Participant: ...I'm learning how truly evil I really am.

Gregory: They already knew that. Who else has issues about being evil? So there is a a strong belief in your own evilness.

For example we've been told that to be angry is bad or evil, so you suppress the anger and get angrier and eventually get so angry that you feel like you could kill someone and then go into fear about being a killer and that is really evil so you suppress even more. It's a negative spiral.

The key to it is that what you judge to be wrong about you is what you've learnt to judge as being wrong. I say there is nothing inherently wrong with any of us. There are things about us all that we've learnt are wrong. When I was young, I learnt it was wrong to masturbate. God was going to get me if I masturbated, that was evil. The Catholic church teaches that's a sin. That's a pretty evil trip to lay on a 10 year old boy; "You play with your dick and make it feel good, and if a bus hits you, you burn in Hell forever, babe'. That is a solid message.

Participant: ...I am constantly judging myself. One thing I am scared of is that I intellectualize so much. I ask myself what sort of intricate story am I scheming together? And I project that on to everyone else and have them think that I do that.

Gregory: So sometimes you do. And sometimes you don't. There's nothing wrong with intellectualizing. It has great value, sometimes. I used to intellectualize everything. I literally had the experience of being cut off at the neck. This thing called a body was my life support system. Where I lived was in my head. I was the pilot up here in my head, doing all this stuff. I had this life support system going. This body was a thing that hung off my neck.

My experience of life was all theoretical because I was totally disconnected. When I did Primal Feeling Release and started connecting with my feelings and my body, everything changed dramatically. That meant I would have experiences and then thoughts about them. Rather than have thoughts instead of the experiences and feelings. That is the difference between understanding and knowing.

I am still able to conceptualize but now do it on the basis of my experiences and being Present, not instead of them. Before I got into Primal, I used to love sitting around with psychiatrists and psychologists theorizing for hours. After I'd done Primal it would drive me batty with boredom at the irrelevance to Life it all was.

Participant: ...That's why I am always restless. I feel the need to constantly have new experiences because I feel such a lack of experience in my intellectualization.

Gregory: For you as a computer genius to acknowledge that is great. So act on the acknowledgement. Go and have five hundred thousand experiences.

Participant: ...Another thing is I've been saying a lot of things like, "This is my problem and this is a terrible thing." And I feel very sad about that.

Gregory: There is no drama running on this planet that is better than our own! We all are Broadway stars in our own lives. I was saying when you do new things you see what you've been doing. You also identify what your own personal drama is. We live our drama. Whatever your life is, I say it's a drama. You've written a movie script, then you act in it, your own life drama. So that is what part of your drama has been. We learn this role of how to be a person. For example, you want to get across something that is serious, so you get yourself sad so that everyone knows that it is serious, then everyone says, "Oh, I feel so sorry for you. Let's all give him some support," and we all have a big hug.

That is your game. We learn all these games. We just keep playing games. It becomes so automatic that it is as boring as shit. I enjoy doing The Living Game Seminar with psychologists. I just love blowing psychologists" minds sidewards. Out through the wall, out through the next block. Guess what! They love it too. One rang me and said, "What do you think of the blah blah blah model?" I said, "I think it's a crock of shit." After a second of silence she said, "Oh, great, I'll do your seminar, I'm so fed up with all the garbage I've been doing."

So, you are not evil. What you've done to yourself is evil. I had a lot of resistance to the word evil for a long time, until I understood that evil is the shit we do to ourselves. My definition of evil is that it is anything that is anti-life. Evil is LIVE spelt backwards. Devil is "LIVED" backwards. Evil is literally anti-life. Religion symbolically externalizes the Devil and the God within you. The Devil, and evil, aren't about doing things that feel good. They are about things that are anti-life, anti-choice.

Participant: ...Just like God is dog spelt backwards.

Gregory: Yeah, see he has a sense of humor. In the beginning was the bark. And the bark was made dog!

Sharing is not holding back on yourself and not doing yourself over. When you share you feel evil, just as you learned. In fact you already feel evil and by sharing you bring forth that feeling and then let it go. In the sex experience you do something that feels bad, and you think, "Oh, I won't do that because it felt bad', but you already felt bad, and doing it just gave you an opportunity to really feel how you actually feel. In fact it is probably good for you because the more you do it the more opportunity you have to release the underlying bad feelings.

Most "bad" feelings occur in sex because you learnt that it was "bad" to do that and if you did it you should feel "bad" about it and yourself. There's the great saying, "If it feels good, it's either illegal, immoral, or fattening."

Rules and morals are more often than not about control and repression. That's all. Rarely do they help create something.

Have you ever had a sore that has become infected and you lance it and gunk comes out, so healing can begin? We don't say, "Oh, piercing that makes gunk come out of my arm so I won't pierce it in future." Yet that is how we sometimes run our lives.

Participant: ...Sometimes I am talking to a man, I'm not really listening. Instead I'm thinking, "Ooh yum" and then I'm thinking, "Oh, is he thinking that?" It happens all the time. The problem is I don't know how to deal with it.

Gregory: Just get in to it. I can just see her walk up to some guy, saying, "I bet you can't guess what I'm thinking about." One of the things to acknowledge is that astrologically you've got Venus/ Mars sextile. You have a particularly strong sexuality and see the world through sex. Everything is sexual for you. You stick a plug in the wall and it reminds you of sex!

Life is based on sexuality for you. Everything is sexual. Life is a process of constant creation, and in that, a totally sexual experience. You're just more in tune with that than most people.

Participant: ...But I'm scared that if I allow it that fully everyone will think I'm a tart, and at work that I am sleeping my way to the top.

Gregory: What is wrong with sleeping your way to the top? If you've got it, use it honey. Some people dress their way to the top. Some people study their way to the top - now that's prostitution. Imagine going to university for three years just to get to the top. Some people backstab their way to the top. You see there are lots of ways of getting to the top. Who is to say that a college degree is better than sex. I mean you are going to have more fun bonking your way to the top than studying your way to the top. Ha, ha. OK, seriously, listen, few woman ever got to the top by bonking their way there. Do you know who created that myth? Other women. Not men. Other women created that myth, I believe, to justify the fact that they didn't make it to the top.

Participant: ...Or that they didn't bonk.

Gregory: Or that they didn't bonk, thank you. You see it is a bullshit myth. No man in their right mind is going to make someone an executive manager of a group or a division or a company because they are a good lay. Unless it's a mattress company. "I can guarantee that these are the best mattresses."

So you get turned on by a lot of men at work. Work your way through them. It's like someone in the desert who hasn't eaten for ten days and you could give them bad meat and that's food man, they are going to eat it. Depriving yourself of sex makes you undiscriminating. You'll bonk anything, or you'll want to. But if you are getting plenty of sex you have choices. That's when you are discriminating.

If you have plenty of food, you're not going to eat bad meat. You'll say, "Not that, there's good food over here." When you are getting plenty of sex, the energy shifts in you. Because then you say, "Oh yeah, he's nice but there is plenty around." See, nothing gives you the power of discrimination more than abundance. Nothing that I know. The minute you've already got what you want, you become very selective. If you walk for 30 miles, you'll drink anything. But after that first drink you'll then think, "What do I want to drink?"

When you come through the door, it's just liquid. It doesn't matter what it is, as long as it's not poisonous, you'll drink it. But after the first drink, you'll think, "What would I like to drink?" You've got your discrimination back because you are not needy.

Participant: ...Can I ask a question? If a woman was having it off with several men, then she would gain a reputation amongst men. So then if you had to compete with those men for a promotion, for example, wouldn't you then be passed over?

Gregory: If that is what you create, sure. If you've got that belief then sure you will.

I worked in hospitals for years. Nurses are the most profligate group of people I've ever met. I mean they're like rabbits. You want to become a nurse, the first thing they do is check your ears. They're unreal. Everything you've ever heard about nurses is true. And I knew nurses who totally bonked their brains out. They bonked their way through the hospital, and everyone knew it and had absolute respect for them. I knew other nurses who screwed around a little bit, and no one had any respect for them.

So it had nothing to do with what they did. It had to do with who they were and their attitudes. Go and work in a company where it's not an issue for anyone.

Participant: ...What about playing a game with yourself so that if sexuality is a big deal in the company, you just laugh it off?

Gregory: You are now suggesting to just pretend that the way it is does not exist. That's like telling a starving man to laugh off the idea of eating food. "Eat sand and pretend it's real." "Oh great, I'm eating fillet mignon, thanks, brilliant."

Participant: ...Can't you allow yourself to see the sexuality in it and then laugh at it?

Gregory: You can, but I am acknowledging that there are specific astrological characteristics that apply to some people that are called, "You live sex. Everything you do comes out of sexuality." It's very powerful sexual energy. Some people live painting. Some people live cooking. Some people live family. Some people live work. Some people live travel. I know people who just have to travel. That's where life is for them. So that is what they do.

There are lots of outlets for those different energies, but what happens for the people who live sex? They've been squashed. So you get to look at how do you create it so that you don't create havoc.

Ultimately when you are clear about where you are coming from no one is going to disagree. I get up in The Living Game Seminar and I say some of the most off the wall, outrageous things to people like you, and what did you all do? You listened and considered it. You accepted it as my okay truth. Isn't that true. I get a 75 year old grandmother in there who says to me, "I'd like you to stop swearing." I said, "Go fuck yourself." And she thought, "Oh, okay. He's not going to stop swearing," and did the seminar, had fun, and after it brought me a dozen roses for being a great swearer!

It's not just what you do and what you say, it's more how you do it. We were at a business meeting recently. The general manager of a very successful business company was sitting with five of his executives. We're going to do business training with them this year, and we were enrolling them into The Living Game Seminar.

A woman in the group said, "What's your background?" meaning, "Who are you, that we should come and do your seminar." It was said nicely, but that was the meaning. I stopped and I said, "Well I guess it started when I was three. I went to live in a psychiatric hospital." This in a business meeting, all wearing suits and doing the whole bit. And please note, my father was promoted to Nursing Supervisor in a country hospital, and part of the job was to live on hospital grounds. Hence, as a kid I got to grow up in a psychiatric hospital!

Their jaws dropped. I proceeded to tell them how I was confronted with the whole issue of normality, sanity and reality, and how I went through it and became a psychiatric nurse, that I went and did Zen meditation, then studied magic in Bali, psychic healing in America, primal therapy etc. I took ten minutes to tell the whole story. My Sales Manager shat himself!

I said, "You've got to stop bullshitting yourself Gregory, you don't want to be a businessman like most people are." I want to be my kind of businessman, and I'm happy to put on a suit and tie because I enjoy that. I think that's a kick. I get bored with sarongs after a while. So I do it how I want to do it, and the message people get is, "Hey, this guy believes in what he is saying and he's having a good time." It's very appealing. When you're clear about what you really want you'll put it out in a way that people get very, very clear. They'll either say, "No thank you," or, "Yes thank you." And any other response will show you your resistance or unclarity in what you're saying.

Three of these people came and did the seminar of the 26 people working in their business. During the seminar they talked about how they would be when they went back to work together. They decided that they'd all turn up together at nine o'clock on Monday morning, and each of them would hug everybody in the office. Everyone in the office would get three hugs each in the following hour. They did, and said it was amazing. Some people fell over laughing, others loved it. Others had to be chased through the entire building so they said, "I'll stop chasing you when you give me a hug." So they got a hug.

I was talking to one of these men a week and a half after the seminar, and said, "How's it going over there?" He said, "It's amazing! People who haven't done the seminar, give other people who haven't done the seminar hugs. People are just hugging throughout the office. Not everyone, some people are still sitting there thinking, "This is a bit weird." That's fine, meanwhile everybody else is having a good time together."

So you could start doing that and create a bit of havoc and a bit of flack, but when you realize that you are entitled to take anyone to bed you want to - assuming that they agree, everyone else will also realize it. If someone comes up to you and says, "Gee, you're a bit of a nympho." You can respond, "Yeah, and I love it." What are they going to say to you? See you only get flack about what you resist and disapprove of in yourself.

You want to end criticism, you agree with someone! What are your fears that they'll say to you or accuse you of, if you bonk half the guys in the office next week or the week after? Yeah, a blond bimbo. So agree with them.

Participant: ...It's not that I want to, it's just that I get in touch with an animal within me.

Gregory: It doesn't work that way. Only acknowledging something isn't always enough. Sometimes acknowledging it makes a difference, but how you turn things around is through acknowledgment, choice and sharing. Another way of saying that is to acknowledge, choose and do something. Sharing as taking action in the world.

So what stops you from saying, "Right now, I'm picking up and feeling some strong sexual messages, and I don't want to do anything with you at this point."

Participant: ...Because that's what I'm thinking, and the message that I get is that it's not OK.

Gregory: Most of the time, if you sense something about someone else, you're having a response to them, then there's something going on there. It's very rare that we act in isolation, or that you're going to sit there and have sexual feelings for someone who hates your guts. If that was happening then on some level you would pick up on that.

The contradiction is that you are getting pissed on by someone you don't want to do it with. That's a problem.

Participant: ...Can't it be that way?

Gregory: Well hang on. If you're getting turned on by someone, why wouldn't you want to do it with them? That's like saying, "I'm hungry, but I'm not going to eat food."

It's the same with anger. If you've got a bunch of anger, it's looking for an outlet. And someone walks in and you go, "I hate your hair AHHHHH."

You become an argument looking for somewhere to happen. But if you release that anger, then people can do all sorts of things that normally would piss you off endlessly, but it doesn't because you don't have an anger hook on it. I see it constantly when people are looking for an argument. There's a Monty Python skit, where you go and buy an argument. Phenomenally funny skit. Everyone related to it because when you're angry you'll find an argument. Whether you mean to or not, you'll find one. I love people who drive cars and have a collision and they stop and they yell at each other. I have this vision of educating them, so that when they'd finished that, they'd then shake hands and say, "Thank you, I really needed that." That's owning it and taking responsibility for it.

Participant: ...I had a meeting one day that got rather heated. A few people said a few things that I could have let hurt me. Then on the way home I ran into the back of a truck. So I got out of the car and yelled, "Why did you stop there for?" I dumped all my anger and then realized I'd never screamed at anybody else before in my life. It was so great, I'd realized why I had set it up for myself.

Gregory: Yeah it works that way.

Participant: ...I find that all of the stuff that I learn and practice and go through, I seem to resist when I go to work. It's very threatening for me to always be honest about what is going on for me, because I feel I'm threatening.

Gregory: The key is called "educating people." To share with people in a way that also educates them. Remember that thing at the end of the seminar, when I said, "When you go home, please speak to your friends in everyday, normal English." It's a question of gradient. So if you went into your boss and did an acknowledgement process in the way, and with the words that you might use with someone who has done the seminar, then you're not acknowledging or respecting where your boss is. I find that offensive. I call that, "Hitting people over the head with personal growth" because there is no respect for them and where they are at or their point of growth.

It's also not about hiding your truth. For me it's about finding a balance between making the acknowledgements that I want to make and respecting the other person. Not ramming it down their throat, or hitting them on the head with it. And in the process, educate them.

This is a simple example; when I went to that meeting that I was talking about, I said what I said, which was very direct, very honest and very upfront, in a way that took into account the fact that I was sitting in a board room with six business people, talking about doing a seminar that would improve business. So I didn't sit there and say, "Oh and you are going to hug lots of people, and we'll probably talk about love and reincarnation ....etc." I didn't get into that, yet it is one version of the truth. I talked about productivity half the time. And in terms of relationships, I talked about them learning communication techniques that would make them more effective and get better results with each other and their clients. That's what they could hear.

Then they get into the seminar you can see the pennies drop; "this will work with my wife, this will work with my kids". Where they start is they're coming to handle their job and by the end of the seminar, they know that was just a small part of it. That's how it works. If you want to communicate, then use the language they understand.

The classic that occasionally slips into the newspapers as a criticism of new age, is that, "New Age people reckon that people with cancer chose it." Some dick-heads who have done personal growth stuff, have read a Louise Hay book and they've met someone with cancer and they say, "Oh, you realize you chose it don't you?" What an insensitive statement to make.

What a brutalizing statement to make! It's very different to say, "Would you like to try some other approaches to your cancer?" and get, "What do you mean?" Then I would answer, "Well there are techniques and approaches that have been incredibly successful in healing cancer. I sure can't promise anything, but hey, neither can traditional medicine. At least I can guarantee this will do no harm. Do you want to hear more?"

It's the same with AIDS. I mean, you walk up to someone who's lost 50 kilos in the last four weeks and they've been given three months to live, and you say, "You chose it." It's like the new age version of "god will get you." It's called "Screw you, I've got some secret so I'm special."

Participant: ...When I took the job, I told him that I was doing a seminar in January and that I need two weeks off. He looked really worried about it and I went away worried. I rang him and summoned up all my courage, and said, "Do you have an issue about me doing a seminar, because if you do I'd like to clear it up before I start working with you. It means a lot to me". He said, "No, don't worry about it." I felt very powerful that I'd summoned up the courage to be totally honest. Since I've been working there, it's been "keep away" and I've gone into not wanting to come across like a weirdo.

Gregory: O.K. given that it is work, what you can do is educate yourself to say what you want to say in a business context. I'm reading a book on McDonald's at the moment, sitting and marking quote after quote. Ray Croc, who created McDonald's, constantly used to tell his staff, "Don't worry about the money, make sure you do a good job and enjoy yourself and the money will come."

Now that's straight out of my prosperity seminar. I'd never heard another human being say it, and here's the founder of McDonalds saying it. So instead of walking in and saying, "Oh I did this seminar with this guy who runs personal growth seminars and HE said...," you quote Ray Croc, "The guy that created the largest food retailing company in the world said..."

There are plenty of people in business, really successful and prominent people who are amazing. There's many of them. One of Australia's wealthiest businessmen was asked, "What do you attribute your success to?" He said, "Vision, clarity and commitment."

There's an audio tape business training course that's been done by thousands of business executives around the world. Do you know what it's based on? Visualization, visualization, visualization. Goal setting with visualization. It's a new age business course that's not called that. This stuff is showing up in every area of life.

***

Participant: ...Our boss is constantly contradicting himself.

Gregory: So deal with this in terms of the relationship that you have: again the first thing is to take responsibility for him. "He's this person in my life who's contradicting himself. What does that tell me about me?" Start looking for where you are contradictory in your life. And then clean up your act, so that you get more consistent and on purpose. Then he changes, or you create another way of having it work with him.

Are you both experiencing him as contradictory? It's no accident that you two work together. You reflect the things you like and dislike about yourself in each other and you both choose to work with him. You contradict each other in subtle ways that you don't see, so you see him do it, and see where you are scattered. And as you get more clear and more focused, so will he.

As you do this, you can also get him focused and support his focus. It's actually very easy. If it was me I would say, "I see where you contradict yourself and I don't know where the hell I am, and that doesn't work for me and it doesn't work for you, because I am wasting your time and money. So I would like us to find a way that we can have clearer, more accurate and powerful conversations so I know exactly what you want. That might mean that as we go through a brief, I actually write down the brief. I write down what you say and you agree to it and then everything stays within that brief."

Participant: ...We've done that, and he came back to us and said that we were making a bit of a problem. How ever we approach him it doesn't help.

Gregory: Whatever circumstances you are in reflect where you are. A good example is nursing. If you want to have a dynamic work career, don't be a nurse. In fact, don't work in the public service. The public service isn't about being dynamic generally. There might be one or two isolated little islands of excitement, there are in fact a couple I know. Basically, if you work in the public service you have a commitment to mediocrity and boringness. That's the game.

I was in the public service and I used to go bananas with the stuff that used to go on.

I'd fight about it, I'd rebel against it, I got involved as a State Delegate of the Nurses Union, then I got the point where I saw that it doesn't want to change, and I do, so I left.

Then I created something much more in line with my vision. After a time I'd see the limitations in that and move on to my next vision.

The risk is that you don't yet know how to get the result you want. The risk is to start, not knowing how to get there. We want to have it all worked out before we take the first step. Life doesn't work that way. The risk for you two is to do something with him. If he blows up, you have a choice; either go into hiding again, or say, "Did you enjoy that, can we get on with the discussion?" So let's say he blows up again. When he finishes, say "and that's not helping me get this sorted out." Just stay with it and stay calm.

We had a meeting the other night with a couple who travel the world with their business.

Others first met with them, and came to me and said, "He's lovely, she never shuts up." I had this warning that she never shuts up. So when I met her I just sat there and let her not shut up.

We sat there and sat there and she talked for 45 minutes non stop. I just didn't do anything. I didn't agree or disagree. She got her record played and she had nothing else to say. Then I had a brilliant conversation with her husband. My Marketing Manager was staggered. She said about six sentences in the following hour. Where there's a will there's a way. I didn't know if this was going to work, but I was clear that I was there to have a successful meeting with him.

It could have been that I said, "Hang on, I'm here for a meeting about this and I'm sure what you're saying is interesting, but I'm not here for that. My time is precious, can we stay on the subject." I've said that in meetings. I used to think that that was incredibly offensive, but I don't anymore.

Be willing to take the first step without knowing what the following step is. Keep your eyes on the result. So if the guy blows up, that's not the result you want, so stay with it. "He's blowing up now and the result I want is to have a harmonious solution." Restate the objective, and the worst that is going to happen is that you are going to find out that you can't come to a satisfactory conclusion. So leave.

One of two things is true. Either the guy wants to maintain chaos, or he wants it to work. You need to find out what he's committed to. If his commitment is to have it work, then you create a partnership to get that result together. If his commitment is to have it stay chaotic, then you need to acknowledge that and see if he's willing to change it. If he's not willing to change it, then what are you doing there?

Also realize that he's unreliable for you, and he may be totally reliable for him. I go to lunch sometimes and come back at five. You need to know what kind of leader he is being and what his ground rules are for the team.

Let me give you an example. There are many ways you can lead and many structures you can work with. The structure that support teams have on The Living Game Seminar is called "Everybody Does What I Say." The commitment to be on support is to do everything that is required, and to have the seminar work, and I determine what that is. I am both in charge of, and responsible for the outcome.

One of the things that would have been powerful for you to say, was, "Ah ha, so that is one of your ground rules." Everything he says is or isn't to happen, is a ground rule. If the ground rules change without you knowing they've changed, that's called creating chaos. What I'm hearing is just chaos, which is pretty typical for the advertising industry. It means that everyone stays very busy and very confused. You need to acknowledge that you are in one of the most chaotic industries in the world.

Do you want to have a structure that is sensible and works efficiently, instead of having a commitment to being safe by keeping everybody else confused?

A common way that people get to stay safe is to keep everybody else unbalanced. It's a major manipulation. If your boss keeps you unbalanced all the time, you'll never get to actually look at him. That's the game and it sucks.

All of this applies exactly to any and all personal relationships, not just work. It's that same sort of chaos, confusion, anger, resentment, feeling devalued, screwed around, missing out and hurt: the whole catastrophe occurs in personal relationships when one or both people are doing what your boss is doing.

The clearer you are about what you are doing and what your intention is, the more powerful your relationship will be. It's like saying, "Let's build a house here. Everybody do what you think would work." That's some house you are going to build. Ground rules set the structure for action, and define what the action will be and where everyone stands.

For example, in tennis you have a ground rule that says that the ball only gets hit with the racket. In football you have a ground rule that says the ball never gets hit with a racket. We resist ground rules because they limit us. They are limitations, but they provide a structure to work in. You cannot relate anything without a structure.

The structure you have at the moment is called chaos, and you produce it perfectly.

You're masters of chaos. If you want a different result, create a different structure.

Participant: ...After I did The Living Game Seminar, I knew that I had to get out of the job I was in. The reason was because I couldn't get any further and the boss wasn't willing to change. I'd been trying to change things for months and trying to get him to do things in a different way, and I realized it was just a waste of time, and I couldn't take that away from him.

Gregory: That's right, he's entitled to do it his way, even if that is ineffective. Then you've got a choice about it.

Some more work examples. A friend's company did a business seminar with me. He's in product and packaging design. After he did The Living Game Seminar one thing that changed dramatically for him was that some high flyer from America was out in Australia looking for a product design company and they had a meeting. At the end of it the guy said, "Well of course, I like your stuff and I'm looking around and checking out what other people are providing, and I'll get back to you." My friend's response was, "That's fine, because we just don't take anybody either, and we'll be checking you out and we'll get back to you."

The American guy fell through his bum. No one had ever said that to him. Have you ever heard an advertising agency say to the client "We might take you." It's the same with the printing industry. A lot of those people come from a powerlessness where the client has all the power. When that was turned around, he blew the guy out, and he regained his right to choose who he worked for.

I do that with business clients. I sit down and establish what my ground rules are for working with a company. I'll only work with a company if the top person is going to be involved, not with a company where the leaders aren't involved. I am only willing to work with a company that is committed to excellence, and willing to look at the way they operate and go for improvement.

I had a meeting last week, and the people talked about why they were interested, and I talked about what I provided, then I said, "And I've got a bunch of conditions, this and this and this." And they said, "Wow!" They loved it because they knew that I know what I am doing and am not going to compromise it. What most people are used to is saying, "Yeah, yeah I'll do that, yeah, yeah, work 24 hours a day, yeah sure."

A lot of people in advertising have done seminars with me, and I don't know how many of them have said to me, "I had to work three days straight and literally didn't sleep because the client needed something." I said, "Yeah, you needed something too. It's called sleep. It's called giving it away."

Sometimes you put yourself into unpleasant situations to realize how much you don't like them. When you've had enough of that, you know that you are not going to take anymore. Then you never create it again.

Participant: …I seem to always have power games with my boyfriend.

Gregory: At some point we have liked to be told what to do because it then means that we don't have to take responsibility. Daddy or Mummy is looking after us but it gets boring, because when you have a desire or want, and this person who has been telling you what to do for however long says, "no you can't do that." That's when you start seeing that it doesn't work. They're sitting there saying, "No, no. Do this, do that." Your response is eventually, "Screw you." It works until it doesn't.

Every now and then I come across a totally strange relationship game. Have you ever met couples where you say, "And how are you today Mary?" and George says, "She's really good." I say, "That's really interesting, you didn't even move your lips Mary. I didn't know you were a ventriloquist." It's the extreme when you get people answering for their partner.

The extreme version of that is called the Story of 0. It's a great game to play, and if you like it, do it fully. Why mess around? If you are going to be a slave, do it fully and really get the benefit. Don't be a mediocre slave. Be a totally into-it slave. "Take me, use me, have me." And get off on it. "Beat me up, whip me." It's a great game to play once you see that it's the game you're playing and either you want to or you don't want to.

By the way, this is the value of acting out sexual fantasies. Instead of doing it in your life, you can do it as part of your pleasure. Shift it out of "This is how life is," and take it into the bedroom and have someone push you around and tell you what to do, and play it as a game, and then say, "Now the game is finished." To me that is the real power and value of acting out fantasies, because you can express that energy in a playful and pleasurable way.

You know that 98% of women have rape fantasies. I assume they don't want to actually get raped.

To act the fantasy out can be really pleasurable. But to act it out in life generally isn't. The bottom line issue is, "Who owns you?" So when he says, "Right, do this," the only response is, "Don't tell me what to do. Ask." It's fine to ask people to do things. "Would you mind not leaving tea bags in the toilet? Especially the unused ones." I can expand your issue with the tea bags up to the point of showing you you're going to become a millionaire with your business.

Participant: ...I am?

Gregory: Yes, you going to become a millionaire with your business if you want to. By the way she makes the highest quality wind chimes I've ever seen in my life, and sells them for crap. So buy them before I finally get her to put the price up! She sells these wind chimes for $25 and they should sell for $130. But that is the point.

Your husband sits there saying, "No, we're not going to merchandise, we're not going to get twenty people to set up a factory, and you're not going to put the tea bags there." And you decide, "I want this relationship so I'll sacrifice my dreams and let him decide." The price you pay is, "Who owns you?" You don't. You get to stay small in your life and big in your body.

See that is what your being overweight is about, by the way. First thing is that you've been waiting (weighting) a long time. Secondly, you're a big woman and the only place you get to express it is in your body. It's not in your check book, although that's getting bigger and better. You don't have a big check book or a big account, or a big customer base, or a big factory, or a big say. You don't have a big thing happening.

So the only place that you are allowed to be big is your body. You weren't even allowed to be big with your voice, until recently. You get it? See the minute that you get that you are big, and you are going to have it big, then if he wants to stay little, that's fine, that's his choice. If he wants to do his hippy little craft trick tucked away up in the mountains and spit out two wind chimes a week and get social security payments, and do that for the rest of his life, that's his choice.

He may really love that. Maybe that is the best path in life for him. The thing that you've been getting to see is that it's not what you want to do. You see it's not about where you put the tea bags, that's just the tip of the iceberg. It's about power, and who is going to own it, and who is going to own you, and who's vision wins you. By the way there is no accident that he is quite thin.

Participant: ...There's a terror that I'll crush him.

Gregory: That's not a terror, that's a hope! Given all the fear you've had about getting here, this seminar is about getting your power and owning it in a way that you fully realize that you are never going to give it away again ...and getting your value, and how much you don't like giving it away. The price you pay is ten miles high and the payoff is about 2 inches high. That you've got this guy who hangs around and sticks it in you every now and then, and part of why you hang on to him, is that you are afraid that no one else will choose you. So you get to manifest your fear.

Day 2

"Be willing to take the first step without knowing what the following step is..."

EMOTIONAL ARMOR - TAKING STEPS - EXCELLENCE/INTEGRITY - SURVIVAL TECHNIQUES - CREATING DREAMS - SELFISH GIVING - RIGHT AND WRONG - HANDLING DEATH - INDULGING

Gregory: A simple thing is to ask is: "Do you want to hear what I thought about that?" That sets up a structure. When it feels like you're shoving it down their throats it's because you need them to hear it and like it. In other words there is a catch to what you are saying, a hook - your need. When you are willing to just say it and leave it up to them to respond, it's not shoving it down their throat, it's just sharing it. They might say, "Oh yeah, that's interesting," or "That's totally boring." That's not the point.

Another way, one that I learnt talking about my seminars with people, was to only answer the questions that are asked. In other words, to really listen to what information people are asking for, and to give it to them. In the early days, people would say to me, "What's the seminar about?" Six hours of talking later I would stagger away. I just saw that that doesn't work. Now if people say to me, "What is the seminar about?" I say, "It's about lots of things, what specifically do you want to know?" Then they'll start refining their questions, and when they stop asking questions, I stop giving answers.

Participant: ...I find that I start giving an answer to a question, and I just keep going and going and going.

Gregory: That will overwhelm them, because they are not ready to hear it all, and they can't do anything with it anyway.

Participant: ...Am I looking for approval by doing that?

Gregory: Well part of it is possibly that you've got a lot you want to share and teach.

What you need to do is find people who want to learn a lot. Use me as an example. I teach at the level that people tell me they are ready to hear. So what I do in this seminar goes beyond what I do in The Living Game Seminar. What I do there, I don't do in a business meeting. I simply teach and share what is going to be heard and appreciated. Then people say, "Wow, that was great." If I walked into a business meeting and started giving them The Living Game Seminar it is inappropriate because that's not why they are there. That's not the purpose and all sorts of things would happen, including they'd get overwhelmed, become disinterested and end up not enjoying it.

There's a wonderful saying - "casting pearls in front of swine." That sums it up. Why do it? Cast your pearls where they are going to be appreciated and valued. How many people have ever been in a relationship where you've had the experience of giving and giving and not having it valued? It is the same process. Part of that is you are not valuing what you give, but it's still the same process.

Participant: ...I'm scared that if people found out how much I hide myself in here, I'll never be touched.

Gregory: O.K. everybody just found out. So who else feels that? It's called armoring. The word for it is the emotional experience of wearing armor.

I love the expression, "We live our lives back to front." It comes up all the time. Here's how it's back to front. It feels like you have to lock yourself in and lock them out and that there is something wrong with you for that. As a child, life was so brutal for you, the only way you stopped being brutalized was to put on a suit of emotional armor, and it worked perfectly. It worked perfectly and brilliantly. It's not something wrong, it's probably one of the most right things you ever did in your life.

Participant: ...Yeah, and I'm still here.

Gregory: That's right, you've made it. What can be more important than that which let's you survive? It's an absolutely brilliant creation. By armoring yourself, all the slings and arrows bounced off. Brilliant. Then we can't remember what was inside the armor that we had to hide.

Because we're sitting on the outside of the armor, it feels like me out here is O.K. but what the hell is locked in there?

We fear what is inside the armor, and we forget that everything inside the armor is what we treasured, and so protected. You don't leave the jewels out on the front porch and lock up your garbage. Do you?

So even if it's just an idea at this point, let's assume everything inside the armor is what you truly valued about yourself. Then what you call you is just the watchman, a technical operator to keep the systems working until it's time to take the armor off when the 'war' ends and it is now safe.

The other thing is that we are far too smart to drop the armor just like that, because we've got 20 or 40 or 60 years of learning that this is how you survive. If I walked in with a gun now and said, "Hey guess what? Guns don't kill you anymore when you point them at your head and shoot" it's highly unlikely that you are going to say, "Oh, right, okay. I've got a new choice." BANG. So we test the waters.

As children, the game was to survive. Seeing unhappy parents we learnt that life is unhappy, and heard from every direction that life is a struggle. Life is pain. Life's a bitch. Life wasn't meant to be easy. Our parents and our neighbors proved that on a daily basis. Newspapers and television has proved that on a daily basis. The message we got was that life was about surviving. So we'd do anything we could to make it. So just as animals develop survival techniques, we developed our own. A common one is the inner suit of armor.

Participant: ...It seems to me that I must protect myself against insensitive and stupid people who I can't avoid.

Gregory: Do you want to deal with incompetence or do you want to deal with people committed to excellence? It doesn't matter whether it's the computer industry or the health industry or the food industry or the seminar industry. It's the same in any area of life. In business, or any area of life, you will find at one end of the spectrum total incompetence, and at the other end people totally committed to excellence and mastery.

Participant: ...Yes very nice to have an ideal like that.

Gregory: No. Stop. I'm not saying it's an ideal. I'm saying it already exists. At every level of operation in any area of life, there already exists everything from total incompetence through to mastery. Then you find the level that suits you. You slot it into at least the moderately incompetent level, or a level where you deal with moderate incompetence. You and a lot of people say, "Well that's how life is. You've got to deal with idiots." Says who???

I used to have a lucrative business giving training days to government departments and I'd come home feeling absolutely wiped out. A lot of the people, not all, who came to those days weren't there with any commitment. In fact, a lot of them were there to get a day off. I decided not to do it anymore and said "no" to a lot of money but said "yes" to a lot of value. Now I sit in business meetings where I state my conditions and I define my ground rules for who I am willing to have as a client. If people don't fill that criteria, I won't have them and they can't have me. Bottom line of that is I get to enjoy the work I do and the people I do it with.

While you settle for less, that is what you will get. The minute you are willing to let less go, you'll get more. I know people in the computer service industry, just like you, who have done lots of personal growth including seminars with me. They have absolute commitment to excellence and to having their clients and themselves win together. The question is, "Where are you willing to be?"

Not everyone armors. Some people do it by anesthetizing themselves. Some people are space cadets; not in their bodies. That's safe: "Kill my body. I'm not here anyway. I am up there somewhere floating around in rose-colored illusion world, so you'll miss the real me." That is a great survival technique. The first step always is to define what you want.

Participant: ...What if you don't know?

Gregory: Then acknowledge that you hide what you want. What you do is disappear yourself, and disappear what you want. You have a basic belief that says, "There's no point being here or knowing what I want because I know I can't have it anyway, so I'll hide it all." The invisible man or woman.

The starting point is to acknowledge that you have disappeared yourself and what you want as a way of surviving. You're very psychic and also quite visionary. What visionary people often do is, because of childhood messages about how much you can't have and what your lot in life is, and because you see suffering and pain, you give up your hopes and visions, or you hide them away where they can't be destroyed.

So if you are given that limit everything else that you envisioned above that, you block it out because you have already been told that you can't have that. It feels much safer to not know what you want than it does to know and find out that you can't have it. So what we do is, we hide from ourselves what we want to protect ourselves from going into despair. If you want it and find out you can't have it, you are left with a big fat nothing, hence despair, or at least that is the fear of what will happen.

The pitfall for people with a powerful vision is that it is much safer to settle for the fantasy, than to actually test it in the world and find out you can't have it.

Participant: ...I'm living as if I have my vision, and the truth is that I haven't.

Gregory: You're pretending to be where you are not for fear that if you acknowledge that you're not there, that you'll never get there. But while you pretend that you are there, you can never get there. You just settle for the pretense. It can be incredibly painful.

After traveling to Bali many times, I had written a book on it. It was a deep behind the scenes look at the culture, and it's fundamental beliefs and so on. I wrote the book in my head. Then I kept saying to myself, "I must write the book, I must write the book." And then finally I got to see that I was not writing the book on paper.

I realized that it was much safer to keep the book inside, as a fantasy, than it was to actually write it, send it to a publisher, and have it go into the book stores where it sells three copies. To my parents! Or to have the critics saying, "If you run out of toilet paper in Bali, buy this book."

Participant: ...I have to go through a process of not having what I want and seeing that it's not bad.

Gregory: That sounds like you've got to create some pain. The truth is that you already don't have what you want and that you never have had it. So it's not that you have to go through not having what you want. It's a matter of acknowledging that you never did have it. Then you decide whether you want it or whether you're just wanking. Start something.

Here is a great starting point. Do you want more than you have got? Yes. So you know something about what you want. Do you want an excellent job where you are well paid and working with great people? Do you want that in a creative sphere? Do you want that specifically in advertising? At the moment yes. Do you want to work by yourself, with a partner, or in a company, ideally?

Participant: ...With a partner in a company.

Gregory: Do you want a fantastic boss and art director, who is really organized and has clear ground rules and guide lines and involves you in decision making and lots of feed back?

Participant: ...Yes.

Gregory: How are we going folks? This is someone who doesn't know what she wants! Do you want to have great sex? Do you want to have relationships with one or many, or both, men or women, or both? Just off the top of your head, at this point?

Participant: ...Yes. All of the above.

Gregory: Do you want your sexuality to be adventurous, exciting, playful, passionate and varied? Yes? So you do know what you want. The first step is to be honest with yourself. We could go through every area of your life and get down to absolute nitty gritty details about what you want. Thick or thin? Ha, ha, ha. She knows what I mean immediately.

The truth is that you know what you want, and part of your disappearing act is, "Oh, I don't know what I want. I don't know what I want." That's not true. Part of your game is that you are also scared of how powerful you are, so if you tell the truth and say, "I know exactly what I want," it will start activating you as a very powerful woman. You get to stay looking cute and ineffective and powerless by never knowing what you want.

The payoff is you walk around like this lost little girl saying, "I don't know what I want. I don't know what I want." Then some idiot man buys into it and says, "I'll tell you what you want. I'll look after you." Then walk in sucker. You get it?

The first step is that you do know what you want. The second step always, and sometimes the biggest one to be honest about is: are you willing to have it? Are you willing to do what it takes? For example, with the Bali book, I could sit down and write a great book about Bali and I am not willing to yet. The minute I saw the fantasy and the reality, I saw that there is a great book in here, and I have had other priorities. One day I will probably get around to writing it, but it isn't my priority.

Participant: ...I know what I want, but I can't see how I can have it all. Like being a good mother, and being a worldwide success as a writer and traveling and doing creative work.

Gregory: So you grab your kids and you say, "I've been busting my guts to be a good mother and sometimes I screw up. Will you support me in being a great mother and tell me if I screw up?" That's the start of being a good mother.

Catch a bus around the city. Is that travel or isn't it? How many people went to Brisbane in the last 6 months from around the world? Millions of people had a trip overseas to Brisbane. You live there and you call it uninteresting. Listen, I'll bet there is enough in Brisbane to keep you occupied for a life time of travel adventures. Yes, even in Brisbane!

How many of the docks in Brisbane have you been onto? How many whore houses? None.

How many police stations? There's three very different cultures to the one you live in. Don't laugh! I'm serious.

One of the ways we rip ourselves off is by believing that it has to be 'out there' somewhere, it has to be a trip around the world. I've met people in my travels, who went on trips around the world, and they might as well have never left their lounge room, people who have gone all over the world and you wouldn't even think they'd been down to the corner shop. That's how much they got out of it.

Travel doesn't open you up. It's you're willingness to be open. If you want to experience different cultures in other countries, the best homework is to start traveling in your own city. If you are not going to walk into a whore house or slum in your city, then what's going to make you do it in India? That's why people go overseas and look for that which is already familiar. And in the process some of the unfamiliar rubs off.

Participant: ...I think I was 18 or 19 and I was living in Melbourne and came to Sydney for four days. I went out every night, and slept around and did the whole lot, because I was in love with the city. I did everything that I wanted to do, but I had to go somewhere else to do that.

Gregory: Being here is a good example. We're here doing what we're doing but the tendency, or the resistant energy, is to go back home at the end of the seminar and stop doing it. That's true for any seminar. It's like, "I can do it on the seminar but I can't do it at home." It's not true, not true.

If you want to get paid for creative work, call your friends and say, "Can I paint your house for $50?"

So you don't do anything because it isn't what you want. Every artist wants to be Van Gogh, and they're not willing to paint houses. It's like that. Start somewhere. If you want creative work, what field would you like it to be in? What would it be if you knew? Watch, she'll tell us. You know, come on.

Participant: ...Writing, fashion and music.

Gregory: That's a great start. So let's start with writing. How big is your picture? Is it being a famous writer? So where do you start? People say to me, "It's easy for you to do this stuff, you're the instructor." Like I was born this way! I didn't get born sitting on a chair at the front of the room sprouting profundities!!

Participant: ...It wouldn't surprise us.

Gregory: Ha. One of my great regrets in life is that someone didn't follow me around for three days with a video camera before I got into personal growth. There are times when I would love to show that video. Lao Tzu said a journey of a thousand miles starts with the first step. You handle huge things by bringing them down to their basics, and starting there.

Getting paid to write could be that some kid doesn't want to do a homework essay, so you say, "O.K. I'll do it for $5." Seriously. Hundreds, thousands of people in the world get paid to write for other people. Start somewhere. Get a job demonstrating the effectiveness of Bic pens in a store, where you get to sit there and write all day. It's an acknowledgement that you've got to start somewhere.

Participant: ...It's like the movie last night, Karate Kid.

Gregory: Yeah, he wants to become a Karate Master and he starts washing cars. He didn't even understand what he was doing. It's called start somewhere.

It doesn't compromise integrity. The compromise is in saying, "This is all I can do," or, "this will do." When you really want more. When you want something that big, bringing it down to, "Where can I start?" means that you're actioning yourself towards it. It's not a compromise. In fact, it gives you integrity, because instead of saying, "I can't be paid to be a writer," you can say, "I'm already paid to be a writer."

Let me give you another example: a great man named Robert Panté. I've never met a human being with such prosperity consciousness. He also happens to be wealthy now. He used to be a teacher, and he's a very theatrical man. He really loves clothes and he's an outrageous queen. He loves clothes and he loves cosmetics and perfumery, etc. He got a job at Bloomingdales in New York with one of the huge cosmetic companies. What he did was simply be outrageous. Bloomingdales is a moderately conservative store, and Panté was outrageous. He would get men in head locks and put lipstick on them. Truckies. I'm not kidding. He used to climb on people. He's only 5 feet high.

He used to attract crowds at Bloomingdales to the point where they had to move him and give him his own section.

People used to go to Bloomingdales to be entertained by the guy. He became the top salesman for this company; he just sent them through the roof. He says that the day his life changed was the day he realized that he was a Living Human Treasure. That's a really lovely expression. Living Human Treasure. I use it a lot in visualizations. He went on to travel the world giving seminars that I did twice. Brilliant man!

The thing is to start somewhere. There's a wonderful saying, "look after the pennies and the pounds will look after themselves." When you attend to small things, the big things handle themselves. Then you start writing and getting paid well. Everything in life that is valid and valuable grows, doesn't it? You plant lousy seeds in the ground, they die. If you plant good seeds in the ground, they live, assuming the ground is O.K. So if you start writing and are getting paid for it, if it's right for you and if it's valuable, it will grow. You don't even have to do anything except keep doing it. Then if that's what you are meant to be doing, you'll absolutely get the message. The universe will send you new customers. Or send you new ideas or send you new publishers.

That's the unreasonable way to run your life. If it's not the best choice for you to be making, it won't happen. I could have written that book on Bali, and it might have made me wealthy, and I would have gone off on tours doing this and doing that and talking about Bali etc. However I wouldn't be sitting here. Guess where I'd rather be? Sitting here. But you've got to start somewhere. Or don't. If you don't want to start then own that choice, and it's consequences. Just don't bitch to me that you can't have it.

The thing with travel that I'll just add is that one of most exciting things about traveling and living overseas is coming home. I love coming back to Sydney as a tourist. I'd say 60% of what I know about Sydney, I discovered in the months after each trip overseas, because when I return to Sydney I am open to it as a new city. It's another city in the world to explore. I come back to Australia and I play it like I have never been here before. I pretended I had some friends who had lent me a place to stay, which was actually mine, and I played that I'd never been there before. I arrived and went and found the kettle and the kitchen and the bathroom and I explored it as if it was totally new to me. Then I went for walks and you know what I discovered? I'd never been there. It really was all new and different this time.

One of the reasons people travel is because travel won't allow you to be on automatic. You have to be aware and conscious. That's the excitement of travel for many people because you can't take anything for granted.

If you walk down the street in Bali, you've got to watch the footpaths. The Balinese have got this cute habit of having blocks of concrete missing. If you don't actually physically watch where you are walking, you may just drop eight feet into the sewer. You can't walk down the street on automatic. You can't do anything automatically. You are making conscious decisions all the time. If you do that in your home town you get to travel in a new home town. Start somewhere, and I say you can do it all. Absolutely.

Look at me. I'm a father. I run a business. I play a lot. I've got lots of people to work with and for me. I go and do business seminars last week. I do a Sex and Relationships Seminar this week. I'm going on national radio again this month. There's going to be a lot of media this year. I've started writing articles. I've organized an editor. I'm creating a really exciting philanthropic project with Peter. We've already come up with some incredible projects and created them. And I created all of that out of nothing but my committed vision for what I wanted my life to be. You can also create your vision of what you want your life to be if you want it enough.

Life is a smorgasbord if you allow it. Start somewhere.

Note that all of this is directly applicable to sex and relationships! It is always a world to explore, expand and experiment, and for many of us if we do not continue doing that then sex and relationships also become boring and we go on autopilot.

Participant: ...Gregory, you were talking about armor. I noticed about myself especially in business and working with people, that there is a certain level that I get to where I let people in. Because of that a few shutters go off, and I don't know why that is.

Gregory: Okay. We'll get into this a lot more. The short answer is that armor is valuable. It's not that there's something wrong with having armor. It's learning how to use it effectively. The knights of the round table didn't wear their armor to dinner or to bed. In other words they knew how and when to take it off.

Have you ever seen the TV show with Maxwell Smart? He walks down the corridor and the doors go clunk, clunk, clunk, clunk behind him. I've met people where, in the first three seconds, twenty doors inside me just go boom, boom, boom, boom, shut. And I think, "Wow, what's going on here?" Then when I actually pay attention to the person, I see that they're a walking toxic waste dump of off energy.

It's like a knee jerk reaction. My senses are yelling, "Warning, Warning, Warning" and all the doors shut, because I don't want to let this person in. Yet with other people it's, "Open, open, open, open, open." That's what I like, having the choice.

In one sense, all personal growth ever is, is learning to open more and more doors, so that you can walk further and further down that corridor. Once you open them, you don't lose the choice of closing them again.

We often picture issues like armor in a context of either/or. Either I always have it or I never have it. I have it all the time, or I never have it.

It's not black and white like that. I immediately open to people who are willing to put their butt on the line. Or who are willing to look like jerks, to take risks.

That's a very powerful statement of trust, and we tend to open up to people whom we trust. The old game is to sit there with six-shooters pointing at each other having 'friendly' talks. And when someone actually says, "Okay, I'm dropping my guns," you relax.

(A participant is trying very hard to ask Gregory a question, but she has lost her voice.)

Gregory: What you're doing right now is literally stopping your voice. It's painful and scary. What you're feeling now, you've been experiencing for 25 years, and you haven't felt it. So now you actually take your voice away, so that you can contact how you feel when you hide what you have to say: that fear of panic and disconnection and loss and inability to communicate and reach out. All those fears and feelings are present and conscious now. This is why we create crises and pain for ourselves. You are going to get to the point where you're so pissed off about hiding what you want to say that you'll never do it again. What you're doing now is really experiencing the price you pay with those feelings sitting there all the time. When you know what the price is, you won't hold back on saying what you want, and don't want. It's very powerful for you, a singer of some note. Ha,ha.

Participant: ...(said with difficulty) I know I block my opinions a lot.

Gregory: Notice her voice has already come back a bit. Just by acknowledging that.

Participant: ...I find at times in my life I get very very excited, and the longer the excitement builds, I get this sense of despair which almost comes at the same time. It's like, "What if it doesn't work?" And then after that it kind of paralyzes me, so I can't act on all these things, and then I just fall into this drop.

Gregory: Yeah that's the same process as what our squeaky singer is having. That you've learned that it's not okay to be excited. And you went into despair. Then you give yourself despair from yourself. So that every time you got excited, you were reminded about your despair of not being excited. So the old message got reinforced and you squashed your excitement and went back into apathy. So it could be that every time you get excited for the next 15 years, a feeling of despair comes up with it. Instead of giving up on your excitement, stay with it, "Ah, there's my old fear of not being excited, and every time I get excited, my despair has an opportunity to heal."

Gregory: What are some of the things that you didn't enjoy about last night?

Participant: ...I was really scared that somebody was going to go for my dick.

Gregory: And do what with it?

Participant: ...Hurting me. I felt vulnerable.

Participant: ...I enjoyed it but I felt like I was on the outside of the group for most of the time. And I was constantly trying to squirm into the middle.

Gregory: Okay, who else felt that? Who felt on the outside? That's how you run your life.

Nothing happens in isolation. To the people who experience being on the outside; my knowledge of you from seminars or socially is that's how you run your life.

Participant: ...That's what I experienced last night. While I was doing the process, I was thinking, "This is exactly how my life is going."

Gregory: Exactly. While you're not conscious of that, you simply have to stay on the outside because that's how you run your life. Once you understand that you run your life by being on the outside, or leaving yourself out, then you have a choice about it. You can decide, "I am not going to be on the outside." It may mean climbing over everyone, and diving into the middle. What usually happens is that you stay on the outside and feel like you're missing out.

Participant: ...When I was on the outside of the group, I came across someone crying, the mother in me stayed and caressed for a while, and then I thought, "Shit, I don't want to be around this," so I forced myself to get out.

Gregory: When the mother in you stays and caresses, it becomes a job. When the human being in you stays and caresses, it is loving and sharing. It's the same with kids as with other people. The roles of Mother and Father are mostly spelt, 0-B-L-I-G-A-T-I-O-N, it's just pronounced differently.

So that when you feel the mother or father role surfacing, you move into obligation: another version of, "I have to take the kids to school." But as a human being responding, "I know how it feels when I cry, and I will hold this person because I know it will make them feel good and therefore make me feel good."

On another level, "That part of me is crying, and I will nurture the crying in me." When my son is crying, I never hold him to be a good father, ever. Because the minute I become "father", I take a role and stop being a person with him. I hold him when he's crying because I own that the baby in me right now is really hurting and I want to heal the baby in me. I can do that very directly, by holding my child out there, I actually feel holding my child in here. And my child in here is crying because he didn't get held enough when he was young, he wasn't allowed to cry. Get it? I'm being totally selfish in that, and my son benefits. And of course I hold him because I love him and he is upset and needs to be held!

I am loving and nurturing myself and that's what my son gets; the experience of being loved and nurtured, not being held because it's the right thing for a father to do. That's the difference.

To come back to the outside / inside thing, there's nothing wrong with being on the outside if you're enjoying it. I used to experience myself as an outsider. I'd see people go to the pub. It wasn't my scene. I'd see people getting into things that were not my scene. I always felt different, an outsider. And as I got into this personal development stuff, and came home to me, started being inside me, I became an insider.

There are always games being played out around me. You know, there's this game and there's that game going on. I have a choice to immerse myself inside the game, or stay outside. Sometimes I want to stay outside. That's my choice, therefore I love being outside: then I'm where I want to be.

Every now and then, I put out to everyone in my life, "Don't talk to me, I don't want to know. Act like I'm not here. I'm invisible for the day as far as you are concerned."

That way I give myself enormous space to be outside of everything. I love it, and it's very nurturing. However I sure don't want to live my whole life there!

Participant: ...I was really scared because all these people were touching me and grabbing at me, and I felt like they all wanted something from me, I couldn't cope, and then a couple of times let myself go and that was okay. It was quite draining. I had to keep up my barriers.

Gregory: You felt like you had to. The barriers you feel in any process, no matter what you think is on the other side of them - the minute you drop the barriers, it gets better. It may be a little bumpy before it gets better. Because you might get some of what I call 'Belief backlash.' In other words it might feel scary for you for a while, then it gets better. Think about it. Walking around with 30 barriers is a heavy weight to carry. Every time you drop one, you get lighter. You literally become en - light - ened. It's true to say that all that enlightenment is about is dropping all your barriers. That's it. When you haven't got any fixed, rigid barriers, you're enlightened. Shine light on them so you have the choice!

Participant: ...I don't know whether I was in the middle or not. There were so many bodies touching me, instead of feeling like I had to give, I felt like I was the centre of it and everyone was just there for me. That freaked me out. I couldn't handle that for very long. I don't know how long it was but I had to get up and get out of it. It was too much to be the centre of that. But I was there for as long as I could.

Gregory: So you got the ceiling of how much attention and enjoyment you're allowed. Who else got that, where you're saying, "Great, great, great," and then you had to block it or stop it?

Participant: ...It's like this isn't just for me, this is for everyone, and I think about it rationally, "They're not all doing this consciously just for me." That's how I felt. I could have continued feeling that the whole time. But it's like, "No, this is too much, I don't deserve all this."

Gregory: One of the opportunities of moving into the wave consciousness, is that you move from, "This is not just for me, it's for everyone," to, "this is totally for me and everyone."

Literally we are all getting all that we want and all winning. The more that I get what I want, the more I have, and the more everyone else can have. That's the other equation.

Participant: ...I felt awkward and stupid. One thing I've been noticing, is that I've wanted to get through the processes to the other side. I just want to get them over and done with.

Gregory: Get them over and done with so that what?

Participant: ...So I can leave.

Gregory: Very good. Anyone else?

Participant: ...I found it really enjoyable because of the wonderful unconventional freedom. And people all agreeing to nakedness, which is not normally done.

Gregory: Margaret Whitehead, the English version of Pat Robinson said, "If God wanted us to be naked, we would have been born that way." Think about it. She said that on national television in England. That is how twisted and perverted social ideas about nakedness and sex get.

Anyone else like to share about last night?

Participant: ...I noticed that I started off on the outside, and knowing that that's what my life is like, I just decided to go in and I got really lost. I just let go. I relaxed and actually enjoyed it. It felt very primal. Now I'm able to just sit and be with people and have contact.

Gregory: One of our fundamental barriers, and fundamental resistances to life, is the whole survival issue, which includes, "Everyone else is the enemy." It's as though your best friends are merely the least of your enemies, so the best you can hope for is to minimize your 'enemy-ship.'

You've just got to make contact. And whatever happens, the fundamental thing is that it confronts separation.

Participant: ...I felt much much safer around the women than with the men. I've never been so close to men physically. I was really surprised how easy it was for me. I had all these pictures of freaking out if a man came near me. I was surprised how calm I felt about it. It really was quite strange.

Gregory: Who else didn't enjoy it?

Participant: ...When I opened my eyes, I didn't, but when I kept them closed, I enjoyed it more.

Participant: ...It wasn't that I didn't enjoy it, it was that I wasn't involved.

Gregory: Did you feel detached? Like it wasn't real? Or just that you weren't a part of it? Is that common for you?

The thing about processes is that while you do everything the same, you're not going to see what you are doing, but the minute you do something different, suddenly you see what you've been doing the same! So you experience being detached and you experience being left out. In the process you then get clear about your issues with men or whatever. It highlights it.

With processes from now to the end of the seminar, what is there for you to play with, and I support you in doing, is this; when a feeling arises that you are not enjoying, acknowledge it. It could be something like, "I'm feeling really scared here. I feel trapped and I feel threatened." Instead of having the feeling there as the reality, step back from it and say, "Those feelings are my choice." Maybe even say, "That's a common choice for me, and now I am choosing to let myself enjoy this."

In other words, have your feelings, don't let them have you.

We learn that our feelings are really real, in the sense that that's how life really is. Secondly that you are stuck with them. And thirdly, that if you change them quickly there was something false about them to begin with. So we justify having them by staying in them.

You feel sad, and people say, "What do you feel sad about?" We have a picture that it must take a certain amount of time and maybe even persuasion or discussion, to emerge from the feeling of sadness. That's socially learned. You can get to the point where you can change feelings quickly, at the snap of your fingers. I'm talking about extreme feelings. You can learn to just access the feeling and shift it really dramatically.

For example, I might be feeling really lost, and sit back from the feeling instead of being in it and say, "I am lost." The truth is that I am not lost, who I AM is not lost, but I am having a feeling called Lost. Step back from the feeling and acknowledge it. The internal conversation could go like this, "I'm feeling lost and what's true is, I am having a feeling called lost. It's an old feeling and I know it well. The truth is that I know exactly where I am. I'm in a room in the middle of a group of people, and I don't know the latitude and the longitude, but it's okay to be here and enjoy it." One of the biggest steps to enjoying your life is giving yourself permission to enjoy your life.

Let's say someone walks past, and spills some coffee on you. Normally, socially that is cause for drama. Isn't it?

The game is that he should stand there and say, "Oh my god, I'm really sorry. I apologize. Oh, oh, oh, oh, oh," and after a while it all settles down and you get on with your life. So you have a choice about what your reaction is, it's not already determined. Everything, every feeling, every thought, every reaction you have to anything, is your choice. The minute you're really willing to accept that, what follows is that you're not stuck with anything at all. It's that simple. One of the biggest lessons we learned as kids was, "Limit your enjoyment." Heaven was where you got to enjoy yourself, not Earth. In fact, the more you suffered on Earth, the more enjoyment you got in Heaven. It's called, "God's superannuation plan." It's called Christianity. "Earth is for suffering, Heaven is for getting the rewards." We have major beliefs and limitations about how much, and what, you can enjoy.

I remember really offending some people; we were having a meal in a restaurant and someone walked in and said, "Joe has died." Now, I vaguely knew who Joe was. And the fact was that the people having the dinner at the restaurant weren't very close to Joe. As soon as someone said, "Joe died," the others used it as an excuse for grief and a major drama. That's what society teaches you to do when someone dies. I just couldn't be bothered. It was just a piece of information. I had absolutely no emotional connection with it. So I just kept on eating my dinner, and meanwhile people were bursting into tears, and wailing, "Isn't it terrible?" and, "poor Joe's parents. Poor Joe's wife."

I couldn't believe it! they weren't family; they had nothing to do with Joe. Yet the words, "Joe died," had magically pressed everyone's death buttons - and an automatic social script/response. This is how we learned to deal with the information that someone has died in western society. In Italy it's different again, it's a dramatic drama, beating your breasts and moaning and wailing and you wear black for the rest of your life.

The best funeral or cremation I've been to was in Bali. Forty thousand people at this huge cremation. They employ professional clowns to entertain the people who were there. There were food stalls, music, and much hilarity.

It's a celebration. It's like graduation. The Balinese believe in reincarnation, so to them the person who died has completed this life's class in their soul education, and they're moving on to their next level. So it's like high school graduation. What cracked me up was the officiating priest. They had the body in a carved wooden bull, and the priest was standing there with incense and there was a cigarette hanging out of the corner of his mouth. He's puffing away and there's ash falling on the body. It was totally irreverent. Of course the bull and the body were about to be cremated so a little extra ash didn't matter! It was just a big party.

Participant: ...You know when you shock people?

Gregory: Who me? Yes, I've noticed that I do sometimes.

Participant: ...Do you just stay with it? I'll give you an example. At the last market, someone died, and it turned out that the guy that died was a man that made wind chimes, as I do.

Gregory: Great business opportunities.

Participant: ...I cracked up laughing and thought, "Oh great, I've got the market now." And it was coming out of my mouth before I censored it. And all these people were horrified ...I do that a lot.

Gregory: What I experience most is that people love it, being shocked. Sometimes they bounce off the walls and out of my life. That's fine too.

Mostly they love it. It's my way of being me, and my experience is that people are so bored with the socially acceptable party line, that it's really entertaining and enjoyable hearing a different view point. "New business opportunities" is what I thought as you started telling the story. Not only that, the guy obviously is supporting the growth of your business to the degree that he died! He is a really powerful supporter of you.

My brother suicided a couple of years ago, and from my end of it, he'd done that in support of me. I needed some big lessons about life and death, and he picked up the job. My brother Kevin was one of my Life and Death teachers. He did his job perfectly. Thanks mate, wherever you are.

Participant: ...A friend of my brother's died in his childhood and we all heard about it whilst we were eating dinner. He came back from the phone and told us and then for the rest of night he was making jokes. But I could tell that he felt a lot of pain. What really pissed me off was that he didn't show it. Because I could see that another part of him just went away.

Gregory: I spent three weeks grieving about my brother's dying. I missed him terribly. It was a great loss. I felt a lot of loss, cried it all out, and it was fine. It was really fine.

My mother was in agony about it, and I helped her process and release it over a period of a couple of weeks and suddenly saw that she needed to acknowledge the part of her that was delighted. He had been sick for nine years and had been a huge burden and responsibility for my parents. I told her to stand at the window at my place, and scream out, "You little prick, I'm really glad you've died."

She just went into horror. She said, "I can't say that." I said, "Sure you can. Move your lips and your tongue." It was such a taboo thing to say. She said it or rather whispered it. And I said, "Okay, say it again."

About the fourth time she really let it fly and then she just cracked up laughing. She said, "He was a shit sometimes, wasn't he?" She said, "I loved him but he could be such a bastard." And it healed it. That's what it took: acknowledging the whole truth and letting it all go.

In that business meeting, when I said that I had my training in a psychiatric centre, I don't say things to shock people, I don't go out of my way to offend or to shock people.

In fact, that's never my intention. I just say what's true for me and sometimes people are shocked, but they get it. There was a man I was listening to on radio the other night who was trying to say things that were quotable, and controversial. I could hear his mind ticking over thinking, "How can I say this in a way that is really controversial." On radio I had a picture of him being really full of himself, therefore what he was saying didn't work for me.

My commitment is to tell my truth, not to be controversial. The truth IS contra-verse-ial.

Participant: ...I see you do that, and be so real and so true, yet in my life it seems that to get where I want to go and to grow, it has to be painful.

Gregory: Growth is painful until it's not. It's a common belief that change is painful. So we have to have it painful to make sure we're doing it. "Oh, I must be growing, I feel like shit." Take some of the unpleasant feelings that you've had like detachment, lost, stepped on, walked on, uninvolved, outside of it. Can you have your vision of sex with any of those feelings running? In other words, does your vision of sex include those feelings? No. So you can't have your vision of you sexually if those feelings are present, especially if they are still running you.

The processes in this seminar are an opportunity for you to learn to master and take charge of those feelings, to have a choice about them again. If you're in a process and the feeling of "I get stomped on" comes up, acknowledge "Yep, that's what I've done, and what my vision is, is that I don't get stomped on, I get loved and nurtured. What I am now choosing is love and nurturing." Then do what ever you can to create that. It may mean that you just snuggle with someone over here and you don't go back into that old feeling. The more willing you are to do that, the more rapidly you move through and heal that feeling, so that you have it the way you really want it.

Participant: ...I beat myself up about having negative feelings instead of saying, "Okay, that's fine." I just get really angry with myself and put myself down.

Gregory: An important thing is to understand that you get a real kick out of being beaten up. You wouldn't do it so often otherwise. Every game has a price and a payoff and the price of being beaten up includes bruises and pain.

The payoff is that it's exciting. Death defying. You get your adrenalin running. You know you're being noticed. You feel Alive! It is for you a powerful way to have life be intense, and you love that.

One of the ways to handle that is to own it. We deny that because a judgement says, "If I walk around telling people that I really enjoy being beaten up they're going to think I'm really weird and kinky and perverted." You are!

So is everyone else, one way or another, and when you get honest about that, then do it in a way that's enjoyable. That's what I said yesterday about creating sexual fantasies that fulfill such wants. Create sexual situations where you get beaten up in a safe, fun controlled game. Find a small Japanese masseuse to walk up and down on your back, "Oh, tread on me, tread on me," and then you get a massage in the bargain. Freedom is when you stop judging yourself and you let yourself tell the truth about what you're doing, instead of having it as a complaint. You beat yourself up for letting yourself get beat up. That's how much you enjoy it!

Once you are honest about it, then it can work for you. Once you're willing to bring it out in the open, you can use it as an asset. Every truly successful human being makes their weaknesses work for them. Makes their faults, their limitations, their handicaps, work for them.

I'll give you an example. My brother was in Amway. He enrolled a man who he used to work with into Amway. This guy had been an electrician and lost his arm in an industrial accident, and he was on what my brother called his 'Chicken List,' which meant that he was one of the people that he was terrified of telling about Amway and asking to get involved.

Anyway my brother showed him the business and the guy became interested, got involved and started becoming very successful. He enrolled lots of other people in his distributorship. One of the things he used to say was, "Get how easy this business is. Here I am with one arm, and I'm creating a successful business for myself." Now that's a great selling point. If a one armed person can get wealthy doing something, what can a two armed person do?

People would say, "I can't do it, I haven't got great health," and he'd say, "Hey, I've got one arm and I'm doing it. You can do it with poor health.

You can do it with this disability, you can do it with this handicap." No one had an excuse. You get it?

The guy is on his way to becoming rich. It's perfect.

If I see something that evokes your sadness I deal with it by simply owning the reflection. I'm sad because I identify with that, so when I then cry, I'm crying for me directly, releasing my own sadness. I enjoy crying because I know that it's doing me a power of good and healing me. So I can go into deep, deep, deep sadness, and cry my heart out and love it and wallow in it.

Participant: ...How do you deal with other people when you do that? Do you let them know, or do you close it off?

Gregory: Depends. I mean I don't burst into tears in a business meeting. It might happen but not as a usual thing.

The answer is that there is no right answer. Make it up for yourself. You're looking for the 'right way' to do it. It doesn't work that way. What works for you? If I'm sitting in the middle of a business meeting, and a huge well of sadness suddenly comes up, I'm sure as hell not going to beat myself up to keep it down.

Participant: ...I often wonder if I'm doing it for the wrong reasons.

Gregory: There are none. See, if you're worried that you're doing it for the wrong reasons, then you go looking for the right ones. By who's judgement are they wrong or right?

It comes back to, "Are you doing it to keep them happy?"

Participant: ...No, it's just that I changed and everyone freaked out.

Gregory: See they're telling the truth, they're saying, "Mike, you're not the same anymore." So sit there and say, "You're right, very observant, you're really perceptive. I'm not."

Participant: ...But I get some doubt about going into indulgence.

Gregory: I hope so. That's a good one. I mean, god help you if you should ever indulge yourself. See you've learnt to indulge yourself with self punishment. I suggest you indulge yourself with self pleasure. Life is an indulgence. Life...is...indulgence! You're indulging in something always. Right now you're indulging in sitting on the floor holding a cup of coffee, and sitting on a comfortable cushion. That's an indulgence. Life's an indulgence. You don't have a choice about indulging yourself. The question is, "What are you going to indulge yourself with?"

Christianity has a thing called indulgences, which are bestowed by priests, and if you pray a certain number of times you get a certain kind of indulgence. So traditionally in this life you get indulgence by suffering more.

Participant: ...It's like a coupon system.

Gregory: Nine missionary masses and you get a reprieve, etc...

Participant: ...That's what the holy wars were for. They used to go to war to win indulgence.

Gregory: Yeah, the only indulgence you could get was by suffering more, or paying up. You could also buy "Get Out Of Hell" passes from the Church! It was a very lucrative business.

If you got a plenary indulgence, that guaranteed that you would go to Heaven, until you messed up again, so you had a period of grace. So you went and did all this study and praying and crap, and got your plenary indulgence. And hoped to Christ that if you were going to die, it would happen soon.

All of you sleeping together in the same room last night is called soul food. Again, Balinese families sleep together. Always. It's not uncommon to stay in a Balinese family home and the bedroom is literally that. It's a room with a huge bed in it. And the whole family piles in on it. So sleeping here last night is like normal procedure for Balinese. Balinese are always in touch with each other. Always. We could call this the Bali Seminar actually. It's real food for the soul.

Participant: ...One thing I've noticed since starting this course is that I've started to like being touched. I want people to touch me because I'm really enjoying it and I want to experience it more.

Gregory: How's your back?

Participant: ...Not too good.

Gregory: So are you ready to do something with it?

Participant: ...Yeah.

Gregory: Okay, close your eyes. Now I want you to give your voice to your spine so it can tell us what is going on.

Participant: ...It's trying to stay straight, but it just wants to crawl.

Gregory: What I want you to do is to move somewhere that your spine would sit if it could be here as a separate entity, where would it sit?

Participant: ...In a room somewhere, lying down, or somewhere away.

Gregory: So it wants to sit away somewhere? Is it willing to be here for a while and communicate?

O.K. Make it this space. Has it got a name? We're having a talk with your spine now.

Has it got a name?

Participant: ...Angry.

Gregory: Okay. Angry Spine, tell us your story.

Participant: ...I don't want to be pushed around anymore. And I don't want to hold anybody else up.

Gregory: Who are you holding up?

Participant: ...Her. Everybody.

Gregory: So what do you want to say to them Angry Spine?

Participant: ..."Get fucked," and, "Do your own thing" and, "Leave me alone."

Gregory: Isn't she polite. Is that how you want to talk to them when you're in a state of collapse? You're still demanding that you do more? You feel like you're dying?

Participant: ...Yes, I want to be free of them to do what I want.

Gregory: Let it out. Express it.

Participant: ...I can't.

Gregory: Tell them that. "I can't yell at you." What are you looking for?

Participant: ...Maybe it just wants to be noticed.

Gregory: Okay That's not Spine. That's Control. That's another person who sits there and tries to work it all out. So while you sit there let the spine express.

Participant: ...I can't tell them to get off my back.

Gregory: Okay. So they get to stay there. Tell them. You feel trapped. You can't make them go, and you can't have them stay.

Participant: ...I can't let you go but I can't have you stay.

Gregory: You're in a bind. That's why you haven't resolved this back problem. It's a Catch 22.

Participant: ...I'm scared that if I tell them to go there will be nothing there.

Gregory: So tell them you don't want them to go. Just feel your left leg. What does it want to do? Go on, let it go.

Participant: ...I have to go away. Just create something, but I don't know quite what it is.

Gregory: Can you feel the bind? See, do you get that even when you're not having spasms in your leg and back you paralyze yourself? What sort of spine are you?

Participant: ...A strong spine. Straight.

Gregory: How do you know that you are strong? What would you like to do?

Participant: ...She wants to run away.

Gregory: Forget her, what do you want to do?

Participant: ...Lash out and be strong, and consistent.

Gregory: So, Spine, what do you want to tell everyone? Not what she says but what do you want to tell everyone?

Participant: ...That I can stand up by myself.

Gregory: So stand up by yourself.

Participant: ...I feel like something is pushing me down.

Gregory: Okay. Come over here and turn around. Now stand up and look at them. I want you to close your eyes and imagine all your pain that's involved in a back spasm. Imagine how powerful that back spasm is. Take that and open your eyes and using all the energy and power in a back spasm tell them, "Get off my back," with your eyes open.

And stomp your feet while you're doing it if you want to.

Okay, let your hands clench. You're going to lose your nice act forever now kiddo...people are going to walk the streets and say, "Don't mess with that one."

While you are stamping open your eyes. Do you want them off your back? Okay. Put it into your voice and tell them. Blow your head off. We'll catch it.

Participant: ...I can't do it.

Gregory: What stops you?

Participant: ...I want to hit myself.

Gregory: Sure. I'm not asking you to hit them. So either say, "Get off my back," or say, "I don't want you to get off my back." Which one is true?

Participant: ...Get off my back.

Gregory: Okay. Stand there and say, "Get off my back. Don't get off my back. Get off my back. Don't get off my back."

Because that's what's going through you isn't it? Part of you wants to say "get off my back" and part of you is saying "no. I'll be left with nothing."

Participant: ...Get off my...(laughing)

Gregory: What is it that you keep seeing?

Participant: ...They're all too nice. I don't want to hurt them.

Gregory: Yeah, that's a risk. Testing a new nuclear deterrent. The dreaded four word sentence. Whole cities are going to be destroyed. Individuals will splatter on the walls. So don't say it. Tell them, "Don't get off my back. Please."

Participant: ...I can't.

Gregory: That's called being stuck between a rock and a hard place isn't it? Say, "I won't" by the way.

Participant: ...I won't what?

Gregory: See when you say, "I can't," you lose it, you become powerless. So say, "I won't tell them," and you own your choice and so you become powerful.

Participant: ...I will tell them.

Gregory: Okay, well, tell them.

Participant: ...Excuse me?

(everybody laughs)

Gregory: That's good! (in a very posh, proper English accent) "Oh I say, sorry but if you don't mind would you please excuse me but if you don't mind terribly..." Say it that way, "If it's not too much of a problem..." You think I'm funny.

(heaps of laughter and pausing)

Gregory: Go!

Participant: ...Get off my back. (laughing hilariously)

Gregory: That's getting there. Say it again. You've been carrying these people all your life.

Participant: ...Get off my back.

Gregory: Mmm. Really? Do you want them to get back on again?

Participant: ...Okay guys get off my back. (said wimpishly)

(everyone laughs)

Gregory: Just the guys. Does that mean the women can stay?

Participant: ...No, no, no...Get off my back ... (cough, cough)

Gregory: Okay. Lets play a variation on the theme. Who are some people who would be good to play you and your father and all those other people on your back? Who here could play those?

Now I want you to stand up around her like this. Just kind of leaning and pressing and hanging on. Don't actually drop your weight on her, right. Just apply some pressure. Alright. Does that match the pressure that you feel inside?

Participant: ...No.

Gregory: Okay press harder. Tell them when their pressure matches the pressure inside you. Is that it? Okay, press even more. This is some backache. Don't break her neck. Okay, now this is your life. How does it feel?

Participant: ...Terrible but good.

Gregory: Yes. Terrible but good. So stay there another couple of years.

(she begins to cry out)

How you get them off your back is you've got to tell them to get off in a way that they get that you mean it. If you say, "Excuse me, would you mind getting off my back please?" That's not particularly convincing. So you have to communicate to them in a way that they're going to hear it and get off.

There's no point moving around because there's nowhere to go. They'll just go with you.

(laughter)

Gregory: See she's not laughing she's crying. That's what I was saying about crying coming out like laughter.

Participant: ...Get off my back.

Gregory: Mmm. That's getting there.

Participant: ...Get off GET OFFFFF!

Participant: ...Get off! Get offff!

Participant: ...Get off my baaack!

Gregory: How much of you wants them to get off? See they're going to stay there because you wanted them there. And it's their job to stay there until 100% of you wants them off. So check out whether you're willing to have them off. It's okay to keep them on. Sometimes choices are very black and white.

Don't say I can't. Say I won't. And if you won't, that's fine. Just tell them, "It's fine folks."

Participant: ...No! ...GET OFF !!!!!!!!!!

(at this point they know that she REALLY wants them off and they oblige)

Gregory: What do you want them to do now, right now, quick, what do you want them to do?

Participant: ...Hold me.

Gregory: Let it in. Just feel how closely they're holding you. Just relax into it totally.

Feel the support. Feel the strength.

O.K. just take your weight back onto your feet again. Have everyone gently move back but stay in touch so that you are all standing up together in contact. And just look at each one of them in turn and say to them, "I've put you in my life to support and nurture me." Or your words for that. Go.

Don't wait for their agreement. It's about you telling them their job. They've got nothing to do except what you want them to do.

Participant: ...I've put you in my life to support me and nurture me and love me. I've put you in my life to support me and nurture me and love me. I've put you in my life to support me and nurture me and love me.

Gregory: Next, step forward. Feel that rocking in your body. I want you to really let that come up and exaggerate it. Really let that build in your body. Okay, open your eyes. Look at them all. Rock your body. Great. Okay. Just look at them all and say, "FUCK YOU!" Don't laugh, just do it. From your body, not from your head. Feel that in your body.

Participant: ...FUCK YOU!

Gregory: Great, and more.

Participant: ...FUCK YOU!

Gregory: Yes, go, go, let the sound out.

Participant: ...FUCK YOU!!!!!!!!!!

Gregory: Let the sound out. Now just stand still, and let all your energy come through your voice. Now say, "Me first!"

Participant: ...ME FIR ...(nearly chokes on it)

Gregory: Or maybe second.

Participant: ...ME FIRST!!!

Gregory: "And if you don't like it, fuck you."

Participant: ...And if you don't like it, FUCK YOU!

Gregory: Keep going. What else does your body want to say to them? Get your head out of the way. Is there anything else it wants to say?

Participant: ...I'm powerful.

Gregory: "And I used to be a powerful wimp."

Participant: ...And I used to be a powerful wimp!

Gregory: Yes, go on.

Participant: ...I AM POWERFUL!!! Yeah, I am powerful.

Gregory: What do you want them to do? What do you want to do? You are powerful aren't you? And you're serious about that?

Participant: ...Yeah. (laughter)

Gregory: It's silly to be that serious. So what I suggest you do, is just give a few whoopees. It's terribly indulgent.

(pause)

Participant: ...I am powerful!

(laughter) (pause)

Gregory: Who gets that she needs to laugh as much as she needs to yell? Yeah. You're a very silly woman. Do it right.

Participant: …I AM POWERFUL.

(laughter)

Gregory: See do you get that you're trying to do it right again? So do it wrong.

Participant: …I AM POWERFUL!!!! WHOOPEE!!!!!!!!!!

Gregory: Very good. How would a fish say, "I am powerful, whoopee!"

(laughter)

Participant: …Do you want me to do it? My version? It would probably be doing it like this …

Gregory: Make sure you do it right though.

Participant: …Fuck you.

Gregory: That's great. You can sit down. Thank you. Do you want to get a clap?

(lots of laughter)

Participant: …yeah.

(lot's of clapping)

Gregory: How's your back?

Participant: …Fine.

Day 3

"You get solidness and stability in life by making and keeping agreements and commitments ...and your truth about them may change."

HEAD TRIPS - RECLAIMING PERSONAL VALUE - NEEDS AND FANTASY - GETTING "BAD" - BEING REASONABLE, OR NOT - KEEPING COMMITMENTS - KEEP ASKING - PARALYSIS - HONESTY - AS WITHIN, SO WITHOUT

Gregory: So who would like to share about the Dynamic this morning or about last night? Yes Squeaky.

Participant: ...I always thought it was other people who weren't giving me what I wanted, when really it was me, not knowing what I like, or not that I don't know what I like, but that I like so many things that if somebody says, "What do you like?" I could keep going for half an hour, and not know exactly what I want right at that moment.

Gregory: That's like being at a smorgasbord, and starving to death because you can't decide what to eat first. At smorgasbords I have something of everything I like. So start by telling them everything you like for half an hour. And then the next thing you say is, "Where do we start? Here's my check list." Anyone else?

Participant: ...When I was younger, I was picked on a lot and humiliated a lot. When I was in the situation where I saw another kid or person let down, sad or miserable I'd reach out to them. I really suffered for them and I was feeling that way yesterday.

Gregory: There's a lot of value in having empathy, and compassion, for underdogs. But you can also waste your life being drained by victims, and it can end up a very painful experience. The distinction to learn is between underdogs who want to stay there and underdogs who want to move on. Then put your energy, love and compassion into those who want to move on, and act on it.

Participant: ...Yeah, but it doesn't get away from the fact that I'm absolutely paralyzed by my worry. I felt fear that all the happiness and strength and joy that I've been getting, may just go whooooph! and disappear.

Gregory: Mmm, pull the plug on yourself. See, does that help anyone? No of course not. It's like someone hanging by the tips of their fingers to a cliff and you're so worried about them, you're paralyzed and so do not help. Does that help? No.

Bring it back to you. One way of looking at it is that you use that fear as a way to paralyze yourself.

Someone hurting or being the underdog doesn't cause you to be paralyzed. Otherwise everybody in the world would be in constant paralysis. It's like fears, or phobias. People attach fears to certain things, like elevators, or heights, water, flying, spiders, snakes, etc. ...They experience the fear as not in here (points to chest), in themselves, but out there in the world. So we literally externalize it, which means we can get on with our own life, and we can deal with our fear by constantly avoiding the thing we've attached it to.

The same goes for paralysis or any emotional response to something out there. I've been claustrophobic in the past. I totally created to get trapped in elevators. The payoff was that I had somewhere to hang my fear. As I was growing up, I wasn't an afraid person, except with elevators. So as long as I stayed away from them, I was okay. Then I realized that I had fear and I blamed it on elevators, and so I stayed a victim of them. What's true is that I have fear, it's my fear and I put it out there. When I acknowledge that, then I can start dealing with it directly, as mine. And I did.

You hang paralysis on underdogs hurting. Some people hang paralysis on wide open spaces. Some people hang paralysis on contradictory demands in their life. And that paralyzes you. "Paralyze" is your word. Stay with the word. It's a valuable and very specific word.

It's your hurt and pain you're responding to. Doing it via someone else is a second hand way of dealing with it. You've got a lot of hurt and a lot of pain, and you feel like an underdog, and you find someone out there who matches that, and then you deal with it through them. That's fine, as a starting place, and it is also healing for you. But to fast track that healing you need to bring it back directly and focus on the hurt, pain and underdog feelings in you. Not them out there. Then it is direct, and when you see it out there and feel that hurt and pain instead of running to them, run to you. Ask your hurt and pain what it is that you need.

You don't need to have all the reasons and memories, to do something about it. Let's say I fell off a set of stairs, knocked my head, knocked myself out, and then fell down and cut myself. Then I wake up and my hand is cut. I don't have to remember what happened or know how my hand got cut, to do something about it.

It's a psychiatric rip off: the idea that you have to understand it all before you can do anything about it.

Participant: ...If you go into delving to understanding it, there maybe one, two, or twenty reasons, but you might not be sure about it.

Gregory: That's correct, so then you still don't know, so you delve more, and you find fifty reasons and you still don't know. Having reasons is different to doing something about it. I spent a lot of years in psychiatry, I knew all the theory, I had all the reasons. I had phenomenal intellectual models about me and for understanding me. And it didn't make any difference. Then I got into alternate personal growth.

Participant: ...But what if it's so firmly ingrained that you can't change it, and you try, but you can't. And you don't understand why.

Gregory: Simply don't believe that you can't change it! When the idea comes up for me that I can't change this, I tell the truth and say, "I won't change it." By the way, "can't" means, "I can NOT." It is saying I have a choice between, "I can not," or "I can do." You get it? See to say, "I can't," is acknowledging that you have a choice to, "not." "I can (choose to) not (do it)."

It's like, "I can no" or "I can yes." It doesn't mean it's not possible. It means it's possible and I'm choosing "no."

Delve into origins and models for understanding how it happened, by all means, that's a fun game, but delving in itself doesn't change anything.

Sometimes it helps you understand why it happened, and then you know how to change it.

(Gregory throws cigarette lighter to giver her example)

Gregory: Did you analyze why, or did you do something?

Participant: ...No I did something.

Gregory: Great, you've just found a new way.

Participant: ...It's not that simple.

Gregory: Looks simple to me. See, you didn't say to the cigarette lighter, "Stop, while I understand this process! Let me delve into the deep and complex reasons of why Gregory is hurling objects at me! Let me comprehend the gravitational forces involved here! Just wait a minute while I do a science degree. Then a psychology degree. Then a degree in inertia and physics. And then mathematics. And then I learn motivation.

Participant: ...What if you do do a lot of different things, and none of them work? And it doesn't change the crux of the issue? Then you have to go back and see why.

Gregory: I do? Or you do? Are you saying that that is what happens to you?

Participant: ...Well it's happened with work. I've got to a point where I can't work, or I can't draw, I can't work for anybody or myself, etc...

Gregory: Stop. You just drew a magnificent masterpiece last night. So don't tell me that you can't draw.

Participant: ...But that wasn't in a work situation where I have to do something.

Gregory: Right, so there's the answer. Create a working situation where you don't have to work - where it's your pleasure and joy! See I can't think of anything more terrible than having to give a Sex and Relationships Seminar like this one just as a job.

Participant: ...But I do want to.

Gregory: When you were at school, did you have teachers who did it as a job, and teachers who did it because they loved it.

Participant: ...Yes.

Gregory: What was the difference?

Participant: ...One was really funny and enjoyable and I learned a lot. The other one was boring.

Gregory: Exactly, so the boring one came to work thinking, "I have to do this because it's work." The other one came to school and said, "I love to do this, so I'm here." And they worked in the same structure, but they did totally different jobs and got different results.

The only way that I know to have work work, is to make your hobby pay. That's the only way I know. In other words, do what you love doing most, and find a way to have it pay.

Participant: ...To do the work, I have to be unconscious, but in graphic design, you have to be conscious.

Gregory: So work in your sleep! Ha, ha. What do you mean that to do the work you have to be unconscious?

Participant: ...That's the only way I can do it. Having to get out what I want to get out.

Gregory: So, what I would call creative, you would call unconscious?

Participant: ...Yeah. It just means that I turn off my brain.

Gregory: That's not unconscious, that's called turning off your brain. It's called being creative. Of course you have to turn your brain off to be creative. You don't think that Van Gogh painted by numbers.

In order to do your work, you have to turn off your mind and turn on your creativity. So what's the problem?

Participant: ...The problem is that I can't do it with other people around me.

Gregory: So don't have people around you.

Participant: ...I tried that. I did that. And the thing was that it was okay doing it. But it just freaked me out presenting it to the other person, and then, just the worry was too much.

Gregory: Okay, so you work by yourself fine, but presenting it is the problem. Okay, so don't present it. Get someone else to.

Participant: ...But then if I don't have any contact and I don't know what they want. It's a Catch 22.

Gregory: The thing is, do you want solution, or do you want to stay trapped in the Catch 22?

Participant: ...Well, I need a solution, but...

Gregory: No, I don't care whether you need one, I just said, "Do you want one?"

Participant: ...Yeah, I do.

Gregory: The key is: Do you want a solution? If you do, then look at the problems, look at the steps, and take them apart one by one.

Participant: ...That's what I was saying before. That you have to analyze the problems that come up.

Gregory: That's not what I call analysis, that's the classic mental wank situation.

I sat in a therapeutic meeting in an admission ward once, it went for ten or twelve hours, talking about the management of one patient. Ten or fifteen so-called highly educated professionals discussed all the possible theories about this woman. And at the end of that meeting, not one decision had been made. But by God, we'd covered the text books.

You can analyze to break down the issues so as to find solutions to them, or you can analyze to try to understand them and never actually take any action about them.

It's a really important distinction. Your mind's a wonderful tool. But tools are only as effective as the use you put them to. If you get a hoe and put it to the garden, it's a wonderful tool, but if you get a hoe and put it to carpentry, it's useless. You won't get very far.

Reasoning is looking for reasons "why." That by itself never changes anything. Hundreds and hundreds of medieval theologians spent literally 200 years trying to get an answer to the question, "How many angels can stand on the head of a pin?" Through reasoning. Finding reasons doesn't get results, looking at what you want and what you don't and what you're going to do about that gets results.

Participant: ...But the problem is that I think, "Everybody else can do it, why can't I do it? Everybody else has a normal job where they can function normally."

Gregory: Who are you kidding? What's true is that most people have a job and most people function normally. And what normal means to many of is boring mediocrity.

In many, many years and many, many jobs and many, many areas of work, I have found very few people who have mastered the job they do.

Most people know the superficialities of their work. And once you scratch the surface, they don't know what they're doing. And I'm talking about every level of success. Or influence, or responsibility. You have an internal myth that says, "Everyone out there has got it together and I'm an idiot." Who else carries that myth, or has? Have a look around. See, it's one of the big cons in our society. Everyone thinks that everyone else has got it together.

Participant: ...I can see that I could really enjoy it. But I just can't do it.

Gregory: Sure. Can you imagine me working in a psychiatric hospital? Wiping bums, washing people, filling in forms, handing out tablets, giving injections. Really, can you imagine me doing that?

Participant: ...In a way I can.

Gregory: Yeah. Can you imagine me doing that now?

Participant: ...No.

Gregory: No. Who I am now was trying to find a way out back then. Except who I was then didn't even know who or where I was going to be. No idea. But I knew that where I was wasn't it. Confused?

It was like a mother being pregnant with her baby. You know there's something on the way. You don't know what it looks like.

The way I know to get there is to be willing to keep trying things. I got here by making lots of mistakes. In other words, I did lots of things that weren't it.

Have you ever solved anything by worrying about it? We have a picture that you get from point A to point B by pushing yourself, but you really get from point A to point B by going to point B.

It's up to you whether you fly, crawl, get carried, or walk over broken glass. It's movement and doing things that gets you to point B. The quality of that is extra. It's a separate choice altogether.

Participant: ...But I don't know what B is.

Gregory: Point B will find you. You have to have your eyes open when it arrives.

It's highly possible that all that you want is already present. In other words, point B is here. And you aren't letting it find you. There's nowhere to go.

Everything you ever want, you've already got. You just haven't unwrapped it yet. There's nothing to learn in life except that you're allowed to unwrap all the gifts. It's the only lesson, plus how to unwrap them.

And some of them are tied with tricky knots. So come back to it. You work well by yourself. I want you to acknowledge something. The second I come back to it the voice in your head say, "No, no, no." It's like, "I don't want to hear it, no, no, no. Leave me in my catch 22. It's safe." You keep arguing for your limitations by continuing to tell me why you cannot have what you want, and you have many reasons to prove it.

Participant: ...But working by myself, I can't deal with the stress.

Gregory: There you go again! Instead say, "I WON'T deal with the stress." See, this is called, "The Yes, But, Game." Have you ever had a conversation with a "Yes, But" person?

Participant: ...Yes, especially with myself.

Gregory: Especially with yourself, yeah. See the, "Yes, But, Game" is also called, "I want to stay here but I want everyone to think I don't want to."

"So I'm going to tell everyone that where I am is a problem and they'll come up with every possible solution on the planet and I'll give them a reason why it doesn't work, then they'll all agree that it's tough and I'll have to stay where I am and gets lots of sympathy from them." Either you are committed to proving that you're right, or you're committed to getting results. It's very black and white.

You either justify where you are, or you find ways to get where you want to be. And it's fine to be where you are. You've just got a judgement that it's not okay. See it's like, you come down from Brisbane to live in Sydney, and push the shit out of yourself to get a job and create something. Your back goes into spasm which gives you good reason to not work, so you don't look anymore, and you have a break. The truth is, you didn't want to go to work when you came to Sydney. You wanted to have a holiday. Except the judge in you said, "No, you've got to go to work Kid. Get up. Go to work. Find a job," etc...

So your recreation director is in a deep, deep coma.

Participant: ...Yeah.

Gregory: You've got this Gestapo officer inside you, saying, "Work will make you free. Work will make you free." Tell him the war's over! Look, most of us push sometime or another. Pushing was a big issue for me. When I did Primal Feeling Release work, what I saw was that in my birth, my mother was heavily medicated. I was drugged out of my brain. She was exhausted, plus when she was born, her mother had died giving birth to her.

So on a cellular level, my mother was terrified that the birth would kill her. She was trying to hold her energy back so she wouldn't die. Which meant I was dying. So I got the message, "Babe if you're going to get out of here, you better do it yourself, nothing is going to help." So I pushed and pushed and pushed for ten hours. That is how my body felt it, and recorded it in my cells.

I got a powerful message that surviving equals pushing. That surviving equals, not just standing on my own two feet, but taking on the burden. Literally, not just doing my job, but doing hers as well.

That was reinforced in my childhood in many ways. Pushing became how I survived.

I also had massive back problems, until I did Primal and released the cellular pattern.

Participant: ...Okay. Can you...Oh no, I was going to say, "Can you analyze..."

Gregory: No, I Primaled it. See, Primaling isn't analyzing, it's feeling what has been blocked, and releasing it. Feelings need to be felt. Trying to think or analyze a feeling is as nuts as trying to appreciate a painting by eating it. Wrong information path!

Participant: ...But that's what I call analyzing.

Gregory: No, the difference for me is, I had hundreds of reasons why I was the way I was. Then I found out what it was.

See it's the difference between my saying, "Here, I've got a box, and there's something in it, what is it?" And you all guess for three or four years. And then I say, "Look in the box," and you all know instantly. That's the difference for me with Primal and reason. Primal feeling release is totally unreasonable. It's my body telling me what feelings are actually there to be felt, expressed and thus healed, rather than my head making up possibilities.

I've had dramatic life breakthroughs that really started with Primal. I've increasingly been letting go of the pushing process, and just learning to let go and relax and trust myself and trust the Universe, to do what I want to do in a flowing movement forward. This year I have had phenomenal success and growth with seminars, with staff, with money and all sorts of things. And I have done less than I have ever done. More importantly, I am trusting that. Just trusting the process, trusting where I am.

The meetings that I've been talking about, I don't go into them by pushing.

I go in there with the attitude, "This is where I am now. Here's a new bunch of people to talk to." I sit and talk with people in seminars. I sit and talk with people in business meetings. I sit and talk with my son. It's just being there, where I am. Being there with whatever comes up. The results blow my mind.

I say it so many times you know, let yourself acknowledge where you actually are, and accept that it's okay.

Where you actually are right now is confused, and not working. You're not sure about what it is you want. Now are you going to beat yourself up for being there or is it okay to be there now?

Participant: ...It's okay to be there for now.

Gregory: Whenever I think that my happiness or my satisfaction or fulfillment relies on having something or someone in my life, I disappear it. Creating that is about loving me so much, that I'm not going to settle for having my value outside of me. It's like fear. Initially we hang our fear on something outside ourselves; it could be AIDS, elevators, terrorists or nuclear wars. Then when we're ready we face it and deal with it directly.

The same goes for value. A lot of people operate unconsciously; everything they feel is outside of them and everything they value is outside of them. Now that's a hell of a lot better than having no value at all, if the only way you can get value in life is to have a new swimming pool then get one.

As soon as my value, or need, or want, or desire, or well-being is "out there," I disappear it. My self-loving choice is to disappear it to force myself to find whatever it is I want out there in here, inside me. To literally own the reflection.

So that I get to the value here in me, or I get the need fulfilled here, or I get the satisfaction or pleasure or happiness here. The minute I get it here, I don't need it out there. And the minute I don't need it out there, I get it by the bucketful. Then I can have it, and enjoy it, but don't depend on it for my value.

We want it to be big and we resist starting with it that big. We think that the thing or person out there will make our lives work better and make us happier, but when we get that love and value in here, within ourselves, our lives are better with or without "the other" person or thing. Which means that we're not dependent on things or people to have our lives work. That's freedom. Now I love living in luxury. I love having money to spend. I love traveling the world. I love having wonderful lovers. I love having wonderful friends. I love all of that, but I don't need any of it for me to be inherently, intrinsically okay with me, and for me to enjoy myself. I am totally unquestionably clear that if everything in my current life disappeared tomorrow, I'm fine. And I'll look around and I'll say, "Wow, it was obviously time for a major change." So then I would grieve for the old, and go and create something new.

I disappeared everything once so far. It was terrifying, but I didn't disappear. To me that is freedom.

Participant: ...Six months ago, I was totally dependent on everything and everyone to let me know how great I was. And when I was on my own, I became so scared because I had no sounding boards to reassure me.

Gregory: You didn't exist in your own right. You existed in terms of everyone else. That's literally dependent existence. That's good cause to be sad, so when you see it happen again, boom, sadness will come up. I suggest you welcome it, the fact that you're seeing it and crying it out now, is proof positive that you're moving on from it. You can't be sad and cry about something until you're leaving it, or ready to leave it. When you're in it, you can't see the sadness of your own situation. You can only see it when you start leaving it and moving into something else. The healing of it is happening.

There's something else I want to say about that.

Very few of us have sex for sex, we use sex for lots of other things, that have no right to be in the bedroom.

If you're feeling empty, and dependent on someone to fill you up, then A) it's not going to be great sex, and B) it's going to block having sex for itself. Why? Because you're not there to have sex, you're there to be filled up. We take all sorts of needs and desires and feelings into the bedroom that have nothing to do with it. A good friend of mine who has done a lot of seminars with me and who works as a high-class prostitute once said to me, "It's amazing how many men have angry dicks." They use their dicks to express their anger. For those men it's not sex, it's an anger release session.

A lot of feelings that have got nothing to do with sex are expressed through genitals. As those feelings appear, look at them and see that you have them; that you have neediness, sadness, anger, etc...

Find other places to express those feelings, so that you shed the dross that you take to bed and your sexuality, your sexual energy and your sexual experience becomes much fuller and more complete.

Participant: ...At the moment I just feel lost. I thought I was getting somewhere.

Gregory: Okay, so you can go into the hurt of feeling lost again and say to yourself, "I'm not getting anywhere, I haven't achieved anything." As

I see it, you've done a lot, you've moved a lot, and you have learnt a lot. Now again there's a challenge to be faced again, and lessons to be learned around the life issue called: "Your Needs" - that need some more work done on it.

You'll do some more work on the issue of Your Needs and then later the issue will come back to you on a new, higher level. It's like building a house. You're building your own temple.

Imagine building a skyscraper, the plumbers will put pipes down in the foundations and then they go away for a while. A few more walls go up, and the construction manager rings the plumbers and says, "Hey come back, we need you again." The plumbers say, "we've already done our job there, why didn't you tell us when we were there the first time?"

You can't do the plumbing for the 20th floor until you have built the 19th floor of the skyscraper. You cannot deal with a certain level of your issues until you have built up to them, learned the lessons and built the strength and knowledge to master them at the next higher level. I often get to a point where I've got four or five issues in my life that just keep coming around at higher levels, like a spiral. So at this level of my life, I handle issues of power and influence, of sexuality and of opening my heart. I play at this level and complete it, and then my life shifts to a higher level. Then I handle those same issues around my power and my sexuality etc. at that level. Then I get that in place and move to the next one. At each level of mastery I get more payoffs, more value, more simplicity and more enjoyment - and more, more!

So it's the same process in a different context.

Sex and relationships are the same. At each level of mastery you open to new and bigger possibilities to master.There's great value in knowing what you're going to bed for and who with.

One of the things that you can acknowledge is that you want to be given to a lot before you get there. Again it's taking a feeling and turning it into a fantasy. Acting out a fantasy, so the fantasy may be that you're the Queen of Sheba, and you get a man to play your totally dedicated life servant. Once you do it for what it is, then it changes.

While ever your need is surreptitious, then it's sneaky, because you're not being clear and honest about it. People will then wonder, "what's going on?" because there is something unacknowledged, that doesn't feel quite right. But once you set it up, two things happen. You become open and honest about being looked after and pampered. And that is given to you. You realize that you can give it to yourself by creating that person there. Then when you have sex without that need, it will change for you, because you know you can have what you want without trying to grab it all the time. It's like not walking around looking for crumbs all the time, because you know there's a room full of bread.

Another version is called, "Getting what you want directly." There are two ways to deal with anything. You can deal with it here/inside or there/outside or ideally with both. Firstly, acknowledge your own need to be given to and showered with attention and pampering and start doing that for yourself in your life, then you will create it directly out there.

My mother was sick through my whole childhood. So I did not only my work, but a lot of hers. I ironed all the shirts and did most of the cooking. I was a servant. I was in service. So I grew up with the belief that the only way that I could have a relationship was to give give give. It almost never occurred to me that I could be given back to. Then I realized that "I want to be given to." I love giving, but I don't love giving endlessly. I don't love pouring it down an endless pit. I also want to get it back. So now I have my tea made for me. I have my room handled for me. I get a lot of service. A lot of people serve me as an acknowledgement of how I serve them; so there's an energy interchange. I give and receive and they're both happening together. To me, that's perfect. The service may be that your boss comes up and says, "Here's some money."

I think bosses should bow when they pay wages. In our society, money is an energy exchange. It's saying, "You've served me, I'll serve you."

Another thing that could be very powerful for you, is a counter-fantasy, where you totally serve someone. When you're feeling really needy and wanting it you don't give it. That's certainly the emotional tendency; "Well I'll start giving it when I get it." That's the pattern of waiting and hoping etc. Break the pattern by doing what you'd like done for you. "Do unto others as others as you will have them do to you." **Participant:** … Last night I just wanted to switch off, a lot was happening around me which made me feel just like withdrawing into a cocoon. It seemed totally unfair that other people were enjoying themselves, but I couldn't. I've been listening to what you've said about creating situations, and finding what you need. In my relationship I have sensed the constant demand for reassurance and that give give give, and I cut off. I would like to find out what it's like to create a situation where my partner just allows me to give what I want to give and not demand anything from me.

Gregory: You can master anything, by breaking it down to it's component parts. For example, a friend of mine had never learnt to swim and was really scared of the water and scared to learn to swim. I said, "It's a piece of cake, I'll teach you on the seminar." To teach someone to swim, there are four steps and you can do three of them out of the water. How we often approach something like learning to swim is to think to ourselves, "OK, I've got to learn to swim, so that if I'm dropped into the middle of the ocean, I'll be alright."

That's not going to help you to learn swimming. Break it down into it's components so that they're so simple, an idiot could do them. That's how you master anything.

You want to become an instructor of the seminar? Start by cleaning toilets perfectly.

I am a masterful toilet cleaner. I clean them with love and dedication. I don't now. But when I was on seminar support teams, and learning to be an instructor, I did. I learnt to put the coffee cups out perfectly. I used to have seminars where there'd be a coffee break, and the participants would walk into the coffee room and no one would drink coffee because I'd put them out so magnificently they didn't want to disturb them. The instructor had to instruct people to drink coffee and tea. I'm talking seminar after seminar, break after break. It ended up being the pattern that if I was on coffee, they'd wait until everyone was in the coffee room and appreciated the artistry, then they'd drink coffee. You get to be an instructor by being a brilliant coffee cup setter; you master every step.

With sex, it's the same. Break it down to it's components. If there is an issue about giving and receiving, spend a period of time doing nothing but giving, so that you have a complete experience of giving unconditionally and in total surrender. Then change it so that you receive and experience total receiving and unconditional surrender. Immerse yourself in the pure experience of it with someone. Once you get that component, move on to a new one.

Listen, one of the biggest mindfucks in our society, is that when you're a kid, you're told sex is dirty, leave your dick and pussy alone they're dirty, it's naughty, it's wrong, it's bad. You then grow up in a religion or you go to school, and you find out that it's wrong and sinful and immoral and only sluts and tarts do it. Right? Then you go through your teenage years where you're hot and horny as all hell but you're not allowed to do it. If you do you feel guilty because you've got to do it secretly. Everyone tut tuts about it. Then suddenly you're supposed to slip this little band of magic gold on, and suddenly all of that should disappear, and your pussy runs wet and your dick runs hard and everything is magic and mystical. Bullshit! IT DOESN'T WORK THAT WAY! It does not work that way.

It's like growing up and suddenly at the age of 23, being told, "Oh, by the way, you're the manager of Apple, now go and do a good job!" And being the manager of Apple is a damn sight less involved than being a sexual master.

One of the most amazing relationships I know of was between two Living Game Seminar graduates who did the seminar years ago. The man was gay. They were both in their forties. Very successful people. Millionaires, and the guy could only enjoy sex with guys between the age of 17 and 20; he could not tolerate being touched by anyone except during the actual act of sex. So when he did the seminar, he literally nearly threw up when people hugged him. His hugs were rigid, he was just amazing. The woman who is now his wife, was also in her early forties, she'd already been married for seven years and had total amnesia about it, and still does I might add, about what happened between the moment she said, "I do," and the moment the divorce was final. She just can't remember anything about it. Now this is not a great start to a relationship. These are people who are 99.99% incompetent in human relationships. Personal relationships. They both wanted to have kids. They were friends before they did the seminar, did the seminar and six months later decided to get married. Everyone who knew them just fell down stunned. Unbelievable.

They made an acknowledgement that is one of the most powerful acknowledgements I've ever heard a couple make. They sat down, did an acknowledgement process together and each one said, "I want you to know that I am totally incompetent in relationships. I know nothing about them. I don't even like your sex. I don't know if I could ever get to the point where I can mess with you. I don't know if I am capable of creating any enjoyment with you, but I like you, and I'm willing to go for it with you on that basis, and on the basis that I have no hopes or expectations for this relationship. However I'm willing to do everything I can to have it work."

After that, there's nothing to hide. What can you hide after that? Why would you need to? So one of them would do something really stupid and say, "Yeah, I warned you," and the response was, "Yeah, you warned me and I knew." There's no need to defend yourself in that relationship. What they said is at least somewhat true for all of us.

All of us have learnt more than they had and most of us haven't learnt much more; we live in the pretense that we know a lot more. Their relationship has grown faster than any relationship I've ever seen. They took off. A year later they had a kid and now they've got another kid. The guy came and did some Primal sessions with me and occasionally I would say, "How's the relationship going?" and he'd say, "Be great if she was an 18 year old boy." He said that to her. He'd be sitting there having dinner with her and say, "Why don't you grow a dick?" She would crack up laughing. And given the amnesia story she'd say, "I will, umm, what was your name again?" They just take the piss out of each other in the most loving way you could imagine.

Participant: ...My version of amnesia is that I just deaden myself. I am afraid that I'll get hit. My father hit me a lot.

Gregory: The first question is, are you alive or not? Yep. So it feels like you're not. You deadened yourself, you didn't die. When your father was hitting you, you didn't choose to die, you chose to pretend you were dead. There's a chasm of difference between those two choices. Choosing to pretend you're dead or to deaden yourself, is light years away from choosing to die. You adopted a play-dead act.

There's no point hitting someone that's dead. So it worked. Very smart, wasn't it? Very creative choice. You beat him to the punch. You got him. You killed yourself off, or pretended to, before he could. And that guaranteed your survival. It worked because you're sitting here talking now. You're not actually dead.

At the same time you say, "I'll pretend I'm destroying me, so you don't have to Dad. I'll do your job for you." That way, you've got him off your back. And meanwhile you've been saying, "Idiot fell for it. It worked."

You've got one problem; you haven't yet registered that he isn't still there.

Participant: ...I let him attack me.

Gregory: Yeah, say that again slowly.

Participant: ...I let him attack me.

Gregory: Cry and say it again. You can go into self pity and beat yourself up again, or you can get through this. Say it again. "I let him attack me."

Participant: ...I let him attack me.

Gregory: Yeah, emphasize the "I".

Participant: ...I let him attack me.

Gregory: You wanted your father to love you, yes or no? As a child. Did you want him to love you or not?

Participant: ...Yes.

Gregory: Yes, what you got was beatings. Okay, I say beatings were better than nothing.

The only way that your father knew to relate to you was to beat you up and the only way that you were going to get contact, was to let him attack you. So you did. Because that beat having nothing with him.

They've done research on monkeys and found that baby monkeys that are hit and get no nurturing when they are young, live. Baby monkeys that are never touched die. Very interesting, there's the value of getting hit. It's possible that if he had totally ignored you, you'd have just died, so letting him attack you was a hell of an improvement on nothing. And it worked. You got here, you survived, but that was then and this is now. The only way that you could get love and attention and physical contact then was by "letting him attack you." You've learnt that love and attention equals getting beaten up, so you create that for yourself. If people aren't beating up on you, it means that they don't love you. Seriously. If people treat you well you don't trust them. Someone walks up to you and smacks you, you're theirs Babe. That's what the books call masochism. But the word doesn't say anything. The truth is that we all learn to get love the best way we can, but then we forget and think that that is love. Then we go and look for it even when intellectually we don't want it.

We've all got our own versions of that.

Okay. The first thing is that then isn't now. You learnt to get love the best way you could then, but there are other options now. The second is that everyone else in your life isn't your father or your mother. Other people have other ways of expressing their love and affection. If you want, you have to learn how to recognize it.

It's like someone else saying she felt like no one was giving her what she wanted. Maybe it was there but she wasn't getting it. In the same way, people could love you but you don't know that that's love yet.

Acknowledge that you enjoy it. Whether you want it or not, is another story. Understand the distinction? You must enjoy it to do it so much but your rational mind says, "That's crazy. I do not enjoy being beaten up. If I did then I'm some sort of pervert. Society has serious judgments about that." Truth is, you wouldn't do it so much if you didn't enjoy something about it.

It's like our mate here who's a committed head banger. Sometimes it's a floor, sometimes it's a problem. He'd rather bang his head against a problem than solve it.

One of my issues was struggle. I struggled so much in my life. Push and struggle. They were my twin friends. Push and struggle.

I woke up with them, I went to bed with them, I took a bath with them. They hung out with me all over the place. Push and struggle.

One of the breakthroughs for me was to realize that I really love struggling. I must. I did it all the time. Then I started asking myself, what is the payoff? One is that I get to know that I'm doing something, if nothing else, and it makes me strong; it's like going and lifting weights. You just sit there and struggle with yourself. Who needs to go to the gym? I can tell everyone how hard it is and get lots of sympathy and condolences like, "Yeah, you're doing a really good job, stick at it."

More importantly, I felt totally safe struggling. I had totally explored and investigated The Land of Struggle. I knew every blade of grass and every flower in The Land of Struggle. But the Land of Ease, which was across the ocean, was foreign territory. I didn't know what was over there. Tigers and dangers and volcanoes that erupt. Who knows? It might be better, but I was not sure, at least I knew where I was here. It was that security of knowing and literally being at home in The Land Of Struggle. For you it's "The Land of Beatings."

You begin to master something by telling the truth, which is, "I've chosen to be beaten up for most of my life. I get huge payoffs from it, or I wouldn't do it."

The challenge is to learn to enjoy it and consciously choose it, instead of being a victim about it.

The immediate fear is that if you start enjoying it then you'll always do it. Guess what?

You've been doing it all your life, have a look at the evidence. When you don't enjoy it, it keeps happening, it follows that if you do enjoy it, there's a good chance that it will stop happening! Or more to the point, stop happening unconsciously and out of your control.

Being beaten up is an old friend of yours. The minute you enjoy it, I say two things will happen. Firstly, you'll have other choices. Secondly, you can still get beaten up every now and then, when you want to be, for old times sake, in a way that you choose and control and so can enjoy, even get pleasure from, like maybe you'll have a really deep massage that hurts in a good way.

Who's ever created a situation where you've got into some beating up, and really enjoyed it? Put your hands right up please. So it can be seen. Was it fun? Was it a turn on? Was it really exciting? Was it really scary? Was it a high point? Yes.

The truth is, we all beat ourselves up and get ourselves beaten up as victims, until we don't. When you own it and create it as a safe fantasy, then instead of it being real life, it is just another "enjoyable game." Another example of it is football. Some people who need to get beaten up go and play football, or other contact sports. A lot of people like getting beaten up in a game. Have you ever seen people coming off a football field? That's serious shit. That ain't fantasy.

That's kind of between victim and fantasy. They come out of the game and they've got eyes popped, and ears ripped off, and their dicks have been strangled, and their legs are broken, and they're saying, "Oh, a fantastic game wasn't it man? Eh, can't wait till next Saturday to get out of hospital and play again."

See we've got all this stuff in our head about what's okay and what's not okay. Whatever is judged to be not okay, like getting beaten up, we'll find a way to do it that is okay. Call it playing football. It's still not okay for most men to cry, or hug, so they create a game called "go to the pub', get pissed, fall over, hug each other and cry. If we could suddenly have a little magic wand, and go, "Bing, Australia, it's okay for men to cry and hug each other." Then pubs would go broke. The beer industry would collapse. Get it?

Do you want to keep getting the crap beaten out of you and feel like shit or do you want to find another way of getting your jollies?

Participant: ...Well I'd like to find another way, but I don't know ...

Gregory: "I'd like to," means that, "If someone comes along and gives it to me on a plate, then I might." It doesn't work that way. Where is your commitment? If you have a commitment to find another way, then you start looking for and creating other ways. There's no energy in "I'd like to."

Can you honestly tell me you're having fun in your life with all that shit going down?

Participant: ...No.

Gregory: The worst that can happen is that you stay having no fun. The possibility is that you'll actually have a lot more enjoyment.

Find a way to get beaten up that's fun. I'm not suggesting you try and be normal. God forbid that I would ever suggest that. But you think: "There are only two choices. Either I go out and get beaten up by a bunch of

Hell's Angels, or I go and be very nice." They're not choices, that's like saying, "Will I eat the rotten apple or the rotten pear?" You don't have a picture that there's a thing called fresh fruit.

It's a choice between, "Ugh" or, "Ugh."

You chose to live, and it comes back to owning that choice. You've chosen to live and you act like you haven't.

Are you willing to own your choice to live, and commit to your aliveness? That's the only issue, the rest is detail. A thing that you do a lot is get scattered in the details. It's like having a tree whose roots are dying, and you are trying to glue the leaves on. Always tend to the roots. Get back to the roots.

Are you willing to choose and commit to aliveness, and health, and well-being and fulfillment and enjoyment? It's okay if you don't.

I know it scares you, what's your commitment?

Participant: ...Mmmmm. I commit to live.

Gregory: That's sounds like some wimpy politician saying, "I'm going to be the President." No, how could he be? Everyone would just yawn.

Participant: ...I choose to be free and live.

Gregory: So say, "It feels really scary, and I choose to live."

Participant: ...It feels really scary, and I choose to live.

Gregory: Now if it is true for you, say, "I always chose to live and hid that really well from myself."

Participant: ...I always chose to live, and fully.

Gregory: Yeah. See it coming? Full power of acknowledgement. "Now I choose to live, fully."

Participant: ...I feel bad.

Gregory: Okay, try this on. Tell them, "I'm a bad bad girl, and I love it." Come on. And then say, "Who wants to be bad with me?"

Participant: ...I'm a bad, bad girl.

Gregory: Now say it fully. Just drop cute and get it.

Participant: ...I'm a bad, bad girl. Who wants to be bad with me?

Gregory: Okay, do the whole thing. I mean right now, the message I get is that your version of being bad is throwing candy at each other.

(laughter)

Participant: ...I'm a bad, bad girl.

(more laughter)

Gregory: Now it sounds like we're going to tell dirty jokes. Say it like this, "I am a bad woman. I am an evil woman." Or your words for that.

Participant: ...I'm scared that you all won't like me.

Gregory: They might not. They may all hate you and judge you. That's the risk and you'll never find out, but while you don't find out, you don't like you.

Participant: ...Who wants to be bad?

Gregory: Have you got another word for bad? The word "bad" is a word that's like, "UGH." What is it that you do that you call being bad?

Participant: ...Having fun.

Gregory: ...Okay, having fun. What else do you do that's called, "Being bad?" What do you do that you judge as bad? Having fun. What else?

Participant: ...Laugh. Being an animal...Being touched ...Screaming ... Being tied up.

Gregory: Tied up. Great, that's kinky. Okay, so there's lots of things you'd like to try. Okay. So now say, "Who would like to do all that with me?"

Participant: ...Who'd like to do all that with me?

Gregory: See. Some do. Some don't. That's how life is. Do it with the people that want to do it.

Participant: ...I don't understand. I need to understand it first.

Gregory: So go and spend 20 years understanding it. You don't have to understand how that sofa got made, in order to sit on it. You can waste your time and energy by going and finding out why it happened, or you can get on with your life.

I actually think it was a climatic change. There was an international Earth Worm convention, and they all came to the surface for this convention, changing the weather pattern. Everyone who started a relationship that day, ended up brutalizing each other. It's as good a reason as any.

You look for it where it isn't, and you don't get it where it is. That's the thing about addiction. When you say, "I am going to have this, and I will attract the person or people that want to have that with me, and I don't give a damn what their names are." That's when you get it.

***

Participant: ...My boyfriend gives me the shits, he's a liar.

Gregory: ...Sometimes. You never lie?

Participant: ...No.

Gregory: Are you going to stand there and tell me you've never lied?

Participant: ...Yes, but he changes his mind.

Gregory: Never? You've never changed your mind? You've never changed direction or decisions?

People are allowed to change their minds. It's a really big thing to lay on someone, that the minute they say something, they must stick with that for the rest of their life. Our truth changes. We've looked for solidness and stability by never changing our truth. But that's denying life, and the reality of life. You get solidness and stability in life by making and keeping agreements and commitments, and your truth about them may change.

I've made commitments where my truth was, "Wow, I'm really excited about this." Then three months later or two days later, my truth was, "I wish I hadn't made this commitment." But I kept the commitment.

You get solidness within yourself by keeping your word, and your truth may change.

There's a subtle difference. People change their minds all the time. That's what minds do. Asking people to never change their minds, is like saying to the ocean, “Be flat, always be flat.”

“B sharp.”

(everybody groans)

You don't have to like it. Every now and then, one of my jokes falls flat ...

(more groans)

Making your mind up is for now. It doesn't mean it's got to stay that way forever. How boring! I mean I made my mind up to come and do a Sex and Relationships Seminar, but I'm not going to live here forever, and I'll make my mind up to do something else after it. Thank you.

Participant: ...Yesterday I acknowledged that I love people walking all over me.

Gregory: Get a Japanese masseur, really.

Participant: ...When people walk all over me, my heart just nearly shoots out and almost hits the wall. I get off on it.

Gregory: It's much easier just to have adrenalin injections, that's why people take speed. There's not enough risks out there.

Try and get someone to resign from the advertising industry. They're addicted to it. They sit there and bitch about their ulcers, but they won't leave.

One of the payoffs of having people walk over you, is that you don't get too powerful before you are ready for it.

Then when you own your power, you don't walk over people. Because you know how it feels.

One thing we sometimes do in life is create experiences of things that we're afraid we might do to other people. That reinforces for us what it would feel like to others if we did it to them, so that we don't.

Instead of you becoming this powerful little bugger, who walks over everyone on the way to your success, you get walked over, so you know how rotten it feels. As you move into success, you will find a way to do it without walking over people because you know how lousy it feels. The old picture is that in order to become successful you have to trample people, whereas you get trampled and force yourself to find another way to become successful.

Participant: ...I was really pissed off earlier so I got up and went outside, because I didn't want to be involved in that. I was saying to myself, "Drama Queen." And then I realized that I'm a Drama Queen. I love drama. And I couldn't bare to see that in someone else.

Gregory: That's another part of it. Thank you. You both love attention. The Leo energy that we have all got that loves to be centre stage. You can do it two ways. One way is to create dramas that force people to notice you. The other is to end your dramas, and emerge as a powerful human being, a shining light, whom everyone notices. Being Drama Queen is a substitute for the real thing.

A good example of that is Mick Jagger. Mick Jagger is the ultimate Leo. He's a double Leo. You've seen him on stage, haven't you? Man, does he just strut his stuff. He loves the attention. The guy is a multi-millionaire and he's still doing concerts. Why? Because he digs the attention. He loves being on stage. And Mick Jagger is so incredibly successful. Why? He loves it, he enjoys it. What else? He owns it. He doesn't get up there and go, "Oh, shucks folks, I'm just here trying to make you happy."

Bullshit. He says, "Eh, dig me. I've got it. You know I've got it. I know I've got it. Let's dig it together."

He owns it, he loves it. I doubt he has the time or energy for dramas.

I keep saying, "Get a Japanese masseur," if you're going to get walked on, you might as well make it a Japanese masseur, and really have it. What a wonderful choice to make in life, no choice is bad, it's having the choice about it. Take procrastination. Everyone says, "Procrastinating is a bad thing," but procrastination is just procrastination. I consciously choose to procrastinate getting sick, and I'm procrastinating dying. What a wonderful use of procrastination.

You can find a powerful and effective use for anything. It's just a matter of using it where it works for you. The button that presses for most people is losing control. Everyone says, "I want to lose control," or, "I'm scared of losing control, but it would be really nice if I could let go."

Great. You want to have a new experience, get someone to tie you up, AND make sure it's someone you trust. Don't walk down to the psychiatric hospital and say, "Will you tie me up?"

Participant: ...I realize that I don't know what my first step is. With everyone here, l felt out of touch and the expression of that is my fear of touching people. I realize that my whole life is untouchable.

Gregory: I'll tell you something you can do about being touched. Set it up with someone to do this with you. Do an acknowledgement process where you acknowledge everything unlovable about you. Everything that you can think of, that you judge to be not valuable, unworthy, disgusting, evil and filthy: everything which keeps you not letting people touch you. You have such a judgement about your own rottenness, that you stop people touching you to protect them. So let them know how rotten you are, then see if they still want to touch you.

Remember that incompetent couple I told you about? When you've got nothing left to hide, you've got nothing left to lose. When you're willing to lose everything you open the space to gain everything. When you've got nothing to lose, you have everything to gain. It's true. And that works with sex, relationships, money, work, health, you name it.

Participant: ...An interesting thing to acknowledge that I've had sex, yet I feel like a virgin. I've only had two lovers, maybe it's lack of experience.

Gregory: In one sense, I think that most people are still virgins. I fucked - and I use the word intentionally - I fucked hundreds of women and I was still a virgin. The truth was that I'd done a lot of vaginal masturbating, but I hadn't had what I now call, "Real Sexual Experience." I'd just had lots of fucks.

Have you eaten food and you have not tasted it sometimes? Then you have a shift in consciousness or a shift in awareness or focus, or something, and you eat food like you've never ever eaten it before. You've never ever tasted it before like that, where suddenly it's, "Wow." That's what I'm talking about.

***

Participant: ...My back is hurting, and I get angry that I haven't healed it yet.

Gregory: This is such a pitfall. Because you don't want it, you don't let yourself value having it, or let yourself have it with ease and fun. It's like smoking. Everyone suddenly decides that smoking is bad, and there's always people saying, "Ohhhhh, it's bad to smoke. Put them out." They give up smoking and take up being self-righteous about it instead. I had the intention to let go of smoking, and in the meantime I acknowledged that I did it out of love and wisdom for myself and had it in my life as a valuable friend and ally, that had been with me for years.

When I started beating myself up about smoking, it didn't help. I just felt more beaten up. So I sat down and did an acknowledgement process with a packet of cigarettes.

I thanked them for being there, for giving me whatever it was that I needed from them, and welcomed them as my friends. I'd light a cigarette and say, "Thank you, I love you, and I acknowledge you for being here for me." It's the same as with your back. You've got it, and while you do not get the message and value it, you get to resist it and it stays. Over time, by owning them I could also let them go.

Participant: ...I just can't function.

Gregory: So maybe the message is, "Have a rest, stop pushing." When you stop getting on your back, and when you stop pushing, and when you give yourself permission to just lie down and do nothing, you won't need your back to give you that message by hurting. In the meantime, your back maintains your health, by forcing you to have what you need.

Let's say you've already heard that it's a good idea to take a break occasionally, but you don't listen. Then, excuse the bad pun, your back is the back-up system. When you don't listen to what you need, in terms of self nurturing and rest, your back comes in and says, "Whammo, now she'll get it, despite herself."

See, here's something to acknowledge your back for. If you didn't have a crook back, you would never rest, you would never take breaks, you would never let go, you would never just stop, you would never relax.

What kind of life is that? Boring and painful. The pain in your back is a hell of a lot less pain than you would have if you lived your life that way. I'm suggesting that you acknowledge your back for that. Thank it for being there and having more brains about your well-being than you've got, and for looking after you better than you do. I would go so far as to invite my back to come back, anytime it thought I needed a rest.

Participant: ...Or wanting affection.

Gregory: That's part of it because you don't give yourself nurturing and rest. You create a crook back which gives you permission to ask for a massage, for example: it gives you permission to be nurtured. You want to get from another person what you won't give yourself!

How to end the need to create a painful back is to make a commitment to take regular breaks, and to nurture yourself twenty times more than you think you need, to have regular rests, to regularly let go of work and the world, and just take it easy. When you are living all of those commitments, your back doesn't need to hurt you anymore because you got the message.

I say we create everything with love and wisdom for ourselves. That includes and means that our creations love us. Your back hurts you because it loves you. Any good friend will tell you if you are screwing up, so you can see and change it. They do that because they love you and want you to have the best. So you can have your friends, and your back, be your persecutors, or you can have them be your teachers.

Participant: ...Yeah, that just cleared it for me! It's stopped hurting! My back just stopped hurting right then! Wow.

Gregory: Something else I suggest you do, on fantasy levels, is have sex where you lie on your stomach and the man or woman gets on your back. At least then, it's fun to have someone on your back. Seriously.

Do you want to hear a good joke? Have you ever heard of Sophie Tucker? Sophie Tucker was an off-the-wall woman in the 1930's in America. This was when Prohibition was on and America was a moral bloody prison. In her act Sophie Tucker talked about a guy called Ernie. One of her jokes was, "Ernie said to me, "Soph, you've got no tits and a tight box," and I said, "Get off my back, Ernie.'"

(laughter)

***

Participant: ...Last night, I asked someone for a cuddle but she'd already agreed to a date with someone else. I always hold back, then when I do something, it might be too late, that's a very strong pattern. There were two other women around and I thought., "Yes, I'd like to ask one of themthe same thing." I knew intellectually that yes, I could, but because I'd had a "no," inside me I just wouldn't do it.

Gregory: Why? What might happen?

Participant: ...It's an old story about, "It's Not Right." **Gregory:** What's not right?

Participant: ...Spreading myself around.

Gregory: He thinks he's a pound of butter. You've traveled from Sydney to come here. That's not spreading yourself around?

Participant: ...The other thing I noticed this morning was that my voice is almost gone.

Gregory: As honestly as you're able to say, did you really want a cuddle, or did you really want sex?

Participant: ...Both.

Gregory: By putting out that you want a cuddle when you wanted both, you present to people that there is something unsafe about you.

Participant: ...I just wanted to feel safe with myself.

Gregory: Okay, did you say, "I'd like to have a cuddle and relax and get safe and move into having sex?"

Participant: ...No.

Gregory: That's called acknowledgement. I must enroll you folks in The Living Game Seminar again!

It's a great seminar where you learn this thing called acknowledgement. Ha, ha.

When you are sneaky or sideways, the other person thinks, "There's something hidden and unacknowledged here, you're not being up front about it." This is a general response. People back off from that. You're not trusting yourself to tell your truth, so you project distrust messages. People back away.

Participant: ...I can't afford to make the agreement more open because I don't like taking risks, so I try and make the risk as small as possible.

Gregory: If you want a cuddle and sex, you're not making the risk smaller by asking for a cuddle. You're lying about what you're asking for. A possible approach would be, "What I want, is to have a cuddle and sex, and I'm not yet ready to take that risk. So what I would like is a cuddle and no more." Asking for less, doesn't diminish the risk. It just wraps it up in a clearer package.

The real risk is to go to bed, cuddle, and have sex. You weren't sure whether you were ready for that. So you ask for less, but hope that you get more by not acknowledging that you weren't really willing to take the risk. If you know that you're willing to go for it all then say that. If the nonverbal message, or psychic communication, whatever you want to call it, doesn't align with the words, then there's a breakdown because your words and your intentions aren't integrated; you don't have integrity, and people get that there is no integrity in the request.

One of the things that I'm coming to see is that when we are aligned inside and out, people will only say "No" because that is their real 100% answer. Remember what I was saying about the business meetings? Six meetings in a row, I communicate to those business people the value to them of doing The Living Game Seminar in a way that has such integrity that they get the whole message and think, "This guy's got integrity, it's the truth. Yes, I'll do it."

When I have some doubt or hesitation or reserve or resistance that I'm not acknowledging to myself, or possibly not acknowledging to them, then I don't get a complete result. It's the difference between someone who walks in and asks, unenthusiastically, "Do you want to come for a swim?" You say, "No." Someone else walks in and asks, excitedly, "Hey, do you want to come for a swim, it will be great. You'll love it once you're in."

Who can resist it? You might. You might be really clear that you don't want to swim, but it also remains very attractive.

Put your hand up if you wanted to ask for a date and didn't. Okay Put your hand up if you asked for a date and you didn't have one. Look around. I want everyone to look around.

Notice that everyone who asked for something, got it. Everyone who didn't get it, didn't ask. 100% result. Ask and you shall receive. The people who asked for something, got it. The people who didn't ask for anything, didn't get it. That's how life works. If you want it, ask for it and if you get a "no," then ask yourself, "Do I really want it, honestly?" If the answer is, "yes," then keep asking until you do get it.

Anyone else who didn't have a date, who wants to talk about anything?

Participant: ...I was being hard on myself for thinking that I should push myself to be as open as I thought everyone else was being.

Gregory: Listen. Your words were, "Everyone else." You hold a picture of the world that, "Everyone else has it together and is having sex." And therefore that proves how useless you are. The truth is, I think it was one-third of the people who were off bonking.

Participant: ...They were very noisy. I went outside to beat myself up for not having it together and not feeling safe enough to ask for it, and I thought, "Oh well, this is where I'm at." And then I enjoyed being where I was at by myself and I had a wonderful rave with someone in the middle of the night. It was great.

Gregory: Okay, and it wasn't what you wanted.

The possibility that existed was that you two got together and shared, "Hey, I don't know quite what I want. I don't feel safe. I'd like all of this, but I don't know if I can have it or if I can go for it," or whatever. You two could have made that acknowledgement to each other, and you could have ended up lying together and cuddling, or caressing, or bonking. Whatever.

The key thing is that there was an opportunity for both of you to have what you wanted, and neither of you had it, because you didn't keep asking. I can't say it often enough. If you keep asking, you'll get it. And it might have meant you started at one end of the room, and went to every person in the seminar, "Do you want a date tonight?" And they say, "No thank you," and you may be the last two to talk to each other, and by then you're thinking, "I give up," and you might say to this last person, "I've asked everyone. All I want is to spend some time with someone. I feel scared. I don't know what I'm willing to have or do, and I definitely want to have some cuddles, and I might feel like more," and you would have had it.

Participant: ...I screwed up.

Gregory: Yes you did, and it's perfect because the opportunity is to learn from it. We stay in 'looking for the perfect partner' or whatever it is. Instead of saying, "Oh well, I'll have this, yes, and this, yes, while I'm waiting, until the perfect one arrives." It's called practice.

If you get a "yes," have it. We miss out on so much because of this.

What I'm getting at is if part of this game is saying yes and part of it is saying no, look at what the no's are, and then handle them. Then decide whether you want one or not. Because once you can see that you can disappear the no's, then you get to really look at, "Do I really want to do it or not?"

Participant: ...Every time I go to seminars, what I look for is who I can screw.

Gregory: Sleaze bag.

(laughter)

Participant: ...I realized I didn't want to have sex with anyone here.

Gregory: So now you'll become an anti-sleaze bag? Two more days and you'll be giving us religious sermons on the evils of sex. Do you think that was a choice or a reaction? Or was it a choice of "I'm just going to have the experience of not trying to screw someone?"

Participant: ...Yeah, I'm going to have that experience.

Gregory: That's doing something new. "I'm going to see what it's like to go to a seminar and not try to jump into everybody's pants." Congratulations. That's a leap for you to go for!

Day 4

"...we identify with our masks, and literally forget who we are. And forget that everything we think, feel and do, is a choice we've made, and we're not stuck with any of it. If you don't like it, change it."

LEARNING TO OPEN - DRUGS - ENERGY EXCHANGE - IDENTITY - ILLUSION - IDENTIFY WITH OUR ACT - EMPTINESS AND POWER - BEING CENTERED - CHI FORCE - BEING AND FEELING - BEING OBSERVER - TAKING RISKS - MORALITY AND HYPOCRISY - SELF TRUST - REFLECTIONS - BREAKING PATTERNS - LEARNING TO PRACTICE - ACKNOWLEDGING - INSTITUTIONALIZATION OF VALUES - PERFECTION - MASKS - REFLECTIONS

Gregory: What is it that you have to do to be open with yourself?

Participant: ...I don't know.

Gregory: You don't know. That's called Catch 22. You're going to live to be an old spinster. Do you want to?

Participant: ...No.

Gregory: You've got a picture of being totally open, your partner being totally open, and having a phenomenal time, but your experience is of you not being fully open. Who told you that you have to be open to enjoy sex? Where did you get that? Did you buy some book called, "Lessons for Living" and it said, "You must be totally open."?

Participant: ...I think it.

Gregory: You think it, yet you don't know how to be totally open? Okay. That's what I call a trap, not just with sex, it's a trap with anything. That's like saying, "When I'm a master carpenter, I'll build perfect furniture. And until then, I refuse to build lousy furniture or make mistakes. I'll only build perfect furniture." How do you do that?

You cannot pick up a chisel and turn out a perfect piece of furniture first time. I don't know any way to. It may be possible but I've never seen it happen or heard of it happening, unless you are an idiot savant. At this point you are as open as you know how to be. You can be that open, and have sexual experiences which aren't how you ultimately want them to be, but can be enjoyable for where they are right now.

It's about practice. How do you learn to cook without using food? Can you? Can you learn to cook from a text book? If you've never used food? No you can't. So how do you learn to be open in sex if you don't have sex?

Participant: ...You don't.

Gregory: You don't. That's correct. If you're waiting to be totally open before you do it, you will wait a long time. If you really want to be open, you're going to have to learn to start somewhere. Remember the friends that I told you about, the couple?

It may mean saying to your partner, "I want to make love, and I feel really incompetent and closed off," or whatever your words are. "I don't know how to do it. I'm blocked off and resistant, and I want to learn. Do you too?"

Some people will say, "yes" and some people, "no" but guess what? The ones who say yes, are one of two kinds of people: they're either people who are where you are and you learn from each other, or they're people who've been where you are and who will teach you, or guide you.

It includes taking the risk of screwing it up. You know what my assessment is of how to maximize sexual experience? There is one component that takes sex through the roof.

Acknowledging what you don't know how to do, and acknowledging what you do know how to do are the two sides to it. Be where you are and speak your truth, whatever happens then will be fine and you will learn from it. It's doing another acknowledgement process. Have you mastered acknowledgement yet? No. The more you do acknowledgement processes and seminars the more you get to grow and the more mastery you have. Same with sex. Same with anything.

Participant: ...Can you get there by doing it with one person?

Gregory: Theoretically, yes.

Participant: ...What about practically?

Gregory: It depends what you want. Can you cook by only using vegetables? Yes, if you're a vegetarian. It's really about what you want. If you're a vegetarian, then yes, you can become a phenomenal cook, just using vegetables, but that's no good for me, I'm probably not going to come to your restaurant often because I may want a bit of meat with my veggies. It really depends on what you want.

Participant: ...I know that if I sleep with 500 different men, then I'm going to get 500 different experiences. And I also know that if I sleep with one man 500 times, I'm going to get 500 different experiences.

Gregory: If he's an exceptional man, you will. That's the problem, there are very few people on this planet, who could come up with 500 different experiences of the one thing on their own. So if you find a man who is going to give you 500 totally different experiences, then SPREAD THE WORD!

Let's put it this way: I've never ever had a lover who's only had one lover who knew much or had learnt much. That's the bottom line, even for me. I lived in a nurse's home for two and a half years. I bonked my brains out along with everyone else there, it was sex and drugs and rock'n'roll for that time, totally full-on orgy. We used to go to work to have a rest.

One of the major values of that experience for me, was that at the end of that time I said, "Well, been there, done that, fulfilled that fantasy, but there's got to be more to sex."

I started looking for ways to deepen sex, getting into energy levels, then tantric levels of it, then the death experience of it, merging with the universe. Down and down and down. Most people walk around with their cock or their pussy in their pants, saying, "Ooh, I wonder what he'd be like, ooh, I wonder what she'd be like?"And that's their first reference point.

Most human beings never get past that one. I don't know many who've had the experience of having all the sex they could ever want, with as many people as they want, till they got tired of it, and looked for something more, some deeper experiences.

It's an experience I wouldn't trade in for $5 billion.

Participant: ...But Gregory, I can go to a restaurant, where there's a first class chef cooking. And he can cook me a steak, and I can eat it and really enjoy it. And I can go to a restaurant where there is an apprentice who cooks it up only moderately well, and I can eat it.

Gregory: But for how long can you eat steak and nothing else and still enjoy it?

Participant: ...I won't get into bed with somebody who's got the experience of a first class chef, and get any enjoyment out of it. Because I'm not fully there.

Gregory: Most people who drink Dom Perignon wouldn't know it from Korbel.

Because they haven't learnt the distinctions. Yet give Dom Perignon to someone who knows champagne and they'll bliss out on it. See, if you give me Dom Perignon, you're wasting your money. Total waste of money. I mean it's not a waste of money so long as there is someone to teach me how to appreciate it. But just to give it to me and walk away, all I can appreciate is the fact that I've got a bottle of liquid that cost $250. I appreciate that, but the actual quality of the flavor is lost on me.

The first time I had Dom Perignon, was with a friend who pointed out the distinctions to me. The problem also, was that I hadn't had enough bad champagne to appreciate good champagne. That's the other value of having lousy bonks. You really appreciate the good ones! It's true.

When I lived in that wage-earning mentality, working in the hospital, I thought it was insane that people could pay $500 for a pair of shoes or $2,000 for a suit. Over a period of time and doing Robert Panté's "Dressing to Win" seminars I learnt what the difference is between a $100 "bag of fruit", and a Zenia Italian hand-stitched $2,000 suit. I now buy excellent clothes for myself, and I love them. That's the difference. With anything of quality, you have to learn to appreciate quality, so have a great coach. That's part of what you're doing here. That's the distinction.

I know that I am an extraordinary lover. I also know that not everyone who goes to bed with me gets it!

Participant: ...How come?

Gregory: Same as you wasting Dom Perignon on me.

Participant: ...Could you teach them?

Gregory: Yes, of course. If someone is willing to learn. That's why I have this Sex and Relationships Seminar, and I'm good enough that I get paid a lot of money for it! Anything is learnable if you're willing to put in the time. You find someone who can already do it and duplicate them exactly, like in The Karate Kid.

Some of the worst bonks I've ever had, and I have had some terrible ones, were very valuable because I really learnt some distinctions from them. You don't really fully appreciate fresh milk till you've picked up a carton and swigged sour milk. You could go to bed with everyone in this room and you will learn something with everyone.

Each experience, each person will be a Lighthouse. Lighthouse's have two purposes. They say, "Warning! Rocks! Stay away!" and they also say, "Welcome: safe harbor, come here." Whether it's a so-called bad experience or a so-called good experience, they are both valuable. All experiences are valuable!

What I suggest, and support people in doing, is just having experiences. Obviously if you're having a bad one, I'm not suggesting you keep repeating it, but in having experiences you get distinctions. And in distinctions, you have choices. Let me give you an example: many years ago in Australia, you could eat good English-Australian food or some take-away Chinese. That was basically it. Then gradually you could get a bit of Italian, then Lebanese, etc. ...Now, in Australia, I think you can eat just about anything except Eskimo food. Very Cosmopolitan. That doesn't mean we eat better. It just means we have more choices. And we eat better. Ha, ha.

I've eaten in many restaurants in Sydney. I regularly go and try new ones. But 80% of my eating out is in Double Bay. Why? It offers a wide range of excellent meals, good service, good consistent food, and it's where I live, among quality.

We have a model or a pattern for what love looks like, we also have models and patterns for sex. If you stay in one pattern, then you get bored, and you also miss a lot of opportunities. The classic 50's pattern is boy takes girl out, buys her a box of chocolates. Second time, a bunch of flowers. Third time, dinner. Fourth time, petting. Fifth time, do it. It's a game. Everyone knows where they stand, except that the games are breaking down. That's where aliveness lives. Outside of patterns. Patterns end up boring you.

When I was in San Francisco, I was really shocked by how many people live and sleep on the streets. I wondered what it would be like: I just didn't have a clue. So I chose to sleep on the street for a night. Not on the street, on the sidewalk. It was an amazing experience. It changed my life. It wasn't until I saw all these people sleeping on the street that it even occurred to me to break my pattern. When you break patterns, you open up new choices, not just in that one thing, but all through your life.

We use a small percentage of the power of our brain. The minute you break a pattern, you create a new possibility - a new pattern, and you use more of your brain. You utilize your brain power by doing new things. You connect more neuronal patterns. You literally connect the dots, seeing more, living more and perhaps most importantly, opening up to new choices and possibilities you did not see before.

One of the ways you will all get extraordinary value out of this seminar, is to risk having a lousy bonk, which may not happen, but if it does, you know what it's like and you've got nothing to fear.

Participant: ...In breaking patterns, I had a one night stand, which was new and exciting, and a lot of fun. By doing that what I realized was that unless I'm connected with someone mentally, the physical just doesn't happen for me.

Gregory: So you got a new distinction.

Participant: ...What I decided was, "Well, if I'm going to enjoy sex, then I've got to be in a relationship with someone who cares about me, and I care about them," and gave myself evidence to bind me.

Gregory: That's called, "Two plus two equals five." You had a one night stand and really enjoyed it, and you realized that what was missing was a mental connection. You got the distinction of, "What I want in sex includes a mental connection." So far, the equation is, "Two plus two equals four." That's great. You added something. But the inequation is, "The only way I get a mental connection is to have a full-on, total relationship."

Haven't you ever sat down with someone and in five minutes, you've created a really good mental connection? Yes or No?

Participant: ...Yes.

Gregory: Have a good one night stand with them. See, "Two plus two equals four" is, "Then have one night stands which are exciting, and fun and great, with people you create a mental connection with."

Participant: ...For me it's a feeling connection mainly.

Gregory: So create a connection. How long does it take?

Participant: ...Hmm, it takes seconds.

Gregory: Seconds. Exactly.

Participant: ...I don't allow myself to take that to bed.

Gregory: Because for you God and the Pope are up there saying, "You'll die, you'll burn in hell." The truth is that with most people you go to bed with, you know within minutes whether you want to or not.

The problem is that we want a mental connection and we want an emotional connection and we want a psychic connection and then we institutionalize that. By the time we get around to having sex, the connection is dead. It's like a solid structure that you're imprisoned in, and the rest just withers.

Think about it. Imagine you meet somebody and they say, "Hey, there's a great movie on, let's go," and you say, "No, I've got to get to know you first." So you get to know each other for two weeks, and then the movie's finished. That's what most relationships look like.

Some of the greatest sexual experiences I've ever had, were with women who I met and it was just there. It was a one night stand, sometimes traveling, for whatever reason, it was then, that was it. There was one night and then I didn't see them again. I cherish their memory, it was really good soul food.

Participant: ...That's what I'm going for, but I'm just not there yet.

Gregory: I maintain that you have a choice. You either have life enhancing experiences, or you have life detracting experiences. I don't care what it is. Work, food, sex, relationships, or whether your bed is really comfortable. Anything. Every experience either lifts your energy, or it drops you down, either fills you, or drains you. I'm committed to fulfilling experiences which doesn't mean you have to have sex with everyone by any means. There's a whole range of experiences that you have with people so if it's there, why not, or if it might be there, why not?? Take the risk. That's my approach and for me it pays dividends.

Participant: ...I had the idea that I could lay down a ground rule before I started that I don't want anyone inside me unless I'm fully aroused, and then it's up to me to say when, but the fear is, that I'll still rush.

Gregory: So own the whole thing. You've put this person in your bed, and the whole thing is for your enjoyment. Find ways to get your enjoyment. For example, some women like a lot of clitoral stimulation, which can be incredibly boring for a man. Sometimes it's wonderful, but the man doesn't want to do that every time. I don't know to how many women I've said, "Have you ever done it yourself?" They say, "What a novel idea." That's a possibility. Turn it into a game, turn that into a fantasy. I've yet to meet a man, who doesn't enjoy watching a woman play with herself. There's an opportunity for a whole new game where you're getting the arousal.

There's nothing worse than demand. If you're saying, "Do it to me, do it to me," that's what you'll get, it will be done to you, but if you're taking responsibility for it, and you're really clear that you are the source of your pleasure, then it becomes a pleasure for a man to join in. But if you think, "He has to do it for me, I do it for him," it doesn't work. I don't think it does anyway.

Participant: ...I know what you're saying, but I don't think this situation is like that. I've never had to arouse the man. The man has always been aroused.

Gregory: You've had it easy.

Participant: ...Yeah, I know. It's been too easy.

Gregory: Interesting that you manifest men who become aroused really quickly, and you are aroused very slowly?

It's a social belief that men become aroused quickly, and women are aroused very slowly.

Participant: ...I can't argue with that.

Gregory: But that's a belief, a conditioned pattern. Therefore most people do it that way.

I once had a lover who was a very wild woman, she was Italian and quite a radical woman. She used to get hot instantly, turned on like a tap.

She said that for many years she was slow getting turned on, and she used to get really pissed off about that. Then she suddenly realized that maybe there was another way. What triggered it for her were taps. She said she just literally walked in and turned on a tap, and she realized she could do that instantly, and that the water was always there: the stream was there. So she gave herself permission to turn her sexual energy on like a tap. And she did. She mastered it.

Whatever experience you have is following a pattern that you've established. Often that pattern is based on a picture, an idea, a belief. So whatever the picture is, whatever you're life movie script is, that's what you get. Change the script, change the result. You can change anything. It may take time. You have to learn.

It could be that you start with visualizations of turning a sexual energy tap on inside you, or that you've already been really hot, and then play with yourself as if you're already hot. To speed the process up, make noise. Just by making noise, you get your energy flowing. So make noise in bed. Most people I've known are silent while having sex. It's incredible.

There are many more processes and techniques to learn for creating such changes.

That's why we do seminars!

Participant: ...I have noticed that when I do a lot of very deep breathing, or heavy breathing I can make energy vibrate all the way up and down my body.

Gregory: So do that. Do whatever works. Try it. It might work for you to have your feet hanging off the end of the bed in warm water. But you're not going to know until you try it. Surround the bedroom walls with pictures of hunky men or women. I don't know. Get mirrors. Just try stuff.

Participant: ...How about turning the tap off again?

Participant: ...Why?

Gregory: That's a good question. Why do you want to turn it off?

Participant: ...When you've finished.

Gregory: There's a difference between sexual energy and being horny. Ultimately your sexual energy is your aliveness energy. You're simply channelling it in different directions. So at this moment, it's called, "In bed with someone." Then it's called, "Having a meeting," or it's called, "Having a vigorous shower."

When I look at it, my picture of sexual energy is that it's about opening myself and allowing my life energy to flow.

I'll use a gardening analogy. My sexual energy is like water in a hose, which I direct to different areas of the garden. So sometimes it's called business. Sometimes it's called seminars. Sometimes it's called bed. Sleeping with full energy. Sometimes it's relaxing: putting all my power and energy into being totally relaxed. As Bagwan said, "Don't just sit there, do nothing." I can go and lie down there for seven or eight minutes and be rejuvenated, because I do it fully. That's how it is for me. And then being horny is something else again.

Participant: ...I think the situation between my husband and I has honestly changed already. I think when we go home, it will change more. It's like, we've created a situation where we just went along, in low-energy patterns, and where we've never tried to make ground rules to help us each get what we really wanted.

Gregory: That's right. That's classic.

Participant: ...In fact, to elaborate even more, we didn't even have to flirt with each other, it was just, I walked into his life and that was it.

Gregory: Always. If you want to change something, own it. You regularly set it up to get half aroused. How you felt was, on some level, resentful and blaming of the man, whoever that may be, that they're not patient enough, and they're not caring enough, and it's proved a whole bunch of beliefs about men for you. And the bottom line is, you choose to bonk half aroused. That's all you've felt safe to have.

Participant: ...I've got that far. And it's getting to the point where there's no arousal.

Gregory: Absolutely. That's what you've been ready for. So one possibility that's really powerful is to give yourself permission to enjoy half aroused bonks.

Has anyone ever had a wank and you lay there in bed and you were feeling a bit horny and a bit not and you thought, "Will I? Won't I?" and you have this little discussion, and you think, "Yeah, it'd be nice." It's like that. It's not the greatest wank you've ever had, but it was nice. Right? Same thing. I just keep coming back to this point. I think one of the major keys for fulfilling sex, is to let go about how good it is. I just keep saying it again. In fifty different contexts I've said it. And I'll keep saying it. To give yourself permission to have what is there. And enjoy that. The minute you start thinking, "But it could be like..." you instantly stop enjoying what you have.

It's like sitting eating a burger, complaining, "It's not filet mignon. It's not filet mignon." You're not going to enjoy it, but if you own your choice to eat a burger, then you can enjoy it fully for what it is. It's another version of being open. To actually learn to enjoy doing it with whatever degree of openness you've got. That's how you get to create the next step.

Just enjoy it how it is. You may not come, you may not get more aroused. Enjoy whatever there is to enjoy about it. It could be the contact, it could be joking around.

Participant: ...That's been the situation for a long time. It's a resentment punishment thing.

Gregory: Sure. Because you're not owning your choice in it, and therefore not allowing you to enjoy what you're choosing. Therefore you go into resentment.

Participant: ...It seems like, "Okay, I'll please him and hope he does it for me," then give up. I've started playing around with, "No, I don't want to," but the end result of that is a sense of almost relief because I've turned him away.

Gregory: That's all story. That's your head's production about it all. All of that avoids the fact that your choice is to have half aroused bonks, and one of the payoffs is that you get pissed off and resentful towards men, and feel hard done by. That's a payoff. So deal with the fact that you're pissed off and resentful towards men, and you feel hard done by and feel like you don't get your share. Deal with that as a separate issue.

Then look at, what kind of sex do you want to have? What you take to bed is anger and resentment and that you're hard done by. You get to experience that in bed, so that's where your attention is by the way. You're not even having your attention on your pussy, or the rest of your body. How can you get fulfillment if you haven't got full focus? Same thing.

The other thing in what you're saying is that I don't know how a man can be fully sexually aroused in bed with a woman who wants to cut his balls off. He may have a hard dick, but that doesn't mean he is sexually aroused. Most men, and most women, fall for the myth that a hard dick equals "turned on". And my experience is that most men haven't experienced sexual arousal because they've bought the myth that if their dick is hard, then that's what sexual arousal is.

Participant: ...Can you elaborate on the fact that a hard dick doesn't equal "turned on"?

Gregory: Right. A hard dick means your dick's turned on. It doesn't mean the rest of you is.

Participant: ...You said earlier about deepening sex. What is at the bottom of the sexual experience?

Gregory: Opening with the Universe. Bliss. That's what death is, moving past yourself, merging with the Universe, bliss. Having a full orgasm is the same as dying, in terms of your mind and your ego. Excellent sex is mindless and egoless. It is also thoughtless and unreasonable, because you've surrendered to your energy. Normally your head or your feelings are in control. When you get past that, you become an energy entity beyond any definition of yourself. Your normal definition of yourself is what I call Ego, or, "This is How I Think" or "How I Feel." "This is what I do." "This is what I believe." Complete orgasm is beyond all that. Remember the best orgasm you ever had. If someone at that very moment said, "What's 6 multiplied by 7?" Could you have answered?

Was your everyday brain functioning? No. It's turned off. Those kind of orgasms are much more than dick and pussy rubbing, they involve your wholeness: the whole of who you are. Ultimately it transcends you, or you transcend your experience of you. It's a merging experience. Merging into the whole. The greater hole, if you like ...

(groans and laughter)

That's where the Indians got Tantric Yoga, they realized that sex was one way to attain connection with the Universe, with Spirit(uality). Tantric yoga created all sorts of processes, we can do some on this seminar, which take you beyond your mundane, everyday self. By the way, my definition of Spirituality is "to live life with Spirit."

What most people experience as sexually turned on is that you go to bed with your ego, your feelings, your thoughts, your needs, your games, your bullshit, etc. ...Then you get hot and stick it in. That's sexual pressure release more than sexuality. In the process, there is some touching, nurturing, and some other needs or wants met.

The sort of deep sex that is available is why the French call orgasm "le petite mort" - the Little Death. The fullness of orgasm is when you can surrender so fully, let go so deeply, it is as if you are dying, because after all, what else is Death except us surrendering this mortal experience?

So it follows that the more you learn how to, and master Surrender, the more fully you open up to orgasmic pleasure of Bliss, of the little death, of the All.

Participant: ...In the past when I've noticed myself feeling, "It could be better," whether it's sex, or a relationship, or whatever, I let go of those signals and they sometimes actually do get better.

Gregory: You can experience everything that your inner voices say as being true. A voice says, "It could be better." That's true, it could be. But it's up to you whether you say, "It could be and it's going to be: the more I practice the better it will be." Or whether you say, "If it could be better, so now is not good enough." See that your voice is actually supporting you by saying, "Yep, it could be better. There's more to go for, more to do, more risks to take." Unfortunately - which means we un-fortune ourselves - we usually hear, "It could be better, it's not good enough, it's not worth it. I'm no good." The truth is, it can always be better.

There's a thousand definitions of ego used. I use the word "ego" to mean: who or how I describe myself. That's a very different one to the psychiatric definition. I describe myself as having these qualities, beliefs, attitudes, actions, games and limitations. The total picture I have of me. My experience of myself could also be called my ego, and I'm always more than that. There's always more to me than I know. I'm always bringing forth more of me, therefore, my definition of me is always changing.

Participant: ...But you said to leave out your ego, and other things when you're making love.

Gregory: Or don't. It's not, "This is how you do it." Though in terms of orgasm, I'm saying the more fully you can let go of any identification of yourself, the more complete your orgasms will be.

Who has had the experience that while you're yelling or crying, the feeling has intensified to a degree where for a moment you've "Been Anger" or "Been Sadness." Who's ever been in the experience where you have a feeling so much that you become the feeling? It could be grief, or hurt. The pain is so great that you are just Hurt. That's a version of egoless because you've become the experience instead of a definition of an experience. We often rip our Selves off by defining ourselves instead of experiencing ourselves. Orgasm is pure experience, and orgasms can be all sorts of experiences as well. It's not a thing, it's a state of Being.

In my early nursing days, there was a woman I met a couple of times. I had a party at my place, I was into dope as a happy Hippie, and everyone was stoned. We were just sitting on a couch, maintaining eye contact, being there, and suddenly I experienced this tube from my third eye to hers. I found out later that she had exactly the same experience. What happened was we started transferring thoughts and had a telepathic interaction. That got to a point where the words in the thoughts disappeared and we were just exchanging impressions, then that dropped away, and we were exchanging colors. Then that dropped away and there was just pure energy going backwards and forwards, which built and built and built, and without touching each other, we both had mind blowing orgasms. I came all over the place. We were fully clothed by the way.

Participant: ...At the party?

Gregory: Yes. I just came like a train. And so did she at the same time, and we didn't touch. So that gave me a whole new way of looking at what orgasm is about.

Participant: ...Were you stoned?

Gregory: Yeah,very.

Participant: ...Have you done it not being stoned?

Gregory: No. I haven't done that. I don't need to.

The next challenge is to open that up without it. Being stoned is fine, but it gets to a point where it turns in on itself. The price you pay being stoned is disintegration, and losing your power.

Participant: ...What do you mean by disintegration?

Gregory: Psychic and emotional. When I smoked, it felt like I could only have valuable experiences when IT did it to me.

I have also often said that marijuana and hashish were my first personal growth seminar. They kept me sane for years. For the three years before I got into primal, I was stoned every day of my life on Menali hash from India, it's the best in the world. The payoff of grass and hashish is that it's very effective for opening doors and dissolving barriers to deeper levels of yourself. That's what I did with it, and I used it very consciously. I read a lot of books about tribal peoples who use drugs in magic and I used it very consciously to open up to myself.

There's a couple of problems with these drugs. The first one is that if you don't learn how to integrate the experience, you can have profound realizations and the next day it's normal life again.

It's like watching a movie. It slides past, it doesn't stay. It doesn't grow you. It's an illusory thing. The ultimate disintegration of drugs is that you start to believe the illusions you're having. Let me give you a really simple example. It's magic mushroom season up here, and lots of people have been dropping mushrooms for years and saying, "Wow man, this shit really makes you aware," and they knock their coffee over. "Wow man, I'm really living in the present," and they fall off their chair. They've bought their own illusion that they're aware, but the truth is, they're messed up and disintegrating.

Participant: ...But you just said that you benefited from it.

Gregory: I did. I had a lot of experiences and openings, but by themselves, they don't stick. I did something about them. That's what I'm saying.

I also want to make the distinction between grass/hashish and hallucinogens like LSD and mushrooms. They are in different worlds. I tried mushrooms twice in Bali. Like Aldous Huxley I got Heaven and Hell. Hallucinogens open the gates to your unconscious so it just floods out. With grass and hashish at least it is a stream that can be ridden.

I think it can be valuable but the pitfall is that you buy it. You buy into it, as THE way.

It's settling for the substitute. I was very actively dependent on hashish. There was no question about it. Then I found another way to reach that kind of depth.

Here's what I mean by integration; I smoked dope for years and years and years, and had all sorts of brilliant insights and flashes, but I still had to wear glasses, I still weighed 240 pounds, I still had back problems, and I was still screwed up in the head. I went and did a month's intensive of primal feeling release where the experiences got integrated. I healed my eyes and stopped wearing glasses. I lost sixty pounds. My back aches disappeared, and my head got straight. That's the difference. Hashish supported me to get to the point where I could do that. So it was valuable. It was wonderful. People called it an escape, I called it an Inscape.

Participant: ...Why do so many people take Ecstasy?

Gregory: Because they are that depressed or blocked and wanting to experience Joy.

Participant: ...It's a love drug.

Gregory: Please, don't insult me. "Love Drug". That's the bullshit we live in. People use different things until they don't have to. How many of you have to have a few drinks before you loosen up and feel free to have sex? Tell the truth! Most people do. Here's a challenge for you. Never ever have sex if you've drunk alcohol. Try that one. See, there's an example of bad sex. I went to bed with a woman who was really drunk, and I'd had a couple of drinks. I was so disgusted by it, I made a commitment that I was never going to have sex the first time again, when either I or my partner was drunk. Or had been drinking. Much more fun. That supports finding other ways to loosen up. Then I discovered massage. Tell you what, getting and receiving a massage before you get into it, takes you a lot further than alcohol does.

Participant: ...Gregory, on death and orgasming. When I ejaculate, I just feel, in an instant, really down, really hurting, and wanting to be loved. I can't remember not doing that, whether I wank, or am with a partner.

Gregory: That means there is no energy interchange. You're giving it all, and they're taking it all. That's one of the things the Chinese twigged to a few thousand years ago. The man not only ejaculates semen, he gives the woman a huge energy rush. Women sit back and think, "Oh, isn't it a bitch. He's gone to sleep." But they don't acknowledge, "Oh, I'm feeling fine. I've got all this energy from him." Women are real good at playing victim. They've mastered it. They've had centuries of practice.

If there isn't an equal giving and receiving, then whoever is doing the giving, will feel an energy drop. There is an energy drop. You just gave it away, because you didn't get back what you wanted. If you are getting what you want, and giving, your energy may drop, that's part of the physiological process, you're building to a peak, and you have to drop away to some degree. When the energy plummets, that's what's usually happening.

Participant: ...So, you can get that energy back.

Gregory: Yes. Stay cuddling and over about twenty minutes that energy will flow back from the woman into balance between you as a lovely sharing and merging of your essence, your essential energy.

Participant: ...Can I just share an experience I had which may be close to what a true orgasm is like? I think I used a vibrator, and I imagined myself sucking all this energy in and swirling it around my body. And then when the climax came, I felt that there was a climax which was longer and more intense than normal. But after that, it felt like I was just swimming in love.

Gregory: That's one kind of orgasm. There's all kinds. One is where I use energy to build and build and build, and it just goes through the top of my head: it's a release upwards. Another kind is like sinking into the ocean, surrendering, letting go. Instead of building, it's dropping. I just get to a place of total surrender which is like falling through the floor. Pleasantly. Or suddenly I become the Ocean. They're two very broad categories.

The big plummet occurs when there is some big expectation of the situation, and all you get is a bonk. If you go into a sexual encounter thinking, "This is going to be it, they'll love me forever, all my problems are solved," what you get is maybe good sex, but not the rest. That disappointment can be a real energy drop.

Participant: ...It would be great if we could transfer that energy over distance for when we are separated. Like over the phone.

Gregory: Maybe. I must tell you a funny story about the Italian girl I mentioned, just to give you a picture of how some people do it.

We were lovers for a while, then she went to live and work in Perth. I was at a party where there were about 90 or 100 nurses, and she walked in, and saw me before I saw her. There were 20 people between us. She is a really feisty little woman, petite but a really feisty, fiery chick with long black hair flowing down her back. The music was really loud, and at the top of her voice she yelled out, "Gregory Charles, I've missed your dick!!!" and just plowed through these people, grabbed me by my dick, and said, "Let's go and do it."

Who could resist? She was an animal. She was just so into it. So we flew out to the car, I lived about nine miles away, started driving back, and she said, "Oh, I can't wait." Whipped her panties off, pulled my dick out, started eating me, and playing with herself saying, "Oh it's great!" Outrageous woman!

Participant: ...Try that over the phone!

Gregory: Yeah, exactly my point.

So I'm going to get you to do a process, I'm going to give you 25 minutes to write down everything you don't like about you. Specifically in terms of your sexuality, what you feel inadequate about, what you're afraid of, what you think is no good about you, the games you play that you don't like, the manipulations you do that you don't like, the trips you pull that you don't like. All that around sex and relationships. Everything you don't like. Be ruthless about it.

***

Participant: ...I'm finding I'm learning to trust myself in this environment.

Gregory: How does that feel?

Participant: ...Great.

Participant: ...Learning to be selfish, to look after and attend to my Self.

Gregory: Very good. What else are you learning? That's an interesting process.

Participant: ...Learning to surrender.

Gregory: Ah, ha. Surrender.

Participant: ...Learning to be rejected.

Gregory: Do you know how you master being rejected and have it not be a problem?

Participant: ...How?

Gregory: Make it boring.

Participant: ...Make it boring?

Gregory: Yeah, get rejected so many times that it's not a problem. Really. When we don't move for fear of rejection, we have a big fear. Right? Then you are rejected, and your big fear surfaces. Drama time. But it didn't destroy you. All fear is about being destroyed. So you do it again, and your fear becomes less. You do it again and again and again. You can get to the point where, if you've been rejected often enough it's got no impact.

Participant: ...I've just discovered another truth. I'm really not turned on by anybody here enough to want to say, "I want to bonk you." I realized that from the start. I like everybody for what's inside them. But there are aspects that may not appeal to me, and may not turn me on.

Gregory: Sure.

Participant: ...And that's me being a perfectionist. I suppose I'm trying to be immediately turned on.

Gregory: There's about 17 issues in there. The one that comes first is the perfection issue, there's so many. It's fascinating. Here's a man who's life is art and beauty who says, "I'm only interested in what's on the inside, or in the inside." One thing about you is that you don't give yourself permission to say, "I only want to have sex with beautiful women." I used to have that bullshit running too, by the way. I used to say, "Oh, it doesn't matter what women look like. I'm interested in who they are." It's a real rip off.

Participant: ...I'm a visual snob. I really like beauty. In a plan. In a piece of art. In a vase. In a person. In clothing. I know everybody has got their own idea of beauty. But I'm basically looking at nature or function outwards. I also think that beauty is a manifestation of what's inside.

Gregory: Do you take this all to bed with you? Must be a bloody big bed to fit it all in!

Participant: ...I may. I may. I'm not trying to maintain that I'm only interested in what's inside.

Gregory: I didn't say you maintained that. I said, I heard you say that. And I've heard you say that several times.

Participant: ...I didn't say I was only interested.

Gregory: ...You're going into mega-defensiveness. Whether you said it or not, what I keep hearing you say, is that you are only interested on the inside. You're only interested in loving relationships. You're only interested in blah blah...you know? You live a romantic myth, and don't give yourself permission to have other things. Watch out for that expression, "My nature." Really watch that one. The inference is that this is natural. There's very little about how we are in life that is natural. We breathe, eat, shit, bonk and sleep. The rest of it is moderately unnatural. Just listen to when you say, "This is my nature," because it infers that that's how it has to be. How you are and must remain.

You swim in an ocean of romantic "nice," which is linked into the perfectionism. You're an artist for God's sake. You're life is about beauty, and you're a perfectionist. One of your romantic niceties is the legend of you as a nice person. You resist looking at anything new that's imperfect.

I'm not saying you don't look. I'm saying, you resist looking. You would like to think that you are also a perfect piece of art.

Participant: ...I liked to think so, but I don't.

Gregory: So then you beat yourself up for that. If your commitment in life is to only have what's perfect, you miss a lot. Yesterday we talked about, "I'm waiting till I'm totally open." It's the same as, "I'm not going to build anything till it's perfect. I'm not going to do a drawing until I can do it perfectly." It's a wonderful way to run your life, to always be going for perfection, but balance the two: it's lovely to go for perfection, but things don't start that way. Which is, of course, perfect.

You learn how to make them perfect. You don't allow the Critic in you. Every perfectionist is an extraordinary critic and rather than criticize, you avoid. Rather than go to bed with a woman and say, "Well I'm not wild about your tits, and your teeth aren't great." The artist is assessing. "But I'd still like to do it with you, because this is what I do like..."

Your perfect woman is someone who's got nothing you can criticize. That's pretty damn rare. A great growth step for you would be to give yourself permission to wallow in imperfection for a while.

Okay, what else have you learnt?

Participant: ...I've learnt how out of touch I am.

Participant: ...Not to force things.

Participant: ...I can release pain through pleasure.

Gregory: You can release pain through pleasure? Very good. Very good. I've got a fantasy for you to play out. This is going to press your buttons all over the place, but I really support you in doing it. Dress up as a Nazi in the bedroom.

(everyone yells, "Whoooo, hoooooo!")

Gregory: He's Jewish, right.

Participant: ...Oh, Jesus.

(everyone laughs)

Gregory: That's why I said it would press his buttons. Give it to yourself. What I saw yesterday was that one of the ways you communicate is with incredible intimidation. How you intimidate people, is you move right into their personal space, with a smile of course.

You're a really powerful guy. And you have the ability to be a very influential man. You have a great ability to influence people. You've got a lot of energy. The way you've learnt to do that is to either go into, "Poor Little Jew Me" or "Slime Bag" or "Nazi."

Just stand up for a second. I saw you doing it yesterday. It's really hard to say no when someone is nose to nose. That's an old cop trick. Cops don't casually say, "Where were you on the night of the 20th?" They stand over you, close, and intimidate you.

If you want to spin people out really fast, invade their personal space.

Participant: ...Our nice Jewish artist was doing that too, during the process yesterday, and it made me really angry, which was good, because that's part of it. Like REALLY angry and I didn't move away. I just stood my ground and felt really invaded.

Gregory: Great. So that's the other side of "nice," The Intimidator.

I see how you control yourself and limit the range of your emotions. You stayed in that mode for just about the whole thing. One of the things for you to do, is to give yourself permission to play with a broader spectrum of emotional responses. That's the link to having never learnt to swim. That fear of water is also fear of emotions, that you know these ones and they're safe, but if you get into deeper emotions, or different ones, you might drown in them. Great.

Participant: ...I woke up this morning feeling amazed at how much I've changed and opened up in just three days. At the same time I feel scared, every time I get close to people I just want to run off. I want to leave the seminar and run away again, and I choose to stay, and get through this feeling. As well I usually create a big drama about it and I don't want to do that this time.

I acknowledge that I don't have enough love for myself and am open to choosing another way. I just don't know what that is, I've never been here before.

Gregory: The other way you are looking for is what you are doing now. There's no drama in what you just did and said. You are present with your sadness and remorse and acknowledging it. At other times you will be present with your excitement or happiness or blankness or playfulness.

Participant: ...For me it's also not wanting to be a victim of pain or being hurt.

Gregory: Ultimately when any of us live in drama, or pretense, or any place other than where we really are right now, we're trying to be something we're not, the bottom line is, "Who I am, and what I do, and where I am isn't good enough, so I'll produce something that's better." That is like killing ourselves off, like trying to get out of your skin into someone else's skin, symbolically, that is killing yourself. Not physically, but symbolically. That includes killing off your feelings or at least deadening them.

The fear is that we've actually killed something and that gets to a crisis point that is so painful, that all that's left as a logical next step is, "Do the job fully and actually kill yourself." It's a perfect example of being back to front. Let's say that's the act you're running and you so identify with your own act, that it feels like the only way you can get rid of it is to actually kill it. That is an illusion.

Kill the illusion. Let it wither on the vine. Drop it. Get rid of it. Forget it. Stop doing it.

Because it isn't a real thing. An analogy would be if you were wearing clothes that you couldn't stand, that were filthy and rotten and maggoty and stinky. Forgetting that they're clothes, you start to think that they are you. You can't stand it anymore, and you think, "I can't stand living with this mess. I'll kill myself." When all that's needed is to rip the clothes off and burn them.

That's a perfect example of how fully we identify with our masks, and literally forget who we Are. And forget that everything we think, feel and do, is a choice we've made, and we're not stuck with any of it. If you don't like it, change it. You made that choice with love and wisdom for yourself. As the best way you knew how to do it back then. But since then, you've learnt other ways of doing it. It's like having new clothes available. What you're doing now is called dropping the mask, dropping the dirty clothes, and literally being here naked ...there's a wonderful saying in Zen: "Before you fill a cup, you have to empty it." Where you're at at this moment, is the moment of emptiness. You've emptied out the bullshit.

That point of emptiness is exquisite. More and more, you'll get to a place where you will really seek the point of emptiness, because that's the point of power. When you're willing to let go of everything you hit the point of emptiness. That's a moment of extraordinary power. In artist's language, it's the choice between doing a painting and spending the rest of your life touching it up, or saying, "Well, that's complete, I want to move on." So you put it aside, and get a new blank canvas.

With a blank canvas it is possible to paint anything in the world. Initially, that's a really scary place to be; artists and creative people talk about the dread of the blank piece of paper, or of the blank canvas. "There are so many possibilities, what do I do?" Do anything.

A key to taking charge of your drama is that you can say, "I want to acknowledge that I want to leave, and I'm staying here." You've got feelings and responses and habits that say, "Run run run. Get out of here." The old way of doing it would be to have a drama about it. Now you can get beyond thoughts and feelings to a point of choice: where you make choices that have nothing to do with how you think or feel about things. That's really powerful. You become powerful and make your choices instead of your old feelings and habits being powerful and making your choices for you.

Your head can produce 400 good reasons to leave, your feelings can produce 400 variations of getting you out of here. It's about having experiences, and ultimately it doesn't matter whether they feel good or bad. The value is in the experience. In the same way, best choices don't always feel good.

See, when you have to make choices that feel good, you don't have a choice. You're a robot that's a feel-good robot, with a feel-good computer program. If you were only a feel-good program, you'd be out of here. Look at the opportunities you'd miss for the rest of the seminar.

So change to a value program: "I am going for value. I am going for experiences. I am going for risks. And some will feel good and some will feel bad. And that's not the point anymore." That's powerful. It's the most powerful way I know to live your life.

***

Participant: ...I'm going to learn how to be light. And I'm learning how to play, and I want to acknowledge to everyone that I'm really starting to enjoy playing with you all instead of being so heavy.

Participant: ...I can identify with that. I feel the mischievous imp in me is trying to come out. I've tried to force different types of emotions without a lot of success. I've produced a bit of crying. And then this morning I visualized myself being in a cot. And my parents were walking out the door. That really pushed buttons. It was just that feeling of being abandoned. I really let go.

Gregory: Gee, we do some amazing stuff. When you were a baby you were a mischievous imp, and had the feeling of your parents abandoning you. In order to survive, you abandoned the mischievous imp, because it couldn't keep you alive, they could. So you became like them to survive, and abandoned the mischievous imp in yourself. Does everyone get that? That's how we become like our parents.

Participant: ...I've also been enjoying playing and not fearing being rejected for it. I've also learnt that there's nothing you have to do, you just have to be.

Gregory: Okay, anyone else?

Participant: ...(with a very croaky voice) I'm learning how much influence my life has had on my voice. When I was a child, people saw me as a singer, they didn't see the child. I used to tell fantastic lies as a child, and

I would beat myself up for it. In the process we did today, I saw that the environment that I was in was full of lies and I was just reflecting it. I had a very Catholic upbringing, and there was a lot of bullshit going down. I'm starting to let go of God as a concept, and coming to terms with Him personally.

Gregory: Fascinating stuff. Whether you're brought up Catholic or not, if you were brought up in our society, you were brought up Christian. This applies for everyone, as our laws, morals, attitudes are all Judeo-Christian.

It's amazing when you actually look at the difference between what Jesus Christ said and what Christianity says. Or how they present what he said. He said, "The Kingdom of Heaven is within you." It's in every Bible. Yet every Christian teacher I've ever heard, says, "You can't go to Heaven until you die." Okay, there's truth in that too, because until you let your limiting masks/games/identity die, you can't enter the Kingdom of Heaven within you.

As a child, I learnt that, "God is everywhere, in all things, at all times, and in all places." That's pure Buddhism. Buddhism says that "God" consciousness existed in isolation but after a few eternities It got really bored with that. So It decided to play a game with It Self, and what It did was to create the game of Hide and Seek. I say "It" in the sense of Universal Consciousness. Actually I like the expression Richard Bach uses, "The Eternal IS." The Eternal Is manifested into form. Or, "In the beginning, was the word, and the word was made God."

So It was like an energy or a consciousness, manifested into forms. Part of the game was, in that form, to forget that It was Itself and pretend that It was something else. So "God" - Universal Consciousness - manifested into everything in the universe, into form, into matter. The game was to then remember who It really was. So It literally played Hide and Seek with Itself. And my truth is that we are all God, hiding that truth from ourselves. All that life is about is to remember who we really Are.

I love it. Buddhists also believe that the walls, the floors, cups and saucers, are "God". Everything is God-stuff. Scientists are now openly saying that everything that exists is the same "stardust".

You know that Buddhists monks don't step on ants? That's a process to stay conscious that all life is Life, that everything is "God". By not stepping on ants, you're also paying attention to yourself, and valuing that everything is a reflection of you, and if you're God, then everything is God - is Life. That is not somewhere to get to. It's something to open up to that is already there in us.

It's juicy. And it's also playful. The thing with Christianity and Judaism is that both project God as this really frightening character. Therefore we're automatically threatened and in survival mode. We've got to protect ourselves against God, and since He knows everything, you're trapped. It's like trying to hide from the Warder in prison. The Buddhist way of viewing the world is very playful: God is playing a big game called Hide and Seek. All of life is a game. Our life game is to remember that.

That adds a new dimension to owning your reflection. We tend to see the world and ourselves as separate and individual beings; everything is separate from us. One of the things that marks our societal culture is separateness, separation and disconnection. Shift your perception and then you see that everything is connected.

(Gregory demonstrates by holding his left hand open with fingers down, with his right hand covering it to show four separate fingers. He then moves his right hand up to show that those four are all actually connected at a "higher" level.)

By the way, the difference between there, isolated fingers, and there, all connected, is also called psychic. Or mystic. We learn to look at the leaves as separate entities, and not see the connection back through the twigs and branches to the trunk. Then even further to the soil, air, and so on. For example, we all have two sets of lungs; one in our chest and the other is a tree out there. It breathes for us as surely as we do. Trees even look like upside down green human lungs!

As for your voice, you said, "All your life you got valued for your voice." You've disappeared it at the moment to find value through other things of and about yourself. The fear is, "If my voice disappears, everyone will leave." So now you're going to test it.

Participant: ...I realized yesterday, that it doesn't matter what I do, I still love myself. Without my voice I can still love myself. It's really a revelation to think that even if I gave it up tomorrow, there's no guarantee or certainty but it's my choice to do it. I had to do it.

Gregory: Remember yesterday I said that in my experience whatever I hang my value on 'out there' in the world disappears. You've done it with your voice. As a singer, you're hanging your value on your voice, so you've disappeared it to make you know that without it, you are still valuable. Let that serve you.

Participant: ...I felt very valuable today with the interaction we were having with the group. I felt really part of the team. I don't get that a lot because I guess from when I was a child, and being in a congregation in the church, and not really wanting to be there. You know, finding it not my scene, like, "This will do you good whether you like it or not." I really feel a lot of unconditional love for myself and everybody here today. It's great.

Gregory: Very good. And there was a lot of sadness in your face and voice when you said that.

Participant: ...Yeah, I guess I am sad because I missed out on that, and I haven't tuned into it.

Gregory: It's been a long time coming.

Participant: ...I did Raja Yoga for two years, it's very much looking at God as a concept and being separate from everything, and I bought the whole package. Then I really beat myself up for getting so sucked in to stuff like that without giving my head a conscious choice. I got caught up in a group and if I decided to leave, I was outcast.

So I've been looking for a group, to find a bunch of people like this who I can relate to and be who I am without having to follow any dogma. Not put up with any shit.

Gregory: That's what makes this group. For me the distinction is, that you can participate by wanting and choosing to value yourself as an independent being. That's the criteria. That is the core game played here! People who don't want that, aren't going to hang out here.

Did you see Monty Python's movie Life of Brian? Do you remember that scene, I loved it, where there was a mob chanting, "We are individuals. We are individuals!" And this little guy says, "I'm not."

There's a video around of Steve Martin in concert, it just broke me up, where he says, "We're now going to do the individual's chant. Is everyone ready?" He's got thousands of people sitting there and he says, "We are individuals." And they all say, "We are individuals."And he says, "We will do our own thing." They respond,"We will do our own thing." He says, "We will not be told what to say." And they just cracked up. Very funny.

I say there are no wrong choices. Everything is God hiding that from itself and God learning how to be God and experiencing all the possibilities of the Universe. When someone kills someone, God is having the experience of killing. Only he's called a killer. Then God gets the experience of the court system, then the prison system, and karma.

I like and play with the idea that anything in life is God evolving Itself, and that as we evolve, we evolve God, not like God is some absolute, but that our truth evolves. As parts of God or expressions of god-ness, we also evolve goodness.

Participant: ...God as a concept is dead. An evolving being rather than just a stationary object.

Gregory: I rejected Catholicism for many years. Then I read a wonderful book called, Autobiography of a Yogi, by Paramhansa Yogananda. He was the first of the Indian Gurus to come to the West. He had a revelation that his job in life was to introduce Eastern religion and philosophy to the West, and be a bridge. He went to California in the early fifties, and set up an ashram and started that happening.

When he died, one of his wishes was that he be left untouched and unburied for fifty days. So they left him in state for fifty days, and his body didn't corrupt, it stayed in perfect condition for fifty days. That was filmed.

His book was profound for me because he looked at Western religion and philosophy from an Easterner's point of view. One thing he did was give the Bible to a Zen Master in Japan to read. The Zen Master made two statements: he said that Jesus Christ was a Zen Master, and that it's a pity that all the emphasis of Christianity was on death, guilt and punishment, and not on how to live, as written in the Bible.

That really got me. There's an enormous amount in the Bible that is really powerful.

In fact, a lot of it, it is straight seminar stuff, except no one ever teaches it in church. I never ever heard a sermon on, "Live like the lilies of the field and the birds in the sky." That's a parable about surrender to, and trust in, the Universe, and trust in Life. That's all it is, but that's not the message that gets out.

***

Participant: ...My head is quiet, my inner dialogue seems to have stopped. I feel like I'm going insane.

Gregory: It's called going out of your head. You're going out-sane!

Participant: ...What do you mean?

Gregory: You're rebalancing. People who are in their heads, detach from their body and live up there. If it was a see-saw, it's like being permanently tipped; permanently unbalanced. Going out of your head is shifting the centre of gravity or the centre of focus or trust, from there, back down to your centre, in your body.

So your head has gone quiet. All that energy was already there. You just weren't feeling it. It's a little like you've got pins and needles of the body. It's been asleep, and it's waking up. Your attention has gone to it, because this is a whole new experience and a balance will come out of that.

The stomach is the repository of many feelings. Many feelings live in your stomach. It's also where the umbilical chord was, so it's the area of nourishment. It's also the centre of power. Things like Karate or Tai Chi are for clearing feelings. I don't mean getting rid of them. I mean feeling them, completing and aligning them. When your feelings are aligned with you your stomach is the centre of your power. It's called Chi energy.

Whereas we in the West identify ourselves with our heads, and see that as who we are, or our centre of gravity, Asian cultures see the stomach, or Hara, as the centre of who you are. Do most of you experience that you're up there in your head? That's where you think, and work things out and come to decisions.

Asians are more here, in the stomach. That's where their experiences are focused. It's a really interesting energy process to visualize actually transferring your brain down there. You can then imagine an eye opening up, and you get to a point where you can actually see from stomach level.

I've done it, yeah. It was amazing. Give yourself the time to just be with the energy and feel it flowing and circulating and moving in you. Then you will present yourself with what to do with it.

Years ago I lived in Taiwan for six months and saw a Pan-Asian karate exhibition and competition. The special guest was a man who was the head of Korean Taekwondo, he looked at least 80, and was about 4 foot 4, tiny, a shriveled little old man. He walked in, and the whole auditorium just went bananas because he very rarely appears in public. He's something like a tenth level Black Belt, a Red Belt. He had agreed to do some demonstrations for the audience.

They had a group of American Green Berets, who were at least Third Dan Black Belt.

One guy must have been 7 foot high, a black dude. This little Korean man maybe reached as high as his crotch. They were really big guys. They did several things including a tug of war. The Korean Master wrapped the rope around his hand, and just stood still while ten of these Green Berets took the other end. They tensed on the rope, and he just stood there. There was sweat pouring off them. Muscle strain. And this little guy just stood still and calm. A miracle.

Next he sat on a three-legged stool so that the only thing touching it was his bum, his hands and legs were in the air. He took the rope again, and they couldn't pull him off the stool. Truly mind blowing.

My mind just shut down, I just went empty-headed. It was not possible and he did it.

They were doing things like running at him to knock him off his feet. Simple: just knock him off his feet. He had ten guys running at him from all directions, and it appeared that he never moved. He just stood there. I didn't see him move, and there's ten huge guys flying through the air. Missing him. Colliding. That's Chi energy. At a high level.

Because you haven't been conscious of it, that energy has been dissipating internally.

It's like having fragmentation bombs going off inside you, and not even knowing that it happens; so you end up scattered and fragmented. This is about letting the energy bombs be directed. Don't rush it. The first step is to let yourself have it. Know that it's safe, that you don't actually physically explode.

Participant: ...I'm learning that I choose to be more accepting of everything, and I like to be alone a lot of the time. I like fresh air. I don't like cigarette smoke. So I choose to do things that give myself comfort and pleasure. But at the same time, I feel a sadness that I've separated myself from other people. And I was feeling quite sad about that this morning. The benefit of choosing that and being accepted, is that I'm getting some pleasures, but I also pay the price in a different way.

Gregory: So what is the imagined price of not being separate? You've learnt that survival means, "Stick to yourself, stay alone, stay away from them." What is the price that you think you'll have to pay by getting involved?

That they'll reject you? Yeah. One of the things about you is that you have very big issues about your own value and lovability. Are you aware of that? Your face is aware of it, it just went red. Are you?

Participant: ...I don't think so. I don't bother about what other people see. I know that other people think that I'm not valuing myself.

Gregory: We all have a varying need to be alone and have our own space. But you make a profession of that, and then justify it. We set up a way of behaving or a lifestyle pattern, and convince ourselves that that's what we want, when in fact, that's how we avoid getting into areas that are threatening, scary or painful. Your fear is, "If I involve myself a lot with people, they'll reject me, so I won't give them the opportunity, I'll stay away from them, then I'll convince myself that I like to be alone." And it worked. The next step is to take the risk of involving yourself and find out exactly what it is you're scared about. Then you can deal with that.

Are you worth it? Let's find out. Kill yourself.

Participant: ...Why?

Gregory: Well if you do, then you'll know you're not worth it. And if you don't, you'll know you are, instead of just thinking you are. So kill yourself. Just once.

Participant: ...No.

Gregory: How come?

Participant: ...I am worth it.

Gregory: Ah. Hear the difference between, "I think I'm worth it," and, "I am worth it."

See, "I am," is a statement of Being. "I think," is a statement needing reasons or evidence or analysis.

When you say, "I am," you don't have to have reasons. You have heard of the American Declaration of Independence. "We declare..." There is no evidence for it. They had no right to do it. No one came up and said, "Yes, you can do this." They just declared it. Declaration makes it real.

Become conscious about saying things like, "I am sad." You feel sad. Sadness isn't your state of being, or your state of AM-ness. It's a feeling that you have. "Valuable" can be a feeling and also a state of BE-ing. Clear that up in your language. To say, "I am feeling sad," is very different to, "I am sad." If I am sad, there's nothing else. I'm just sad. It's like the difference between me saying, "I feel like a dog," or "I am dog." It's ridiculous. But I can feel like a dog. That's fine. Woof.

A very powerful thing to do is that whatever you want to be, declare that you already are it, unreasonably.

Participant: ...I've done this before but it's still there.

Gregory: Sure, that's like saying, "I've weeded part of the garden but there's some still there." Sure. Do it more.

Participant: ...Yeah. I feel frustrated that it's still such a big issue.

Gregory: Have you ever weeded a big garden? Is it frustrating? Bet your balls it is.

Especially four weeks later, when half of them pop up again. Getting frustrated doesn't acknowledge what you've already achieved. What we tend to do is weed the garden for four days straight, and clear 20% of it. Then we think, "Oh my God, there's still 80%. I'll never get there," instead of thinking, "Wow, that's 20% handled, if I do that again four more times, it will be finished."

Is a cup half empty or half full? Most people say and act like it's half empty. They look at what's not there, and base their life on that, instead of looking at what is there and basing their life on that. We can do that in every area of our life. One thing I stopped doing was judging myself in terms of what I haven't achieved, and started patting myself on the back and acknowledging myself for what I had achieved, then taking the next step, then the next one. But if you think in terms of three thousand steps that are yet to be taken, you might as well crawl under a rock and give up, which is what most people do. If you look behind you, and see that you've taken 330 steps, all you have to do is keep going.

A journey of a thousand miles may start with the first step, and I would add that it ends with the last step and progresses one step at a time. For me, the value of personal growth is that I learn to take bigger steps and to identify the fastest route.

Anything that gets worse in your life, is getting closer to completing. Remember that you can't change something until you acknowledge it. Sometimes, in order to acknowledge something fully, it has to be sitting up in front of your face, and you say, "Aha, that's it." While it was in the distance, it could be ignored or avoided. It gets closer so you can acknowledge it more fully, but it often feels like it's getting worse, which means it's getting nearer to completion.

***

Gregory: Imagine an oak tree with legs, that's how I'd describe a friend of mine. He's a big guy and a very powerful guy. He'd done the seminar and other processes and knew he was very angry. Then he realized that a lot of his anger was about not being treated like a King. He often does his own personal growth in a very innovative and unusual way, and he got this idea that in a past life, he was the Egyptian god Ra, or King Ra. Right? And that his anger was that he had forgotten that, and that everyone else had as well.

So what he did was that as soon as he'd start feeling angry, or feeling like he wasn't valuing himself, he decided he'd remind himself by yelling, "RAAAAAAAAAAA!" King Ra, right? We'd be in a restaurant, and some waiter would tell him he couldn't have something, and he'd go into agreement with the waiter instead of insisting on it. And the waiter would walk away and he'd be yelling, "RAAAAAAAAAAA!"

If you want a whole new perspective on life, do that!

It's outrageous. He breaks social rules. When he first went to Brisbane he was driving a cab. A woman walked up to the cab and said, "Could you help me in dear, I'm handicapped?" He said, "We're all handicapped honey, jump in." So she did.

He has a unique way of cutting through bullshit.

He has this amazing ability to not buy into what people think, and he takes it to the limit. At one stage, he was quite broke and was really looking at issues around poverty consciousness and money. He put a $50 note in his pocket, and every now and then he'd take it out and say, "Gee, aren't you lonely in there? Why don't you invite your friends around for a party?" Then he put it back.

He'd do it anywhere, it could be in a meeting, it could be anywhere, and he'd just start talking to his money. It was wonderful. People would look and ask, "What the hell are you doing? What are you doing?" So he would tell them and they would crack up laughing.

***

Participant: ...I'd like to acknowledge that the reason for me coming on the seminar is I feel like I'm being emptied. I've got no job, no direction and lots of bloody bills at the moment. I don't even know where I'm going to be living. On the East Coast somewhere. I feel like a spectator.

Gregory: Here, or in your life, or both?

Participant: ...Here. I made a choice to put everything into this, and I'm determined to do that, but I still feel like a spectator. This is what? The fourth day, fifth day.

Gregory: He's counting the hours. "I'd better get it quick."

Participant: ...It's like, "Shit, if I don't get this, what am I going to do?"

Gregory: Stay confused. Who else feels like a spectator? Hoping you'll get it? Okay, quite a few people.

One of the things about being a spectator is, the minute you relinquish action now for later instead of just being here, you're thinking, "What am I going to do later?" In a sense, you do become a spectator, because instead of staying here, you go up in a helicopter to look into the future. You also have a serious judgement, that being a spectator isn't okay. Where is a footy game without spectators?

There is nothing wrong with being a spectator and as it happens you're not being a spectator. You feel like one but the truth is that you are participating fully. Right? You're here doing it. You feel detached and you feel like a spectator, there's a distinction. There's two things happening: you're here with the feeling of detachment or spectating. Then you judge that, negatively.

Call it the Observer, there's a difference. A spectator isn't necessarily involved in what's going on. An observer is, if you like, an active spectator as a conscious choice to watch. You can see something happening on the street where you're a spectator, but you have no connection or involvement. But if you are an observer, then you're not doing it, but you're a part of it by choosing to focus on and observe it. Just by changing the name of it to "Observer", it changes how it works and your experience of yourself, here.

The Observer is a very important and necessary role in you; sometimes Commentator, sometimes Analyst and sometimes Guard. The Observer stays above it, checking out the world. "I'm here doing it, but I'm checking out the rest." My experience is that the Observer shows up when I'm feeling unsure or insecure, unsafe, scared or threatened, in any new situation.

It serves a valuable and powerful function for you. To diminish the Observer's energy or size, have a talk with it, imagine it as a person then let it know that you know that you're safe, and it can relax.

It can be observing as if it's standing in full armor with guns loaded, or as if it's sitting on a beach in Bali. Either way it can observe, and it has value.

That's the first thing. Next shift that feeling of being spectator by creating your version of yelling, "RAAAA!"

In other words, do what you would never normally do. That gets you real and in the Present very fast; when you are on automatic, you've gone away, and left the Observer there. Automatic pilot can be another word for Observer. So if you want to get you real present, be outrageous - whatever that means for you.

On a Living Game Seminar there was a forty year old guy who's a Bank Manager; he had this problem in extremis: being a bank manager was a disease for him - he had become a walking mental calculator instead of a person. I had him up the front of the room and I said, "Listen, do you really want to break through this one?" And he said, "Yes." So I said, "Do the most outrageous thing you can imagine right now." And he stripped, he even took his knickers off, which really impressed me, and he did it as a full striptease, he was great. He even took his socks off so he'd look sexy.

Then he went back and sat down naked, and just spent the rest of the session naked.

It transformed his life and his work. He had been running his life like a bank manager. It shifted his energy dramatically.

Just do stuff, it doesn't have to be hugely dramatic. It could just be to say something that you would normally never say; off the wall stuff, break your own patterns. Really go for breaking them. It's very powerful and you get back into the present because alarm bells go off. Have you ever seen movies where there's a ship cruising across the ocean? Half the crew's asleep and half the crew's eating, and suddenly the alarm bell goes off. What happens? Everyone comes alive. When you do that, every part of you is on alert. And you're really aware of the present. Very exciting. High risk stuff is very exciting. That's why people jump out of airplanes and jump off cliffs and do things like that, because it gets all of you present and very focused.

After the last Sex and Relationships Seminar we went up to the Blue Mountains where we had held the seminar, and went abseiling, you know, rappelling. For me abseiling was really interesting because for years I've been leaping off cliffs inside me, and knew it would be interesting to see what it would be like leaping off a cliff outside me. So learn to abseil inside yourself.

Participant: ...I connected with a part of me that really enjoyed the movie, Quest For Fire. And I started being like a real cave man, ape man. Then I started to feel like a real killer. Like I'm a monster. When I'm playing monster with kids, I really enjoy it. It was good. I mean, if any of you were scared, that was the intention. And then it went to laughing at people. You know. Laughing at them being scared. And laughing at their wimpiness.

Gregory: It's called, The Jew Wimp Strikes Back. What a movie!

Participant: ...Yes, that's me alright! In a process on a Living Game Seminar with Gregory, I drew a picture of me at school: a bully who punched me, and then there were some other guys around me laughing. And Gregory said, "You are the Bully, you are his Victim, and you are the person who laughs at others. You are also the person who doesn't understand." And at first I said, "No I'm not." And then after that, I was able to cry and start to end that inner battle. Today I feel a real communion of everyone here and letting myself be all the people that I am. And I was just sending forth energy, to and from the universe.

Gregory: Stunning. This is the beauty of identifying masks. Your masks aren't who you are, they're roles you play, and by safely acting out your fantasies, whether they're sexual or not, gives your mask appropriate validity as roles you do, and it gives you a distance between Who You Are and What you Do. Who you Are is the chooser - the one who chose to act out certain masks and roles in your life.

Set up fantasies where you act the nazi or the bully or the wimp. Get tied up and slapped around, and have fun with it as a conscious game that you're in control of, and then you go on and live your life, instead of acting them out through your life as if it was real. You get the difference?

It's like a hungry man. If someone's hungry, what obsesses them? Food. Everything in their life, they see through eyes that see only FOOD. They can't get past that because it's not complete for them. Yet how we run our life is to block other aspects of ourselves and become unconsciously driven and obsessed by them.

Once we know we can have it, it gets completed. We know that food is over there, we eat, and then we get on with our life. You don't walk around 24 hours a day thinking about food or trying to act out eating, do you? You just do it when you're hungry. The rest of the time, you're doing the rest of your life. As you identify those parts of yourself, and give them their space it becomes the same. Then you have a choice about it and you get on with other new activities. It's no longer running you.

Something that is very important is that you are different with everyone you're with. Different people are different reflections of you, and access different parts of you. So with different lovers you get to experience different facets or capacities of you as a lover and as a man or a woman. That opens you up to new parts of you and then you can access them and bring the whole collection with you each time into bed. And have a choice about it.

***

Participant: ...Even though I've often had unconditional, fantastic sex for a couple of years I still felt responsible for my ex-wife, and involved.

Gregory: Stop right there. Just try and step out of yourself for a minute, and look at the mess you put yourself in. It wasn't so much that your girlfriend was insecure about the relationship with you, but the bed wasn't big enough for everyone and everything you took there - in your thoughts. You had your ex-wife, the other people, the other factors, work and the other situations, all the responsibilities, all the things you've got to be nice about. All that got crammed into this bed, and your girlfriend got knocked out over the side. There wasn't room for her. That's another version of what I'm addressing with you, which is that you don't make a stand. You're so goddamn nice, it's sickening. What's sickening is, I don't know where you are, and you don't know where you are.

Where you are is like living in this fairy tale land made of ginger bread houses and sugar palaces. Being so goddamn bloody nice to everyone that you disappear. Your ex-wife has just about cleaned you out financially, and you still feel responsible for the bitch. You're still letting her decide what you can have, and your obligational responsibility to her comes first before your happiness and well-being. I'm telling you, get very unreasonable. The perfectionist wants to be 100% sure about everything. If I had to be 100% sure about everything I did before I did it, I'd still be living in a baby's cot wearing a diaper.

There are no guarantees in life, mostly what we do is act in uncertainty. For instance, I'm confronted with choosing a new seminar centre to move into. I'm so unsure about either of the places. I'm unsure about whether I can pay for it. I'm unsure about whether I want to make the move. I'm unsure about whether I want to go for that expansion. I'm unsure about the whole thing, but I'm going to do it anyway, and I can't find one good reason to support my decision that gives me a guarantee.

It's totally unreasonable. My head works on the problem like my Mac, "Chug, chug, chug, chug." I've looked at the situation from every possible angle, and guess what? It spat out a little piece of paper that said, "No conclusions possible. Make up your mind." And guess what? I may mess it up totally. We may take on this new centre and go broke in three months. Sorry about that. But if I do I'll learn something. You get it?

Participant: ...Yeah.

Gregory: Yeah? If I had to be sure about every woman I took to bed, I'd be a virgin. If I only went to bed with lovers who fulfilled my total picture of the perfect lover, I'd be the world's greatest wanker. Start speaking your truth, and putting that out before you know what other people want. Don't check out what they want and modify it. Decide what you want, and when you get it, then decide whether you still want it. If you create it and you don't want it anymore, then at least you've had the experience of going for something and getting it.

Participant: ...Now I've got to find out what my truth is.

Gregory: No you don't. Make it up. Pick something. It doesn't matter what it is. Really. I'm not kidding. Ever read a book called The Dice Man?

Participant: ...No, I haven't.

Gregory: In the book The Dice Man, this guy would come up with six possible things to do, and he'd throw the dice. Which ever number came up, that's what he'd do, that became his truth. Whatever your truth is, you've made it up anyway, and you can change it any way. If you sit around waiting for the ultimate truth before you move, you never move. So, pick a truth that will do for now, and see how well that works for you, and that will clarify your own truth even more.

Participant: ...I've got to work out what I want to do.

Gregory: No you don't. Look, all of that keeps you not doing anything. It keeps you inactive and mutual and passive. If you have to wait to work it ALL out, you never will. Start somewhere.

When you're ready to leave home you think, "I want to go and live somewhere." How do you find out where you really want to live, ultimately? You go and live somewhere. Who had the experience that the first place you moved into after you left home was crap? No! I bet it was a palace, at first? Wasn't it just the greatest place you'd ever lived? Then after a while, rats weren't that much fun? At first it was exciting, "Hey, I've got my own rats!"

The first place you move into is fantastic, and then you start seeing what doesn't work.

So then you know that the next place you move into is going to have a sink, and a toilet. You move into a place with a sink and a toilet, but then you think, "Wow, broken windows aren't that much fun." Each time you get to learn what you do and don't want, and you refine your truth - through experience, just doing it.

I sat in Bali with a man named Ida Bagus Tilem, who was Bali's greatest wood statue carver and one of the greatest carvers in history.

This man was amazing. I spent quite a lot of time just sitting with him, and walking with him. He didn't talk a lot, but he talked to me about how he carves. He'd get a piece of wood and meditate on it. In other words, he just sat with it for maybe half an hour a day for two or three years. How he approached carving is that the carving is already in there, in the wood. His job was to get rid of the excess wood. You get it? It took him anything up to three or four years, to find, or to divine, the carving that's waiting to come forth from inside the wood. Then it took him three weeks to carve it. Once he started carving, it was a flurry of activity, because he knew what was in there. It was amazing watching him carve, he'd be all over the place, and there'd be this mess. I'd say, "How do you know when to stop?" He'd say, "At the edge of what is emerging." For me, life is a lot like that, it's like this block of wood, except, I don't know what's in there, consciously. But I trust that I do know what's in there, then I start chipping away the pieces. And I say, "Well that's not it," and keep chipping, or, "Yep, that's it" and keep that part. But if you sit there, and never pick anything up and never look at it, it's still going to be a piece of raw wood in fifty years.

Most of the experiences of my life resulted in the conclusion of, "That's not it." Those get me closer to the "Yes, that's it" moments.

Participant: ...I've had a lot of experiences like this. Great successes and great failures.

Gregory: Great, fantastic.

Participant: ...And I do a lot of risk-taking in life.

Gregory: Yep. But what you need to do, is pick an action and commit to it, not knowing if it's the right one, not knowing if it's your real truth, not knowing if you are going to get the result. Follow it through, irrespective of what anyone thinks or says. That will be a breakthrough for you.

Participant: ...Well, I've got a funny one. It came to me a couple of days ago. I thought it would be amusing to do it.

Gregory: What is it?

Participant: ...Learn belly dancing.

Gregory: Great. Great.

Participant: ...I went to a belly dancing concert two weeks ago. It changed my mind about the idea of night club belly dancing. I'm in contact with a couple of people.

Gregory: Okay, that's after the seminar. What are you going to do now?

If you are not willing to have it already, you're sabotaging your effort to get it; you won't get it. If you're putting more energy into how to retreat than how to advance, then that's what you end up doing. Because that's where your energy is going.

There was a Zen Master and a student walking along the roads of Japan. Buddhists monks aren't allowed to touch women at all, not even shake hands. It had been raining and there was a huge puddle right across the road. On their side of a puddle was a high-born woman; very well dressed. She had stopped at this puddle because she didn't want to get her clothes wet. The Master and the student reached her and the Master said, "Would you like me to carry you across the water?" and she said, "Yes thank you."

So he picked her up and took her across the puddle and put her down. She thanked him and went on her way. The Master and student walked on another ten miles, and finally the student said, "Master, I don't understand it. We're taught not to touch women, and yet you carried that woman across the water." The Master replied, "Yes, but the difference is, I left her at the other side of the water, you're still carrying her."

Anyone else? How was it for you not having a date last night? Would you have liked one?

Participant: ...I think I would have liked one.

Gregory: Okay. What I already know is that you are quite scared of sex. You judge yourself for it, and you are a virgin. Correct?

Participant: ...Yes.

Gregory: Yes. You're a virgin. And you haven't had many sexual experiences with women?

Participant: ...No.

Gregory: Right. And you have some very severe judgements about yourself, like you'll come too quick or you won't satisfy. Right? What I suggest you do is make an acknowledgement of yourself that goes like this, "Hey folk. I'm a virgin. I don't want to be. I want to learn to enjoy sex. I feel incompetent and I feel scared. I invite any and all of you women on that basis, to ask me for a date, and teach me how to do it." Is that close to the truth?

Participant: ...Yes, but I'd also like to ask them.

Gregory: Okay, so give them your version of that, acknowledge the truth about the situation. See, you keep yourself away and don't create it, for fear that they'll find all that out. If you own it up front, then they know, and maybe then all the women run away. Then you deal with that as the next lesson. But first give yourself the opportunity to be present with where you are now. And give them the opportunity to respond to where you are, rather than where you're not. So put out your version of what I just said.

Participant: ...I have never had much experience with sex. I want to get more experience. That's one of the main reasons why I've come on this seminar. I have a lot of apprehension about sex and past experiences that suggest that future experiences might not be good. I want to learn to have good sexual experiences.

Gregory: I suggest you add one thing that just occurred to me. Just add the statement, "And I'm asking a lot and promising nothing."

Participant: ...And I'm asking for a lot and promising nothing.

Gregory: Great. Isn't that powerful? Thank you.

(everyone applauds)

I don't know about you women, but I would find that an irresistible invitation. Has anyone else got a version of that that they'd like to share?

Participant: ...I came on this seminar to experience my sexuality and learn how to play again. I will ask a lot of people for a date and I'd really like to be asked for a date, and just play.

Gregory: Great. Anyone else?

Participant: ...I did come here for sexual experience. To discover myself. I want to know about my feelings past and present. I know I am sexy but I can't promise anything. I feel like a disappointment, but I still would like to ask people, and if anybody would like to ask me.

Gregory: Okay. Hang on. Just change that to, "I am going to ask people, and I want you to ask me."

Participant: ...I am going to ask people, and I want you to ask me.

***

Participant: ...What is the deal with astrology?

Gregory: An astrology chart is a map of where the planets are in the sky, above and below the horizon, at the moment someone is born, looking from the place you were born. Then there's a system called the houses, which define the twelve major areas of your life.

Astrology is a mixture of art and science. The old idea was that the stars make you do it, the stars cause things. How I look at it is that you've chosen your birth and that everything in the universe is connected. The concept is called Synchronicity. In the same way that your watch doesn't cause time to pass, it measures the passing of time.

The positions of the stars don't cause things to happen, they measure the passing of things, they measure the movement of cycles. Simply by empirical observation over thousands of years, the early astrologers noticed that when there are certain planetary configurations occurring, certain things happen in people's lives.

There was a man in France named Gaughelin, who was totally cynical and skeptical about Astrology. He was a scientist, and he set out to statistically prove that Astrology was bullshit. What he did was take about 20 or 30 thousand Astrology charts, and analyzed them in extraordinary detail with details of the lives of the people those charts belonged to. The result was that he statistically proved the accuracy of Astrology!

He went from being an absolute skeptic, to a true believer. This man called Gaughelin, a scientist and a skeptic, wrote a book which statistically, mathematically, scientifically proves the validity of Astrology.

He looked at specific things like: traditionally people with Mars on the Ascendant are either surgeons or generals. Incredibly boring book. Unbelievably boring book. All statistics.

More recently an American professor in Jungian Psychology and Philosophy, Richard Tarnas, with his students researched correlations between historical events and astrology, as well as famous lives and astrology. He published his 30 years of research in an amazing book called Cosmos and Psyche and he too started out as a complete skeptic, and as the research progressed was fully convinced that astrology worked.

For myself, I have done countless astrology readings for people I had never met, and the most common thing they said after the reading was that I knew them better than their best friends! It is a map of your life.

Incidentally it always amuses me when religious people say astrology is the work of the Devil. The Three Wise Men who visited the new-born Jesus were called the Magi, which was ancient Greek for Astrologer. Who else would be following a 'star' in the sky, predicting the birth?

***

Gregory: Whatever is in your life, loss of a parent, loneliness, incest or anything else painful as you grew up, either you chose it or you didn't, and either it was valuable or it wasn't. Either you or your Higher Self wanted it or you didn't. It is also your choice which way you look at the above questions and which you decide is true. And how you deal with the answers.

Write down what happened as if it was a game you really wanted. Sure, we learn that it shouldn't be, and that we have no choice in such things, but that just keeps you a powerless victim of it.

Once you see your choice in it, then you can act it out and really have it. You can act it out with someone. Absolutely. But acting it out probably won't be enjoyable until you know that it was your choice. Then you can re-choose it consciously and safely and play it out and enjoy it. My experience is that many women who didn't have the experience of incest who act out that as a fantasy, love it. Sure.

We who pride ourselves on being such an advanced culture, still have barely acknowledged that young people are sexual, we ignore and deny that. Then we look the other way when they begin their fumbling in the back seats of cars, and wonder why suddenly they are into drugs, alcohol and rebellion. Of course they are. Adults have given them messages that they are not seen in their life, why should they listen when they begin to have the ability to independently act on their own? Think back, did you listen to adults or think they were blind hypocrites?

So we send these young people off to learn to explore this amazing and wonderful thing called sex with others who are just as unsure and scared and inept as they are. Would you go to learn painting from a blind man, or ethics from a politician? You would go to someone who already knew what you wanted to learn, would you not? It's so obvious, yet we seem to have an innate ability to miss the obvious and do the stupid, often based on a bizarre set of things called "morals", which successfully keep us ignorant, afraid and unhappy victims. Then we get older and need to come to sex and relationships seminars to discover our previously hidden truth for ourselves!

Would anyone like to share about this morning's Dynamic or last night's process?

Participant: ...Yeah I got heaps out of last night. The truth was that I didn't want to do it, and as soon as someone said, "I'm going to do it," I said, "Yeah, I'm going to do it," only more like, "I better do it." Then I realized how many times I've just given my power away by doing things to prove myself to other people, and not really wanting to do them for myself.

I got angry. I stood up and I walked out and then I started beating myself up. Then I saw that it was fine for me to be able to do that. I started going into, "Everyone else is having a good time, and poor little me is sitting out here not having a good time, again." I just said, "Piss off voice. It is my choice not to be here." There was just so much freedom in doing that, then people came up to me and started talking and sharing. I've just never been in that space before. It was amazing.

I realized that I'm going for being with people on an energy level sexually rather than a particular type of person. I just want to acknowledge that it's really scary and I don't know what it's going to be like, but I know that that's what I'm going for and that's what I want.

Gregory: Very good. Who's getting in touch with, and trusting your own process? Very good. It's about getting to trust, that whatever you create, and produce, is taking you where you want to go. Ultimately it's just about trusting yourself and going for whatever you present to you. Yes?

Participant: ...Someone touched my hair and then I knew that they knew who I was. But I hid it for a while and it was really good.

Gregory: The value of anonymity is that it opens the possibility of getting past your limited version of yourself. You don't have to act like you usually act. So there's a huge space of freedom in anonymity.

It used to crack me up reading stories about John Lennon when he was living in New York. He used to dress up, or dress down rather. Mostly he'd dress as a hobo or a bum, and put on a false beard and wear daggy old clothes and just be nobody. He used to truck around New York like that.

With that freedom of anonymity he could get out onto the streets and not have anyone know that he was John Lennon.

Participant: …I noticed how much I feel intruded upon, and I just withdrew.

Gregory: The feeling of being intruded upon can be a statement of how much you fear closeness. We all have a personal space, obviously, and sometimes it is just intrusive, and sometimes it comes out of simple fear of closeness.

One of the things that you're not owning in that, is that you've chosen everyone who's here. Given that you've also chosen everyone to be here, you can make them up as dangerous, or not safe, or you can make them people that have each paid thousands of dollars to come here for you to be safe with.

If I didn't have that belief totally, I couldn't get up in front of people and do seminars. It would be terrifying otherwise. If I thought that people were dangerous, I'd be terrified; especially when you've got a six foot six angry guy who just wants to kill someone, a repressed accountant for example! I simply make it up that everyone who comes to a seminar is an old friend, who so much wants to be with me that they pay to be with me. And that they've just come to hear what I've got to say and learn what I've learned. I did that right from the start.

Have that one going, so that when you feel that intrusion then acknowledge, "Yeah, I feel scared of that closeness, and I'm safe. I am safe. These people have traveled a long way, and paid a lot of money to just be here with and for me, because they love me. I'm safe to be with them." When you get that one, then you can expand it to encompass the whole world.

Participant: …I find it very hard to do that.

Participant: …Yeah I do too.

Gregory: There's a poster I saw that said, "There is no such thing as strangers. Just friends we haven't met yet." I love it. Having acknowledged that, and yes, it's a big one for you, then start somewhere. Start doing it and each time you simply say, "I'm safe," you start growing that experience of safety.

The point is that for years you've walked around with a voice in your head saying, "I'm not safe, I'm not safe," and that got to be your truth and your experience. Whatever the "I am" voice says becomes your truth and experience. That's how it works. It's then a simple matter of directing your voices towards the truth you want and enjoy. Yes?

Participant: ...I just feel very safe with men and being touched and I think I've now learnt how to claim my space without looking for it.

Gregory: Okay, given what you connected with in the past few days about not asking for what you want, not putting it out there and not owning yourself - in other words, being nice and passive - that posture in life generates enormous fear, because if you're playing it that you'll go along with everyone and everything: some maniac might come up and say, "Okay, let's go and slaughter a few hundred people." The fear is you'll say, "Yeah, okay."

If you keep putting yourself in a submissive and passive role, you then withdraw so that people can't control you. If you're not present, then they don't have the opportunity to make you do things. The more you step forward and claim what you want, and state what you want, and be willing to say no, then the less you experience that people can take you over. So the safer you get the less you need to withdraw.

Participant: ...I feel guilty when I say no.

Gregory: Tough. See at this point it's, "Feel guilty, or withdraw and feel ratshit." So start saying no. Like I said yesterday, after you've said it fifty or sixty times, your guilt will burn out.

Participant: ...I put a picture on myself that this is a sex seminar so I should be allowing myself to be touched all the time. And sometimes I don't even want a hug.

Gregory: Just say, "No." When you don't want it say, "No." And when you do, go and look for it, don't just sit there waiting for it to come. Go and find it. Then instead of having to be on permanent withdrawal you can be on, "Yes," or "No," or some other choice.

Participant: ...What I'm getting out of the seminar is that I'm relating to being with my experiences as they happen, rather than thinking, "Gee I really want the ideal," and just enjoying everything for what it is. Being where I am is just really amazing; being happy where I am.

Gregory: It's called, "Being there."

Participant: ...Some people are desperate, where my response is, "Get off, get away from me." I hated it.

Gregory: When people felt desperate, you hated it, and what we were talking about yesterday was, when you come from need that's like desperation. It's great for you to be on the other end of it, and know what it feels like.

Whatever you don't like in someone else, you can either keep not liking them, or you can own the reflection and see that it is also a part of you. Then change it in you. My experience is that maybe 19 out of 20 times when I do that, suddenly this miracle then happens and they don't do it anymore. If they do, it is no longer an issue for me.

It's not even learning to live with it. Once you're willing to own it, then do something about it. Whatever it is that you don't like in someone else, you have. When you really get that you have it, then you can do something about it.

The value of creating someone out there doing or being something you don't like or that's really painful, is to reflect back that part of you that you don't like. It's really motivating because once you own it, you'll want to stop doing it, because you see how painful it is for them and for you. Stop doing it. Do something different.

So you see someone holding back on himself, and you think, "God I can't stand it. I wish he'd just get out there and do it." So bring it back to yourself. "Ah, ha. I see him holding back on himself. I don't like it when he does that. I own the reflection that I hold back on myself too, and I don't like it when I do it, so I'm not going to do it." You get to see what it looks like more clearly.

His job in your life is to show you how painful it is to hold back on yourself, and he's doing his job really well for you. Because you haven't really seen what it looks like when you do it, he gets to show you. Then you stop doing it. He is a mirror to reflect you. We all are!

Participant: ...I spent last night with a woman where I was really open and she seemed to put up barriers.

Gregory: You created a date with someone who put up her barriers. So the opportunity is to own the reflection of how you put up your barriers. You open up for a while, and then put up barriers, and you may not even be aware of it. In other words, how you put up barriers is to get someone else to. Put differently again, you get to have barriers exist in your relationships by choosing to be with women who put them up.

You can sit there if you want to and be self righteous and think, "Well I'm wide open and she's the one who's withdrawing and putting up barriers. Not me." So you're a bit tricky about it. Bring that one back to you, and see the price you pay for putting up and creating barriers, whether they're in you or anyone else.

If I'm sitting here, and you're sitting there, and suddenly you build a wall between us, I can sit here self-righteously saying, "I didn't build a wall. He did it." That's true, but I'm the guy who put you in my life to build a wall between us, so I'm the wall builder through you. I've still ended up with a wall between us. But I got you to do it, so I didn't have to own that I put walls up. Many years ago I never ever ever ended relationships. I was a 'nice' Libran person, I didn't reject people. I was a master at unconsciously manipulating the woman to end the relationship when I'd had enough of it. Then I saw that I still ended relationships, so had a new choice about whether to end them honestly, and to take responsibility for doing it.

Day 5

"When you feel how much it hurts to not love and value yourself now, warts and all, that's when you really start doing it."

DISCONNECTING - AWAKENING - REFLECTIONS - FAST TRACK - BOREDOM - REALITY - POWER - DETACHMENT - CLARITY - INNER VOICES - COMMUNICATIONS - BOUNDARIES - HARD OR SOFT - CLEAR COMMUNICATION - FEELING RELEASE - MONEY

Gregory: Good morning all. Who'd like to share?

Participant: ...This morning I refused to do Dynamic, and someone woke me up because they intended to do it, and I thought, "FUCK YOU." All this rebellion surfaced. When it's that strong I normally fight it and do Dynamic, but today I just wouldn't. Then I became really sad that I've always fought my rebellion and resistance.

Gregory: Rebelled against your resistance. Ha.

Participant: ...I do a lot of things that I don't want to do because I think that I should work through my rebellion. I just got really sad that sometimes I don't want to do things. And I've never been allowed to be rebellious and say no.

Gregory: Saying "no" doesn't have to be rebellion.

Participant: ...It always has been.

Gregory: For example, "Go and hit your head on the wall."

Participant: ..."No."

Gregory: Stop being rebellious and do it. See, "No" is not always rebellion.

Participant: ...Just doing stuff that I don't want to do. Last night was really good, because there was stuff that I didn't want to do, and it was easy for me to not do it. I didn't feel that I had to push myself so I could get this seminar faster.

Gregory: In fact, that's the way to not get the seminar. Pushing yourself because you have to get the seminar, is how you don't. Just like life, eh?

Participant: ...(begins crying) It has come to a point where I have heaps of love for people, and can say the words and go through the actions, and I don't know how to communicate it. I just want to acknowledge that to you as a group so that you know that, and so there aren't any expectations that I know how to express my love.

Gregory: By saying that, you're doing it.

Participant: ...Yeah. It's really hard to make that acknowledgement. I've been pretending for so long that I can show my love, and I have an incredible vision of what I could do, and I just can't do it yet, I'm going to, I know how to do it. I'd like your support in making it happen.

Gregory: Great. Very good. Yes?

Participant: ...I put up a wall or something and keep people away, I'm not sure how to let it down.

I don't even know whether I'm ready to let it down because it's been with me for years and it's been a real protection for me. Now I'd really like to open the space with everybody, I feel a real love for you all, and I feel that you've got a lot of love for me.

Thank you for listening.

(everyone laughs)

Gregory: Isn't it funny? We say, "I don't know how to reach out" and by saying it, we do it. You reach out by reaching out! Someone else?

Participant: ...I feel really pissed off with myself for not being able to connect.

Gregory: What's the process whereby you disconnect? What's your internal response and process?

Participant: ...I do want to know, but I get pissed off because I don't let myself know.

Gregory: So you are disconnected from your truth and honesty. So when they show up, you disconnect from them as well. So what else scares you so much that you disconnect from it?

Participant: ...Revealing myself.

Gregory: Yeah. What might happen?

Participant: ...Rejection.

Gregory: What else?

Participant: ...I'll get trampled on ...I could lose myself.

Gregory: Where would you go? Or, what would take over? Or, what would be left if you lost yourself, what do you get to feel?

Participant: ...Nothing.

Gregory: You got it. "You're already in the place you fear." You disconnect from your truth, so you lose your truth. What you feel is nothing. You do that because you're afraid that if you show your truth, you'll lose yourself and feel nothing.

What truth do you need to bring it back?

Participant: ...I want to be with people.

Gregory: Again louder.

Participant: ...I want to be with people.

Gregory: I can barely hear you. (In a soft, distant voice) "I want to be with people. I love people, but I don't want them to hear that." Say it loud.

Participant: ...I want to be with people, and I love people.

Gregory: That's like a loud whisper. Okay, say it really loud. Sit up and say it so it comes from your diaphragm, not from the back of your throat. Sit up more. Yeah. Let that sound out. Just notice how when you sit up and get more seen, you immediately shut your eyes and lower your head, like, "Don't notice me." Okay. Look at them and tell them.

Participant: ...I want to be with you all and I love you.

Gregory: And?

Participant: ...And I'm scared.

Gregory: Of?

Participant: ...Of being rejected.

Gregory: How are you going to feel if they reject you? Really.

Participant: ...Maybe sad.

Gregory: How sad? Think about it. If no one wanted you, and you couldn't contribute to anyone, how would you feel?

Participant: ...I feel like I wouldn't want to live.

Gregory: Tell them directly, "If you don't want me, and I've got nothing to give you, I don't want to live."

Imagine you drive down streets and the word goes out, "He's coming!!" All the hotels put up "No Vacancy" signs. Shops close at midday, bus drivers crash just in case you wanted to get a ride. You walk down the streets and people are committing suicide in case you touch them; mass suicides. The word gets out in the global media that you live in Australia, and tourism ceases overnight.

Real estate developers pay you millions to go and live in suburbs to depress property prices. Cooks in restaurants jam food up their noses in the hope that they smother before you eat their food.

Tell them. What you're really terrified of them finding out is how much you need them.

(intense crying and yelling)

Gregory: Do you still feel disconnected?

Participant: ...No. Thank you.

Gregory: My pleasure. What would you like from these people right now?

Participant: ...(more crying) Some love.

Gregory: What does that look like for you, practically? Being held? Getting hugged? How do you know that you're being loved? Don't think about it. Ask your heart.

Participant: ...Being hugged.

Gregory: See, you can wait until you save the world, and then everyone will love you and appreciate you and touch you, or you can get love and hugs first, while you're saving the world. Personally there's nothing I can do that's more powerful to heal the world than to heal myself first. There's no point me saving the world and being in despair, all I'm doing is adding despair to the world. There's enough of that already. Yes?

Participant: ...Throughout this seminar I have related quite strongly to that despair with my partner and it came to a head this morning.

Gregory: You gave each other head this morning??? Go on.

Participant: ...This morning I had my first erection for a long time.

Gregory: Hooray. It's good when life's hard isn't it?

Leadership, anger and erections are connected. What you do with them is your choice.

Some people use the anger, leadership and erections to be destructive, some to be creative and constructive. There is nothing wrong with erections, anger or leadership. It's up to you whether you use them or abuse them. You've made sure you never abuse them by sending them on a trip to outer space. Your leadership. Your anger. Your erection. Now what you're doing is bringing them back safely. That's great.

Participant: ...Doing the Dynamic, I actually had a feeling that my balls were growing.

Gregory: Great. They probably are. Stranger things have happened in my seminars!

Participant: ...I want to acknowledge that I've really cut off with you, and I don't like it. I'm sick of hearing that I'm not good enough being the way I am, I don't know how to change it. I feel good enough and loving enough, but I freak out about getting close. I've left it for so long, it hurts.

Gregory: Yep. That's there for everyone. Acknowledge where you are. Value and love where you are. What you're doing now and what quite a few people are doing is connecting with the feeling level of those words. When you feel how much it hurts to not love and value yourself now, warts and all, that's when you really start doing it. If nothing else, the value of your hurt is that you see that it's painful to disconnect, and it's painful to leave it that way for a long time. Seeing that is a damn good way to motivate you to do something else. There's no need to change it until you really see how much it hurts the way it is, that's why connecting with your pain is extraordinarily valuable.

Participant: ...In the past twelve hours, three people have come up to me, and have told me they love me, and that they feel safe with me, and I can't feel it.

Gregory: Yeah. Yet. Every time you say, "can't," add, "yet." It lets you out of the trap straight away.

Participant: ...I feel like I'm pushing them away.

Gregory: What I say is true, is that you do feel it, and you're scared of it. So you push them away. If you truly didn't feel it, you wouldn't be crying now. You're not crying because you don't feel it. You're crying because you don't let yourself feel it fully. You feel it and block it, then you get sad. Like everyone else, you block it because you fear being that close and connected.

It's called "taking a risk." If you actually let in how much those three people love you, then you've got no choice but to respond: to open up your heart. You've got a lot of messages that say, "If you do that, you're going to get the shit kicked out of you, and be broken hearted again."

We all learnt to deal with feeling broken hearted by metaphorically sticking a big morphine injection in it, and putting it to sleep. Then you don't let yourself know that it's actually still feeling, and anesthetized. Again, we've done that to survive, and it worked. Now find other ways to have it work that are more enjoyable.

I had an operation on my eye when I was twelve, to cut a muscle behind my eye that was too short. I was unconscious for the surgery, it was just to cut across under my eye, slide the scalpel under, nick the muscle, and then suture it. It's not a huge operation, but my body felt it totally, my consciousness didn't. I was unconscious to what happened to my body, but my body was present for it.

When I did Primal, in one of the sessions I consciously experienced the operation. I actually had a session where I experienced and released the pain that my body had felt, and stored, in the operation. In the session, it was like having the operation without pain killer. That was so acute that while I was having the session, I was even recalling what the doctors and nurses were saying, which I had heard while asleep. I felt the scalpel cut. I felt a drop of blood going down my cheek, and the doctor saying, "Wipe it."

I tell you that because that's what happens when we block ourselves. It's not that you don't connect, but you're just connecting in a way that you're not conscious of, because you put your heart to sleep. Bringing any part of yourself awake like that comes with pain. It's like when your leg goes to sleep and it starts waking up: if you've ever had severe pins and needles, you know it's bloody painful. Especially if you try and walk around on it.

The pain you're feeling is from waking up; pins and needles of the heart. Acknowledge how important people are to you, how much you love them and want to connect with them, and how scared you are of that. Then you start giving yourself permission to feel what's already happening, which is strong connections with others.

Participant: ...I keep saying all those things, yet I can't feel it.

Gregory: Saying the words isn't as important as feeling how much it hurts. That's the next level of acknowledgement. The verbal is the first level, feeling the results of that is the next level of acknowledgement.

By acknowledging the deep feelings it will shift for you, and in the process you're connecting with yourself. Which is where it all begins.

Participant: ...It clicked this morning that I'm really frightened of being rejected, and that I live my life trying to avoid it happening. For me, a lot of sadness arose yesterday and today. I've had a lot of fantastic experiences and because I haven't had sex during this seminar, I'm going bananas. I must be resisting it because it's getting worse. I just felt this huge resistance growing in me just to risk anything.

I don't care what you think of me. I know I'm a jerk at times, but I really don't care. I want to give a lot. If I feel that I can't get something, including women, that I really want, I sometimes go for second best. That's a predominant pattern in my life. Even women who I really want, I create that they don't want me.

Gregory: Okay, I know a bit about what that is about for you. There are some things you need to acknowledge first. You really depend on people's acceptance of you, and ultimately they screw you. One of the things about sex is that it's the ultimate acknowledgement.

Think about it. It's the ultimate acknowledgement. Some people connect on a level of, "Hi, how are you?" That's where the acknowledgement is. Some people are more important to each other and might have hugs and cuddles and spend hours together and go to dinner. Some people are more important.

Given that your pattern is that you "want people to like you and approve of you," the epitome of that is sex. You need to own your choice to disappear sex. You do with sex what the two singers here have done with their voices. They know that they're valuable through their singing. And they get a lot of acknowledgement for that.

During this seminar they've totally disappeared their voices; i.e. that which they think is valuable about them, in order to open other ways to value themselves. If they could have been singing for the last six days, they wouldn't have got to the point of growth that they have already reached here.

Okay, what you've disappeared is sex and the opportunity is to value yourself with or without it. I went through a period where for two and a half years, I didn't have a relationship. In two and a half years, I went to bed with about 5 women once or twice each. For me, that is the Sahara Desert and the water bottle is empty! For about 18 months I went bananas. I was climbing the walls! I'd been acknowledging my creation of it and suddenly realized that meant I was choosing to have no relationship. That was a radical place for me as a Libran to get to.

I then saw that the value of this was to force myself to create a deeper relationship with myself.

Over the next twelve months, I still wasn't in an external relationship, but I was actively and consciously creating one with myself. I had no sex for that period of time.

I was absolutely clear. I was sitting out on the verandah, surrounded by lots of lovely trees, and I felt totally complete. I actually thought to myself, “It's fine if I never have a relationship, I'm really feeling good.” Three days later I was in a relationship that went for two and a half years.

You're disappearing sex to force yourself beyond seeking approval from others. You have spent your life running around looking for women to approve of you and wanting to bonk you, to prove to yourself that you're okay.

Find another way to approve of yourself. You don't take a woman to bed to make love with her. You take a woman to bed to prove that you're okay. There's a great possibility that the most powerful thing that could happen for you in this whole seminar, is that you don't have sex with anyone.

While you're not approving of yourself how can anyone else? You're walking around projecting, “I'm not approvable” messages, and because everyone loves you, they'll agree and fulfill your beliefs for you.

Participant: ...How can I change my own self approval?

Gregory: That is the unreasonable thing. Are you valuable to you or not? If no one ever wanted to bonk you again, are you valuable? Can you have a happy, enjoyable life if every woman on the planet sent you a telegram tomorrow saying, “In answer to your enquiry, no way.”?

Participant: ...No.

Gregory: Exactly. So when the answer is “yes,” you'll need a guard dog to keep them away!

Participant: ...Is that possible?

Gregory: Of course. Until that's possible, you're addicted to sex. There's no difference between heroin and sex, in the sense that both can be addictive and destructive. If you're using it because you need it to feel good about yourself, it's an addiction. Not a choice.

Participant: ...I can't comprehend that you can live without a woman.

(everyone laughs)

Gregory: I'm not for a moment suggesting that that's an ideal way to live. I can't imagine choosing celibacy as a path to enlightenment. That's not my thing at all. In fact, my choice is exactly the opposite.

I'm not saying it's an optimal ideal to be celibate. I'm saying that while ever you need to have sex to feel good about yourself then it's an addiction. Just like needing to have heroin to feel good. When you're clear that your life will work with or without sex, then you're not addicted to it. It's a choice. That's when you get to have sex for sex. Not for addiction.

The same thing goes for money, for relationships, for everything. If people have to have money to feel okay, they're addicted to money. Some people know that it's nice to have money, but that's not what makes their life work. So then they get to enjoy their money.

Have you ever met a millionaire who doesn't feel wealthy? It's a great experience. I've met people who've got their two or ten million dollars and who are going for more millions the same way that people who've got four dollars are desperate for the next four. That's poverty consciousness. I call them the miserable millionaires.

More importantly, they're addicted to money. They need it to try to fill the emptiness within.

I know people who've got millions of dollars and who have filled their own emptiness. They play with money. Money isn't the reason for their happiness. So it's the same with relationships and sex.

The answer is to fill your own need. Whatever it is you get out there in the world, learn how to give it to yourself, then you don't need it from out there. The simplest level of that which we talk about on The Living Game Seminar, is that it hasn't been okay to acknowledge ourselves, we have to get others to do it for us.

We get into a situation where we say, "If you acknowledge me, I'll acknowledge you," because it feels good to have acknowledgement - and thus create dependent relationships with others. "I need you to acknowledge me so I feel okay and I'll acknowledge you so you feel okay."

The first step in the seminar is to learn to acknowledge yourself. Then you don't need others to acknowledge you. Of course, the minute you're acknowledging yourself, you attract acknowledgement from other people. The same goes for sex.

Find out how to give it to yourself and start doing it. Then you don't need it from someone else. Then you can accept it and share it as a beautiful experience and gift. That's freedom.

Another example: I saw years ago that I was not going to become a millionaire until I didn't need to become a millionaire. I created inner wealth, I made my life rich. I'm a very wealthy man, and money is now catching up with me. Last year I earned ten times what I earned 8 years ago, and it's growing exponentially.

Guess what? If I had 20 million dollars now I'd be sitting here doing this seminar! What I do in my life is not determined by money, but by what I want to do in my heart.

The relationship you have with money is like the relationship you have with people.

Money isn't stupid. It doesn't want to have to give all the time, it wants to be enjoyed and played with. That's why money avoids poor people. Think about it. Poor people are resentful that they don't have more money. Then money turns up at the front door, and they angrily say, "Where have you been?!" Would you hang around? Now wealthy people have a few more thousand drop in their pocket and they say, "Let's play together," Money works like people. After all, people created it. You'd rather hang out with people who are having a good time than with people who are miserable. So would money.

We created money in our own likeness. Those of you with a religious upbringing would like that one. Trouble is, we make it a god in our lives and forget that we are.

***

Participant: ...I don't feel like I've had a lot of lovers in my life.

Gregory: That's true. What you fear finding out is that you are unlovable and unloving. Also that you just might want to bonk.

Participant: ...I do sometimes.

Gregory: What else is reject-able about you?

Participant: ...That I'm a bastard at times, and maybe perverted and kinky.

Gregory: Ah ha. Who sees his kinkiness? Who sees his fear of it?

Participant: ...One of the women said to me that she wanted to dress me up as a woman.

Gregory: Great. I'll tell you something else about sex. While you don't acknowledge and connect with your kinkiness and your perversity, you're scared of it. Then you disconnect from yourself to try and be something different from that; then what people pick up is that you're scary and disconnected. They're scared to get close, because there must be something wrong because you're scared to get close.

One of the major breakthroughs I ever had in my life was on a seminar years ago, telling everyone that I was a very kinky man. It felt scary, like I was supposed to be this pure personal growth teacher type, etc. A "nice person". Caring. Everyone loved it, and wanted to know more. That was the genesis of this Sex and Relationships Seminar.

Participant: ...How do I get into my kinkiness?

Gregory: It's not even about getting into it. First acknowledging it and let yourself know it's okay. Give yourself approval for it.

Participants: ...I can see him in a black leather G-string ...With thigh length black leather boots ...And a girdle ...And a nazi helmet ...Singing "YMCA."

Gregory: A part of it is owning the Queen in you. Not everyone is going to want to play with that with you, and some already do.

Whatever it is you do, people will show up who agree. While you aren't approving of your sexuality, then people will show up in agreement with you in that too. Remember in The Living Game Seminar, we identify two things about people: everyone proves whatever they believe, and everyone agrees with everyone else's beliefs. We are the most agreeable creatures on the planet. If you choose to experience your sexuality as rejectable, everyone will agree with you because they love you. They'll prove you're right. We always support the whole planet, and every person in it, in having it however they want it. Your belief and therefore your reality is that your sexuality is rejectable, so everyone supports your reality for you and stays away from your bed.

You don't connect with it because you believe it's unacceptable. The minute you accept it, then the agreement changes. People will then agree with the new agreement.

Participant: ...If you reject yourself, everyone else will.

Gregory: That's right. Absolutely. To see what you reject in you, look at what others reject about you. If you want to know about yourself, look at your reflection and you'll see what you haven't been seeing. Yes?

Participant: ...I want to acknowledge that I'm scared of people who I think need me because I see that as a reflection of myself needing people, and I want to be independent but I also really need people. That makes me feel a lot stronger because I feel that I can be independent and have people.

Gregory: The truth is, we do need people. We human creatures need other human creatures around. That's different to being needy. To need relationships is different to being needy IN relationships.

Participant: ...I've got something I have to say about last night. We were in the bathroom.

Gregory: That's kinky, a married couple having a date. Wow!

Participant: ...He shaved my pussy last night.

Participant: ...I couldn't leave myself alone when I shaved mine, it felt so good.

Gregory: There's some great advantages in it. The first one is that women actually get to feel their pussy on the outside. So does the man. It just opens up a whole new world of erotica and sensuality, and it can also be much more pleasurable for a man to have sex, because he's not ripping his dick with hairs.

There's a whole lot of new things open up that you can do with your dick and pussy: playfully and sensually and sexually, especially with oil. It just opens up a whole lot of fun. I recommend it, it's amazing.

Okay. Some more on reflections. Sometimes when we look out there we see aspects of others that we don't like, that are painful. Common reactions to that include to ignore or avoid it, to block it out, to make it illegal or immoral, to try to stamp it out, etc. ...

I run seminars selfishly. Whatever you or other participants present that's painful, I see another level of that in me, then I can heal it by dealing with it out there. The value is extraordinary, as shown by my growth over the years.

What most seminar leaders or therapists do when someone presents something that's painful is avoid it.

If you cry in psychiatry, most psychiatrists will end the session. They say you are having a catharsis. "That's not therapy, it's catharsis." The truth is, they can't deal with their own sadness or pain, so if you present it, they have to run away or push you away. They are trapped in their minds and disconnected from their emotions. If you really want to grow, go for the stuff that you avoid or resist in others, and find a way to get past that with them, then you get past it in you.

If you put up a lot of barriers inside, you are going to avoid other people who put up barriers inside, so make it your job to get past their barriers, and you'll get past your barriers. As I have said since I was a nurse and saw it: some people are in a job for 30 years and they have 30 years of experience. Some people are in a job for 30 years and they have 1 year's experience 30 times.

It's your choice whether or not you keep repeating the same patterns and experiences year in and year out, or whether you seek new breakthroughs and new choices.

If you want to fast track your personal growth, look for people whom you resist. In the process you learn about yourself. That's one way to get major breakthroughs for yourself. If you hang out with the people you like or feel safe with, then they're likely reflecting what you've already handled. That's cool, just not a challenge.

That's very loving and nurturing. It's not great for fast tracking your growth, because the tendency is to stay and stagnate there. Anyone else experience resistance like that?

Participant: ...I have this huge fear of the maniac in me. That men could just turn into animals and eat me or kill me or something.

Gregory: So one of your fears is that if you actually start having it, you'll become a sex maniac.

Participant: ...I have felt that.

Gregory: Because that's a fear in you, you see it in him and you avoid it because it's not something you're ready to deal with in you. So you go into Ice Queen because your fear is that the other side of Ice Queen is raging nympho. And nice Catholic girls don't do that.

Participant: ...In my life I attract a lot of men, and I just brush them off and think, "No, they're not good enough for me" and I set up to go out with a model.

Gregory: And then end up really disillusioned, no doubt.

Participant: ...Sure. The caring Cancer in me wanted to go to bed and cuddle up to him and be open to where ever that would lead, but then there was just something stronger saying, "I'm not ready for that."

I know that I could take him to bed and show him a good time and make a real impact in his life, and I feel like I'd come out of it thinking, "Yuck." This all feels really risky to say.

Gregory: It's great. You feel yuck a lot.

Participant: ...Yeah. And it's so easy to put it out onto him and not be bringing it back onto me.

Gregory: That's exactly what I'm addressing. Just notice in what you've said, all the conflicting energies and thoughts and feelings, "Part of me wants to nurture but part of me doesn't, something happens, and I become shallow and I go for looks, but I feel disillusioned and yucky and I don't want to because if I do I'll..." Blah, blah, blah.

It's like a can of worms, where do they begin and end? While you stay put, it stays confused. When you step out of the comfort zone, and into a new experience, suddenly that starts sorting it out. Have you ever had a knotted fishing line?

Participant: ...Yeah.

Gregory: Have you ever tried to unknot it bit by bit? If you try and get this bit out, it pulls something tight somewhere else. You have to move back from the knot and work the whole thing, don't you? Gradually the whole thing unfolds and then it just sort of falls open.

What I'm saying for all of you, is that while ever you stay in your comfort zone, you don't solve the next set of problems and challenges: you'll only do that by stepping into the next risks. Again, if you want to fast track that process, look for what you resist or fear.

It may not be enjoyable. In your case it may bring up all sorts of confusion about the mother in you and fears about becoming like your mother, or fears about reaching people on deep levels and feelings of "yuck" and all that. Your next step to resolve all those. You can't resolve anything until you see it clearly: it's called acknowledgement.

See the truth is that you can all see yourselves in every one of the people in this room, you connect with different parts of yourself with each one, and the tendency is to connect with the parts you already feel safe with.

Trust that whatever you create is of maximum value for you. So as we saw earlier if someone is trying hard to get laid it may be that he will get maximum value out of this seminar by doing the whole seminar and not getting laid. What's already happening is that by not getting it, he's getting angry and starting to connect with his anger and learning how to turn that around.

We have such integrity with ourselves, that we won't let ourselves have 'B' until we have finished 'A.' Trust the process and the steps.

When you don't get what you think you want, trust your own choosing. Then own it as yours. Understand that you've obviously chosen this because this is what you got, so own your choice. "This is my choice. It's not what I thought I wanted to choose. This is apparently what I actually wanted to get maximum value, at least for now." The only other possibility is that your life is out of your control, and you are a victim of circumstances.

Participant: ...It's got to the point for me where everything seems a risk. I get really confused and I don't know why I'm here. To learn? I've made those acknowledgements before, but it doesn't feel like anything has changed. I just feel dull and confused about what I'm supposed to be doing here.

Gregory: You're here, and your head doesn't know why yet. A lot of my life like has been like that. I create my life and I don't know why. My head goes off on all sorts of interesting explorations of the question, "Why?" At some point out of owning the choice, I get the why, not as an idea or possibility or a question, but for what it really IS. Yeah? So are you willing to be dull and confused for a while?

Participant: …Oh yeah.

Gregory: It might just be to show yourself what it is to be really present with being dull and confused.

Participant: …Yeah I get dull and confused quite a bit.

Gregory: The difference is, you're conscious of it now. Until you are present with it, in fact fully allow it, you don't have a choice about it.

Just maybe the whole purpose of your life at this moment is to learn to fully experience being dull and confused! Then you master it. Then you have new choices with it.

Now, I've got a really great process for you all.

You're all going to get undressed, and all the women are going to sit in the middle in a group facing inwards, and they're going to have girl talk. As if they were by themselves.

To start, the women talk about sex, about what you like, what you don't, what you bitch about, things that amuse you, funny or boring or exciting bonks and other sexual times. You're talking as if there were no men present, you all know what that's like. Don't you? Let it get nitty gritty, it may include things like how you like dicks that bend up or to the left or the right or what you don't like or just criticisms. Normal girl talk.

Participant: …What do the men do?

Gregory: Stay quiet, listen and learn. Then it's the men's turn later.

The myth is that men talk about their conquests. The truth is that women do it far more. Men very very rarely discuss their sexual exploits. And very rarely discuss the ins and outs of them - if you will excuse a bad pun! Women are obsessed by it. If you have two women together, you have a sexual discussion.

Participant: ...Especially if one of them is me.

Gregory: That's true isn't it? Sometimes it's camouflaged, but often it's not. Are there any questions from anyone about this process? Yes?

Participant: ...If I don't feel comfortable with it, can I just sit and let it flow and then join in when I feel right or should I force myself to try?

Gregory: No, it's not about forcing yourself. Give yourself the opportunity to ask the other women the questions you would have liked to have asked and never did, or tell them the things you would have liked to have shared and never did. Or simply sit there as a part of it all.

Maybe you'll find out you're one of the herd. Maybe. It's also about mixing with the girls.

So be scared or shy and do it anyway.

Chances are at first you're going to feel self conscious and strange. Let that be there and simply get into it and keep going and at some point you'll relax about it and probably crack yourself up laughing and get on with it. So, men out, women in, clothes off.

***

Participant: ...Gregory, yesterday I started off the day feeling great and then I seemed to go downhill so that I felt that I was losing the feel of the seminar, feeling absolutely spaced out. I lost track of time. By the end of the night I was fine, sort of peaceful and nonchalant. I don't know what went on.

Gregory: When you all did The Living Game Seminar, you opened up a huge space and then it contracted somewhat. That's how it works. Your old beliefs say, "Whoa this is a bit much." So you pull it back until you feel safe and grounded in your life. And you've also got the knowledge and experience of having been there to work towards.

The more you do it, the more you create safety, then you're ready for the next step. Until you learn to recognize it, you do it by pushing your energy back down, then you feel drained and it's like going down hill. Once you recognize the process, you just let it happen without having to suppress or repress yourself.

Who else has ever had that feeling, "God I've lost it," with all the great feelings and knowing that you've opened up to and grown in seminars?

Participants: ...(many voices) Yeah. Heaps.

Gregory: I haven't gotten to the point, and I don't know if I ever will, where that has stopped happening, except I now give it different words. I used to call it, "I've lost it. Oh my God. I've lost it," until I saw that I am it and I haven't lost me. Now, the the name for that feeling is either, "It's time to have a rest," or, "It's time to move again."

For example: remember when you learnt to ride a bike and it was really exciting and challenging and scary and you were very aware of learning to ride a bike. Then you mastered it and became casual about it and it wasn't so exciting. It was just a form of transport?

Then it got dreary because you wanted to have a car. At that point you could say, "Oh, I've lost it. I've lost the excitement and the challenge." That's true, but you haven't lost the ability to ride a bike, you've mastered that. When you master something, it's time to take on a new challenge. Find something new to learn, something new to go for, and immediately you're back in it.

In a sense, "lost it" also means it's getting boring. The minute you get bored you're not taking risks or challenges, not stretching yourself or going for something new, then things get ordinary again.

There is always more. You can do 20 years of personal growth and be just as bored as if you never did any, you're just bored at a much higher level. The same is true in every area of life.

Participant: ...That's particularly how I felt. I had a threesome date last night. And I didn't even get an erection.

Gregory: What did you actually do? Since you didn't get an erection, I assume you didn't have sex.

Participant: ...Yeah.

Gregory: So what did you do?

Participant: ...We just caressed and played.

Gregory: So that's what you wanted last night. Your head thought, "Oh wow. I'll have two bonks tonight." And what your body said was, "No, the next step for you to learn is to get comfortable and relaxed with two women."

Then if you create another threesome, it may be that you're as horny as a rabbit because you've taken that step. Again, trust the process.

Participant: ...What went through my mind that I was sort of getting bored with sex.

Gregory: You might be. So do something different. I guarantee you can get bored with sex. It doesn't matter what you do. If you have 430 orgies in a row, you're going to get bored with orgies. You're going to want to get really kinky and just sleep with one person - in the missionary position!!

Anything will get boring. Look at Prince Charles. Being the future King of England looks like one of the most boring things on this planet to me. How he gets to stop being bored shitless, is to go and give talks that rip on the architecture in London. He stirs up an international controversy over urban architecture.

Anything can get boring, so do it differently. If you're doing the same thing, do the same thing differently. It's like driving to work. If you drive to work and you take the same route every day, what happens?

Participant: ...Automatic.

Gregory: Yes. Automatic. You get up, have a shower, get dressed, have breakfast, you're in the car, drive three or five miles or one hundred miles. The next thing you know, you wake up and you're actually at work and it's 11:30 in the morning. That can't happen if you have breakfast in the shower and drive a different way to work. Or get a cab, or get someone to drive you. Catch a passing helicopter.

Doing something different just wakes you up. That's one of the most powerful processes you can ever do in your life, find new ways to do ordinary things, for no reason whatsoever except to wake up.

In the Carlos Castaneda books on Don Juan, the Yaqui Indian, there is some good material about what reality is, and how to stay real. He says the perfect way to live your life is as if you're going to die in five minutes.

If you knew you were going to die in five minutes, nothing you did would matter, and everything you did would really matter. You'd be incredibly conscious of everything for five minutes. But nothing would matter. Being in that place, where you love and value everything but you're not attached to it, is the place of Power. That's when you've got a choice.

Also note that we all have a terminal disease - it's called Life! It amazes me how people get told that they only have a year or two to live and immediately they set about doing what they always wanted to do in the time left to them. Well I'm here to tell you that you only have somewhere between one day and a hundred years left to live, so get moving!

One of the concepts from Asian philosophy that's been translated and twisted is the idea of detachment: that it's good and spiritual and right to detach from the world. Westerners often think that means that nothing in life matters, and we should not want or own anything of this world. That is a Christian distortion of a Buddhist idea. For me detachment is about not attaching your value as a human being to things and actions outside of you in the world. So I am detached from money in the sense that my value doesn't live in how much money I've got. At the same time I have, use and enjoy money.

The difference is that I have money, it does not have me.

When we make anything, be it a relationship, money, house, car, success, looks etc. be the source of our personal value, or status, then we are attached to it like parasitic lympets, and it owns us.

To be detached from the world in that sense, and at the same time value and love your world, is very powerful. Either way, staying asleep or waking up in your life is an okay choice, you just get different results, so in a sense it doesn't matter. Just another choice: more or less value and aliveness.

Hear that phrase? Matter is literally that which is real and solid. It's material. It doesn't matter. You do. You do the act of making matter. When you create something, you literally matter it; you materialize it. Which is to say that you make it matter. You of course only put your energy into what matters to you, what is important to you. You've created everything in your world so that everything matters; you've mattered it.

Participant: …Yeah, I was saying, "Oh it doesn't matter. It doesn't matter."

Gregory: Everything works some of the time. It's very powerful to give yourself the experience that nothing matters, but that's not the whole truth, because the other side of it is that everything matters.

Spend a day as if nothing matters, then spend a day as if everything matters. You will start to integrate the two opposites. It's like spending a day saying No to everything, then spending a day saying Yes to everything. You will start to have a real choice about your yes/no responses, where mostly we say yes or no on the basis of old unconscious patterns and comfort zones. Just as we have learnt that certain things do or do not matter, or have relative values in how much they matter. My truth is that whatever matters is where I choose to invest value or importance.

I'm a master of paradox, and to become a master of paradox you live both extreme opposites as if each is true, and then you start to get the point of resolution in the middle of a paradox. Give each reality it's separate space.

To give yourself permission to do both at different times, you start to have a choice about either all the time. And with concepts like, "It doesn't matter." "And it does." "It's all real." "It's all unreal." "I make it all up." "No, it's all fixed." All of those are true. I think it was Einstein said that the true sign of genius is the ability to entertain opposing truths at the same time. That's how I did it. So practice being a genius!

Give yourself time and space to entertain different realities, especially opposites, and develop your own genius.

Participant: …That's powerful, but can you imagine doing that at work, it would be a bit ineffective.

Gregory: Work also becomes interesting when it stops being boring. Work is also a part of life, believe it or not. I know that's not a popular idea! Everything we are talking about here applies to work. Or family. Or sex. We are identifying underlying principles that always apply in life.

***

Gregory: I've said many times that to release feelings works. It's a healing process.

Most of our feeling patterns were set or developed in the first year of our life. Probably all of them by the time we were seven.

A feeling like abandonment could have even first occurred while or before you were being born. It's not uncommon for mothers in childbirth to become scared and pull their energy back from the child. The unborn baby feels abandoned on that fundamental life energy level.

Then you have or create other experiences as you grow up. When parents aren't there when you want them to be you feel that abandonment again. That's a feeling that comes between us and our wholeness, or the fullness of our Selves.

As adults we create experiences in our lives which force us to feel these feelings that stand between us and experiencing our fullness and our joy. One level of living is survival. A higher level is fulfillment, wholeness and joy. In other words, attaining the God within. Anything that stands between you and that, you will keep coming back to it in order to heal it. Our true state is to be whole and healthy.

If you cut your arm, your attention and focus will stay on that wound. Suddenly, all the other things in your life don't seem to have the same importance anymore, because that's where your attention needs to go, and it will keep coming back to that until it's healed.

The same process applies emotionally to return to emotional wholeness. One of the things that people fear is that if they open up to their hurt it will never end. People often say to me, "I cry and I cry and it feels like it doesn't help, it feels like there's always more. It feels like I'm not getting anywhere," etc...

The thing to remember is that as babies we felt things totally. You didn't as a baby feel abandoned, you were abandoned. You became abandonment. It wasn't a feeling within, it became your total reality, if only for a second. For many of us it was for hours, many times. Yet the nature of it is that we blocked, or suppressed the feeling, it being too scary, too big, too painful to deal with. Once you, as an adult, experience that feeling in it's totality, it disappears: it is done, it becomes completed and so can be released. Then when someone leaves, they are just leaving, not abandoning you.

To the degree to which you experience or "feel" the feeling, you disappear that amount of it. For example, say you have a feeling of abandonment and you could measure it and it was ten feet high. Last night, you felt 1 inch of being abandoned, you cry it out so what's left to experience is 9 feet 11 inches more. You've healed 1 inch of it and literally released that much. It's not that nothing is shifting, it's that you haven't felt the totality of it, yet.

The totality of it when you were a child was terrifying, which is why you blocked it, and you still carry that fear of feeling it, because when it happened it was so big and so real. Our fear is that if we feel something that intensely, it will become real again, and we will discover that we truly are abandoned. Then what we do is abandon our feeling of abandonment, reinforcing that we can be abandoned, and that internal abandonment is actually happening, again.

The same goes for all feelings you block or suppress. In other words you get to be in the place you fear. You fear that if you let your anger out, you'll be a killer, so you kill your feelings of anger and become what you fear; an anger killer ...of your feelings.

You fear the possibility of abandonment, so you abandon your feelings of abandonment, proving to yourself that you're abandon-able. Each time you let yourself feel those feelings, you give your whole consciousness - body, mind and spirit - new experiences which give you the message, "Oh, feeling that much abandonment was safe." Then it gets to be safer to feel that more fully.

Gradually you build confidence and strength in your own ability to feel your own pain.

At some point, hopefully, you get to totally experience the feeling of being abandoned, and release it. Nature can't stand a vacuum, and it can't stand incompletion. Whatever is incomplete returns to be completed, hence the saying, "A stitch in time saves nine."

Have you ever swept the floor and not done the last bit which is to sweep into a pan and put it in the garbage?

You've just left it in the corner where a breeze catches it and it blows it around again and you have to sweep the floor again? Nature can't stand incompletion. We have enormous drive to have complete experiences, and to complete past incomplete experiences. What happens is that issues that are incomplete simply keep coming back - repeating in our lives in different shapes and forms - until they are completed.

Participant: ...Is that why, last night I developed a pain in my throat, in my larynx, and I was remembering when we were shifting house a lot when I was a child and I was feeling really sad and unsafe.

Gregory: What happened then was that you were feeling scared and unsure and you couldn't express it in sadness so you expressed it in tonsillitis. You suppressed your sadness. That's why so many kids lose their tonsils. Their sadness becomes jammed up in their throat, and instead of being released, the tonsils express it through pain and swelling. They go to a hospital and their sadness is cut out. They sacrifice their tonsils to survive their sadness. It's literally a modern hi-tech ritual blood letting.

Participant: ...I can relate to that. I had tonsillitis when I was four and it went on until I was about five. I vomited a lot.

Gregory: Really sick of what was going on huh?

Participant: ...Then they cut my tonsils out.

Participant: ...It's amazing how many doctors encourage that when there are other ways to do it.

Gregory: They don't know that there's another way of doing things, plus they have a big investment in not knowing. There's only ever been one psychiatrist who completed The Living Game Seminar.

Participant: ...Where is that psychiatrist?

Gregory: He's a German psychiatrist who was out here on holiday. There have been a lot more psychologists, but only one psychiatrist. When I get into the healing aspects of all this, the most defensive people are doctors. When I say, "We are God in our life," the religious get their backs up. When I say, "Through the education system we get to control our citizenry," the teachers have a turn at being miffed. The doctors have got a lot invested in being right. Everyone has a lot invested in being right about their way of doing life, until they don't. While you've got a lot invested in being right, you're not only not making changes, you're not looking for change, because you believe you're right.

Let's call it professional institutionalized self-righteousness. Doctors are the last people to want to look at alternative ways of approaching medicine, that's their competition!

For centuries doctors have been sitting at the top of a power structure as absolute experts, modern gods, dictating down to people who couldn't possibly know about or take control of their health and bodies. The world has changed and that structure hasn't - it had no reason to.

What isn't being acknowledged in society is that the structures that have existed for hundreds, even thousands of years still exist, but they're been eaten out from the inside. And they haven't all yet collapsed.

That collapse is so serious in medicine that the Sydney Morning Herald reported the head of the Australian Medical Association saying doctors HAD to get into alternate medicine to maintain their income, so great has been the flood of patients away from them!

If you want to create change, appeal to the hip pocket nerve!

Participant: ...But that structure is our creation.

Gregory: Sure. And society is moving away from the traditional structures. Marilyn Ferguson called the process the Aquarian Conspiracy. She sees the New Age is a conspiracy in that it's not happening from the top down. It's a grass-roots movement happening from the bottom up. The old power structures are still intact and they're being rapidly eroded. It is often not obvious, and it is gaining momentum.

Those power structures were created in an era when people believed that they were not powerful. Power existed in someone "up there," be it God or the Government or the priest or the doctor. Others had power invested in them and came to quite like the arrangement.

However, the world has changed. We live in the age of information, which IS power, we no longer need others to decide for us. We are also demanding results back from those in power, and when we don't get them, we are looking elsewhere. In the process all the old assumptions are being put under close scrutiny to see where the truth and the bullshit lies. Then we are extracting the parts that work and discarding those that don't.

So with medicine we have some amazing miracles evolved and evolving. If my hand was cut off I'm damn sure I'd want a microsurgeon, not a seminar! However medicine is now almost passe´ for general disease and healing. It is valuable for crisis situations and what one surgeon friend calls "crash repair."

You can see that erosion in simple things like union membership world wide has declined yearly for years. Unions are still powerful, but their power base is eroding. Same with medicine. More and more people are seeking other ways of healing and taking responsibility for their healing, including doctors. On the surface, the medical profession is still in the same position, but it's eroding.

Practice what you teach is my motto. Once you start telling people about a concept that you're not practicing, then it sounds false, it starts sounding like theology, dogma or ideology. When you share from your experience honestly, then people either see your authenticity or they don't. And not everyone can see it.

Participant: ...Sometimes I feel that I want to share some of my knowledge, just for the sharing. Then I ask myself, "Am I looking for approval for doing this?"

Gregory: It could be. Or it could be that you want to show off or it could be that you want to share. The important lesson of sharing is called, "Don't throw pearls in front of swine." Some people simply haven't got the ears to hear it yet. That's not a criticism of them, it's an acknowledgement of where they are or where they're not.

For example, most doctors don't have the ears to hear that alternate healing has any validity. Most media commentators do not have the hearing for that either. This is the true definition of ignorance, because they ignore other possibilities, they have closed minds. Lots of people have.

I would rather spend my time with the people who want to hear it, than with the people who can't or don't. Ultimately if I spend my time with people who don't want to hear it, I'm devaluing me. What I hear with you sometimes is that where you come from is called "conversion." Like the religions do. That comes from your desire to share and your excitement and the value you get BUT telling it as if you have THE value, which disrespects other people's choices and paths. Turn that around and say, "I did this and this and it was really exciting and I got a lot of value." Then it is up to them. Inform, not convert.

Some people will say, "Oh that's nice." You might as well have said, "I've changed my laundry detergent." Why spend your valuable time talking to that person? If you want interaction, find something that you are both interested in.

Several times in the seminar some of you have made the comment that you've become aware of how you don't listen, and have acknowledged me for my capacity to listen. A communication where you listen to questions is very powerful because then you're both talking about what you're talking about, instead of what you're not talking about.

Often conversations are like two people on different planets having a conversation with themselves in front of each other. And what happens is that each one politely listens until the other one shuts up so they can get on with saying what they wanted to say. That's what most conversations sound like to me.

It's like when I asked you all what you take to bed with you …what is between you and having good sex? What is between you and good communication? If it is the desire to convert, the desire for approval, the need to boast or the need to show off, then behind that are your criticisms of yourself doing those same things and then behind that is your doubt of yourself and the doubt that they will see how good you are. Then behind that is that you feel alone really want to have a cry and behind that, etc…

You approach someone with 9 layers of your own conversations between you and them. They've got 9 layers of their own conversations between them and you, and you talk through 38 levels of communication. It's like having a committee of 18 censoring and monitoring what gets through. Have you ever played the Chinese Whisper game?

I whisper to someone, "The moon will probably rise tonight." He whispers it to the next person. By the time it gets around the circle back to me it's turned into, "Dogs run after breakfast."

The more you own the different parts of you, the more you have a direct communication and hear what is being said. I'm constantly shocked by the degree to which people don't hear what is said.

Participant: ...How do I make my inner voices change?

Gregory: By acknowledging them and getting them on your side. A simple example of changing an inner voice: I used to have a very severe Dickensian judge, an old-fashioned English High Court judge, who sat on my shoulder in his black robes with a wig that went down over his shoulders. Everything I did, my inner voice judge said, "You blew that. That wasn't very good." That was his job. It didn't matter what I did, good or bad, awful or great - his job was to criticize me. I'd hear his voice. It felt like he was in charge and I had no say and I never felt good enough.

Then as I saw how I did that, I took responsibility for my creation of him. I played the game that I created him with love and wisdom for myself. I lay down and did a visualization of him, and I said to him, "Okay, I just realized that I created you, and I gave you the job you're doing, I don't know why. Tell me why. As your creator, I am commanding that you speak to me." And he said, "It's really simple. You gave me that job to make sure you never went into resignation, never settled for less than you were capable of doing. Your fear was, that if you did a good job, you would settle for that. My job was to sit on your shoulder and never let you think it was good enough, which meant I forced you to keep doing more, and doing it better and bigger."

That's a lot of value. If I hadn't had him there there's a lot of things I'd have settled for, for sure. Then I said, "Okay, I'm now clear that I'm not going to stop growing and living and expanding, so I'm now giving you a new job. Your new job is that after everything I do you say, 'Hey that was really great, and guess what? There's some more you can do to improve it even more, and you're doing brilliantly.'"

Now he sits on my shoulder and says, "Gregory, that was really great, and you can improve by doing this and this IF you want to."

Participant: ...I find that words are always open to interpretation, what one word means to me, may not necessarily mean that to you.

Gregory: Part of powerful communication is to make sure that we're talking the same language. If you want to have clear, powerful communications, take responsibility for ensuring that you both understand the language. There are some limitations because our language has limited words for some very broad experiences. "Love" is a good example.

We've got a few words for "snow." Eskimos have got 20 or 30. We need about 943 different words for love. We've got one. Acknowledging that, if someone says they want to have a loving relationship or a love relationship with me, I want some clear communications about what is meant by that. Otherwise I guarantee some crises and learning experiences as we accidentally stumble along "in love."

The word commitment is another. When I ask you, "Is that a commitment?" you know that means that if you say yes, it means yes. A lot of the rest of the world may say yes, but what they mean is, "Yes, if something else doesn't happen." I had some learning experiences where I said to people, "Is that a commitment?" They said, "Yes" and then I got a phone call saying, "Oh I can't, because this has happened." I said, "That's interesting, but you've got a commitment."

"What? You expect me to keep that commitment even when that's happened?"

I said, "Yes, that's what commitments are about." They understood a whole different meaning of the word. It actually is a statement that, "I will." They mean it as, "I will if it suits me at the time."

Participant: ...How do you handle a misunderstanding like that?

Gregory: First I get to take responsibility for the fact that I created a misunderstanding by not clearly defining my meaning.

It's not that they're wrong and I'm right, it's that we didn't have a clear communication.

In a sense, because I'm a lot more conscious about communication, it's much more my responsibility to handle that, and to then do what I should have done before, which is have a very clear conversation about what I mean by commitment, and to then have them make a statement about whether they're making a commitment or only have an intention to do it if it suits them.

Again, it's the thing that's incomplete. If my communication is incomplete, I have to go back and complete it. Thinking, "Oh, aren't they stupid," doesn't get me the result I want, which is a clear communication where we both know where we stand. If I hadn't completed it, it was my job to complete it.

That's why I often ask, "Have you got that?" To ensure that my communication to you all is complete for you all.

To an extent, it's a romanticized idea that, "We don't need to talk to have this wonderful understanding." I might say something to you all and I see a lot of facial expressions which can accurately say anything from, "I've checked out," to, "My God, that's profound."

Communication isn't an accident. We evolved it. How do you communicate a request that asks, "Will you pick up the towel and take it to the washing machine?" without using words? The only way is to act it out and by then you've done it anyway. There's no need to ask!

***

Participant: ...Sometimes I've wanted something and I concentrate.

Gregory: That's telepathy, and it's a great thing to develop. In the meantime, words have great power. "In the beginning was the word, and the word was made God." By using words, you create your world. The degree of clarity in the words you use helps determine the degree of result that you achieve.

People say things like, "Gee, I really feel like an ice cream." My response is, "Thank you for sharing, that's an interesting want." Nothing is going to happen. If someone says, "I'd really like an ice cream, would you buy me one?" that's a whole new ball game. That's a request for action. My experience is that people often don't ask for what they want. They don't state their intentions. They're not up front and clear about it.

The game is that everyone's supposed to sit around and ponder: I say it obscurely, and then you've got to sit around and make enquiry or guess. And it's a big wank. It's an interesting game if that's what you want to do. But it's just not very effective if you want results. If you want attention, one game is, "What's wrong?"

"Nothing."

"I can see that's something's wrong."

"No, really I'm fine." It goes on for hours.

Participant: ...So why do people play that game?

Gregory: Because it gets lots of attention. You might say, "Gregory, would you get me an ice cream," and I might reject you with, "Go screw yourself mate, get your own," so you don't take the risk. The game is to be a crab, sideways, approach things indirectly or circumspectly. You say, "Gee, I'd really like an ice cream," hoping that I'll say, "Oh, I'll get you one." If I don't, you won't feel rejected because you never asked!

You're coming from powerlessness and you're supporting the other person in being powerless. To say, "I'll get you one," has a level where it's also being powerless, because I'm buying into your powerlessness and saving you from the embarrassment of asking or fear of rejection.

Participant: ...Is there a way to do it softly? I don't know a way to do it softly.

Gregory: Change your pictures of what's soft and what's hard. Socially we have a picture that to be direct is to be hard and to say "no" is to be hard, so just change your pictures and definitions about that. Socially we have a picture that to fire people from a job is to be hard. So people in business work get themselves into all sorts of shit to avoid being seen to be hard. Then they are not seen to be hard, they're seen to be incompetent. They buy into the incompetence of the person that they want to sack, and they become incompetent too, not hard. Everyone says, "Gee, isn't the boss a nice guy? He's incompetent but he's a nice guy."

I worked with many people who were described in those terms when I was a nurse. I couldn't believe it. I used to be really hard in nursing. There were lots of crazy people in the ward. Obviously, a psychiatric hospital is where you find crazy people!

I used to have this "hard" rule. "Any patient who hits any of my staff, I will personally take out." The reactions I used to get from doctors and psychologists and supervisors was incredible. "That's harsh. You're a nurse. You should be loving and caring. I said, "I am, I care about my nurses, first." The other rule was, "Anyone who hits any other patient, I take out." One of the results was that I became hard, but almost no one ever got hit. And when they did, I took them out. They knew I meant it.

In other wards where they were nice and "soft," people got hit all the time. You get what you resist. By being soft they had a hard time. I was hard, and we all had a soft time, including the patients!

One of the social workers on my ward was hit and wanted to have the patient sent to a security hospital. I said, "What's the problem? You're the one who was bitching that I stood up on behalf of the nurses. You didn't want me to do that. So I'm not standing up for you." I turned around to the patient and said, "My ruling only goes as far as the nurses. If you want to punch her out that's between you and her. She doesn't mind." Wow, did she turn it around? She got "hard" real fast.

Then a couple of doctors got punched out. And they got to learn that being hard was much more preferable than being beaten up. Stepping back from it, how else do you do it? You've got a choice. You set a ground rule and you stick to it, or you don't, and get beaten up.

The irony was that the administration moved me to that ward because there were so many staff and patients getting hit! Two weeks after I got there no one was being assaulted! In the process the patients got a lot saner because they knew the limits and felt safer.

Participant: ...Is there a time when it's not appropriate to be hard. For example, if I see a girl that I like and I go up and say, "Hey I like you."

Gregory: At that point you probably are feeling "hard."

Participant: ...But I really mean, "I want to fuck you."

Gregory: To walk up to someone who you've just seen and say, "Hey I want to fuck you," sometimes is appropriate. At that moment you might pick up that that's a real possibility.

There's a difference between being clear and hard. There's a difference between being direct and hard. There's a difference between being clear and direct or insensitive. Clear and direct doesn't have to be hard. If I walk up to you and your job is to collect the mail, and I say, 'will you collect the mail?' or, 'collect the mail now,' it's clear and direct. If I say, "GO

AND COLLECT THE MAIL YOU IDIOT!!!!!" that's being something else; clear, direct and bloody, and in a package that could be called harsh. Most people go into soft wimpiness and disappear, rather than make clear statements, so they disempower themselves.

Participant: ...I am accused of being hard and harsh a lot in my life. Sometimes I do say things in anger, and sometimes it's just, "cut the crap" kind of stuff. Then I see that people don't like me, so I don't do it.

Gregory: They accuse you of being hard because they don't like such clarity. They want it to stay undefined because then they never ever have to actually do anything or deal with anything. It's all peace and groovy man. They get to stay unaccountable and irresponsible.

Day 6

"The only meaning that life has is the meaning you give it."

ORGASM NOT EJACULATION - HOMOSEXUAL FEARS, FANTASIES & FEELINGS - AUTHORITY - ROLES & VALUE - POSSESSION - ENTITIES - SAME SEX COMFORT - LOST & SEARCHING - TRUST - LETTING GO - CONFUSION - LIVING TREASURE - COMPLETION - BEING PRESENT - BELONGING - OWNING OUR DRAMA

Gregory: How you get to have sex for hours is to be totally clear that you're not there to have an orgasm. You're there to have the sensations that lead up to orgasm. Usually, as you get hotter and hotter, you go up up up up and you hit a peak where you don't have a choice anymore. And it's like, a little switch goes click, and you know you're on the "vinegar stroke" as they call it. But you know that from that point you're going to come. You're going to ejaculate.

So instead, what you do is build energy until you begin to approach that point, but don't go there.

Slow down, stop, have a rest, think of England, whatever so that your energy drops back. Then build it up again and leave a good margin so you don't come. When you've got that one, then take it a bit further, then a bit further. Learn to stop a hair's breath before the switch goes on. Stop and come back down. Up. Come back down. By this point you're going nuts by the way.

Participant: ...What about the woman?

Gregory: You're going crazy, "AHHHHHH." She's going crazy, "Ahhhh." Some women like to do it quickly to get you out of the way but a lot of women really enjoy that.

That's how you learn to extend it. And simply make love for longer periods. Once you master that, the next one to go for is that when you can stop that hair's breadth away, take it to stopping a tenth of a hair's breadth away so that you actually start having orgasms without ejaculation.

Participant: ...I've done that Gregory.

Gregory: Who can do that regularly? Not many. Right, you're missing a high point of sex. Right?

Really, put it on your list of priorities to master. Several reasons for that.

The first one is that you can have sex for hours, you can have 25 orgasms and not ejaculate.

The second is, you can have fantastic sex any time of the day and not wipe your energy out. If you practice that, something to go for is to have all the sex you want and all the orgasms you want and don't ejaculate for a month.

Now, several things will happen. Firstly you'll be climbing the walls for a while. You'll have so much sexual energy you won't know what to do with it. Secondly you'll be walking like a bandy legged person because your balls will ache from here to breakfast and back. They will, I tell you. Have you ever had lover's balls? Lover's balls is what you used to get as a teenager when women would play with your dick and balls and then stop. Some call it "blue balls."

It's extraordinarily painful. The irony of this is that I'm teaching Indian lovemaking techniques to an Indian man. I love it.

Participant: ...Why is it so painful?

Gregory: Because the physical release doesn't happen. Most of you have shared some version of sadness coming up, you block it and your throat gets sore. It's like that. When you have sex and don't ejaculate, there's an enormous amount of physical energy there ready to release. Except it doesn't get out so your balls get sore.

It can be REAL AGONY. Like, "Please carve me up into little pieces to put me out of my pain." So just be wary of that. Don't begin doing this if the next day you have to go for a jog or play football or something. Make sure that the next day is going to be a day where you can sit around and hopefully never move. It's worth it. It might take a week of pain but that too will pass.

The payoff is quite extraordinary. It gives you a whole new range of choices, and then you men can have multiple orgasms too. It's lovely to lose count at 15.

In a sense we have sex automatically, until we don't. It takes conscious intention to take charge of the process, and every step in the process. I suspect it's more important for men to learn it, because men have a much bigger push towards orgasm, to get the ejaculation. Women are usually more languid about pleasuring themselves, they don't usually have that pressure.

***

Gregory: Sadness can be a result of feeling happy. My experience is that every time I open a new level of joyfulness, i.e. enjoyment, what arises as well is sadness. The sadness is for the knowledge that I didn't have the good feelings before. By releasing the sadness, you grow the good feelings. You're sitting there feeling happy, and you're sad about the fact that it's taken this long to sit here and feel happy. By releasing the sadness you will be here and more present, and you let go of past sadness or unhappiness. Kahlil Gibran wrote, "Your joy is your sorrow unmasked."

Participant: ...I'm finding this hard. The people that I feel the need to connect with ...I'm doing exactly the opposite. There are many combinations of either being able to get on with someone or of sometimes feeling a close connection and taking that for granted on their part and then they're feeling intruded upon. I need to do it differently. This has caused a lot of sadness, which is also connected with envying the popular people.

Gregory: Feeling your sadness is you opening up to your sensitivity to yourself. You are now being far more sensitive to you than you have ever been. That makes you more sensitive to other people. You can either envy the people who have learned things that you haven't yet learned, or turn them into your teachers. The whole issue of human relationships is a vast area to master, and probably a lifetime one.

Open yourself up to how other people do it if you're willing to learn, or you can sit back in resentment that they've got it. The chances are, they got it by being willing to learn. No one on this planet that I've ever met, and I've met many thousands, was born a relationship master.

We're all born with certain skills and talents. And some people are born with them and don't develop them. I have a skill and talent for communication and I honed it and grew it over many years. I'm not aware that I was born with any particular skill or talent for relationship. In fact, being a Libra, it felt much harder for me, because relationships are SO important, belonging is SO important and connection is SO important, that my experience was that I had to learn every bit, bit by bit. I'm still learning.

I've had an absolute commitment to get to this level of mastery for decades, and sweated blood to get here. It's quite easy NOW but it wasn't automatic for me to be here.

The simple truth is, if there's a quality in someone else that you envy, then you are capable of developing it. For instance, some people have the quality of being absolutely brilliant book keepers. I don't envy it. I don't desire it. You get it? And I really respect their ability in that. But it's not something I want.

On the other hand, the minute I see something in someone that I want and feel I haven't got, I instantly know I've got it; it's just latent in me. If I don't want it, it's because I haven't got it and it's not my path.

Robert Panté says, "Desire is Nature's way of letting you know that what you want is on the way." When we start desiring something and think, "Oh I can't have it," we invite envy and resentment.

That's just your particular bag of stuff to clean up. Everyone's got their own bag of stuff to clean up. You just think that your bag is bigger and badder than everyone else's bag of stuff. It's not. Life's very fair. We are never presented with anything that we are not ready and able to solve or resolve. We all get our own bag. But wise people look for ways to put more stuff in their bag to further challenge themselves to get there faster.

***

Participant: ...Last night was for me one of the most amazing experiences I've ever had in my life.

Gregory: Tell us about it.

Participant: ...Being dressed up as a Drag Queen for the first time in my life was exciting and I wanted to do it, and when I was out here dancing I felt ridiculous at times but I wasn't afraid of it. And I got, really clearly, "I don't give a damn what you think of me." It was just...I've never ever been in that place. I mean completely. So free! It was so good to finally express that fantasy, that part of me. I felt ridiculous too, and today feel more manly than ever!

Gregory: Got it.

Participant: ...This morning one of the people said to me that the first time she met me, she thought I was gay. I said, "Yes, it's been mentioned before." And I went away and started thinking about it and decided to look at the possibility and try and see what that is. That terrifies me because it's ...it's fine for other people ...I've shared a house with a gay person and had a great friendship. But I didn't want it for myself. I don't think I'd be happy being bisexual, from where I am now. And when I thought, "Yes I would explore the possibility," my response was, "What will Mummy think?"

Gregory: She'll shit. If you tell her, "Dear Mummy, is it alright for me to be a queen?" Ha, ha.

Participant: ...It's really amazing.

Gregory: If your sex is an expression of your life force, why not express and share that with men and women - the human beings in your life. How far you take that is another issue. You as a man can also love a woman and not express that sexually. We all have both male and female, Yin and Yang aspects to ourselves.

Participant: ...Well the issue on that is, when we did the process, lying here and touching men, I realized that I could get into touching men, but the thing with homosexuality is that I'm really not turned on by bonking a man or a man bonking me. Not at all.

Gregory: Have you done it?

Participant: ...No.

Gregory: Then you don't know if you're turned on. You're not turned on by the idea of it.

Participant: ...The idea. Alright, alright.

Gregory: Vast difference. I'll tell you something. I used to work with a delightful man named Neil who was very openly gay. One of his excitements in life was that he never had sex with gay men. He liked to take a walk on the wild side. He only ever seduced straight men, and occasionally he got a beating for it, but he said, "Well you know, that's part of it."

It was really interesting for me because he said that 99% of the men that he approached went for it and loved it, and went through all their guilt about it, etc. ...My experience also is that all so-called straight men who open up to that possibility enjoy it, or enjoy some aspects of it. That's so for women also. The bottom line is that it can be an enjoyable experience. That's the bottom line. Ohh that's an appalling pun. My apologies. It can be an enjoyable experience. Obviously. People wouldn't do it if it wasn't.

A religious nutter was on Geoffrey Robertson's BBC TV Show "Hypotheticals" and the subject was AIDS.

The nutter got quite hot under the collar and said, very emphatically, that he wanted people to know that anal sex was NOT an enjoyable experience, like it was propaganda put out by homosexuals to recruit new members. Another guest, whose timing was impeccable, looked at the clergyman quizzically and said, "And are we speaking from experience, Fred?" The audience went bananas.

Participant: ...It's still not complete for me yet on that issue. I have had a homosexual experience and I have an averseness still about being close to men.

Gregory: What was the homosexual experience?

Participant: ...Fucking, sucking, stuff like that.

Gregory: Did your body enjoy it?

Participant: ...Yes.

Gregory: Did your mind?

Participant: ...Yes.

Gregory: Where did the aversion come from?

Participant: ...The hairiness and hardness of a man's body. I don't like the feel of it. I tend to associate that with this idea that I don't want to get close to a man.

Gregory: So one of the ways you get around that is to have a hairless soft man. You could put a woman with a phenomenal figure and beautiful eyes and sensual lips, who's got hair all over her body in front of me, and it ain't going to do a damn thing for me. It's distinguishing what does and doesn't turn you on. And make it up so it works. If you enjoyed the experience and your body and mind enjoyed the experience, but you don't like the flavor called 'hard body hairy,' go get soft body, no hair. Then you get to have it all work.

***

Participant:...I have a lot of resistance to authority. While we were talking I saw you as a father figure, and I found that within me there's a real resistance to figures in authority ...to authority itself. I saw that only I can fill myself. The seminar can't do it for me. It's my ability to get from the seminar what I need. Then I started to feel a lot of pain in my back for the first time in years, and instead of trying to get rid of the pain, I thought, "Just be with it." It's still there, trying to tell me something, I'm not quite sure what.

Gregory: Authority is very simple. The word authority comes from the word 'author.'

Hence, AUTHOR - ITY. So that you speak with authority when you are the author of what you say. It's that simple if you want authority in your life. In other words, write your own script. Tell your own truth in your words, your way.

(everyone applauds)

Gregory: You like that eh?

Participants: ...(everyone) Yeah.

Gregory: Did I say that with authority?

(everyone laughs)

Gregory: It's that simple. You can say the same thing in many ways. Taking responsibility for your choices and making choices releases power. Power in that sense is authority. You are the author of your choices, through personal experience, not through concepts. That's the difference between an expert and an authority by the way. There are a lot of experts who speak without any authority, but who speak with lots of concept or opinion. The definition of expert is: "X is an unknown quantity and a spurt is a drip under pressure. X-spurt."

Participant: ...In my childhood I always saw the church as being the authority.

Gregory: The church was the authority, and you followed the script it wrote. So it had authority over you. The more you own your own life script, your truth, the more you take back authority. You know?

The medical profession has authority over a lot of people, because it authors a certain script about health, and a lot of people buy it, and live that script. They then have no authority - or power - about their own health. It's the same in every area of your life. When you speak from experience, you speak with authority and thus are auth-entic.

Saying, "Having homosexual experiences doesn't turn me on," is speaking from concept, not authority, if he's never done it. So he was speaking about an idea or an opinion. When he says, "The idea of homosexual experiences doesn't turn me on," then he's speaking with authority.

A lot of resistance to authority comes from a victim place, where there's someone, something or an organization 'up there' which has the authority, which equals control. "They do it to me and make me do it." We give our power away to other's authority.

When you take your power back, when you begin to author your own life, then you become the authority. If I say, "Do this now," you can think, "Oh, he's the figure of authority and he's making me do it," and that is powerlessness. When you think, "He's the human being who speaks with authority on subjects that I want to learn about and I have authored him into my life," then you are the authority in your life. Then you listen to the authority of what I say, and you decide what you use from it.

So all I ever do is sit here and talk my script: my life, my experiences and what I have learned from them. In other words, what I've authored. Notice that I have no attachment to what you take on board from that!

Participant: ...I understand that I am the author of my script, yet sometimes I feel that I'm not scripting what is happening ...it feels like it's out of my control.

Gregory: Play the game that you are the creator in your life, therefore you chose it, you created it, and you didn't know you were doing that. So make an acknowledgement like:

"I wasn't conscious of the fact that I was choosing to create what's turned up in my life, but if I'm the creator, then somehow I created it. So I will take responsibility for my creation and get the value of what I have created with love for myself." The other option is to say, "I didn't want it. I've got no control."

Regarding your back pain - by taking that degree of authority back you have the experience of then not getting on your back. That releases feelings of tension on your back. You're letting go of the burden, and the first step is to feel the burden. That back ache has always been there, it's just been anesthetized. Now that you're waking up to it, you feel it again and then you can release it.

Participant: ...It's owning the fact that I heal myself.

Gregory: Yes. You are your authority. Ideally, in any situation that involves more than one person, everyone owns their own choice, it is co-created. What happens when you own your authority is that you stop experiencing me as an authority figure. You see that I'm a human being sitting here doing what I do with great authority. Instead of resenting that, you respect it more as you own your own authority more.

Participant: ...So you are an equal, rather than up there with us down here.

Gregory: Yes. We are equally human beings. We are of equal value. I'm of unlimited value and you're of unlimited value. And I do this better than you, that's why you're sitting there. Tomorrow I might say, "Hey I'd like to learn conga drums," and then you're sitting here and I'm sitting there, and you're teaching me what you know: drumming. One of the greatest teachers in my life is my son. I learn more from him than just about anyone else in my life. Because he does a lot of stuff with a lot of authority.

He constantly shows me new ways of doing and being and approaching. I'm always on the look out for teachers. When I want to learn something I will find someone to teach me that thing. I don't give a damn what role they play in life. It may be you teach me the bongos and it maybe some fifteen year old kid who is a bongo master, or some derelict down in Chinatown who happens to be sitting there with a bongo. And I say, "Hi, can I sit down and see how you do that?" And he says, "Yeah sure, bongo bongo bongo." His mind might be scrambled: I want to know whether he can do it or not.

We get sucked into roles. We start treating roles as though they're real. People go to doctors because they've learnt that those in the doctor role are healers. Very few doctors are healers. But they act the role of it. The title becomes more important than the person, or their abilities.

We buy the title instead of who they are and what they can actually do. It constantly staggers me that people go to psychiatrists for ten, fifteen years. Wouldn't you think that if it hasn't worked by then, it is not going to work. It doesn't seem to me to demonstrate a huge amount of intelligence. How many times would you take your car to the mechanic without getting a good result?

You're not going to take your car to the mechanic 25 times in a row if every time you get it back, you haven't got the results you want. Because it's a psychiatrist or whatever, people don't look past the role and instead say, "Oh he's a psychiatrist, he must know what he's doing." Ha, ha, ha. Sure.

Participant: ...The other side of that is when you can do it and you can prove you can do it. You don't need qualifications to sit there and be an instructor, and wave a bit of paper.

Gregory: That's a perfect example. People settle for paper qualifications. They say, "What are your qualifications?" Rather than, "Let me find out who you are and what you can do." It's been many years since anyone has asked me what my qualifications are. People used to ask, "What are your qualifications to run this seminar?" I'd say, "I get results."

What else could I say? Being a psychiatric nurse isn't qualification. I used to sell encyclopedias when I was a teenager. That wasn't qualification. Nothing I've done 'qualifies' me for what I do. And everything I did in my life qualifies me for what I do. Ah, I love such paradoxes.

The word qualifications implies that you can deliver quality in that area. Rather than test the quality, we accept that someone with a piece of paper saying they are qualified must be. We do not look at the quality of their quality, the degree of quality they deliver or the quality of their degree to deliver. I know some mechanics who are qualified and are great, others who are incompetent. The same is true for teachers, psychiatrists, seminar leaders and so on. As I said, I am interested in who can get the results, they are the truly qualified.

One of the huge pitfalls in life is to relate to roles and not to people. They did some brilliant research experiments in an American university. They got a class of university students who all knew each other, then split them in half and said, We're going to play a game called "Prison." They built a mock-up prison in the university with quarters for the warders, and cells, the whole bit.

They put the warder half of the class in prison warder garb and the prisoner half in prisoner garb. Then they put them in the prison together. They had to call the experiment off after three days for fear that one of the warders would kill a prisoner. It took three days for it to end up as a totally totalitarian prison where warders would beat up prisoners for the slightest error! They were all class mates. It took some of them months to come out of the experience. That's where roles mess people up, and how fully we buy them.

Another experiment that horrified me even more, was that they got students and set up another game, an interrogation game that went like this: you sat at a table and I would ask you a question and try and get you to answer. You've been instructed not to answer. On the table, I had a little buzzer where I was told to give you a little electric shock if you didn't answer.

What would happen initially, is that the students who knew each other would sit down and say, "I have to ask you these questions, I really want you to answer them because if you don't, I have been told to give you electric shocks to make you answer."

Just one more example of "I was just following orders. I have been told." The others said, "Oh no, I'm not supposed to answer." They played for a while and it became more serious. They'd say, "Okay, so what's your name?"

"I can't tell you." BZZZZZ

"What's your name?"

"I can't tell you." BZZZZZ

Then they changed it so that they could vary the amount of shock that they gave. Across a table, they would give little shocks. Then they put the interrogator in uniform and once they were in uniform, the shocks got bigger. Then they put sunglasses on the interrogators and the shocks got bigger. Then they put the interrogator further away from the prisoner and the shocks got bigger. Then they put them behind a one way mirror with a microphone and the shocks they gave their student friends were huge.

They were giving shocks that were nearly knocking the 'prisoners' unconscious. I saw that the more distance we have from people, the less sensitive and more brutal we are. Much harder to be brutal with someone who's close to you. There's a direct correlation between the amount of contact you make or don't make. When you are playing a role, or relating to someone else as a role, you have created total personal distance from them. Most Nazis went home and still hugged their wives and cuddled their children. It was when in uniform, in role, that they lost their humanity.

Roles are a game, so if you understand the game, that's fine. On the seminar, people have different roles. I have the role of instructor. Someone has the role of support team leader. Some people have the role of team member. Others have the role of participant.

That has nothing to do with the value of the people involved, it is an acknowledgement of who's mastered what. Rather than see it as a pyramid, I see it as expanding, concentric circles, and the more you learn and master, the closer you get to the centre of the circle. Just as taking responsibility and making your own choices means you're altering your own life, authority shows up as a real quality with responsibility. And some people don't want the authority or the responsibility. Becoming the authority in your life is taking more and more responsibility for your life. That means becoming accountable.

Participant: ...In response to what people were saying about authority... last night I went out and screamed, and I got to screaming at this God figure that's still there for me, and which was very strong when I was a kid. I let out one really good curse and lightning went 'zap' and I went, "Uh oh."

Gregory: Was God zapping you or were you zapping him? He's probably in a critical condition now!

Participant: ...I realized how scared I was of this God figure striking me down because I expressed anger. So just to let him know that I was still going to scream at him I yelled, "SCREW YOU GOD!"

Gregory: Ha, ha. Basil Faulty arises. The God you're talking about isn't God, it's the role you learnt about. Ultimately it is a superstition. There are thousands of Gods and Goddesses to choose from!

Participant: ...Yes I know. It's an image that I created when I was in Kindergarten to watch over me and I thanked him for it.

Gregory: You created him to do exactly what you needed him to do.

We create God in our own image. It would fascinate me as a Catholic child when they'd say that God is all powerful and unknowable. God is so unlimited that he's indefinable. Then they proceed to define him. Not only define him, but say what he liked, what he didn't like, how he liked it, what he wanted and didn't. Even as a young child I saw the bullshit in that one.

***

Participant: ...In the movie last night I had to leave. I was sitting outside thinking, "Am I running away from that in me?" When I see things like that, it changes my whole perception. I have these rose-colored glasses that I really like then I'm quite happy with it all.

Gregory: You're a Pisces.

Participant: …Well everybody else seems to be able to handle it and not be affected by it.

Gregory: That's part of the rose-colored glasses you see through. You look through rose-colored glasses at the world and think, "Everyone else is handling it." Let me jolt your reality further. Who found aspects of that movie hard to handle? Look around you and join the human race. You decide that they're all handling it and you're not, therefore you're different and you have no right to be here.

'Rose-colored glasses' is a Pisces expression, just as Librans say, "On the other hand…" You make up this nice pretty picture of the world and then when some evidence appears that shows that it's not like that you feel disillusioned. Guess what? You are disillusioned. That means removing your old illusions: dis-illusioned. Looking through rose-colored glasses means looking at a bunch of illusions, not at what is real.

Pisces want everything to be so nice that they take mud cakes and put frosting and a candle on them.

Then they get afraid that if they look past the frosting they'll find a mud cake. They don't see that mud cakes are really just mud cakes, and deal with them as such.

Which part of the film did you go blank to?

Participant: …The part that lost control and went ape and tore things to pieces and the man was getting hurt.

Gregory: So the common denominator is destruction, in both movies. You find it difficult to look at your own destructiveness, the part of you that wants to rip and tear and go ape shit. Pisces are nice people. They don't want to bite, chomp and scratch and tear and eat dead burnt bodies and stuff like that. The rose-colored glasses are saying, "I'm not going to look at this shit. Not me. I'm nice." It presents the stuff you don't want to look at in yourself, because you have a judgement that if you're like that then you are bad. Everyone has that capacity. That's why we're showing these movies, to connect with it.

Participant: …I went and I did a drawing and went back into my own little world.

Gregory: Of course you did, pretty sweet things; tied ribbon bows and tinkle bells and tickle the gold fish in the pond. Eat packets of Amplex so your farts will smell sweet. You probably do.

Participant: ...I'm shutting doors, it's the same with aggressive people. I've shut the doors. So I become one.

Gregory: Of course you do. The starting point is to acknowledge that you are capable of destruction. You are capable of bloodletting. You are capable of rip and tear stuff, and of being an animal.

While you deny it, you don't have a choice about it. You either attract it in videos and you attract it in people, or you create it in yourself. Once you see that it's there, then you have a choice about it.

That's the beginning acknowledgement. As anger comes up, express it. Don't bury it.

You bury it because if you let it out then it will prove that your rose-colored glasses are just that. The truth is that the only way to attain your ideal world of everyone being happy and at peace is to release your own anger and destructiveness. Then you don't have to create it. Then you are really at peace.

Participant: ...Releasing it physically and acknowledging it and releasing it.

Gregory: Either scream or beat up pillows or have some feeling release sessions. It's classical that Germans are very repressed and controlled people, and they start a world war. Japanese are very repressed, controlled people. America seems to be always at war with someone or something. They are probably the three most militaristic countries in the world, and three of the most repressed advanced countries in the world in terms of expressing emotion.

Participant: ...Every time I see supernatural films, they scare the shit out of me. I actually had to leave the room yesterday.

Gregory: So what's the fear?

Participant: ...Usually when I'm in my room by myself I put all the lights on. I'm scared that I will see spirits or ghosts.

Gregory: Yeah. What's the fear though? That's what you're scared of rather than what is the fear.

Participant: ...That they will talk to me.

Gregory: Right. What might happen if they talk to you?

Participant: ...I'll freak out.

Gregory: You're afraid that your reality will be shaken, but what's real? Which reality do you choose to live in? Supernatural stuff is only that stuff in nature that we don't understand yet.

Participant: ...Yeah.

Gregory: So on a daily basis, we all do things that even 50 or 60 years ago would be called supernatural. We use computers. We send rockets to the moon and back. Fly airplanes. Holograms. Beat your eggs with an electric mixer. Watch television. Clean your teeth with an electric toothbrush. See, if you'd have walked into that Quest For Fire movie with a box of matches, they'd have made you a God. You get it? Or they'd have eaten you to get your spirit.

Participant: ...So how do I not be scared to stay by myself at night?

Gregory: Firstly you need to get specific about what the fear is. If someone says, "I'm scared of Ferris Wheels," it might be the height, or how fast it will go, or that it will stop with them at the top, they'll fall out, the carriage will drop.

Participant: ...I'm scared of something showing up in my apartment. Something that doesn't have legs, that floats, that's got lights. That's what I'm scared of.

(everyone laughs)

Gregory: That's what you're scared of, but what is the fear? What will it do that is so scary? Or what is it capable of that's so scary? Or what might happen to you that's so scary?

Participant: ...It could take me over.

Gregory: Aha. So, you're afraid of possession?

Participant: ...Yeah.

Gregory: Very good. There's a big difference between, "I'm scared of the dark," and, "I'm scared of being possessed." So what might happen if this thing possesses you? What will happen to you?

Participant: ...I will lose myself.

Gregory: Yes. How?

Participant: ...That I will no longer be me, I'll be somebody else.

Gregory: Okay. I say that's already happened. And that you're already in the place you fear. Everything you fear in the future has already happened otherwise you wouldn't know to fear it. If I say there's a gollywomp arriving here this afternoon, you'll say, "What's a gollywomp?" You can't fear that because you have no experience of it. But if I then say, "Well it's 18 feet high and it eats people alive," you're going to start yelling, "I'm out of here!" Though you may not have had the experience of being eaten alive, you at least have an idea of what that may be like.

What you're fearing might happen, I say has already happened. In the past, you had the experience that something possessed you. You became someone other than who you are, and the real you got lost.

Participant: ...Yes.

Gregory: I say that you have lost contact with who you really really are, and are acting out a role that you've chosen, and you have believed that the role was the real you.

Everyone of us is possessed until we're not. Until you own yourself and all of your choices 100%, who or what does? Someone or something else, and the someone else could be a partner.

It could be your anger that possesses and controls you, or it could be your rose-colored glasses, or your fear of your anger that possesses you. Most people are at least possessed by their fear. Their fear decides what they do and don't do, when, how and why they do, with whom they do or don't do. Fear, anger and sadness possess most people, or the fear of them. Possessions even possess some people.

Things that happen that you don't take responsibility for possess you. If I can find out what your need is, I can possess you. The need for approval possesses you, so all I've got to do is tell you you're no good every time you do something I don't like, and then gradually let you know what I do like, and because you need to be approved of, you'll do it.

If people need the 'answer', you tell them you've got the answer. Put on saffron robes and ring some bells and wear a turban and chant, "Om." And they'll say, "Give it to me. Give it to me."

Another way of saying "being possessed" is giving your power away. Money possesses some people. The need for sex possesses some people. The need for love or approval or comfort or security or whatever. Youthfulness possesses some people. Possessing even more possessions possesses most people.

(applause)

Whatever you give your power away to "out there" you don't own. You don't possess it. It possesses you. My judge used to possess me, he ran my life. Not me. Once I "owned" him, owned my choice to create him to serve me, then I possessed him again and freed me more.

In exactly the same way, some people are possessed by psychic entities. Quite a few are.

But it's not a big drama. People have an illusion that spirits are all sorts of intelligent beings. That's not true. There are spirits on all levels. See, there are spirit levels.

(everyone laughs or groans)

We are entities incarnate, in body. Literally in-carne, in meat. There are entities discarnate on every level of evolution, and variation. There are angry entities out there - they're just pure little anger balls flying around. Have you ever had an anger ball thrown at you by someone? No words, just the anger?

You can bet they've got a little angry poison entity sitting in them. The point is, nothing happens without your agreement. You also attracted it and allowed it, even if unconsciously.

So no-one becomes possessed against their will. Whether they're doing it consciously or not is another ball game. If someone feels terrified by life, they may even welcome a dangerous entity. The agreement is, "You can live here," and the entity gets to stay connected to a human form in life so it has a taste of being an alive human to feed off. The trade off is, "You protect me because I feel so terrified and weak."

The entity says, "Sounds like a good deal for me." It is literally like a parasite or a leach. "Parasite" is a much better word than "entity" in that sense because it's a specific entity that sucks life energy in return for some service, but it is an agreement.

Participant: ...My fear is that I will create all of that.

Gregory: You probably already have. Whether you bring in an outside entity or whether you create one in yourself is irrelevant. Especially you nice people. Tell the truth, who's ever sat there being nice, but aware that there's a voice in you that says, "I'll put up with this shit, but if they push too much, I'll kill them."

That's called your killer entity. It's something that stays hidden, but you can call on it if need be. You don't own it, you separate it from yourself. When you own the killer in you, you'll just acknowledge your anger and do something else, like tell the person to shut up or piss off.

Participant: ...But that's so mean.

Gregory: Exactly. So you create a mean entity that's got nothing to do with you. And it can sit up there in the background ready to slash and tear, but if it does, guess what you will say? "Ohh I don't know what came over me. That's not like me, I am such a nice person."

Participant: ...I used to do that all the time.

Gregory: Exactly. It's irrelevant whether it is an external entity with a life of it's own that you've done a trade-off with, or whether you create your own internal entity with a life of it's own, like an inner killer created from your blocked anger and your need to be nice. Voilà!

Participant: ...What I have to find out is what is missing that I'll be afraid of.

Gregory: Exactly. And what is present that you've been scared to admit to to yourself.

One of mine was anger. I had such a "nice" act going. I was totally disconnected from my anger. Twice in my school days I got hassled and hassled. In one case it took me six months of putting up with shit from a guy at boarding school, then I just snapped. I put the guy in hospital.

He was built like a footballer, and here was I, this little fat kid wearing glasses. I just went into cold rage and I literally pulled my glasses off and threw them against the wall and went through this guy like a dose of salts. I broke bones, I injured organs, and it terrified me because it felt like I wasn't in control. Then I had to stuff my anger down even harder, and be even nicer, to stay with my illusion that, "I'm not that kind of person."

Participant: …I want to learn how to use my anger in a positive way.

Gregory: Take responsibility for it, own it, scream it out, express it, then it stops being anger and simply becomes energy which you can use any way you want. To use a biblical phrase, it's internally turning your swords into plow shares. You can put your energy into creating and maintaining destructive self-protection or you could put it into growth and development.

I see that you're really, really terrified of your compassion, so you cut it off in order to survive. The fear is of opening up. I think your fear is very much like mine. Before I went to India every time I went overseas, I'd think, "Will I go to India this time?'"And I got a big, "No."

One of my fears about going to India was that I'd arrive and just fall in a crumpled heap on the roadside, sobbing and sobbing for ten years, totally overwhelmed by the pain of humanity. That's so strong for me that I feel sadness just thinking about it. If I ever want to cry, all I have to do is imagine myself in Calcutta.

It can be something as beautiful as your passion, or compassion, that is the entity, or part of you, that you fear possessing you. It feels like if it takes you over, then you'll be washed away.

Acknowledge it and start opening to it. Let yourself connect with the sadness of the human condition. We shut that off when we thought we couldn't do anything about it, the situation seemed hopeless and we gave up hope and went into despair. Our compassion was wrapped in despair. For me, regaining my compassion is a process of simply seeing me, and people, regain hope and act on it.

Seeing people not giving up in seminars. Seeing people instead saying, "I'm not going to take anymore, I'm going to do something with my life," and seeing them heal their hurt, and over a period of time, seeing that the world can heal itself. I get to learn how to have compassion for myself and the tragedy of living life the old way.

Life is a very sad place to be, until it's not. The tragedy of millions of starving people in Africa, or hundreds of millions of dirt-poor hungry Indians is incredible. That's the tip of the iceberg. The tragedy of a mother who hits her children is also overwhelming for me, because that pain and fear and destructiveness is not necessary. Hell, it's not even getting the result she wants. The tragedy of someone going to hospital and having organs cut out is overwhelming, because it is so often not necessary.

For me, tragedy is where pain occurs unnecessarily and can be ended.

As I gain more evidence for that, I am able to bring forth my compassion and change my belief that it's not hopeless. I go to places at times and I feel that it's hopeless, so I cry my heart out. Then I sit there and think, "Well what are you going to do? Are you going sit here for the rest of your life, or get off your butt and go again?" No choice for me anymore.

***

Participant: ...I'm feeling very confused about giving at the moment. I want to use you as an example.

Gregory: You going to make an example of me?

Participant: ...Yes. I feel very given to by you, I also want to give to you but was too scared to ask you for a date, even though that's ultimately what I wanted. So I said I'd like to massage you and that's still true. It's the same with everybody. I have what I want to give but I get really confused as to how to get some response from them.

I get confused about what I want, what they want, and what I want to give. Maybe it's because I don't tell them enough. I only tell them that I want to give. I just feel confused about power.

Gregory: So the answer is to sit down with me, and say, "What I want is to have a date, and I'm not ready for it, I'm too scared to go for that now." The steps are: A - acknowledge what you want, and B - acknowledge where you are.

Acknowledge what you want and where you are and what you're really willing to give.

And acknowledge the difference.

Participant: ...Sometimes I want to just give, I want to do, and I don't know what to do, so it becomes, "How can I reach you?"

Gregory: I'm hearing that you feel something wrong with that. To wholeheartedly say to someone, "I want to do something for you, what would you like?" is to me, the highest level of giving. What most people give is what they would like to be given. It's like the old classic; the father buys the kid a toy train because he never had one as a kid instead of finding out what the kid really wants.

Everything works sometimes. To say, "I would like to give you A, B, C, D, E, F, G, do you want any of them?" And they say, "Yes, I'd like A, B and G," is one way. Another is to say, "What do you want? Because I want to give you what you want." That's a much higher risk because if you say that to me and I say, "I want you to scratch my back for the next three years," I expect it, or you're full of shit.

Participant: ...I'd do it. Ha, ha.

Gregory: To say, "I want to give you what you want," is a really high commitment and most people simply aren't capable of that.

So, don't say it unless you're really clear that you are going to do it. Why mess around? You talk a lot about giving, but not getting. It's very important for you to acknowledge what you want out of the situation. And one of the things you want is the opportunity to give safely.

Participant: ...Yeah.

Gregory: Right? That's one of the things you truly want selfishly, is to give.

Participant: ...Yes.

Gregory: But there are also things you want back for that. It might be a simple "thank you" but there are things you want back. Learn to communicate what you want from the situation or you'll feel ripped off.

You can't ever give more than your truth, and your truth includes what you want out of the situation, and your truth may change.

I've talked through the seminar about getting away from judging things in terms of good or bad or right or wrong and getting back to the value of the experience. Ultimately I don't care what you tell me, so long as it's your truth. It doesn't matter whether I like it or not, or whether it presses my buttons or not. It really doesn't matter what my reaction to it is. If I know you're telling me the truth, I know that I'm loved. And if you're lying to me, for any reason, you're insulting me.

Participant: ...So what you've done by creating seminars is to provide a venue for people to check out their truth.

Gregory: Sure, seminars are about creating a space for everyone to focus on what their truth is and if it works for them. Or if they want to change it. There's a wonderful thing I often quote in my business seminars from Winnie the Pooh. Winnie the Pooh is going bump bump bump down the stairs and he thinks to himself, "I wonder if there's another way to get down the stairs, but I've never got time to stop bumping to find out." Seminars are for setting time aside for people to check out whether they want to keep getting down the stairs by bumping down them on their bums, or whether they want to find a new way to do it. They might even decide they don't even want to keep going down the stairs!

***

Gregory: Does anyone want to share about the process last night? Anything that came up for you?

Participant: ...It was fascinating touching another man's dick.

Gregory: You've not done that before?

Participant: ...No. Just letting myself feel it with my body.

Gregory: Very good. Anyone else?

Participant: …I've had a very traditional background against touching; touching men in particular. I found that I overcame that, and there was no sexual connotation on it at all, just touching. I felt quite comfortable.

Gregory: That's fantastic. Yes?

Participant: …I felt connected to everybody in the room.

Gregory: Great. Yes?

Participant: …I still have numbness in my body.

Gregory: You store anger, sadness, and fear in your body. Then you block it. One of the ways to block it is to send it numb, put it to sleep. As you allow that to wake up and be released, you won't have to keep your body asleep.

Participant: …I chose not to let it become sexual.

Gregory: Why did you make that choice? That's your resistance. That's like saying, "I'll eat the food but I'm not going to taste it."

When you eat food, the primal level of it is for nutrition, but it can also taste good and look good. Now, if the opportunity is there, why wouldn't you have good nutrition, good taste and good look?

What I'm saying is, given the opportunity, why would you choose to not have it sexual? That's like saying, "I'm going to eat this food, but I'm not going to look at it." Or, "I'm going to look at this food but I'm going to spray my mouth with zylocaine and numb it so I won't taste anything, but I'll get the nutrition."

So tell me, did all the men get to touch a dick?

Participant: …I didn't.

Gregory: You chose not to. If you are not comfortable with men's bodies, remember that you live in one. The same goes for women. If you women are not comfortable with women's bodies, you live in one. One way to see what is uncomfortable inside you is to do it outside. Whatever you resist in here, will come up out there, so to speak. As you get more comfortable with yourself, it will become easier and vice versa. If you don't know how to deal with it in here, create it out there and deal with it out there.

Participant: ...It's interesting you say that, because I've experienced some women not to like dicks or not to like men's bodies. I also feel that I'm not completely at home with men's bodies even though I haven't experienced them fully. The opportunity is there to see what women are on about, for starters.

Gregory: Of course, but I go further. That's why celery drives me nuts. I approach experience not just to try it but to master it. If someone likes something then there's something of value in it and I'm a value hunter so I want to get the value from everything. I don't like celery. And I have been eating celery on and off now all my life because I want to know what it is people like about celery.

Anyway the starting point is, "What the hell, I'll give it a try." And the next possibility is, "I'm going to do this until I feel 100% comfortable with it and get the value. Then I have a choice."

So which women got to play with a pussy? Put your hands up. So who didn't? Okay. Put your hand up if you've never played with a pussy. Women?

It's the same thing for women as it is with men. To explore other women's bodies has extraordinary possibilities for you. If you stop rejecting yourself and reach out, you might still be rejected. If you do, then you're back where you were anyway. So you've lost nothing.

Participant: ...Logically that makes sense. But it doesn't feel like it makes sense.

Gregory: Of course it doesn't. Feelings don't make sense. That's why you've got a mind. Yeah?

Participant: ...I got into a real head trip last night.

Gregory: So what was your body scared of?

Participant: ...The closeness. I think the idea of enjoyment conflicts with the social beliefs that I've been brought up with, that it's wrong to masturbate, and therefore to touch someone else.

Gregory: Anyone else?

Participant: ...My fear is that maybe I won't make the break. Maybe I won't be able to do it. Maybe I won't be able to handle it. And then I will really know. Then everybody else will really know. I want to make some acknowledgements to the group.

I acknowledge that I've pretended a lot in my life. The truth was I didn't know where I was. I want to belong and I'm really afraid. I know I have a lot of potential and a lot to give, and I'm afraid that if I really put that on the line, I won't make the grade, and that I'll feel really broken hearted about it. I also want to belong to the group.

Gregory: Is that it?

Participant: ...I don't know. I don't know what I'm doing here. I'm trying to do something but I don't know how to do it. I don't know what it is that I want to do.

Gregory: So what are you going to do about the fact that you don't know?

Participant: ...I feel like I want to go nuts.

Gregory: Okay, so that's what you feel like. Is that what you are going to do?

Participant: ...No.

Gregory: So where are you at? What do you want?

Participant: ...I'm too scared to know what I want.

Gregory: One thing I know is that if you don't know what you want, you definitely won't get it. Which means you stay sitting there spinning. What I suggest you do is simply acknowledge that you enjoy being where you are right now.

Your way of avoiding change is to ask questions and seek support and seek advice and counseling. So have it. Stay miserable. Stay in pain. Stay spinning on the spot. But at least, at least have the courage to own your choice in that and stop wanking. Because it's ugly and you're ugly when you do that.

So is there anything you want to say or act or do or anything?

Participant: ...I'm building a life for myself with me in it.

Participant: ...Can't hear.

Participant: ...I SAID I'M BUILDING A LIFE FOR MYSELF, WITH ME IN IT. And that's scary, and I can do it. I'm willing to risk everything I've got to make sure that that happens.

Gregory: Okay. Then do something different. Step out of your usual you and do something different. You know, it's like your version of him? Pay attention, because he does his version of this. What he acknowledged this morning is his version of what you do. He has disappeared on himself. He has buried himself so deep and so far away and then made up a version of himself that he bought 100%. He doesn't know who he is. And you don't know who you are. What I'm talking about is: are you willing to find out if there is someone in there? Under the performance. Under the rightness and the hurt and the whole bullshit game?

Participant: ...Yes I am.

Gregory: Good, then find it. Do something, say something with someone in here that reaches beyond your total current experience of yourself.

Participant: ...I feel paralyzed.

Gregory: Yeah. Paralyzed is the word. So stay paralyzed for the rest of your life. Stay a powerfully pathetic performance for the rest of your life. It's okay with me. Just notice how you're starting to enjoy the drama of this.

Participant: ...Please someone tell me what to do. I've never known what to do. I feel like a cripple.

Gregory: It's a safe place to be. Cripples get looked after. You don't know what to do because you don't know where you want to go. You're like someone who hasn't decided where they're traveling sitting in the car, paralyzed because they haven't got a destination, so they don't know which way to turn.

Participant: ...I just want to know.

Participant: ...What's that look like?

Participant: ...Standing on my own two feet.

Gregory: Anyone else?

Participant: ...I procrastinate. The world's greatest procrastinator. I'm going to change that. A part of me knows what I've got to do to change it but I've built it into a toll gate and locked up the keys and put iron bars on it and then go off and say, "Well tell me what I've got to do?" And they'd tell me what it is and I'd wonder if I should and I lock the door again. And I forget about it and I go off on another performance.

Gregory: So what's the payoff of that?

Participant: ...The payoff is to give away my responsibility.

Gregory: Simpler than that. That can be a perfect answer that says nothing. Anyone know?

Participant: ...Safety.

Gregory: Safety. Getting closer.

Participant: ...Attention.

Gregory: Getting closer. What does it guarantee?

Participant: ...Never getting there.

Gregory: That's one thing. The payoff. What's the payoff?

Participant: ...Never being rejected.

Gregory: Yes. Like the song lyric, "If you leave me, can I come too?"

Okay. So it's, "You tell me how to be, then I'll know you'll never reject me." So what's there to do? It's so radical, I'll bet none of you get it. It's obvious. I warn you. Be really specific.

Participant: ...Acknowledge.

Participant: ...Be willing to be rejected.

Gregory: Getting closer.

Participant: ...Be rejected.

Gregory: More obvious.

Participant: ...Know exactly where you are and own it.

Participant: …Play it all consciously.

Gregory: More obvious.

Participant: …Be a jerk.

Participant: …Make a fool of yourself.

Gregory: Simpler.

Participant: …Do nothing.

Gregory: No.

Participant: …Be with yourself.

Gregory: Yeah. They're all just circling. You're like little birds hovering.

Participant: …Stop asking.

Gregory: No.

Participant: …Experiment. Just acknowledge it.

Gregory: Definitely not that one.

Participant: …Hide his truth.

Gregory: No, but it's very close. They said. "Stop asking." I said …

Participant: …Ask yourself.

Gregory: Thank you. Ask yourself what you want. If you keep asking other people what they want you to be so you'll be acceptable and it doesn't work in the process you have the experience of being empty and losing yourself. It follows that if you ask yourself what you want to be, and follow that, then you can never be rejected by yourself, and instead of being empty you'll be full. I told you it was obvious!

Eventually we see that it doesn't work to ask them so we stop asking. But we don't take the next step which is to ask ourselves. It's another measure of how much we leave ourselves out of our own life.

To own and value where you are includes creating structures in order to be spontaneous. That's called structured spontaneity instead of spontaneous spontaneity. But that's a hell of an improvement on no spontaneity. It's one step forward at least. Once you've done that and got bored with it, you think, "Wow, what's the next step?" To be spontaneous without structures.

The value of rebellion is you get to learn who you're not. And to maintain a semblance of independence and the illusion of independence. That's the value of it. The price of it is huge. Firstly, everyone else owns you. If you're in rebellion, you're totally controllable. I can just tell you to do the opposite of what I want you to do. Of course I don't, because I want people around me, not puppets.

If your habit is to identify yourself through rebellion, then when you find out what it is that works that you need to get where you want, you're automatically in rebellion about that. It's like when she says, "What do I need to do?" And I tell her, so she doesn't do it. You get it?

Participants: ...(everyone) Yeah.

Gregory: Right. And one of the things she needs to do is own her rebellion and own that she chooses to be there. But she won't so she stays stuck. One level of this is called, "I'm going to reinvent the wheel. I can do it. I'm not going to let anyone teach me how to create the wheel. I'm definitely not going to go and buy one already made because then it might look like I need someone or depend on someone, or that someone else has got something I haven't got. So what I'll do is I'll reinvent the wheel."

Over thousands of years of history we've actually learnt some things of value. You don't have to work it all out from scratch. But she does. Yeah? Because she's got to prove that she can do it. Yep, she can. A couple of hundred lifetimes and she'll get there.

Except by then the world is going to be a couple of hundred life times ahead. Then she wonders why she feels left out. It's because she is. Because she makes sure she's left out. Because she's afraid that if she's in then she'll forget who she is. But she's already forgotten that. She just doesn't want to remember that she's forgotten. Do you want me to keep going or have you got the gist of it?

Participant: ...You're talking about me as well. I do that a lot.

Gregory: I'm talking about everyone. Do you see what we do? That's called "CRAZY." That's what one version of real madness looks like. Please give yourselves the opportunity to see that in yourself.

Participant: ...I feel really alive for the first time in a long time. And what's happened, you've ended my work bind.

Gregory: Which was?

Participant: ...Your directness, I got a BOOM. As if I was standing there and at the end of it was a big "Yes" and I felt really alive and not paralyzed, and the realization that I'm fine. "I'm just doing this." It was a release for me.

Gregory: It's the power and magic of acknowledgement. It's very powerful to be acknowledged and you've used that to break through. But what she does because of all that stuff she's got running is take the power of my acknowledgement and vampirize my energy with it. And not act on it.

Participant: ...And I do a part of that too. That's my act.

Gregory: Sure, that's what committed victims do. They look for rescuers to vampirize off. Like, "Fix it for me. Help me." You know. And the last thing they want, the last thing, is for someone to actually make it different.

Participant: ...Ultimately no-one can give it to you or do it for you.

Gregory: Of course. That's also true. Another paradox.

Participant: ...I know I vampirize you and your giving, I suck from it, and by simply saying, "I'm here, this is my goal," and trying to be that goal I'm allowing myself to crawl, and make mistakes, and be laughed at, and be rejected, and just be who I am where I am and do what I want to do here. Now because I know in what we were talking before about experience I'll be where I want to be. I can't get there without learning those steps.

Gregory: Yes. It's a mark of your power and growth that you get to rebel on that level.

The phrase I use is "Trust the universe" or "Surrender to the universe." I trust and surrender to whatever gets presented to me in life. And I want to add it has taken years to master that ability. Now if something shows up in my life, I am very adept to automatically say, "Wow, I've created that for myself." Or, "The universe has sent me this," and it might be a lesson, it might be a reward and it might be a challenge, but I trust that it's okay and I'm okay with it. It's now a rare occasion that I react to my creation.

And it's one of the most painful things I know to do to myself. So I don't do it.

The only meaning that life has is the meaning you give it. Someone can receive a gift and invest huge meaning into it, it means a lot to them. Whereas to you it's just a bit of pottery. It means nothing to you.

Life's like that. You invest meaning into it. For instance, right now in the Middle East, the meaning of life for a lot of people is to kill the other tribe. That's where meaning lives. The Muslims, the Druze, the Christians, the Jews - they all kill each other. And I think, "How can you have meaning in that?" But it means something to them.

As your truth expands your meaning expands as well. And I don't know if there is some ultimate meaning to it. I strongly suspect that the meaning of it all is that it's just a great game. I really think that 'God' is a humorist, a bit of a character. It's all a game, and the game is that it's up to you what game you play.

Participant: ...This morning I said to you I feel boring and bland today, then during the lunch break I announced to everyone at the table that I was being boring and bland today and it was just hilarious. After about ten minutes of being consciously boring and bland and turning it into a game, it just got boring being boring. I ended up pretending to be a man and I had a banana in my pants!

Participant: ...Did you enjoy yourself?

Participant: ...Yeah. I think I'll get bored more often!

Participant: ...You said the universe has presented you with either a lesson or a gift or a reward or challenge or an opportunity. I get really confused when I have a whole lot of different opportunities and I think, "Which one's the right one to choose?"

Gregory: There isn't a right one. It's like going into a smorgasbord and saying, "What should I eat? What's the right choice?" It's exactly the same.

Participant: ...In that situation I think, "Okay. Just trust the universe." And I can't. I have to trust myself.

Gregory: Same thing. For me, saying, "Trust the universe," is the same as saying, "Trust myself. Or saying trust my Higher Self, whatever that means for you."

I can live my life like I am here, an isolated little widget of flesh and blood. Or I can invest the meaning that I actually have a place in this universe. In that place, then either the universe, God, creation, other people, whatever you call "the rest" are dangerous threatening things, or they're on my side.

I believe that they're on my side and the whole universe has nothing to do except agree with me, so if the universe sends something, it's like getting a gift from a friend. So when I say, "Trust the universe," it's like, "Yeah, not only here inside me is safe and valuable and okay but everything and everyone out there is too." And sometimes it doesn't feel like it.

Or it doesn't always feel like it, but there are no wrong choices.

Participant: ...I can sit around and procrastinate and say, "I don't know. I don't know. I don't want to make a decision," not willing to take responsibility for my life out of fear of making the wrong decision.

Gregory: Then not getting where or what you want to get, which you hide from yourself anyway.

Participant: ...I don't know where I want to go. Someone asked me what to do. I don't know. I mean, don't ask me of all people.

Gregory: You hide it from yourself because you're afraid you won't get there.

Participant: ...Or that it will be too big to complete this life time.

Gregory: So you sit there and do nothing.

Participant: ...I screw around. I don't know what I'm doing. It's bloody boring. It's so stupid. Two days ago I felt like a cripple, I was crying, "Oh my God it's so terrible," then this morning I just cracked up laughing. It's so stupid. The whole trip.

My whole life is just so ridiculous. It really is. All the dramas and the pain are like one big joke, and I still don't know where I'm going.

Gregory: Somewhere.

Participant: ...I know. I'm going somewhere, and I do get little flashes of it. I do have a vision. A sort of vague vision about what I want to be and how I want to be in my life and what I want to do, but it's never clear. I don't set any ground rules of how to get there or make any decisions.

Gregory: So that's how you're getting there.

Participant: ...Just by pissing around?

Gregory: It's as good as way as any. It's just not very enjoyable while you resist it.

Participant: ...I think there might be a quicker way.

Gregory: There is.

Participant: ...What? Tell me.

Gregory: The minute you complete something, it disappears and you move on. It follows that, if you want to fast track your life, complete a lot of things. You can sit for 20 years facing the next risk and not taking it, or you can take two minutes.

Some people get a year's experience in thirty years. So progress is slow. Some people get one hundred years experience in thirty years.

If people find out what I've done in my life and also if they do seminars with me, a common question or acknowledgement I get is, "How have you done so much in the number of years you've been here?" And I say, "By doing a lot." Ha, ha.

Participant: ...I waste so much time.

Gregory: I have done so much and I also often feel like I waste a lot of time, that I don't really do much. Then I look at what I've done and think, "Wow, who was that?" Often we are really resting, pausing, replenishing ourselves for the next chapter of our life.

Participant: ...I feel like I have done a lot in my life as well. And I still sit around wasting a lot of time.

Gregory: Doing around 20 personal growth seminars and two Sex and Relationships Seminars and a trip around the world for a year by yourself by the time you are 20 isn't too bad!

Participant: ...I know, but you can't compare yourself to other people like that.

Gregory: Oh yes you can.

Participant: ...It's normal for me, that stuff.

Gregory: Of course. That's where you don't value it. It's no effort for you to do that so you do it and don't value it, or your ability to be able to do it.

Participant: ...Everyone says the shortest sentence is, "I am." The shortest sentence is actually, "Do." When I was overseas instead of going on about, "Who am I? Who am I?" I realized it doesn't matter: just do something. I might never find out who I am, and it doesn't matter, so I just started doing anything. And that's my answer to all my questions.

Gregory: The point is, if you're god in your life, the creator of your life, and if god is truly unlimited and undefinable, then you can't define it/you. JC said, "Through their actions ye shall know them."

I add, "Through your actions you will also get to know yourself." Asians have a saying I love, "Don't listen to what they say, watch what they do."

Participant: ...Yeah.

Gregory: Who I am isn't a thing, it's a process. Just as an action, a doing, is not a thing but a movement. It's like, "What is life?" It's indefinable. "What is love?" It's indefinable because it's not a thing. You can only define things. You can't define processes.

Kids who grow up in the centre of Australia and who are 16, 18, 20 years old have never ever seen rain. They've heard about it, but they've never seen it. You can't define rain. You can describe it, but not in a way that you get the experience of it. Then it rains and they know rain. The question of who you are has an analogy with the ancients who said you can't look directly at the Sun. Who you are is like the Sun. You can only look at it indirectly.

You may see the sun rays, or you may look at sunlight reflected off the moon or through shadow. But you can't look at it directly. In the same way, you get to know who you are through your actions and choices. It gets back to people keeping their word and doing what they say. The quality of who we are can be power and integrity and freedom and ease and love, but they are not things. They are results. They are experiences. They are also choices.

I know I have integrity because I see my integrity show up in the world. I hear me say something then do it. I experience my own integration, the integration of my words and my actions. So I can say, "I have integrity",' which is an expression of who I am.

There's a place where "Who am I?" gets to be a navel-gazing wank. The powerful question to ask isn't "Who am I?" it's "What do I want to do, to create?" That is what's powerful. You have numerous opportunities and choices in front of you so have a look at each and ask, "Which one turns me on most? Which one expresses me best?" then go and do it and you'll find out more of Who you are.

Participant: ...I am 20 and I have three passports, so I can live in three different countries and it really confuses me. People say, "Oh wow, three passports!" But it makes it harder for me because I've got too many choices. As an indecisive Libra I am now learning to just say, "Alright, this one," and do it. It's really good.

Gregory: The other way to look at it is that you've got three passports, but you only have to choose which country you live in for now. You can live in all of them. When there's a smorgasbord, it's not, "Which one will I eat because I can only have one choice?" We have unlimited choices. It may be that you want to have a bit of everything. You can have it all. It's called making a feast of life. Life IS a Feast!

***

Participant: ...I've been feeling quite a lot of pain and tension in my neck.

Gregory: All tension is holding on and resisting. Often when it's around the neck and head it's about fear of blowing your top or losing your head or going out of your mind. Always when you look to understand body symptoms, or dis-ease, the answer is always very direct and simple. So head stuff can also be about fear of getting ahead. If it gets down into your back then it's often about you or someone else getting on your back. So check out what is going on that you're resisting or holding on about. There's no accidents. Tension comes, you don't have it all the time do you?

Participant: ...No.

Gregory: That's correct. Stop. Stop and hear that. You don't have it all the time which means you have it sometimes. Now it may be a lot of sometimes, but each time you have it, it's a reaction or a response to something that is going on in you. It is a loving message from your body to get your attention ...notice ...at tension!. You happen to do it a lot. So check out right now, what is going on or what has been happening that you are tense about.

Participant: ...I was feeling some anger and I swallowed it. I didn't let it out.

Gregory: So scream and yell and stomp your feet. Anger comes up and you don't have a picture of you as an angry person so you push it down for fear that if you let it out you'll blow your stack or you'll lose your head. So then your neck and shoulders grab on even stronger and block your expression of anger even more.(Gregory speaks in a squashed voice) ... Now make sure you don't lose your head. You keep it all stuffed in so you get to walk around like that. But you don't feel angry do you? Ha! Like hell you don't! Do you recognize that it is suppressed?

Yes. And all it takes is to just acknowledge, (in squashed voice) "I'm holding onto it and this is painful and I sound ridiculous."

So then acknowledge what you're doing and get clear about whether you're willing to let it go or not. Reassure your body that no-one has ever been known to actually physically blow their head off by yelling. Then as you yell, several things may happen. It may just come out clear and it maybe that you're hands move around, (squashed voice) and you're sounding like this.

It could block at your throat. It could block at your jaw. Some people get angry and sit there and clench silently because it's got past their throat to their jaw. It's like putting an imaginary hand over their mouth. Just let the sound out and as you release it, the tension relaxes. If you don't do it, then get that you want to keep the tension.

Participant: ...Until now on this seminar I've had reservations about what's coming up next all the time. I'd like to be able to understand why I don't feel like that anymore. I just feel totally relaxed.

Gregory: It's called experience or practice. The more you do it, the more you get to see that whatever comes up you can handle, so it stops being scary. You're getting to a point where you're thinking it and your body knows it too, that, "Hey, I've been through all this stuff and it's fine, so whatever comes up, I'm going to get through it and it's fine." It becomes safer to let things come up.

***

Gregory: You get angry because they keep reminding you about the acts and masks you still hold onto.

Participant: ...I hate my act, and I hate thinking I have to find an act so that they will like me. When I do love people, or when we acknowledge that we are acting together, I love it when we know the game together, and that the game is not reality.

Gregory: When you're clear that you don't want to do that anymore, do something different. If you keep surrounding yourself with people with a lot of acts, then you're choosing to be in that environment with your acts. The risk is to put yourself in an environment where people don't do that because then there will be no room for you to do it. You're doing that now. By being here, you're surrounding yourself with people who are dropping acts faster than trees drop leaves. Think about it.

Participant: ...I can't tell anymore though.

Participant: ...What's an act?

Gregory: Aha. Your dumb act is getting stronger by the hour!

Participant: ...I get confused because when I think I'm being myself, then I think, "Well maybe that's an act."

Gregory: Maybe it is. The difference between running an act and being yourself is whether you choose it or not. It's like being bored. Being bored is something we can all act at, but when you're being bored as if that's reality and you've got no choice, then you've got a bored act running, and the minute you own it, it's different. You might still be bored but it's your choice. It's, "I am at this point choosing to be bored, or express or act boredom. And I have a choice."

Earlier we looked at the question of "Who am I?"

Who you are is he or she who may choose to be any way you want to be. When you choose boredom, you can be bored and say, "I am choosing boredom," or, "I feel bored." For example I cried two or three times in all my life before I was 27. Those few times were terrifying because I would feel my sadness so fully that it felt like my whole truth was "I am nothing but sadness".

After I got into Feeling Release, I allowed myself to allow my sadness and really enjoy it.

One of the most exquisite experiences in my whole life was the first time I really cried in a Primal session. I cried out sadness for two hours and at the end of two hours there was no sadness left to cry, for then. Then I thought, "I don't want to stop," so I didn't. I cried for another hour for the sheer physical pleasure and release of it. I realized how enjoyable a good cry is.

Some people have a crying act. They cry at the drop of a hat, but as victims. They don't feel that they have a choice. If you acknowledge that you are choosing to cry and choosing sadness and can choose to enjoy it then suddenly it's a whole new ball game.

Once you do that, it's very hard to stay bored. Earlier someone said, the minute she saw that she was choosing boredom, she got bored with it very quickly. Same as the minute you own your choice to be angry. In short bursts it can be enjoyable and a good release, but it's really hard to consciously sustain anger or sadness. Because it's not much fun. And you need to be in victim mode to keep at it.

Another paradox: if you are sad and feeling that you have no choice about it, then you get sadder about the fact that you have no say, and your sadness remains and grows. When you own your sadness it starts to heal, complete, and disappear.

I am appalled by the ignorance and stupidity of all these macho, terrified, shut off commentators who put down anything to do with feelings and releasing them as "wimpy" or "animalistic" and stay in the old myth that feelings should all be held in. Hell, those feelings will eat at you for a lifetime. It's like resentment. I've heard people express resentment that they've carried for 20 or 30 years, acid eating their guts, when all they have to do is confront the person they resent, acknowledge it, and let it go.

You can then think, "Been there done that, let's choose something that's fun." It's back to, "What do I really want to do?"

Participant: ...Yesterday I was really sad, I started crying and I was able to be here and listen to what was going on while crying. I was enjoying it. I wasn't very conscious about crying, I was just crying. I've never experienced that.

It's great to just connect with crying just for the crying and not having to be blocking the feeling, or conversely, lost in it, or have to have a reason for it. When somebody reached out to me I thought, "Hey what are you doing? Leave me alone. I'm crying."

Gregory: Yeah. "Leave me alone. I don't want to play."

Participant: ...That was a reaction which I've never had. Usually I'm crying and reaching out at the same time.

Gregory: That's the paradox: on the one hand it's very valuable to let yourself have your feelings. On the other hand it's also powerful not to buy into them.

Participant: ...One of the things I've found here, is that I can experience a feeling then let it go without holding onto it, allowing myself the freedom of the changing feelings.

Gregory: Tell me if this is correct: you can do all this stuff here and then you'll go back home as if it didn't happen, because you have a judgement that if you change, then somehow that will invalidate how you were as not being real.

Participant: ...I've experienced that with my family. For example I cried on the phone to my Sister and then say I'm happy. She thinks it's a load of bullshit. Then the next time I try and talk to her, if I cry, she'll come back at me with, "It's a load of bullshit because tomorrow you're going to be thinking something else." So I got into the trap that, for her to listen to me or for me to get sympathy from her, I have to play sad. Which I didn't want to do.

Gregory: That sounds like you put people in your life who require you to be a certain way.

Participant: ...That's what I've done for a long time and I'm sick of playing that game because it doesn't allow spontaneity. My feelings change like that. I used to cry, and then laugh and forget about it. I used to feel that I had to really hold it down, because everybody else went into depression and I could never really be like everybody else.

Gregory: The step to take is have people in your life who are open to that changeability. Who can handle you doing that, being authentic in that moment, and it's fine for them. Great. Anyone else? Yes?

Participant: ...I'd like to do something about my slow pissing.

Gregory: You disappear into being nice out of great fear of showing yourself. One of the things that happens physically when you're very scared is you either piss your pants or you can't.

By the way, the kidneys are the organs associated with fear, among other things, and one of the first places you hold on is your bladder, then your bum and then the rest of your body.

Ultimately how you end that slow pissing is: (a) Stop being sweet and (b) Take the risk of stepping out and saying what's true for you and risking rejection. Then you discover that you aren't rejected, or that you are and it's okay, and your fear will diminish. As your fear diminishes, your body will relax. When your body relaxes you'll piss flowingly.

You disappear into Hansel and Gretel Land where everything is made from candy and sweetness. Where you fart perfume and crap Mints.

You've got a lot of Pisces energy. You're like a slippery fish. You just disappear under the water. You were there a minute ago, then it's back into that sweetness. The fear is that if you make a stand and actually say what's true for you, that someone will hook you. There is nothing more powerful for you to do in your life than have a talk with your internal censor and let her have a holiday. Start saying what's true for you and risking that everyone throws up and leaves. There is nothing more powerful for you to do right now. Anything else is a distraction.

Participant: ...What's true for me is that I have a lot of fear.

Gregory: That's a great start. Okay. I want you to tell me, who in the room you don't particularly like, without a story to explain why. Just a name. Don't think about it. You already know. Thank you. Who else? Don't think about it, you already know maybe a thing about them. Just name something you don't like about someone. Who?

Participant: ...I...

Gregory: No story, just a name.

Participant: ...I get a fear...

Gregory: Ah ah. That's a story. Just a name.

Great. Who else? It doesn't matter. Who else? Quick.

Who else? Quick. Don't think. Who else don't you like much? Or is there something about them you dislike?

One more person. It's alright. Anyone. One more person. Just feel how you disappear. Can you feel it?

Participant: ...No. Well ....

Gregory: Just be with what happens. It's like part of you is saying, "Whoa, let me out of here."

Participant: ...Yep.

Gregory: No story, just one more name. The minute you start explaining it or justifying it you lose it. Is there one more person.

Participant: ...I'd like to get it clear that...

Gregory: Aha. She's going to say, "I really do like him, but there's just this tiny little weeny bit, like he hasn't cut his toe nails." You haven't given yourself permission to say, "I don't like you much Fred. I haven't got much in common with you. I'm sure you're an okay person but I don't like you much." You haven't given yourself that permission yet.

Participant: ...There's a fear...

Gregory: Heaps of them. You can sit there for the next three years looking at the fears that arise or you can get past them by saying what is there to be said, i.e. your truth. When I went abseiling, I realized I can sit at the top of that cliff and ponder and contemplate and understand my fear for fifty years, and I still wouldn't have gone down the cliff. Or I could go down the cliff and my fears would disappear, to whatever degree.

Name one person.

Participant: ...Fred.

Gregory: Great thank you. What don't you like about Fred? No story, just details.

Participant: ...He has the combination of the Buddha and the Devil.

Gregory: Great. I think that's very perceptive. What don't you like about John?

Participant: ...I have a fear of homosexuals. I suppose of being homosexual.

Gregory: So you don't like the fact that he's homosexual.

Participant: ...Yeah.

Gregory: Right. What don't you like about Mike?

Participant: ...The animal.

Gregory: Great. Who was the other one?

Participant: ...Me.

Gregory: Oh, butt head here! What don't you like about him?

Participant: ...The animal and the letch in him.

Gregory: Great. Fantastic. Fantastic. Now, what is the fear of what might happen if you say those things? The biggest fear?

Participant: ...I suppose that I'm ...that they'll dislike me...

Gregory: Do you dislike her for saying that?

Participants: ...No, it doesn't worry me. I don't care ...Not at all ... Doesn't worry me.

Gregory: Great. And I'll bet 50 others would say something like, "I already knew that." You get it? So his response is, "That's fine." His response is, "Eh." His response is, "Bugger off." Great. Whatever.

Now you know where you stand. And they know where you stand. You've just made a stand. You have just appeared in their life. By the way, all those comments I agree with. I think they're very perceptive. You have instructor eyes. Very perceptive. Also very visual. You see a lot.

Participant: ...Too visual.

Gregory: No, no, no, no, no, no, no. You see a lot, and then judge that it's not okay to say what you see, or even to see what you see.

Participant: ...I'm a bit of a headfucker. Instead of using my heart I use my head.

Gregory: One of your fears is that if you say what you see you'll also mess people around. What it does is it sorts out the weak from the charm. Firstly you get to get honest with who you want around you and why you want them. And you get to have people around you that you really love and you're not bullshitting yourself about what is missing for you with them. In other words like her you take off your rose-colored glasses. I don't know anyone who's more forthright and direct than I am, it makes life very simple. Some people piss off and some people come and do seminars and get to be in my life. They know what the deal is. You get that?

Participant: ...In other words, say what I think.

Gregory: It's called Be As Honest As You Can Be. That will change your life. Dramatically. And you'll piss easily. You, your truth, will be flowing and so will your pee! No longer holding back and therefore no pissing off from yourself.

***

Participant: ...As far as the relationship between my wife and I, I've been sitting here wondering why I feel so good because I know that she's not taking any shit. It just clicked that her doing what she wants to do without worrying about what I'm going to think about it, and me not worrying about what she is going to do. I feel great, and I feel closer to her than anytime I can remember. I'm delighted we are doing this together.

Gregory: Fantastic. What I see you two creating here is what I talk about in The Living Game section on relationships. You each take responsibility for fulfilling yourselves and then share that with each other without constraints, without controls, manipulations, demands; without all that crap. It's really inspiring. Both of you are.

And you are inspiring everyone else. They get to see what a relationship can look like, and it will encourage these people to either transform their own relationships or create relationships in that model.

For me the ultimate pleasure in relationship with someone is knowing that they're enjoying themselves, and when they want to enjoy themselves by hanging out with me, that's great, and when they want to enjoy themselves with other people, I know that they're fulfilling themselves that way.

What results from that is that each time you get together, you have 100% messages that you're there because you want to be, not because you're expected to be. Phenomenal.

Participant: ...I'm confused about being with people and speaking my truth and if they don't like it, they can piss off, because there are a lot of people in my life that, well, I just don't need. There's not a lot of people I value in my life.

Gregory: So when you get honest with yourself, there won't be a whole lot of people in your life for a while. Then it will fill up again with people you do value. Before you fill a cup you have to empty it. While you keep people in your life that you don't value, that's what you get. Not much value.

When you're clear that you're not willing to settle for that, it's a statement of you valuing yourself. Then the people whom you don't value and who don't value themselves won't be able to hang around with you anymore.

People who don't value themselves hang out with people who don't value themselves and each other. When you change and start valuing yourself, all those other people have a new choice: they either shift with you and start to value themselves, or they stay where they are. Which is called "Somewhere Behind".

Participant: ...There are people I value but there are so many ancient games involved that I get really confused about.

Gregory: Acknowledge the games. Acknowledge what is, and how you'd like it to be. Where you are now and how you'd like to have it. Then you see what they're up for.

Participant: ...I'm seeing a lot of stuff about my value and my skin and I'm really relating to it well. I can accept my choice to have my skin the way it is. I've gone out looking for someone to show me how to fix my skin, then just think, "Screw you," because I don't want to fix it. Now I see that I'm choosing to have my skin the way it is, and it's totally fine for now, rather than continuing to push myself. One of the things I wanted to get out of this seminar was clear skin, but I've let go of that.

Gregory: Here's how it goes. You may never have clear skin, now what are you going to do with your life?

Participant: ...I'm going to make it okay to have it exactly how it is. And accept that the way it is, instead of wasting people's time and energy.

Gregory: And yours.

Participant: ...Yeah, and mine, trying to make myself be something that I think I should be or I think they want me to be. Thank you.

Gregory: I used to work with a nurse who was one of the clearest human beings I've ever met. She had a really large birth mark on her face. And every man in the hospital wanted to take her to bed.

Participant: ...Why?

Gregory: Because she was great. She was just a stunning woman. The first time you saw the birth mark it was like, "Oh," you know, it was really unsettling. Second time it was okay. Third time you never saw it. It just disappeared. The force of her personality and who she was, was simply bigger than any handicap she had. It was that simple. People forgot she had a birth mark. Because she didn't have a birth mark. She didn't make any deal about her birth mark. She totally owned it, "That's what my skin's like. And, I'm special." She knew who she was and did not identify herself as a reaction to her birth mark.

So everyone agreed and forgot her birth mark and saw that she was special. She was gorgeous, and she was really really plain looking. Objectively I couldn't find anything visually attractive about her. Except who and how she was, which was a beautiful woman.

***

Participant: ...When I'm scared that an answer I've got will not work, then it doesn't work. Just last night I was looking for something not to work, I decided to just do it and may be it would work, not even caring if it did or didn't. I don't even know if it worked. I feel better today.

Gregory: I keep saying, everything works some of the time. So if something's not working now, try something else. During that two and half year period that I was out of relationship, I went and had a holiday in Bali. Before I went I saw how desperate I was to create a relationship. I'd been doing all these acknowledgements and processes and scripts and choices etc. Then I just thought, "Screw it. I'm going to Bali for a total holiday. I'm not going to do anything when I'm there."

So I acknowledged that I wasn't going to acknowledge anything, or "work on myself," and I moved through miles of stuff. Everything works sometimes. Hit your head with a shoe. That might work sometimes. Who knows? When you don't know what to do, try something. Yes?

It was also at that time that I real-eyes-ed that," You can't have a better relationship with someone else than you have with yourself." So I decided to just enjoy me enjoying Bali.

Participant: ...I just want to acknowledge that in coming to the seminar, I had a voice saying, "Oh great. After the seminar, I'll get everything I need."

Gregory: You've already got everything you'll ever need. Life is not a matter of finding what you need, it's giving yourself what you've already got - which is everything you'll ever need. After a month of intense Feeling Release sessions, I came out with a realization that I hadn't added one thing. What I had done was lost a lot of blocking of what I already had.

Whatever it is you want, you've already got it, it's just a matter of finding out how to let yourself have it, digging up treasure. The treasure is already there. Remember, you are a Living Human Treasure.

Participant: ...I want to heal my cyst. And when I mentioned that yesterday you talked about the energy process. Shall I wait until tomorrow?

Gregory: All of this is healing your cyst. The most important thing in changing anything is the desire, willingness and commitment to change it. The rest is gravy. Simply making the statement, "I'm choosing to heal my cyst" is the most important step. When people come and do The Living Game Seminar, I say, "The hardest thing about this seminar is getting through the front door. The rest is easy." It's true.

Participant: ...For the first time on this seminar I feel love and value for myself. In the past it's been a concept - I've said that I have but it hasn't felt like it. Through that I've seen how much I love and value you in my life and don't show it a lot. The way that I can show it is to love and value myself, that's where I grow. I really value my creation of you in my life. I just want to thank you for that.

Gregory: Thank you. You loving and valuing yourself is a huge gift to me too. Telling me completes the circle. That way you have acknowledged both the people in the process: you and I. Anyone else?

Participant: ...I'm just noticing how hard I find it to own where I am. I feel like I don't care about anyone and just become withdrawn and sad and committed to a bad time. It's really hard but I fight it. Struggling.

Gregory: Once you let that be okay then the rest of the truth can surface. Yesterday morning you connected with just how totally you cared about people.

And the flip side is, "I don't care about people at all. Screw 'em." Right? To use that as an example, we then say, "Well I should decide on one or the other," and then hop between them. The truth is, both are true. Sometimes you care passionately about people and sometimes you couldn't give a damn about them. You see that?

You end conflict and struggle by ending opposites in your life. And when you can totally give yourself, "Screw everyone," and you put a big sign on your house saying "Human beings, GO AWAY until further notification." And in brackets, "I don't care how bad it is. I don't care how big your drama is or how much you need me or how much it hurts."

An amazing Australian woman named Faye Druitt is a quadriplegic and a staff trainer for the State Government. She wrote a book called I Always Wanted To Tap Dance. The opening line is: "I know there are lots of people worse off than me. But I don't care about them." Isn't that great!

Then you sit at home, and you totally have your space to yourself. Have an answering machine on that says, "You have dialed my phone number. Please hang up and don't do it again."

Now I don't actually do that because in a week or so I mightn't want them to piss off and by then they've pissed off, so I do it inside me here. I just project it out, "No entry. No disturbance. I don't want to know right now."

Everyone gets the message. What works is to stand up and say, "EVERYONE PISS OFF UNTIL I SAY OTHERWISE."

When you want it, maybe five minutes later, you say, "I'm back on deck!" I do it with people in my life, just to let them know I'm not here, not available for a while.

You're either here or you're not here, being present. But it's real hard to be not quite here, which is where a lot of people spend a lot of their time. Most people are not fully present in the Present, the Now.

Notice that the Present (this moment) is a present (a gift) that was present from the past!

Your thoughts, actions, choices and commitments in the past got you here to this moment of the Present. If you want a different Present to show up in the future, then send yourself that present by doing new choices, actions etc. that are aligned with your vision for then, and it then happens.

Participant: ...I spend a lot of time sitting on the fence, and I see that reflection by creating a lot of people to feel uncomfortable with me.

Gregory: Your body is here but your consciousness is somewhere else, you've stretched yourself way away, then you get scared that you mightn't be able to get back. All sorts of things go on. Then you become confused and lost, etc. Very unpleasant. If you're going to be Here, have all of you here and if you're not, take all of you and go.

That's Zen, doing everything perfectly and consciously. Have all of you where you are 100%. Have all of you where you are. So sitting here saying, "Er, er, er..." and thinking about that over there and that over there and that over there, you're not being 100% consciously Here.

Practice doing things 100%. It's easier to practice that with things you don't normally do. Once when I was in Bali, I became absolutely intrigued with an ant's nest, so I picked an ant and followed it around for half a day.

Participant: ...Where did you go?

Gregory: Wherever it went, and it went everywhere. It was amazing. Tourists thought I was crazy but the Balinese really enjoyed it.

I actually felt very normal in a crazy way, it was great. I was learning to be a little bit like an ant.

Because I didn't just follow it around. My intention was to be ant-like in my following.

Participant: ...Did you walk on all fours?

Gregory: Yeah. But the way ants walk is really funny. They have this swimming gait.

Participant: ...Had a little red bow around it's neck. He knew which one it was.

Gregory: Ha. They also walk differently when they're carrying things, they carry them in their mouths. It's funny carrying things in your mouth.

The Balinese would come up to me and say, "What are you doing?" I'd say,

"Being an ant," and they'd say, "Oh. That's fine. That's as good a thing to be as anything."

Participant: ...They'd lock you up if you said that here.

Gregory: Oh, of course they would, but the point is, that to be an ant, you really have to pay attention and anything that forces you to pay attention, gets you all Here. Especially when there are other ants around that could bite you, you really pay attention.

I loved Aldous Huxley's book, Island, where mynah birds walked around all the time saying, "Attention attention, (be) here and now boys."

Participant: ...Did the ants enjoy it?

Gregory: I couldn't tell. They were getting their own ant-lightenment!

Participants: ...(everyone) Ooooohhhhhh!!!

***

Participant: ...I'd like to acknowledge something I've never acknowledged publicly before. It's that my body is fat.

Gregory: She's noticed. I told you she was perceptive.

Participant: ...I made it fat. And I did that because it had a lot of value for me and I really enjoyed it, and I intend to stay fat until at least the end of the seminar. And yeah, I really like it.

(everyone applauds)

Gregory: Very good. I once had a very fat woman do the seminar, a really really fat woman. She raised some issue and I said, "Okay, Fatso, up the front." Everyone else crapped, and she cracked up laughing. What she said, and I knew it, was that everyone else pretends she's not fat.

Participant: ...Me too. I pretend. I don't own it.

Gregory: Yes. Exactly.

Anyone else? No? Burn out time. It's a great place to get to when you've got nothing to say. So keep doing it. "Before you fill the cup you must empty it."

Participant: ...I find it really hard to let go of having to get results.

Gregory: That's how you get results. Have you had any results so far?

Participant: ...Yeah.

Gregory: Yeah. Were they the ones you were expecting?

Participant: ...No.

Gregory: The problem with having a result in mind is that you miss all the other possible results. Have you ever been to a party, for example, where you really want to meet someone, and you ignore everyone else, then when you finally get to the someone, they're really boring. You turn around and everyone else has left the party? Have you ever done that?

Participant: ...It's very painful.

Gregory: It is very painful. That's when you let your head get in the way. John Lennon wrote, "Life is what happens while you're busy making other plans."

Participant: ...I'm just feeling I've got to let go.

Gregory: Find the balance between going for the results that you want and being open to the results that are best for you. It's very Libran. I keep doing this, but for me it's about balance. Mostly I'm clear about the results I'm going for but I'm also open to new possibilities, so I might head off that way, go three steps, and suddenly see there's a new possibility or a more exciting way, or something else.

Participant: ...Or, "Here I am somewhere else." If you're heading over there, sometimes you end up, like I'm here but I am somewhere else.

Gregory: Yes. Here I am somewhere else. That's very good. There are many roads to the top of the mountain.

Participant: ...And enjoy them.

Gregory: Exactly. What I'm really interested in is that I'm enjoying the journey. That's why it's so important to love and value yourself and acknowledge where you are. Then you get to enjoy where you are, which means you enjoy the journey. But if you say I'll enjoy it when I get there, that means I'm practicing not enjoying myself now.

How do you master enjoying yourself by practicing not enjoying yourself? Darned if I know. I get to have it all by practicing having what I've got and enjoying that. Then I get to increase my ability to enjoy and have it. Then I have more. Once you master where you are, you move on to the next place or stage in your life.

Participant: ...I'm noticing how I get stuck in being righteous and thinking I know it all.

I'm very much a fence-post sitter which can be quite painful. I always see both sides of things, so I often find that I never get to do what I want to do. What I'm realizing is that if I get angry because my lover wants me to clean up the house and I don't want to, that's my choice because I didn't think of it first, I've put her out there so that somebody supports me to have me and my environment conscious, starting with cleaning up the house.

Gregory: That's right. You can get angry about it or look at and decide whether you want to clean up the house, or do you want to pay a cleaner?

Participant: ...She gets on my nerves because I keep refusing to listen to myself!

Gregory: Ha, ha. That's exactly it. You're resisting your creation of her in your life. Yes?

Participant: ...I've been trying to relate what's being said to my life and I gave myself a headache. Then I thought, "Well, I don't have to work it all out. Just let it go."

Gregory: See, I don't "understand" a lot of what I'm saying and most of what I say, I never figured out intellectually. You really get it after you do it. Before you act, you have understanding. After you act, you have knowledge and experience. Then maybe some wisdom.

Participant: ...With my skin again, I was thinking about making a commitment not to pick at it again, while I'm on the seminar, but in acknowledging where I'm at, I'm not sure whether I'm up for keeping that commitment yet. Taking responsibility for it is something I haven't done before, but I'd really like to ask everyone's support in my being conscious, because I go unconscious about it. I'd just like everyone's support in helping me stop pick it.

Gregory: What I suggest you do is make the commitment not just to stop picking your skin, but to stop picking on yourself. What you do a lot is put stuff out and then pick on yourself for what you're saying. Then it dies away and you lose energy and you don't get to say what you want to say, and in the process you don't get to stay with what you see and know.

Participant: ...For the first time, through acknowledgement, I'm beginning to feel my heart open. I feel really sad, and I feel good.

Gregory: Very good. That's the heart opening process. That's how you get to open your heart, and it includes acknowledging what you don't like and letting it be okay, then giving yourself permission to act on what you've judged to be negative.

Participant: ...I just want to acknowledged that I've never taken the risk of showing my ugliness to the degree that I have today, and how stuck I am in it. The acknowledgement I want to make of myself for being willing to stay in how stuck I am and show that and expose that in me. The other thing is that my fear has been that if I show my ugliness, no-one will ever want to be around me. It is my intention and goal to heal that ugliness and I want to let people know that if they have something to say to me, I don't care whether it's just that they think that I'm no good, then come, or I'll go to them, just for me to take the step to connect. My mask, which keeps everyone at a distance, I've never shown before to this degree. I know there are big payoffs in doing it that way.

The truth is, I don't know any other way, I'm just starting to test that out. It took me doing it to this degree and in reaching out for another way. Underneath all of that is the paradox of wanting everyone to piss off and on the other side having a need and want to connect with you all.

Gregory: Acknowledge that fully. You just slipped past that a bit.

Participant: ...Right. I really need and want to belong and be part of this group and I've never had that before. And I don't know ...

Gregory: Okay, stop. Go back to the first part. Don't explain the acknowledgement. Just tell them again, "I need to belong to this group."

Participant: ...I need to belong to this group.

Gregory: Louder please.

Participant: ...I NEED TO BELONG WITH YOU ALL.

Gregory: Yes. And again.

Participant: ...I want to belong with you all.

Gregory: How much?

Participant: ...With all my heart.

Gregory: Yes. How lonely has it been?

(lots of crying)

Gregory: Just open your eyes and feel how much you've wanted to be with them.

(lots of crying)

Gregory: What are your hands doing? What do they want?

Participant: ...To reach out.

Gregory: Well let them. Stay with it. Just stay with your hands. Just feel your hands. What do they want to do now?

(lots of crying - she starts to hit her chest)

Gregory: It's not dead yet. Kill it. You haven't killed your heart yet. So what are you going to do? What is it that your heart wants that you keep trying to kill?

Participant: ...Love.

Gregory: So tell them.

Participant: ...I want love. I want a lot of love.

Gregory: Stay connected with your heart. Feel the bind again. Feel the new bind. What's the bind?

Participant: ...I want to run away.

Gregory: Why?

Participant: ...I'm scared they'll get me.

Gregory: Yes. Why will they get you?

Participant: ...I don't know.

Gregory: Okay. Keep breathing. Keep your eyes open. Just be here and feel how scared you are that they'll get you. What does getting you look like?

Participant: ...That you'll all want to come and rip me apart. Because they don't like me ...Because I make trouble.

Gregory: What's wrong with you?

Participant: …I've seen too much. I don't agree with them all. I don't fit.

Gregory: Keep your eyes open. So tell them how you want it to be and what you want. Keep your eyes open.

Participant: …I want to be here. I want to be able to be in a group and be myself. That's what I want. I want you to be okay with me being myself.

Gregory: So who is yourself? Keep your eyes open. Tell them now so they know what to expect.

Participant: …I want to be a powerful full-on woman and nobody gets in my way when I want something. I want to have everything I want. And I want to do what I want to do. And I want to be a part of what everybody else is doing as well. I've never been in a group before. I want to know what that's like. And I don't know whether I can be in a group.

Gregory: What is it about you that might stop you?

Participant: …I'm afraid I might destroy it.

Gregory: …Okay, So tell them, "I'm a destroyer."

Participant: …I'm a destroyer.

Gregory: Sometimes.

Participant: …Sometimes.

Gregory: What else is wrong with you? Or what else is it about you that you try and hide from them?

Participant: …I get angry. And I lie, and I don't have a lot of time for people sometimes. And sometimes I just want to be on my own. I really value that. And I see a lot of what goes on …I don't know whether I've got anything to give.

Gregory: "Except bullshit."

Participant: …Except bullshit …And deceptions.

Gregory: So what do you want to say to them? What is missing?

Participant: ...That I don't have a lot to offer. And I really want to be a part of this group.

Gregory: Stop looking for an answer. If you don't know what's missing, have the guts to say, "I don't know what's missing."

Participant: ...I don't know what's missing. I'm really scared that I don't have anything to offer and you won't want me anyway.

Gregory: Very good. Try this one on, "I want to be the centre of attention, and I've got nothing of validity to do that with, so I'm going to keep throwing dramas." Try that one on.

Participant: ...I want to be the centre of attention.

Gregory: No, you're going into blank.

I'm not invalidating that you're having some intense pain and some intense feelings, but that's where you go to avoid changing. Your pain is safe, so you keep going there. Very dramatic, very impressive. Most people would think, "Oh poor thing. Isn't she trying hard?" But it's just boring for you. Other people need to access those levels of feelings, for you it's a deception and a hiding place. It's a safe place for you to come from. For other people here it's a risk. It's no risk for you, it's a drama. You dramatize it.

Participant: ...Yes. I don't need to do that.

Gregory: No, you don't need to do that, it doesn't progress you or advance where you are at all.

The two things you did that progressed you somewhat were actually acknowledging things that you do in a way that I saw was coming from truth. The second was that you acknowledged that you didn't know - that was coming from truth. The rest of it, the acknowledgements were true, coming from drama. Yes?

Look, you're doing it again. You're telling us what you're not going to do, you're not telling us what you are going to do.

Participant: ...Right. I'm committing to handling my stuff without any dramas.

Gregory: And if feelings come up, that's a separate issue? Yes?

What I'm telling you is that you can handle your drama and you can have feelings, it's like, you can walk down the side of the swimming pool or you can dive in. You automatically dive in as a way of hiding.

Day 7

"Do what you want, and if you want to be a Master, then master what you're doing."

FEAR REJECTION - ACCEPTANCE - DISCRIMINATION - HYPOCRISY - CAPITULATION - COMMITMENT - PERSONAL POWER - LEADERSHIP - SERVICE - SURRENDER - TRUST - MASTERY - LEADERS IN OUR OWN LIVES SURRENDER TO OUR COMMITMENTS - NOT SELLING OUT - GIVING OURSELVES PERMISSION

Participant: ...I don't like rejection, or rejecting anyone.

Gregory: I know a woman who lives down the road and I've got her phone number. She's an 80 year old leper, she's got wet leprosy by the way.

Participants: ...(everyone) What's that?

Gregory: Bits come off.

Participant: ...Is this a story?

Gregory: No. She lives in isolation down the road. To give you the experience of not rejecting anyone, I suggest that I bring her up as your date for the night. I know she doesn't get a lot of sex these days, and she gets pretty horny. What's your response to that?

Participant: ...Forget it.

Gregory: Thank you. That would be my response. Saying "no" isn't a rejection, though it can be. If you decide it is then it's a rejection, but if you decide that someone saying "no" to you is simply sharing what's true for them then you don't experience it as a rejection. Another level of that is that we all discriminate all the time. You discriminated about where you sat in the circle. You had discrimination about what clothes you wear and the rest of your clothes are in your wardrobe crying with the unfairness and rejection of it. Or they are lodging an appeal with the anti-discrimination board, who will make you wear all of your clothes all the time or send you to prison, where they discriminate against all your clothes and don't let you wear any of them as punishment for not wearing all of them!

You could walk around wearing clothes you don't like and be feeling like shit, and having one voice saying, "Gee, you're a really good person because you rescued these clothes from everlasting rejection." When you've got clothes like that in your wardrobe, give them to a charity store. Then they'll give them to people who'll really appreciate them. Then the clothes are happy because they're getting worn all the time and they're really being enjoyed.

It's the same with people, exactly the same with people. One of the most insulting things I can experience, is someone being with me so I won't feel rejected. It's horrid.

If you're not willing to change it, and you're not enjoying it, then say, "this isn't working for me," and go to bed.

Mob mentality says, "Oh this is what everyone's doing, so I've got to stay and do it too. It's not okay for me to separate from the mob." It also is the end of individual thought, discussion, perception or opinion. When the mob rules, as it so often does, there is only one acceptable way to be and think and act. It is called Political Correctness. Government by the Mob, for the Mob.

South Africa was a great example of this in terms of discrimination against discrimination.

That country had a highly discriminatory policy to blacks and colored people, called apartheid, literally, apart-hate. The rest of the world said, "You have no right to discriminate against them for being different, and to force you to stop doing that we will discriminate against you." So the world created a policy of discrimination and hate against South Africa for doing the same thing. It's called fighting fire with fire. It appears to have worked. My point is that within it's own hypocrisy, the West does not, EVER, acknowledge that it's own policies are often discriminatory. It is one of our blind spots.

Also the mob backs this policy of hypocrisy, so that if anyone in any way questions it then the mob brands them as supporting discrimination and therefore bad.

Remember that hate fills the space between the love you want and the love you get.

Fulfillment is to love your choices. When you withdraw that, then you start hating your choices out of a judgement that it's not okay to choose that. The only way that I know of to get rid of the hate is to choose to do what you do because you love it.

You're scared that if you tell everyone what you really want they'll hate you, so you hate yourself first, and everyone thinks, "Oh well, I don't need to hate him because he's already hating himself." That's a real subterfuge that we use to deceive the world.

The key is to give yourself permission to be the author of your life. There is nothing right or wrong about any choice, but every choice has it's consequences. The foundation stone of everything I've learnt and teach is, "It's your choice, and you're entitled to your choice." It's the basis of real, true freedom and democracy, which in some enlightened future may occur on this planet.

If you only want to bonk six foot tall blonde women with big tits because that's all that turns you on, be proud of it. If society says, "You're a male chauvinist pig because you only bonk women with big tits," great. Fine. You're the one that's getting your rocks off the way that you enjoy, and they're the ones who are walking around bitchy and miserable. Who's winning? You, and the six foot blondes with big tits!

You say that there's something wrong with you, it's like an apology. I'll play out a little game. Go and change your shirt. Go on. Change your shirt. It's really weird. It's unusual. What a wimp. Do it. Okay.

That's how you've played your life. "Oh okay, someone's told me to do it. I better do it, whether I want to or not." You end up angry and resentful and poisonous. Hence the Wimp Jew/Nazi Killer masks you get trapped in. So play this one. When I tell you to change your shirt say, "Get fucked. I'm not willing to change it."

Go and change your shirt.

Participant: ...Get fucked. I'm not willing to change.

Gregory: I'm not convinced. Who's convinced?

Participants: ...(everyone) No.

Gregory: I reckon three more times will have him. Go and change your shirt.

Participant: ...Get fucked. I'm not willing to change.

Gregory: Getting better isn't he? Do it, you're a naughty boy.

(everyone laughs)

Gregory: Okay, I'll tell everyone, so if you want me to like you, go and change your shirt.

Participant: ...Okay.

Participants: ...(everyone) Ohhh. Wimp. Gave in.

Gregory: See they can't stand it because they just saw themselves. Now that's perfect.

(he turns his shirt inside out and puts it back on)

Gregory: See what he did?

He changed it by not changing it, he turned it inside out. That's how you go into deception. That's where you pretend to go along with what's going on, and behind it is a massive "Fuck you".

And that's where you become dangerous and poisonous. You act like you have changed your shirt, but you haven't. Now, turn it around again and really give yourself the experience of playing the game through a new way, not capitulating. See, whether you actually change your whole shirt or just change it inside out, it's still coming from the place in you that says, "I can't do what I want to do. I can't have my whole full choice."

So this time really stay with you're not going to change your shirt. It's your shirt, it's your life and it's your body and no-one has the right to tell you how to use or live that.

I'll start at the last point which was, c'mon mate, change your shirt.

Now look, you're being silly, you're being rebellious, you're being naughty. You're acting like a child. Now you know that the best thing to do is change your shirt and then everyone will be happy. Now, change your shirt. Come on. Stop this screwing around will you? Everyone is waiting for you to change your shirt. Then we can get on with things.

Participant: ...I am not going to change my shirt.

Gregory: Getting there. Hear it?

Participants: ...(everyone) Yeah.

Gregory: Right. Change your bloody shirt. Come on. Cut this shit out.

Participant: ...(in German accent) I'm not to change my shirt.

(everyone cracks up laughing)

Gregory: Very good. You beat me to it. (in German accent) You vill change your shirt Jewboy. Do it now.

Participant: ...No.

Gregory: Okay my little friend. I've got three young beautiful virgins out there if you change your shirt.

(he almost takes off his shirt)

Participants: ...(everyone) Ohhh.

Participant: ...Nearly got him.

Gregory: See his price for capitulating on his own truth? Find out what yours is!

When you being in charge of you is the only thing that matters, you don't have a price. You're near-capitulation then means that you're worth three virgins. I can buy you for three virgins. I can make you jump through hoops for three virgins. Do you see that?

Participant: ...Yes.

Gregory: If your truth is that, stick with it. Here's the catch: it may be that at that point you have a look at whether or not you really want your shirt. If you change your position, you make that choice. Say, "I'm not selling out to my choice or my truth, I really see that this shirt is not worth three virgins." So sell your shirt, not yourself. You get that one?

Participant: ...Yeah.

Gregory: It's not about going into being totally stuck, "I can never change a choice because if I do I'm selling out." That's not what I'm talking about. But if you're clear that something is true for you, don't let what others think, say, want or do, change your truth, or you are selling out.

And it may be that someone comes along, you know, Gregory walks in and you've been absolutely clear that that is the best choice you've got for you in your life, and suddenly here's a new choice that opens a whole new bunch of possibilities that are much more fun than wearing a shirt. And you want that.

Then you choose that because you want to change. It doesn't matter what it is, the minute you give yourself permission to make your own choices, it shifts. It's easy. Sometimes we don't want to change, sometimes we're not willing to change. I'm absolutely clear that there's a whole lot of things in my life that I am unwilling to change at any price. Because I like and value them so much.

Down the line I might think, "Okay. Now I want to change that." But I decide. So each time there's something about you that you hate, cut through it by saying, "Yes, I hate it because I haven't let myself have it and I'm entitled to this choice. It's my life."

When my son was about three and a half or four, he was living with his Mum, and he used to spend every weekend with me. I'd picked him up and we'd gone over for dinner at a friend's who has a daughter around his age named Mary. We all had dinner and Luke and Mary went off to play.

It was Friday night and I went in and said, "I'm getting tired and I want to go in about ten minutes," and Luke said, "Oh, I'd like to stay here the night." And I immediately went into, "Gee mate, I haven't seen you for a week, I'm really hanging out to see you." He just looked me straight in the eye and said, "Dad, it's my life."

What could I say? I got it. So I said, "Fine, I got it. I'm leaving in fifteen minutes so if you stay here, don't change your mind in two hours because I'm going home to bed. It's absolutely fine with me for you to stay the night." So I set up my end of, "It's my life too," with him. So he was really clear that he had that choice, and so was I, but I also knew that I had choices in my life, and one of them was, "I'm not willing to come back in three hours when you've finished playing and have decided you don't want to stay the night."

He thought about that and he said, "Okay. I'll tell you in 15 minutes." And in 15 minutes he said, "I'll come home with you." The issue wasn't about coming or not coming home with me. It was him testing whether or not I would respect his choices. Once he saw that I absolutely respected his choices, he didn't need to stay there. The underlying truth was he wanted to spend the weekend with me, but he also wanted to know that he had a choice about that.

Participant: ...For me to say, "No, I'm not willing to change my shirt," I find that I either use anger to get my point across, like, "Piss off. I'm not going to change my shirt," or resignation or something else. I go into different feelings to get my point across rather than just being able to say it. I often gage it on how the other person is. If the other person requests something, then I'll say, "No, I'm not willing to," but if someone else demands it, then I'll get into anger like, "No. Absolutely no."

I find myself fluctuating and allowing myself to fluctuate according to where they're coming from.

Gregory: That's the point. Your response is based on where they're coming from, not what your choice is.

Participant: ...So how do I have my truth and my intention and just be with that 100%? And not allow myself to be affected by their energy, or their approach?

Gregory: The key is to give yourself 100% permission to make your own choices. Until that happens you will take being demanded upon seriously. If someone came up to me and demanded something from me, I'd probably crack up laughing, it's that silly.

The demands you put on yourself are excessive, so when someone puts demands on you, you flip out and go into rage, because you've already put enough demands on yourself.

Participant: ...Yeah.

Gregory: If you'd handled or resolved all your own demands on yourself, if someone came up and said, "You've got to do it," you'd say, "Says who?"

Most people love taking the easy way out. Don't look at the hard basket, just deal with the easy basket, but some people overwhelm themselves spending so much time in the hard basket. It isn't about beating up on yourself or giving yourself a hard time, it's about being willing to handle the stuff that creates problems.

We seek the path of least resistance and think that it's going to work. It often doesn't. For example, you find it difficult to reach out and make contact, so after you've tried for a while with no result you think to yourself, "Oh well, they can come to me," and you sit back and wait for them to come to you. Then it's, "Screw it, they're not coming to me, so I don't really care. I didn't want them to anyway." You disappear on yourself, you don't just live a lie, you live a double or triple lie.

My sense is that you do care very deeply and then you resign from that. Your job is to find a way to reach out and express your caring. That's your job and you resigned. Your next job was to wait until someone cares. But you resigned from that too.

You don't wait until someone comes because they care. You resign from that. Then you pretend you "don't care at all". That's your third job, which you resigned from by starting the whole thing again. You don't hold down any of the jobs. Your commitment isn't to any of them. Ultimately, any of them will work by the way. If you keep reaching out and keep that job until it's complete, you'll get a result. If you sit back and are willing to wait forever, eventually someone will come.

If you think, "I totally don't care," long enough, it will happen. All roads lead to Rome.

The problem is, you don't commit to any of them. You sit there thinking, "Oh this doesn't work, and this doesn't work." Instead of, "I'm not making this work."

Let me tell you a story. A man went up to a Zen Monastery in Japan in the 16th Century.

He walked in to the Abbot of the monastery and he said, "I want to become a Zen Monk." And the Abbot said, "Go away. Get off the monastery property." So he went out and he lived at the front entrance of the monastery. And every day he walked in and said, "I still want to become a monk." And the Abbot said, "Go away."

For six months he lived outside the monastery. He'd go and find work around the village or the town through the day to keep himself alive, right through winter in snow out in the cold, in the open. He's nearly dead. Every day for six months, "I still want to be a monk."

"Go away." And after six months he cut his hand off, and he walked in with his hand in his other hand and said to the Abbot, "This is how big my commitment is to become a monk, and if you tell me to go away again then tomorrow I'll cut my foot off. And the next day I'll cut my other one off. Then I'll crawl here." The Abbot got his commitment and let him in.

I say that there is a level where none of you know what commitment even begins to look like, and I don't suggest you cut your hands off.

Participant: ...I heard in that that his commitment was killing him.

Gregory: You would. You've heard me say 100 times, nothing and no-one can stop you having what you want if you're willing to do what it takes. That's what it took, and he got the result. And he became one of the greatest Zen Masters ever in the history of Japan, probably the greatest.

Participant: ...That's a true story?

Gregory: That's a true story. That's not a parable. It's a true story in the history books of Zen Buddhism in Japan.

You're thinking, "Isn't it enough that he slept outside for six months?" The answer is, for that Monk and that Abbot, it wasn't enough. And I would suggest that, if the Abbot had let him in the first day, he never would have become the greatest Zen Master in history.

When you have a commitment that big, a hand is nothing.

Sometimes what seems to be the hard way is what is needed. We have such a strong inclination to take the easy way. Most Westerners would have turned up at the monastery and said, "G'day great Abbot, I want to become a Zen Monk." And he says, "Go away," and they do, and then spend the rest of their life bitching about it. See, the Abbot couldn't stop him becoming a Monk.

Participant: ...You said you can't refuse someone who is totally committed.

Gregory: Of course not, why would you want to? You cannot resist it. How can you resist that? If you were running your business and someone walked up to you and said, "I will do whatever it takes to work with you and learn your business, including working for free. I'll clean your house. I'll pick you up. I'll drop you off. I'll do your shopping. You tell me what you require and I will do it." What would you say?

Participant: ...YES!!!

Gregory: Exactly. But what people do is say, "I'd really like to learn your business but you've GOT to pay me this and you've GOT to do that and you've GOT to do this." It doesn't work that way.

Participant: ...I've seen other people stand up to do a process to clear something, and I've been crying with them and also crying for myself when I see the rejection, my version of their issue. And I'd already seen it before, and didn't do anything about it, like go and talk to them or offer some support.

Gregory: Okay, so what you do is to make it all too hard; you don't connect with the pain in them, you don't connect with the pain in you, you just distance from the whole issue.

What it comes down to is you see something, then walk away from it and leave it up to me to do it.

The question to ask yourself is, when are you going to start becoming the Instructor in your life? Are you going to wait until someone else handles the problem for you?

The possibility is that you see what's going on in others, and it's a reflection of what's going on in you, but you're not willing to deal with it in you so you don't deal it with the other person, so you stay distant. The question is, how long do you want to keep doing it that way? The other way to do it is to be clear whether or not you want to deal with that in you, and if you do then handle it in yourself by handling it with them. But you give up, that's my point. You would walk up to the monastery and say, "Can I stay and become a Monk?" The Abbot says, "No." You say, "Okay," and leave.

The truth is, you don't care. An important distinction; whatever you feel, the truth is you don't care. Your feeling may say, "This is the most important thing of my life," but if you don't act that way, you don't care.

"Don't listen to what they say, watch what they do."

If you say, "Okay," and walk away, then the truth is, it didn't matter that much, and whatever you say about it is interesting, but so what?

That's one of the big lies we pull on ourselves. We say, "I really care. I'm not willing to do anything about it but I really care," but that's really where you bullshit yourself. I'm talking to everyone. If you don't act on it, then it's not that important to you, and you're doing a nice big, "I am a caring, loving person," routine on yourself, when your truth is, "I don't give a damn."

I would rather see you tell the truth which is, "I see her doing that. Then I see myself doing it, and I don't give a damn. I'm not going to do anything about it because it's too hard. I'm going to distance myself and live my life in a state of distance, that's my choice." Then at least you're being honest with yourself. What a lot of people do, and what you do, is become distant and then from a great distance say, "I really want to do something about this." Everyone agrees saying, "What a caring person! Yeah, isn't it terrible?"

It's painful. But that's fine, because when you see that it's painful and that you have that choice, then you do have that choice, or you do something different. Or you don't.

You get angry when you're demanded upon. The first thing to acknowledge, it's that it reflects the demands in you that you resist, and you become angrier because they're reminding you of what you don't like about yourself.

The whole other level to anger, or to any response, is called matching. I'll give you an example. It will take a few minutes but it describes it well.

At the beginning of last year after the Sex and Relationships Seminar, I decided to create an event called Feast For Famine to bring attention to the fact that we can end world hunger if we have the commitment to do so.

One of the seminar graduates is a friend of the manager of a major Sydney radio station, and so she said that she would like to connect me with him. So I went and had a meeting with the manager who is this absolutely zany, bizarre guy. He really loved the idea of Feast For Famine and we talked for an hour then he said, "What I want to do is set up a meeting tomorrow with the National Media Manager, so he can sit down with you and work out how this radio station can help you. It will be fantastic, and I've talked to our top celebrity about it and he loves it." I went away thinking, "Wow, wow. Big win, big win," and was really excited.

I turned up excited the next day to have the meeting, given that I'd just had an hour's solid input the day before with statements like, "Listen mate, I get 1000 good ideas coming through this door every week, and this idea is hot. It's great. You're a genius."

I sat down with this buttoned-up corporate executive, thinking that this meeting is to decide what they will do to help. I was wide open. I learnt a lesson out of that. This guy just absolutely attacked me. He said, "Oh he's told me about this idea. It's an alright sort of idea but you're really an amateur, and I don't think you can make it work." It was like being in the ring with Muhammad Ali. I'm not kidding. I was bruised. I was punch drunk after five minutes; just didn't know where I was. It was really brutal.

As it happened after ten minutes of this, one of the radio station celebrities stuck his head in the door and called the guy out for a minute. He went out and stayed out for five minutes, and meanwhile I was thinking, "Where am I? What do I do with this?" Then what jumped into my head was, "Match him." In other words, give back what he's giving me.

He came back in and by then I'd pulled myself together. He sat down and said, "Where were we?" I just took an enormous leap and said, "Well I don't know where the hell you are, but I feel like a bag of shit dropped from a great height you fucking abusive hypocrite." I just went for him. Inside I was shitting myself. It was a very difficult thing for me to do. Nice Libra and all of that.

It sat him on his bum so fast that he just said, "Oh look, you've got it wrong. You've heard me wrong. That's not what I'm saying. It is a good idea and I'm concerned..." He just totally turned around. That's matching.

At the end of the meeting, we had a hug and he shook my hand and he said it was fantastic and he loved it and he would do anything he could and he'd commit that the Corporation would help in any way they could.

At times anger is incredibly appropriate if used well, and consciously.

Participant: ...I'm not going to take off my shirt and I don't give a damn of what all of you think. And I just want to let you all know that I'm committed to myself and I hope you can all appreciate that I'm giving something to you all now. And if you don't, go away.

Gregory: What's the thing that you're giving everyone?

Participant: ...That I'm committed to myself and that I know that I might mess up, and I know that I might continue being nice and continue beating myself up and I'll enjoy beating myself up.

Gregory: So you're giving your truth, and your commitment. That's great. Anyone else?

Participant: ...I had an interesting feeling after the leadership process this morning which I found very educational and satisfying, but when I finally sat down and relaxed I felt a real fear coming through my body.

Gregory: What was the fear?

Participant: ...I suppose of telling people what to do.

Gregory: Right, but given that you'd already told them what to do, they'd done it and you sat down, what was the fear?

Participant: ...I couldn't believe how great everybody was in doing it, it gave me a great feeling. The fear is I don't think I'm connected to it.

Gregory: What would it be if you knew?

Participant: ...Saying what I really want.

Gregory: Ah ha.

Participant: ...I think I do realize that I have a lot of personal power.

Gregory: That's absolutely true. It's really interesting what we do with leadership.

Every time you get into a cab, you take on the mantle of a leader. You tell someone what to do and where to go and they do it. You don't waffle, and you don't mess around, and you don't play nice social games. You just get in and say, "Take me to Sydney." Leadership. Every time you walk into a restaurant you do it. The truth is you already practice a lot and you just didn't know you were.

You catch cabs and eat in restaurants don't you? You just never called it leadership before. When you get that you're a leader in a cab, you move closer to being a leader in all of your life.

As well, to be alive is to have personal power! The question is, what do you do with it? How do you use it? What do you create with it? You can be a powerful Victim, or a powerful Creator in your life. Choose! But get that either way you are powerful.

Participant: ...I find it very hard to actually tell people what to do, I like everyone to be happy.

Gregory: Does that make them happy?

Participant: ...I've always had very happy, unbelievably happy times in my work.

Gregory: Right. I didn't ask what you feel. I asked does it make them happy, not does it make you happy.

Participant: ...At the moment I feel friction with my girlfriend with whom I work. But apart from that, we work pretty well together.

Gregory: That keeps you happy. So who's the leader? In other words, who's the dirty four letter word "boss" at work?

Participant: ...I believe I still am.

Gregory: Decide who's going to be the leader in your work, it might be that your girlfriend won't accept that so she leaves. The other possibility is that you hand over leadership to her and you stay or leave. Yeah?

It's just a choice. What do you want? You freelance to maintain your independence, and then become dependent on maintaining peace. Leadership in life is about you deciding what game you're going to play and then inviting people to play it with you, and their leadership is them making the decision whether they do or don't.

Either you're the leader in your life or someone else runs your life. It's that simple. Either you do what you want to do or you do what someone or something else wants you to do. The issue is, do you want to be a leader?

Participant: ...So it doesn't have to be aggressive.

Gregory: It doesn't have to be aggressive at all. It can be as aggressive as, "Will you pass me the salt please?" It's not about being aggressive. It's about stating the truth. If you want to own the leadership of your business, it goes like this: "This is my business. Either you're working for me or you're not in my business. I created the game." See, we've got a lot of business bullshit that goes on too. And work bullshit, like, it should all be democratic. Crap. Absolute crap. It doesn't work. Ultimately someone decides.

Participant: ...I can remember saying that I was the leader and was open to any suggestions at any time.

Gregory: That is the perfect statement of leadership.

Participant: ...I felt it was democratic too.

Gregory: No. Nothing democratic about it because there's no vote about it. There's no vote in it.

Participant: ...I didn't want to play dictator.

Gregory: But it is dictator. "I will dictate the terms." Be a benevolent dictator. The only good leader in a business is a benevolent dictator. The rest are wimps. And no-one knows where they're going. Who's ever worked in a situation where the boss was so terrified of being a dictator he or she was a wimp. You'd say, "Can I have a decision on this?"

"Let me think about it," then he or she'd say "Yes," to you, "No," to him, "Maybe," to someone else in order to keep them all happy.

So you got totally contradictory decisions, and no-one knew what the hell was going on, so everyone would hunker down behind their desk and hope they got paid next week. The energy just dies. That's why politics is rarely leadership, politics is symbolic war. Instead of killing each other, we elect groups to represent the two major tribes or three major tribes, called the

Labour Party tribe and the Liberal Party tribe. They go to a symbolic war together. Nothing much is meant to happen except to prevent bloodshed. And we do that very successfully. But as far as leadership's concerned, forget it. Rare.

Politics isn't about leadership. The politicians price to change their shirts is called, "a poll" or "getting elected". Often it can be a contribution. Remember politics is called "the art of the possible", not the art of the exceptional.

Leadership isn't democratic. Unless it's a democratic leadership. And I have rarely seen one work, ever, because it's ultimately about being nice. To have leadership work you pick someone to make the decisions and then do everything you can to make it work. Good leadership only happens when there's good "follower-ship". And you can only be a good leader by learning how to be an excellent follower. Until you master follower-ship, you can't be a leader, as General George Patton pointed out in an interview when he stated that he was a great leader because he had been a great follower. By the way, Patton, one of America's greatest ever Army Generals, also totally believed in reincarnation. In fact, he believed that in every life he came back as a warrior to fight in great and necessary battles! I wonder if they teach that in Military History at the Pentagon! Ha, ha.

As to the fear of being a dictator, in the usual sense of the word: that kind of dictatorship is distinguished by the fact that the followers are coerced, abused, threatened and punished and have no conscious choice, or control, in whether they are a part of the game or not.

A successful leader may have a dictatorial style, but if you don't like it you can always leave! Teams work when the person with the most experience makes the final decisions and everyone else acts on them, having fully owned their choice to be there. In that they are the leaders in their lives. So everyone participates fully as leaders from the position in the whole structure that they occupy.

Take a football team. Can you imagine a democratic footy team? The captain calls a play and someone objects, so they stop play and have a discussion, followed by a vote. Minutes are kept in triplicate, etc. ...Ha. No way. How about a democratic orchestra?

In going on the team you accept the leader and the ground rules, then go for it to the best of your ability. A football team is actually a powerful model for getting a team to work, as is an orchestra.

Within that, a good and smart leader will also draw from the ideas and experiences of everyone on the team, but in the final analysis it is the leader's decision. "The buck stops here."

Participant: ...I don't let myself have as much enjoyment as I want by not communicating exactly what I want.

Gregory: When I know I want something, but I don't know what it looks like, it's like being in a field where I know that I want to get to a house, and there's a heavy fog, so I can't see where I'm going. I know where I want to go, I just don't know what it looks like. All I can see is the step in front of me and then fog. So I take the step in front of me and then all I can see is the next step in front of me and the fog. So I take that step. And all I can see then is the next step and the fog.

Sometimes the universe tests my intention by only showing me one step at a time, so it's like a treasure hunt. Only the determined find the treasure. The people who say, "Oh, I can't see it. I won't bother," don't get to get the treasure. How it works in that situation is that the universe always lets me know the next step clearly. Even if the next step is, "I don't know what to do, so do something." I might suddenly hit a wall, I don't know what to do, and I know if I keep walking forwards I'm just going to walk into the wall, so I find another way to go to get there.

You can rip yourself off by being in a situation thinking, "Oh, this isn't what I wanted." but you never would have known that if you hadn't been in the situation. You have to do it to know what it is and isn't that you want. There'll be things that you really like, so you do them more, and things you don't like, and so won't repeat but instead will try something else. The next step takes you closer to your vision, your perfection. Have you ever seen people who cook without a recipe?

I don't consciously know anything about cooking. So I go down to Chinatown, buy a whole bunch of spices, buy a chicken, buy this and that, buy a paw paw, buy a mango and just get all these different foods that I've never seen put together, and then I come up with a concoction. If I just threw it all in, stuck it in the oven, it would probably come out tasting like shit. So the trick is to take a step at a time. So I put the chicken in, and then I think, "Okay, I'll make a sauce." So I sit there with nine different ingredients and put a bit of this, a bit of that and if it's something I've never tasted before I have a sniff and a taste and add a bit of this and that till it tastes great.

I don't even know what the result is going to be but I know that by taking the steps the results will eventually be fantastic. Or they'll be awful, in which case I get to start again, and hopefully I've learnt what doesn't work!

Participant: ...One thing in that that doesn't make sense is that I don't know what the result is going to be. And I say that you know because to make a meal with a chicken ...

Gregory: Yeah. That's true too. And I don't know what the result's going to be in the sense that I haven't got a clue what it's going to taste like.

The value of taking one step at a time without seeing the goal for me is also that sometimes I get where I actually want to be and then take another step beyond that and see that I've already been where I want to be.

That means also enjoying the trip. The steps are important. I see the results in my life from taking the steps.

And of course the completion's important. The truth is, everything happens step by step. Sometimes the steps are a lot bigger and sometimes people can take three steps at a time; that's their stepping pace. But you have to take the steps. A fast runner takes a mile of steps in four minutes where someone else takes an hour. Yeah?

Participant: ...I believe that I've got the potential to be an amazing leader, and I never do it because I live with this stupid illusion that I can do it anyway. I just sit back and not be a leader.

Gregory: I just want to interrupt. It's not a stupid illusion. It's true, you can be a leader, you just don't. It's like the difference between, "Don't listen to what they say, watch what they do." What you say is, you can be a leader - and you can. It's absolutely true, but what you choose is to not be a leader ...yet.

If you want to be a leader, how you do it is become a follower first. Master following.

That's what it takes. What's the difference between someone who's worked up through the ranks to become a manager, and someone who comes in as a manager from a university?

Participant: ...Experience.

Participant: ...They know everyone's job.

Participant: ...Made mistakes.

Participant: ...Authority. Because he knows all the levels.

Participant: ...She's earned her merit.

Gregory: He or she has earned it. Yes. Which also means that he or she can coach you in how to be an excellent follower. The person who comes in as an academic manager doesn't know how to make your job better, and doesn't know how to support you in having your job better. They literally don't own the situation.

Did you know that in the McDonald's corporation, of the top 1600 executives world wide, there are about 20 with degrees. They value experience much, much more.

Ultimately leadership is about embracing everything in the situation. I got to be an instructor of the seminar by being on the support team and absolutely mastering cleaning toilets; cleaning them as an instructor would. Then I got to master coffee cups. I got to master every job on the team and then mastered being Support Team Leader, then Assistant to the Instructor, then I became Instructor and from that place knew everything there was that anyone on the seminar had to know or do.

Participant: ...Where I bullshit myself as a follower is that in the past I've agreed to be a follower and then I've been a covert leader.

Gregory: And resented the leader, because you weren't where you wanted to be and knew you could be. It's called sabotage. And topping from the bottom.

The next step is, "In order to keep my illusion going that I really should be the leader, I'm going to mess the leader up to make sure that he or she doesn't look too good because that will show me up as better even more."

Participant: ...Sometimes I don't want to lead or follow. I get a job where I supervise six people and then I get really pissed off with that so I quit and I go and get a job as a house maid in a hotel. I just go from one extreme to the other and I don't fully surrender to either one. I don't know how to surrender.

Gregory: The truth is that every follower is a leader and every leader is a follower. By choosing to be a follower, you are being the leader in your life. You're saying, "I am going to lead myself into following." By choosing to be a leader, you have to follow something, whether it's your ideas, your intention, the plan or the vision. So in seminars that I lead I'm also a follower. I follow the seminar, and where the people are at to ensure they get full value. So the whole issue of service is creating something bigger than you to serve, so that you're serving your Higher Self and therefore growing towards it.

It never stops because whatever level you're at, there's always something bigger to serve, and master.

My version of that is moving from serving seminars to serving the world. Obviously I'm serving the world through seminars, but now I'm doing that in practical projects like Feast For Famine and Ethiopia Aid Tonight (EAT) as well as through writing, media and so on.

When we serve a vision or project bigger than us we grow into being more and more our Higher Selves, our Bigness. If we don't then we serve staying in our "lower self," or our smallness.

Participant: ...How?

Gregory: Remember the conversation yesterday about what possesses you? If something possesses you, you're serving it. If your anger is running you, you serve your anger. That's what I call your lower self, the small version of your capacity.

Get a Vision that you enjoy to possess you, and then serve your Vision. Then you serve your Higher Self.

***

You have all already mastered surrender. But you surrender to your own shit, to your fear, to your anger, to your sadness, to your resistance, to your smallness. He surrenders to three virgins. He surrenders to peace and quiet, or the fear of conflict. Many surrender to money, or security, or superannuation, or status.

You're already in surrender to stuff you don't like, so you might as well learn to surrender to something you really enjoy. You don't have a choice about being in surrender, you have to surrender to something. A lot of you surrender to your fear of surrender. It owns you. You totally give into it, and so you grow it. Whatever you surrender to and serve grows. If you serve something that you value, then you grow value in your life. If you serve something that you're afraid of, you grow fear in your life. You don't have a choice about that.

You don't have a choice about surrendering and serving, you have a choice about what you surrender to and serve. I've made my choice. Given that I teach that we have unlimited choices, the paradox for me is that as I move through life, I have less choices. By that I mean there are many things I could choose, but why would I? Once you let go of smallness, why would you ever choose it again. It is called Choiceless Choice.

Participant: ...You're clear about what you want.

Gregory: Well, it's like getting on a roller coaster; you don't have a choice once it starts, except "jump out".

Participant: ...Something you've been working up to for so long that there's no choice. Is that what you mean?

Gregory: It's not that I've invested so much in it that I'm staying stuck with it, like doctors often are with medicine, avoiding new alternate developments. It's because I want it.

Participant: ...So you're open to change.

Gregory: Absolutely. In order to create my visions I am always looking for better techniques, developments, mentors, approaches, ideas, technology, whatever.

The more I do what I want to do, the more what I want to do owns me. I become my Purpose. So in that sense I don't have a choice; all the other choices are less interesting or appealing for me.

When you surrender to your fear, you don't have a choice, you run away. When you surrender to your Vision - your Ideal - of yourself, all there is to do is to move towards it and create it.

The choice not to is always available. You've got a choice to put your service into, and surrender to, shit, or beauty and value. When you really understand that, that's the only choice in Life that really matters because then everything flows from that. Why would you choose to fill your life with shit? Many do!

This applies everywhere. For example, some people pooh-pooh name brands like Rolex and Mercedes, and deride those who buy them as "buying the name". What they miss is how that product got to BE a name!

It happened because the makers made a commitment to excellence and then surrendered to, served, that vision. The result, apart from excellent products, was that they contributed value, brilliance, quality and beauty to the world, for those who appreciate that.

After I became an instructor I was learning to create my own structures and my own game and my own business and when it felt difficult what used to come up for me was, "Well if it fails I'll go back to nursing." Then I suddenly stopped and listened to that voice and I said, "Who am I kidding? Me? Me go back to nursing? Now? No way." Then I knew that I didn't have that as a choice because I wasn't willing to choose it. If I'm not willing to go that way, then I'm going to go another way.

Participant: ...I felt very good last night that in my relationship with my wife we were making milestones in simply letting each other be ourselves here on the seminar, but then started to feel that she was enjoying herself more than I was.

Gregory: Nothing's completed until it is. For a long time you two as a married couple have handled stuff a certain way, and that included monogamy. Monogamy often occurs as a way to avoid feeling what you started feeling last night.

Monogamy is often the path of least resistance. "If I can nail her feet to the floor and if she can nail my feet to the floor, then we know that we're never going to have to deal with the feelings that come up when she or he goes with someone else." The source of monogamy is that it's often a way to avoid pain and to avoid a whole lot of feelings like rejection, and, "I'm not good enough," and, "Will she come back?" and a million other unknowns. You have taken huge leaps in that, but that doesn't mean that it's complete for you yet, and in the future, those old feelings may still surface occasionally.

Then you will be there with them and feel them and decide what to do with them. You affirm your right and hers to live your own lives - and be in relationship together. The old marriage game is that if she's having a good time without you, you must feel like shit, so she should feel like shit with you. After all, the game is to do everything together and share everything. So you both lose. At least if you're feeling like shit and she's having a good time, one of you is winning! The perfect solution is to acknowledge what's going on and then move on, and you can have a good time too, which is what you did. Perfect.

Pain occurs when you resist or block your own truth.

Participant: ...Yeah.

Gregory: That's the thing about choice-less choice. It's a paradox. I have total choice and I have no choice, because I can choose anything, I can do anything with my life. So I think, "What do I really want to do?" The minute that I know what I really want to do, there's nothing else to do except what I really want, so I don't have any other choice.

You hurt yourself when you don't acknowledge what you want. I'll use you as an example. You know that your path is to be involved in these seminars and be an extraordinarily, powerful woman on this planet. You know that already and you've known it for a long while.

Participant: ...Yes.

Gregory: Given that you're 20, that's pretty amazing, but then you get scared about that because it's such a big vision, and you forget that you know all that in order to deal with the rest of your current shit.

Participant: ...Yep.

Gregory: The payoff for you is that you get to deal with the rest of your crap. In that sense one of your burdens is "the burden of knowledge". Knowledge carries responsibility. And people who have knowledge have a choice about whether they accept the responsibility that goes with it or run away from it. Every time you're in a situation where you know that you can contribute something to someone and you avoid it, you are abandoning the responsibility of knowledge.

Say you have a power saw in your house, there is a responsibility attached to that. If you leave it sitting on a bench, upside down with the guard locked back and there's kids in the house, you are highly irresponsible.

In the same way if you know something and you back off from it, you are abandoning your responsibility to knowledge and ultimately to yourself. What happens is that the universe will stop giving you knowledge because you don't use it and so abuse it.

If you want more knowledge, then use what you've got as much as you can. See, it's the same with you too. Your version is that you have said, "Give me knowledge about how I can change this." And I've given it to you. I represent the universe at this moment. So I have said, "Here." I've got that knowledge and my responsibility to that knowledge is to share it with you.

So I fulfill my responsibility and I share it. I say, "Here is the knowledge you asked for."

I have given her a gem in the form of knowledge. So I hand the gem to her. Now if she doesn't use it and then she comes back to me and says, "I want another gem." I'll say, "No way. You threw the other one away." The universe does that with you too. But if you keep it and treasure it, don't just look after it but treasure it, that's how you become aware that you're a living human treasure, and until you show that you appreciate what you've got, you don't get past that.

It operates on every level. I grew up with a then middle class Australian attitude to quality. "Buy cheap. Save money. Put it into buying a house." I didn't value simple stuff like clothes. I didn't value quality. Clothes were only what I put on my body to cover myself, or stay warm. As I learnt to value them, I started to buy quality clothes that I valued. Then I moved to Double Bay which is a centre for quality clothing, among other things.

Now I'm surrounded by clothes of quality because I value them and I wear quality clothes. I am giving me quality, because I'm a quality person. I started seeing it with clothes, then with everything. What is that great old saying? "The quality is remembered long after the price is forgotten."

One of the things that people hold back is trust.

It's like getting on a roller coaster. Roller coasters scare the hell out of me, but I regularly ride them. The only thing that gets me on a roller coaster, given that for me getting on a roller coaster is like putting my head in a lion's mouth, is being absolutely clear about the question, "Am I choosing to die?"

"No." I'm not kidding. That's the only thing that gets me on it. Then I think, "Well I might be, and I can trust my choices."

So I get onto a roller coaster willing to trust myself, and maybe die.

Participant: ...Yeah. That's what I'm learning how to do. After the last Sex Seminar, I acknowledged that I totally trusted you. At that point I totally trusted myself.

And going overseas I taught myself a lot more, and the issue isn't whether I trust you or not.

Gregory: Exactly. That's why I'm saying all that. It's a wonderful place for you to be when you can say, "Gregory, I totally trust you," but that's not the end point. Because when you get to say, "Gregory, I totally trust me." That's when you are centered. That's the completion.

Whatever job you do, imagine walking up to your boss and saying, "I totally own my choice to be here and have you as my boss. I am here to make life excellent for you and me. Anything I can do to help you be a wonderful boss and have it work for you, let me know. Also, if I think you're screwing up or hurting yourself, I'm going to tell you because my commitment is to have it work for you too."

Trusting and surrendering isn't about becoming a mindless "Moonie" or "yes" person. That's not trust and surrender. That's called "becoming a mindless Moonie yes person". That's non-participation, it's capitulation. That's why people are so afraid of it - it is an extreme version of what they are already doing it in their lives!

Participant: ...I don't know what capitulation means.

Gregory: "I give up. You look after me, you do it. Tell me how high to jump. Tell me what to wear." It's like Hare Krishnas, "Tell me when I can have sex." See, that's capitulation. That's fine, they're getting value, they need to do it, but I don't see it as an ideal. That's a structured way to give your power away.

Participant: ...Not willing to own my choice.

Gregory: The fear of trust and surrender is that to surrender is to lose power. But if I make a choice and surrender to my choice, that's when I am truly powerful. A simple example, I had a guy do the seminar through the year, a big young angry man. There was one point where I was handling him at the front of the room and I got that he could kill me. I mean really, actually lose control and kill me. He was so possessed by his rage in that moment.

The support team were at the back of the seminar room and gasped in fear because they saw it too. He wasn't noisy about it, that was the problem, he was just in deep, unconscious, homicidal rage. What went through my head was, "He can kill me." Then, "No he can't, I'm not choosing to die here, so he can't kill me." So I walked straight up to him, put my arms around his neck and shoulders, looked him in the eyes and said, "I love you and it's okay if you're that angry."

If I hadn't, he just might have killed me, or he would have damn well tried. If I hadn't done that, I would have been killing my most basic human response to another person. And by letting me kill that off in so-called "self protection", he would have attacked me. It was like everything in my body said, "Stay away." Everything I'd ever learnt said, "Stay away," except what my heart said which was, "This guy is terrified. His only way of protecting himself is that degree of rage." The minute I walked up to him it just disappeared, just melted away.

He was also reflecting the mad murderous part of me, and I can kill it off - therefore being even more murderous - or embrace and heal it. I did with him what I would want done for me. It's a great example of, "Do unto others as you would have them do unto you."

You trusting me is not going to fully empower you. That's empowering but it's not where power comes from. If you create a situation in your life with an angry dude like that, and you're thinking, "I trust Gregory," it ain't going to help much. Ah, but you know, when you trust yourself ...

Participant: ...With the trust thing, I've had times of hope and self-trust and I've totally trusted myself, but I lose it sometimes, and that's when I don't know what to do. While I was overseas by myself not being able to ask anyone, "What can I do? Help me." I had to do it myself. And so I built my self-trust even more. And I'm still building.

Gregory: You and I are both clear that your version of going for your Higher Self is called becoming a life teacher, and it's also true for some others here. For those of you who are clear that that's not your path, don't beat yourself up, don't go into, "Becoming an instructor is the best way to do it." That's bullshit. All I do as an instructor is share what I've mastered. You can do that anywhere, in anything.

Do what you want, and if you want to be a Master, then master what you're doing. Do what you want and master it. That's why Japan nominates people as Living National Treasures. Some of those living national treasures arrange flowers. They are nationally acknowledged for their contribution to the quality of life and their contribution to art and people and tradition by arranging flowers. There's a possibility that Japan could create a living national treasure with a street sweeper. Do you see that?

It's not what you do, it's the quality you do it with. It's your commitment to excellence in it and the degree of mastery you go for, and it doesn't matter what you do. People become world famous chefs because they are totally committed to doing it perfectly. Other people just cook. My dad taught me that from childhood. He'd say, "I don't care what you do when you grow up. Just do what you love and be the best you can be." That is what he did in his life. He walked his talk.

One of the people I talk about a lot in my life is a waiter named Vladimir! I meet a lot of rich, powerful, and influential people and their impact on me is like a butterfly wing. Vladimir is a waiter in my favorite local restaurant. He makes an impact. He makes a difference in people's lives. He makes a huge contribution into my life, being a waiter. "Waiter" is just the story, the role. That's not where it lives. It lives in Who he is, and his level of mastery of what he does. So he has a big impact on people.

Day 8

" ...until you can honestly say no to someone, you can never honestly say yes."

ESCAPE - FEAR - LIVING LIES - EVIDENCE - BEING REAL - SAYING NO - RISK - DETERMINATION - COURAGE - EMBARRASSMENT - SELF IMAGE - FORGIVENESS - CONSEQUENCES - AGREEMENTS - ACKNOWLEDGING MISTAKES - TRUTH - COURAGE TO STATE IT - OUR GREATEST GIFT

Participant: ...Are we just rebellious by nature? Like kids, don't they just rebel?

Gregory: No they don't. Most of them never ever hear about learning. They don't rebel against learning. They rebel against not learning.

Kids rebel in their school because what they're really saying is, "You're not going to tell me how to be. You're not going to push junk down my throat that doesn't even work for you." It's like Luke saying, "It's my life, Dad." Kids aren't taught to learn. Kids are not educated at school, they're conformed at school. They are told how to be good, acceptable little citizens, told what the mold looks like and forced into it. They're being told to, "Get in your boxes. Shut up and die." They're being taught how to be robots, just like you and I were. Of course they rebel, just like you and I did. If they are honored for who they are and allowed to become themselves as they grow up they would have no need to rebel!

Participant: ...They're encouraged to be the same.

Gregory: That's right. They give kids at school stars for not shining. Think about that!

They learn that life is back to front. They are rewarded for doing nothing new or different or individual, for being nice, passing academic tests of often questionable value, and fitting in.

Participant: ...One teacher got across to me the value of her knowledge.

Gregory: Wow, one whole teacher! I had two or three teachers who were actually teachers.

***

Participant: ...I just realized that having one foot in and one foot out is what I've been doing in the past in my relationships. As soon as I get into a commitment or a relationship, the first thing I'd do is act like it was a room and go to the door and make sure the key is there so I can open it and escape, step out of it anytime. I feel like that in my relationship with the seminars and with you as well. So I would like to give you the key back if you want it.

Gregory: I didn't know I'd ever not had it!

(everyone laughs)

When you get honest about what you want, then you can make commitments about it.

Remember I told you about the Italian girl? I told you about her coming to the party and yelling out across the room, "God I've missed your cock!"

She was amazing, and when we got together we quickly realized that we didn't want a "normal" relationship. We really enjoyed each other's company, and we had fantastic sex together. I had a breakthrough when I said to her, "At this point I don't want to create a serious relationship with you, but I really want to spend time with you and have sex with you." And she said, "Fantastic."

We used to ring each other up when we wanted to hang out and bonk. That was the relationship.

Sometimes it wasn't for two months and I'd ring up and ask, "What are you doing this afternoon or tonight?" And she'd say, "Nothing. Come over." The commitment was very clear about what it really was. We weren't trying to pretend that it was something that it wasn't. That also allowed that she went to live in another city and after a year she can come back and in the middle of a party and say, "God I've missed your cock." Instead of, "Gee, it's nice to see you again."

One more thing about that degree of honesty and aliveness is that it often looks outrageous. 1,000 other women in that situation would have walked in and said, "Gee, it's nice to see you again," and thought, "Gee I've missed his cock!" She spoke the unspeakable, all the time. She was outrageous.

She was a general nurse doing three months in Psych to get experience. Patients would come and say, "Do you think I'm alright?" and she'd say, "No, you're as crazy as a loon. Why do you think you're in a Psych hospital?" And they'd say, "Oh right, of course." She would constantly speak the 'unspeakable' truth. Amazing woman.

***

Participant: ...I'm getting clearer about what my resistance and fears are about surrender and service and commitment.

Gregory: You have a huge vision. You are a powerful woman and you put all your power into all that shit you were into yesterday.

You start moving towards the vision then your fear arises and sometimes you surrender into and through your fear and move closer to your vision. What often happens is that your fear appears and you run back to that other known, safe place because you know it, but pretend that you're still going that way.

Participant: ...That's right.

Gregory: Your mind says, "Oh I'm still going for it," but the truth is you've given up on it. That's another way we bullshit ourselves.

Participant: ...That's the lie that I've been living in.

Gregory: That's one of them. I'm not going to let you get away with just one!

Participant: ...Ha, ha. No. Part of all that is seeing how much I lie and seeing the lies I live in. I've avoided the unpleasantness by thinking I'm going for it. Now I've just let myself stay with the unpleasantness, instead of trying to run away from it, or jump into something else. I'm letting myself feel where I really am.

Gregory: Right. It's like there's a picture that you have that says, "I've got to go back for a while." I say no. Keep moving forward and take your shit with you.

What you do is, you acknowledge that you've got a few bags of crap and start taking them with you. And on the journey you start emptying the bags along the way. My experience of that was a time when, a couple of years ago, I was absolutely broke. Totally in debt, and a thousand dollars worth of bills to pay immediately, and I had a seminar to give. What was there to do according to my vision, was to take all that with me. You can use your baggage to stop you going where you're going, or you can go where you're going and take your baggage with you until you learn how to drop it.

So I gave a seminar telling people, "You can create it all. You can have your vision. You can have it all work, etc..." And right then my life was in the middle of a nightmare, and I acknowledged that and said, "And it doesn't feel like it sometimes. Right now I'm creating major screw-ups with money and I'm owning my choice in that as a learning experience. I will master this experience and move on." Everyone on that seminar got it. You get it?

I could have thought, "If I go and give a seminar with all this crap going on, then I'm a hypocrite. So I won't do it. I'll wait until I get my money sorted out, then I'll give the seminar. Or, I'll go into the seminar and pretend everything is honky dory."

Either way is bullshit. Integrity is to keep going and take it with you until you learn how to drop it, and being honest at each stage of the journey.

Participant: ...So be where you are now?

Gregory: That's it. Once I was in a seminar and right near the end of the seminar on Sunday night we were sitting in a circle and this female participant turned around and said, "I think that you're setting yourself up as a Guru and manipulating us." I just freaked out. Here we were, everyone was feeling blissful and wonderful and it was all great and suddenly WHAM.

I just went blah, blah, blah saying something and then we had a dinner break. I looked at what she had said and saw where it was true. There's always some truth in everything that is said, at least for the speaker.

What I did was simply walk into the middle of the dinner break and say, "Down forks. I need to acknowledge something. Here is where my manipulation lives. This is what I did and didn't see that I was doing." And I acknowledged that and turned around to this woman and said, "I really thank you for pointing that out to me and serving me and having the courage to do that." They just all burst into applause and she gave me a big hug.

See, I can use evidence to prove that I don't have a right, or it's too risky, or I should wait, or I should hold back, or I should learn more. Or I can step forward absolutely knowing that I'm going to do the best I can and I'll screw up sometimes. When I screw up, in order to maintain my vision and integrity, I will acknowledge it. Then learn from it and move on towards my vision again.

Participant: ...I'm clear that I'm not willing to give up on me, you, and anyone else in the world, and that I'll stick with it even if the whole thing falls to pieces. I also have much fear that I will give up on me and everybody else, and it sometimes feels like I might. I'm also prepared to feel both of those things in me and not worry about going either way, because they're both really true.

Gregory: Right. So, if you say, "I'm not going to give up," or, "I shouldn't give up," out of judgement that it's wrong to give up then it doesn't work.

So give yourself total permission to give up. And then see if you really want to.

Participant: ...I don't want to give up. And just acknowledging that there's a big fear that I will one day.

Gregory: Yeah. So give up sometimes. Say, "Tomorrow I'm going to give up for the day," and by the end of the day you'll be bored and you'll think, I'm really glad I don't want to give up. Giving up is an invitation for boredom and despair. So do it every now and then as a process so you remember how boring it is!

***

Participant: ...I see that everyone here is my instructor.

Gregory: Yes, and the trick is to see what they're instructing! Some people teach me how I don't want to live my life. So they are my loving instructors in how not to do it, whether they know it or not.

Participant: ...Before I basically said to you all, "I want you to like me and if you don't you can piss off." I mean that, but I want to say that I'm still going to keep reaching out and I might be creating you all as assholes so that you all piss off, but it's okay because I want you to be that so that I can keep on reaching out. And until you or I realize that it's O.K. or I suppose until I get that it's O.K. for me to want your love and to still have me being an asshole to you.

Gregory: That sounds like you're absolutely lost in your head. Some clear feedback from me is this: I don't want assholes loving me and I don't want them in my life. If you want to play the asshole game, hang out with assholes. If you say to me, "I'm an asshole and you're an asshole so I'll reach out to you," that is you shitting on me. I guarantee with absolute certainty that I will shut the door on you, if that's where you are coming from.

I gave up being crapped on years ago. I don't enjoy it. I don't like it and there's many more fun things for me to do in my life. So if you want to keep experiencing me personally as an asshole in your life, that is your problem. You get to be surrounded by assholes and I have enormous sadness for you. Having assholes around you means you are surrounded by a lot of stink.

Secondly, if you don't like yourself, I don't see any way that you're going to create others to like you. You said you're going to keep everyone an asshole and reach out to them because you don't like yourself. You don't like them. That's like saying, "I'm going to feed you shit until you enjoy it." It just doesn't work. That's fine. Keep doing it by all means. You might get sick of it one day.

Participant: ...What I'm trying to say is that if you reject me, then I'll say piss off.

Gregory: So what are you going to do? Are you going to tell me to piss off and then reach out again? I'm not going to be there, am I? You tell me to bugger off mate, I'll agree with you totally. I won't be present for you to reach out again. I am not a head banger like him over there.

(everyone laughs)

When I discover that a wall is hard, I simply stop banging my head on it.

Participant: ...I feel like I have a lot of anger that I've got to express.

Gregory: The starting place is to see how much you reject you and how angry you are with you, and stop hanging it on everyone else, stop wanting them to do what you won't do, stop wanting people to compensate for your refusal to deal with your rejection of yourself and your anger. It doesn't work.

Participant: ...I want to give myself the freedom to sometimes be an asshole. When I say no to someone, I feel like a real bastard.

Gregory: There are two totally different things there. Saying no to someone is simply saying no to someone. What you feel about it or what they feel about it is something else. Being an asshole is a different thing. If you come into my house and crap on the carpet, just get that I'm not going to invite you again. Because I also have rights and choices. I don't choose to have people shit on my carpet. But if you come into my house and I say, "Will you make a cup of tea for me?" and you say, "No," that's fine. Saying no and being an asshole are two totally different games, and sometimes they become entwined.

Participant: ...Sometimes I can tell you to piss off by saying no.

Gregory: Yep. And if you tell me to piss off by saying no, I'll see that you haven't got the guts to tell me to piss off directly. I'm not stupid. Neither is anyone else. What I'm getting at is that it's fine if you want to be an asshole around people sometimes. It's fine. But if you pour water on the side of a hill, don't bitch to me if it runs down the hill. There are no wrong choices, just different consequences.

So if you want to be an asshole, own that and own the consequences of that, which is you're going to be lonely, because people don't want to hang out with assholes. Except other assholes. So you're going to surround yourself with people you can't stand. That's fine, lots of people do it.

Participant: ...I'm not though.

Gregory: Well that's what you're setting up. See, if you want permission to be an asshole to anyone in this room any time, you can do it, once. But don't bleed to me about the fact that they've told you to piss off and never turn up in your life again. They have a right to do that.

That just may be the consequence of your actions, but maybe someone in here devalues themselves enough to have you around treating them like an asshole. Go and find people with no value of themselves and they'll love you because you confirm their lack of value. Treating people like an asshole is another version of, "I don't care," and it's a lie. Fundamentally it's a lie. The truth is you do care, you just don't have the guts to risk finding ways to open up and express it, so you take the chicken way out of acting like a tough strong asshole.

Like when we dealt with her version earlier we saw that she cares so much it nearly tears her heart out, but rather than learn how to care that much safely, she shuts it off and says, "I don't care." You have your version of that. So get clear about what the result is, then test what you're doing in terms of, "Does this get the result I want?"

Participant: ...Sometimes if I say "no" I feel like I'm saying piss off.

Gregory: Then there's a very good chance that you're actually saying piss off.

Sometimes you say, "No," like you mean, "Piss off." Sometimes you say, "I love you" like, "I want to kill you." Sometimes you act like an asshole.

You have a choice whether you dump that in people's lives or take responsibility for it and do it in a way that is not going to have that consequence.

Be creative. Find ways to play being an asshole like it's a game, not like it's real life because when you play it like real life people respond in real life. Create a fantasy game. Where you and someone else or a whole bunch of people sit around being totally abusive as an acknowledged game, and the game is to be vindictive and poisonous and rude. Set a time on it, say 15 minutes and at the end of 15 minutes you all crack up and give each other scores. Then you can enjoy that choice.

By the way, until you can honestly say no to someone, you can never honestly say yes.

Participant: ...I find that with my husband when I want to say "no" and I don't, I just feel that I'm wicked.

Gregory: So he keeps doing whatever it is you wanted to say "no" to. You take it out on him by not giving him the opportunity to be real. I'll make up a silly example. Let's say he had body odor and he came up to you and he said, "Have I got b.o.?" And you say, "No," being nice. So he goes off stinking to high heaven, driving people away from him in masses. You got him.

It's irrelevant whether it's a yes or a no. The issue is the truth. The minute you share your truth, you are loving. That is a loving action, love in action, making love. The minute you tell your truth then someone has something real to deal with.

Let's say he says to you, "Let's go for a picnic," and you don't want to go for a picnic but you say, "Yes dear." Then you go and have a miserable picnic together. Did he win by having you agree?

Participant: ...No.

Gregory: No. He had you like a miserable big black cloud darkening the picnic. But if you'd have said, "No, I am not interested," then he might have said, "Oh, okay fine. I won't go." Or, "Yeah fine. I will go." Then he turns around and he asks others, "Who'd like to come for a picnic?" The neighbor hears him and says, "I'd love to picnic." And the friend down the road hears it and he goes and has a picnic with people who want to have a picnic. And they have a ball. Meanwhile you're doing what you want to do. You have a ball. At the end of the day you've both had a ball. Then you get together and share what a great day you each had.

You may wait another three years before he says, "Hey, we're not very honest in our relationship. Let's do something. We've sat here wasting three years in bullshit." What is it going to take? When do you start? Either you start, or you don't. Either is fine. Just don't lie to yourself about that.

By the way, until you start, you're saying "no" to your own honesty. And the bottom line is, you might start telling the truth and he freaks out and leaves. So what, really? The choice is, you then get to have yourself as an honest integral person in your life, which means that you then create some more honest integral people to hang out with.

You will never know until you take the risk. If he leaves, what you've done is saved yourself forty years of bullshit. In one instant. Then he goes to create another relationship with someone who bullshits him. That's the possibility. That's always the risk. He might love it and want to keep doing that.

My mother did the seminar when she was 59. My father was bouncing off the walls. He was terrified that she'd change. He was really anxious that she'd leave. Finally she just said, "Listen, you're a pain in the butt about this. You've been angry and nasty and unpleasant and rude and you can keep doing that but I'm doing the darn seminar. You tell me now, are you going to act like a human being or are you going to keep this crap up? Because if you're keeping it up, I'm moving out until after the seminar."

That's courage in action. My mother is one of the most courageous human beings on this planet. Really. She did the seminar and he was fine with it but then she would start talking about the seminar and he'd freak out and panic. And that went on for a couple of years. Every step of the way, he got more real. And she just wouldn't back off. And she'd confront him on it. She'd say, "Look, do you want me to sit and lie to you? Is that what you want? Do you want me to treat you like an idiot and just tell you lies? Or do you want to hear what's true for me?" And she kept turning it back to him to choose. He finally came and did the Turning Fear Into Power seminar with me, which was a HUGE growth step for him. You get it?

She is ruthless in her commitment to her own honesty, and she goes through terror sometimes about it. Really goes through enormous fear about it. It is hard for her to do it but she does anyway. That is courage.

Participant: ...Well I've already started but I haven't got to that stage.

Participant: ...Yeah. I feel the terror.

Gregory: Yeah. One thing about responding to other people - put yourself in their shoes. Do you get a payoff out of growing more honest with yourself? Do you want people to be honest with you?

Participant: ...Obviously.

Gregory: Right. Are you and he human beings?

Participant: ...Yes.

Gregory: Is there a reasonable chance he will love it given half a chance?

Participant: ...Yep. I can see that he'd really like it.

Gregory: Exactly. My father is a transformed man. Out of Mum and I both doing the seminar, my father has shifted more in the last few years than all the rest in my life. He loves it and he resists the hell out of it at times.

My father's a Cancer and he's a really full-on Cancer. Home is everything. He's very attached to home. He was born at Parramatta, a suburb of Sydney, and he grew up in Parramatta. He's been there for the last 20 years. Mum had always had a vision of living overlooking the ocean in Manly Beach since she was a kid living in the countryside, and she'd given up on it because she thought he would never agree. She did the seminar, she scripted that vision, she went back home and she said, "I'm moving."

(everyone laughs)

Gregory: I mean, this is serious! Then she added, "And you can come with me if you want to." And he freaked. He freaked. She simply confronted his greatest nightmare. And it took them two years to move. To find the place they wanted and sell their place and so on. And in the process, he pulled every trick in the book. I mean every trick in the book to delay it, to slow it down, out of his terror. At one point she rang me up and she said, "I've had it. I can't stand it." I said, "Then leave him," and she crapped. She said, "You're telling me, your own mother, to leave your father?" "Yeah," I said, "you're miserable. So bugger off. Have a fresh start. I totally support you in that." It just freaked her out. So then we went through all her issues.

And what she got to was, that if it came to the crunch, being with him was more important to her than the new house by the beach. She connected with how much she loved him, and how important the relationship was to her, and that that really was her priority. I said, "Now tell him." So she did. She sat with Dad and she said, "I got absolutely clear you don't want to move. You've been resisting it. You've been fighting it. You've been arguing about it. You've been moody about it. And I've been hassling you to move. And what I'm clear about is that our relationship comes first to me. I love you more than I love moving to a new house. If you tell me that absolutely in the deepest deep of your heart you don't want to move, I'll drop it. And I'll live here and make it work for me." He burst into tears and said, "We'll go." They were in a new home overlooking the ocean within a couple of months. She got to have her childhood dream and of course he loved the new house with the ocean views!

Participant: ...Yeah. I totally trust you and you're the person I most trust and love and value in my life. I see that with you and my next step is to bring that back to me.

Gregory: That's right. You use me as a mirror, as a practicing board and as a testing board. That's what you all do here in seminars. That's my job. It's my game.

Participant: ...You do that job really well.

Participant: ...I remember in my seminar you said one of your fears in becoming an instructor was that people would put you on a pedestal and turn you into a guru.

Gregory: That's correct, and I've learnt how to stop you turning me into a guru. I am not going to be anyone's Guru. (Gregory blows a raspberry) Boring job. Be clear that I mean the "I have all of the answers you need" type of b.s. guru. In fact the word just means Teacher. In Asia when a school class starts, all the kids say, "Good morning guru" to their teacher. So I get I am a teacher-type guru, that's ok.

As well, a friend with a great sense of humor, and word play, told me I am a guru because all I do in life is say to people: Gee, You are You! Get it? G, U-R-U. I like that one! Ha, ha. I'm a G,URU type guru! Ha!

Participant: ...I want to give you a hug. (She gives Gregory a hug)

Gregory: Thank you. We see the difference between ourselves and others and then resist them or avoid them or fear them. The truth is, everyone of us is different from everyone else. We are all different, and we're all the same. I look for the sameness in everyone: that which I share with everyone, then find a connection with that. Then everyone becomes safe for me. That guy at the front of the room who was a potential killer, he and I are very different. We have very different lives, but I can connect with the part of me that has felt like he has. I've handled it differently, but I can connect with the sameness. The minute I connect with the sameness I create safety, and recognition. Then I can act. There are always similarities.

You're a brilliant artist. I'm an amateur artist. But I can draw, so there's a sameness. I get pleasure from it so there's a sameness. You can always find sameness. I talk to people, so do you. I say wise things to people. So do you. I support people. So do you. I screw up. So do you.

Participant: ...Do you get embarrassed?

Gregory: Oh sometimes, terribly. Strange things embarrass me.

Participant: ...What embarrasses you Gregory?

Participant: ...Go on. Tell us,

Gregory: Admitting that I get embarrassed! How embarrassing. Sure I get embarrassed. I often get embarrassed when I am acknowledged for something.

Participant: ...Is that because you feel you're not worthy of it or what?

Gregory: Oh no. Secret delight. Embarrassment isn't about devaluing yourself, it's someone seeing something that you like which has been a secret pleasure. SPRUNG!!

Participant: ...When I acknowledged you for your depth of understanding the other day, I saw you get embarrassed.

Gregory: Yeah, sure. I quite like being embarrassed, it connects me with the innocent boy in me. It heals me.

Participant: ...About your embarrassment, was it the story you told about a bonking incident.

Gregory: Oh no. She's going to remember it all. OH GOD. What's it worth to keep quiet? Shh, shh.

(everyone laughs)

Participant: ...Oh I remember.

Gregory: What was it? Okay I can own it.

Participant: ...Wasn't it about the cow.

(everyone laughs)

Participant: ...You fucked a cow?

Gregory: No, I didn't fuck a cow. No, someone else I met fucked a cow.

Oh I remember what she's referring to. When I used to nurse many of us would take a perverse delight in bonking at work a lot. It was a game that really took something to get organized. I got caught a few times. One time I got caught and we were bonking on the ward trolley. It was about eight o'clock at night.

Fortunately it was one of the rare times that I was using missionary position because there wasn't a lot else you could safely do on the trolley, especially as we were both almost fully dressed. The night Charge Sister walked in and opened the door. She was really stern. She said, "What's going on here?" I said, "I'm teaching this nurse mouth to mouth resuscitation. I'll be with you in a minute." She was so shocked she said, "Oh good," then left, and locked the door.

(everyone laughs)

Gregory: Two nurses bonking in the medicine clinic and it was an alcoholic ward. All the "alkies" were really cool about it. I'd say, "We're going into the clinic to count the drugs now," and they'd all say, "Oh good," and laugh.

Another time I worked with this very kinky Seventh Day Adventist nurse who was really into wrestling, a delightful and very very masochistic girl. She really loved being tied up and being spanked. We were really hot for each other so I organized to get an overtime on the night shift, then sent the other two nurses up to count all the inventory. We got right into it and we were wrestling in the living room of the ward!

This is embarrassing. We were bonking our brains out and I looked up and one of the patients was standing there, a guy. He was a really cool guy. And he just smiled, saluted me, and went back to bed.

(everyone laughs)

Gregory: When we finished and got it all together, I went in to see him, "What is it Joe?" He said, "I just wanted an Aspirin but I didn't want to disturb you."

Anyone got a funny sex story?

Participant: ...I once did it on an ant nest.

Gregory: Oh you didn't. With ants?

Participant: ...No. I was teaching Tai Chi and there was a woman in the class I got to know, and we went out after class one time and decided that we were going to bonk. The only place we knew of was out at a reservoir where she knew there were trees for cover. It was just great.

Full moon, the whole bit. When I woke up next morning, I said, "What have I caught?" I did all my classes that day and I got home and this woman called and she said, "What's your butt like?" and I said, "It's bloody sore," She said, "So is mine." So we met that night and compared back sides. I was so sore I couldn't sit down for two days.

Participant: ...I think I did it at the same venue with a friend of mine!

Participant: ...Can you tell me what the patients you nursed were like, what sort of people are they?

Gregory: It varies from people who are feeling depressed through to people who are waiting for the Martians to come and take them, totally out of it. Gone. No-one's home. At another end of it are people who are just literally vegetables, human shaped vegetables.

Participant: ...Can you tell a story about someone who stopped being crazy?

Gregory: Yes. I had a guy who was about forty who came and did the seminar. He'd been in psychiatric treatment on and off for twenty years and on medication daily for twenty years. He was diagnosed as a chronic schizophrenic. He spent all of the first day like a zombie, even dribbling sometimes. By day two I'd had enough and I said, "Aren't you sick of this mad act?" Then I just really went for him, for who and what I was seeing, including the simple fact that he had brought himself to, and paid for, the seminar.

As I acknowledged him, a smile began to come over his face and it lit up, and his eyes came down and he said, "You bastard." He just dropped it, sat back, wiped his mouth and that was it. He scripted that he'd get a relationship and a job and live in the country. He'd always wanted to work on the railroads. He reckoned it would be really healthy for him because he'd get outside a lot and it wasn't demanding.

It would give him plenty of time to think and paint. He loved painting and he was a really thoughtful man. He wrote his movie script and on the day after the seminar went and visited his psychiatrist, shook his hand, thanked him for being his friend for twenty years, gave him his tablets back and said good-bye. Within six months he'd done it all. Moved out to the country, got a job on the railway, created his relationship, started painting and got his house.

A lot of people withdraw into the game of madness as a way to say, "Stay the hell away. Leave me alone. I want to get on with my truth." That's part of the payoff for some.

Participant: ...I just wanted to share a funny fuck I had in Melbourne. I was just about to have an orgasm and a bee stung me on my bum. And it was really like VOOM. Really added to it and I just kept going.

Gregory: Tipped you over the edge.

Participant: ...Yeah, I just put my hand up, pulled the sting out and just kept going. It was great.

Participant: ...Gregory, I'm interested to know if the seminar is going the way you want it to go.

Gregory: I don't have a pre-set picture of where the seminar is going, I respond to where it's going.

I do have a picture of the end result, that it will be incredible, valuable, powerful, transforming, amazing and wonderful, healing, freeing and fun for all of us. And I don't know how we will get there. I come into the seminar with a whole grab bag of possible processes, subjects, things, directions, and my whole life experience, knowledge and abilities, and then see where it goes. I don't have an attachment to where it goes or how it gets there, just a commitment to the outcome. Like life really.

Participant: ...I would like people to tell me how they really see me physically. I have issues about it.

Participant: ...I like your smile.

Participant: ...Great eyes. I love your bum.

Gregory: All you've got to do now is learn how to walk around with your bum forward and exposed.

Participant: ...Put bums all over me!

Gregory: Or have a photo of your bum on your chest.

Participants: (various) ...I like your general shape ....I like your arms and your legs. They're kind of really strong. And they've got definition ...You've got beautiful balls ...And you've got nice teeth as well ...You remind me of statues or pictures of Greek Gods.

Participant: ...(everyone) Yeah. Greek Gods.

Participant: ...Me? Fuck!

Gregory: Let that one in. Okay. Put your gear on again.

Participant: ...Thank you. Do I have to?

Gregory: No. No. It's just not a bad idea if you're chopping vegies for lunch.

(everyone laughs)

Gregory: Sausages for lunch folks. Ha, ha.

***

Gregory: People make mistakes. So if the minute someone breaks a cup, you cut them out of your life, it's not going to take long before you're alone.

But if you give them the opportunity to compensate that, to take responsibility for their breaking the cup and replace it, and their response is "no" then they're saying, "I'm going to keep smashing your environment." If you don't want that, that's when you say, "Finish." Why would you want someone in your life doing that?

If they say, "Wow. Hey, I'm really sorry," or if they just turn around and say, "I'd like to replace that," and they come back with a cup to replace it, fine.

If they come back with a dinner set or they come back with a cup and a rose, then you both know where you stand and you know what their intention is with you: they are serious about making good and showing their apology in real terms. If they don't come back with that, why would you keep them around?

Participant: ...I keep forgiving a lot of people, giving them another chance.

Gregory: That's fine. When I went to work in a medical ward, I had quite a reputation in the hospital as a maverick, and I was. I'd made a lot of enemies as a result of that. I went into work in the medical ward and the Senior Charge was a great guy named Johnny Tribe. He took me into the office and he said, "Okay. Here's my deal. In my ward the first time you screw up I'll tell you and teach you. The second time I'll kick your butt. The third time you're gone. Do you agree with that?" I said, "John, you'll never have to tell me a second time. That's my commitment. You tell me once, I'll get it."

I worked with him, and he was a beautiful man and a really obsessional man in the sense that he broached no screwing around from anyone because it was a medical ward. It was, "Either do it or leave. We've got lives on the line here." So he took it very seriously and if you did too, then you had a ball with him.

He was an outrageous man. We used to do things like have a hectic period for four or five hours, then he'd hook the garden hose up and run around spraying everyone in the ward with it, just playing. And the third time anyone stuffed something up he would walk up to the main office and get them out of the ward. That was it. No questions.

He asked for me to remain in the ward and I ended up staying there for 18 months, and I ended up very good friends with him. I really loved him, and I was absolutely clear that if I did mess something up three times I was out too. He didn't take his shirt off for friendship.

Participant: ...What I realized from that process was how much crap I carry around about my body, and I would say, "I don't like my dick," and at the same time I'd say, "I like my dick." Two sides. Identifying I don't like it and I also like it. It serves me very well.

Gregory: The point of integration is, "There are some things I like about my dick and some things I don't." Or, "Sometimes I like my dick and sometimes I don't." It doesn't have to be either/or.

Participant: ...I actually really like my body and still criticize it.

Gregory: Oh sure. That's the game.

Participant: ...What game is it?

Gregory: That's one of the things I expected to come up in the girl talk process. "Oh, but I don't have this and I don't have that."

"My tits are too big."

"Oh, mine are too small." There's a whole trip that goes on about it. You like your body, great. Give yourself permission to love it unconditionally, and enjoy it.

For much of my life I didn't like my body, because I don't look like a movie star. I didn't like my body by comparison with others. The truth now is, I really enjoy my body. I'm a hedonist. I love my sensuality, I love my sexuality. I love food. I love being massaged. I love my body. And yet I didn't like it.

Then I thought, "Yeah, I could do this and that and get all muscled up etc..." but my commitment wasn't there to do that. So I'm really clear that I don't have my own ideal body, but I love my body, therefore I can sit and criticize it or just love it. And I've got my own ideal dick. I've absolutely got my own total, perfect, ideal, dick. And I love it. You can criticize it, or you can enjoy it, or just have it be as it is.

Participant: ...The other night when I was with one of the men, he said, "I like your blubber." I took that as an insult, even though he was saying that he liked that there was something to hold on to on me, I went into, "Oh, I'm not skinny," and started criticizing myself.

Gregory: Very diplomatic. Yes?

Participant: ...I heard that someone did a survey many years ago on how men prefer women's bodies. Assuming that they weren't perfect, would they prefer a bit more weight or a bit less? And the vast majority of men said extra weight.

Gregory: Sure. The other thing about bodies is that it's very cultural. Very cultural.

If a large white woman like you walked down a street in any part of Arabia, you would be mobbed.

Participant: ...By Greek men.

Gregory: Yes. By Greeks and Arabs, and Indians. A lot of cultures love big women.

Most of you they'd take one glance at you and think, "Oh, scrawny chickens." They wouldn't be interested or turned on. I saw this when I first went to Bali. I was really overweight at 220 pounds, and I had a beard down to here and I had hair half way down my back, and I'd walk down the main street ...the whole hippy trip, you know? Leather head band ...

(everyone laughs))

But really, I was fat and big and solid and hairy. I'd walk down the main street of Denpasar in Bali and stop traffic. The thing is that I'm a Greek God in Asia. Why? Asian men don't have body hair, Asian men are thin, and in Asia, being fat says you've got plenty of food. That means you're wealthy. Same with a long fingernail! So does having white skin. It means you are not a laborer out in the sunshine.

What turns people on culturally is often survival stuff. A man's driving around in a Maserati, what's it say? He's got lots of money. The equivalent in Asia is a man's walking around with a paunch, he's got lots of money. He's wealthy. That's a turn on. Lots of hair, turn on. It's survival or it's contrast.

That's why many Western men go bananas over Asian women. Many Western women go bananas over black men, or at least the fantasy of them. It's that contrast thing. Mind you it might also be the search for the BDP - the Biggest Dick Possible!

At the time it was just amazing for me because at that point I had an appalling body image and suddenly I'm walking down the main street of this city and I'm not kidding, cars were stopping in the middle of the road and people were getting out and women shoppers just stopping to look at me.

Oh, the other thing is that I've got quite a prominent nose and God knows where this came from but Asian women believe that men's noses indicate the size of their dicks.

Participant: ...You proved the theory wrong,

(everyone laughs)

Gregory: Quite right, my nose is just not that big.

(everyone laughs)

***

Participant: ...I'm really aware that I have to really monitor all my actions. If I be spontaneous, I take a risk.

Gregory: My experience is that you've come from monitoring all your actions. You get committed to doing it right so that no-one will see how messed up you are, so you take your shirt off whenever someone says that's right.

I really like that. Isn't it wonderful, the language we create? I say, "Take your shirt off," and everyone knows what I mean. I can just see you folk going home saying to someone, "Oh, you'd take your shirt off for a quick bonk," and they'll say, "Um, yeah, I usually do."

(everyone laughs)

Sure we monitor it. We've all got monitors, ideally checking out options in terms of what you want.

You'll screw up sometimes, or you'll do something then see what was missing that you didn't want, or what it was about it that you didn't want, like, "I thought I wanted that and now I see it doesn't work."

But monitoring it for you is heavy censorship. Do you see the distinction?

One of the most powerful things you or anyone can ever do is to acknowledge, "I've screwed up. What can I do about that?" If you attach a huge drama to that fact then that supports you in not dealing with the fact that you screwed up, and in doing something about it.

It's highly arrogant to assume anything about anyone. Have you heard this, "To assume makes an ass out of you and me?"

Participants: ...No.

Gregory: Assume is literally ASS-U-ME. You just proved it. When you assume something you make an ASS out of YOU and ME.

I've said it a lot today and I'll say it again. What is required is that you ask. If you want results, ask. Get all the information you need in order to act, so that you're not pissing up a wall.

There's no rule that says you have to make a commitment. Also, you can put time limitations on commitments. You can say, "For the next three weeks, I will do such and such, then I'll check it out."

Participant: ...So you're open to negotiation. If you say, "For the next three weeks I'll do this," then one and a half weeks goes by and you've changed your mind, you negotiate the other half of it?

Gregory: Let's say you made a commitment with me for the next month, and after two weeks you come up to me and say, "Gregory, I'd like to renegotiate the commitment," also acknowledge, "I'm absolutely willing to keep it, and at the same time I'd like to look at renegotiating it. Are you up for that?"

Then I either say, "No. I require that the agreement continues." In which case you complete the commitment. Or I say, "Yes, I'm willing to have a look at what you want to negotiate." And you say, "Well there's five changes I'd like." I say, "That one works for me. That also works for me. That doesn't. Let me think about that. I'll tell you within 24 hours and that's fine." I might say, "Okay, you can have all those five but I'm going to require something to replace them. You don't have to do those five, but instead I require that these be done."

If you really want those give me these, it's up to you. It's not about being nice or fair, it's that I've got to win and you've got to win. If you don't want to do what that takes with the changes, then stay with your original commitment, and understand how important it is to you to do so.

Requesting to renegotiating your commitment isn't breaking it if you acknowledge, "I'm willing to fulfill the commitment."

If you say, "I'm breaking my commitment, I won't keep it, and I want to renegotiate," what's the point? You've just told me you're going to break commitments, so why waste my time renegotiating a new commitment with you? You might come back in 24 hours and break that one too. You lose your credibility and my trust.

Participant: ...I get confused if I've got a commitment with someone and they break it, they don't turn up or whatever. What's my end of that? Of creating that? That's what I don't understand. When I create other people to not do things that I've made commitments to with them.

Gregory: Your end of that is that you continue to waste your time with people who mess you around. You let yourself get messed around, until you don't.

There's a catch in what you're saying: if someone breaks a commitment with you then yes, it's true that you've also broken the commitment, but there is a difference. Yes, you created that, but you didn't do it. Do you get that?

Participant: ...This is what I'm trying to understand.

Gregory: That's the thing about action and responsibility for action. I take responsibility for the fact that I create killers in my life and my society.

Participant: ...But you didn't do it.

Gregory: I own the killer in me. I own the fact that I and every human is theoretically able to kill. I am capable of doing that, but I didn't do it and don't intend to. It's a real important distinction.

Participant: ...So if someone breaks a commitment with me, after I've felt the anger and I've done all that stuff, I should start to take it back to myself and look around to see where I'm breaking my commitments.

Gregory: Very valuable.

Participant: ...I don't always do that. But I'm doing it more and more and sometimes it takes a while after it happens for me to see where I'm not committed, but why do I create these situations? Is it because I'm not committed in things?

Gregory: Yes, let me give you another example. I'll see if I can make this really simple.

If someone is breaking commitments around me, my creation is to have people around me breaking commitments. But I didn't break a commitment.

If someone breaks a commitment with you, you didn't break it, you created someone to break it. You get it?

So it's not quite true to say you broke the commitment. What you did was allow someone in your life who breaks commitments. If you drop my cup and break it, I didn't break the cup. That was not my action. My action was to have someone in my life who breaks the cup.

It's an important distinction. So what I have to look at is what I break in my life, and more importantly how I keep creating people to break things in my life. Do you see the difference?

Participant: ...I don't know what to do. A girlfriend of mine, I've given her so many chances.

Gregory: To do what?

Participant: ...I continue making commitments with her to meet somewhere.

Gregory: So do you get there on time?

Participant: ...Oh yeah.

Gregory: So you continue to keep your commitments. And you continue to let people jerk you around.

Participant: ...Yeah. I got really pissed off with myself because I should have known better.

Gregory: Exactly. You've mastered commitment, she hasn't. What you haven't mastered is putting people in your life who keep commitments. That's your lesson. She hasn't even learnt to keep them. So she can't get to learn your lesson until she's learnt how to keep her own commitments.

When people come and do the seminar with me, I see extraordinary trust and surrender and commitment. I have people walk into a Living

Game or some other seminar who've never met me in their life, who know little about me. Their friends have said, "Look, it's a great seminar. The guy is very cool. Do it." So they walk in, sit on their bums and if I say, "Jump," they say, "How high?" Why do they? Because they are that committed to value.

The level of trust and surrender is extraordinary. That's the thing about commitments: if you make them then keep them. Then you and others trust you. Just surrender to your commitment.

Don't listen to what they say. Watch what they do. Don't buy the bullshit that's delivered in the space between the actions and the words.

One of the distinctions between commitments and agreements is that my commitment here is to do the very best I can with love and integrity. That's my bottom line commitment. I make up the agreements and change them to get that result. Agreements often work differently, often you don't have a say about agreements except that you either buy it or you don't.

If you want to play tennis, the agreements, the rules, have been set for years, you either take it or leave it. That's your choice, there's no room for negotiation. You don't wear football boots on a tennis court, no-one wants to negotiate that.

Invariably an individual or a group has been given the choice to determine the agreement. In football they changed the tackle rule after 100 years, then there's a new agreement and if you want to play football you play by the new rule.

As the creator of this game or the creator of the context of this seminar game, I set the agreements, and I can change the agreement, as I already have, when I see a better way.

Participant: ...With commitments, there's the little everyday commitments like having a date or meeting someone at the movies, and then there are overall commitments to career, etc.

Gregory: Contextual commitments.

Participant: ...Yeah. And what I feel with my partner at work is that she works very hard and we work long hours but there's no overall commitment to get the job done. I do the same thing sometimes. It's,

"I'm hungry, I'm tired, something is upsetting me." I can see that I do that too and I feel really ripped off that I can't be stronger about trying to stop the game. I'm impotent with what to do about it, because I don't want to lose the relationship.

Gregory: You take your shirt off for the work relationship and let that run you. It's another form of marriage, like any relationship. "If I tell the truth, she might leave. I can't tell the truth, I've got no power, I'm impotent." Yes you're right, and when you're willing to have her leave, then you will be with your truth and she gets to make an honest choice and you are back in potency. Until you're willing to be with your truth, you support her in not being honest, and vice versa by the way.

Once one of you is willing to tell the truth, the other one has to start being honest about it, and that's when you look for the difference between their actions and their words. If you say, "I want an absolute commitment to work and this is what it looks like for me. You don't ring your boyfriend through the day. You don't do this. You don't do that. We sit down and we start a job, we go for it until it's finished." It's always important to describe what you mean by commitment to the job, to what it looks like.

If she says, "Got it. I'll go for it," and two days later she's on the phone to the boyfriend there's a difference between what she says and what she does. So then you say, "Hey, hang up. Talk to me now. You said that you were going to do this work and you're not doing it."

Participant: ...Whenever I say, "you said" to her, she freaks out.

Gregory: Ah ha. Why does she do that? Have you asked her why she freaks out?

Participant: ...No.

Gregory: That's the next question, the next step. You stay something, she freaks out.

Where do you give up? Do you take it to the end or do you give up? The next step is, "I see you freaking out. What is that about? Freaking out isn't going to resolve this, it's just telling me that you don't want to hear me." A great way to get someone to stop saying, "Hey you said...," is to freak out. It stops her being accountable to you, so she stays irresponsible and keeps breaking her commitments.

Eventually you learn that if you say, "You said...," she'll freak out and won't deal with it and it's not worth it, what's the point? Decide if you are willing to have that shit go on? Ultimately it's irrelevant why she does it. The fact is she does it and it doesn't work for you. It's her job to get clear whether she's going to keep doing it or stop it. That's not your job, anymore than it's mine. She must choose between work and drama.

Your job is to be honest and clear. It's her job to define her commitment and her bullshit and deal with freaking out. Either she does it or she doesn't. If she does it, great. If she doesn't, cut her off. Or acknowledge that you're not willing to do that, and your commitment is to do anything to placate her to keep her around including putting up with her bullshit, dramas and really, her control trips.

Stop bitching about it. "Yeah. She throws pies on the walls and spills my coffee and craps on me and spends half the day with her boyfriend, but it's worth it because I want her around." You get the difference?

Participant: ...It feels like it's tied into not allowing myself to be great, not truly letting my sun shine.

Gregory: Own your reflection. What she does shows you what you don't like about what you do so you can stop it. Then it's up to her whether she stops it.

***

Gregory: It's a little bit like what I used to do with money. I used to say, "I want a million dollars, I need a million dollars. When I've got it I'll be alright."

I let go of ever having a million dollars, ever. In other words I resigned from the million dollars. In order to force me to find it in here, in me. I said to myself, "Okay mate, what if you never get a million dollars? What are you going to do then?" That's a really powerful statement. Whatever you think you need out there, just say to yourself, "What are you going to do if you never get it? Are you going to live your life like this?"

Once you do that you start looking for another way of creating it all without the million dollars. That's very powerful.

What's missing is owning choices. For instance support teams on the seminar. Who hasn't been on support? I thoroughly recommend it, it's quite extraordinary. It keeps getting more extraordinary.

I loved being on support teams. Okay. Just to fill everyone in. The seminar Support Team agreement includes that you commit to be there fully and give 100% in support of the seminar. And to get back more than you give. Also, to do whatever is required by the Support Team Leader and in turn the Instructor. Literally from the moment you go on support team you don't have any new choices, until the seminar ends. You totally put yourself in service to your Team Leader.

That's in recognition of the fact that the Team Leader knows a hell of a lot more about what is required and how it's done than you do. So you also put yourself in a position of learning, you're fully acknowledging that you don't know, here's someone who does, so teach me.

The Support Team Leader says, "You wash the cups now, and you do the chairs now." There is a way to wash them and a way to put chairs out. Very specific. There's latitude for creativity within a structure. You're there to do it. In a similar way you do the same thing at work, you just don't do it with the same degree of clarity and consciousness. In other words you go and get a job and someone says, "This is what you do. This is where you sit. This is how you do it," and you do that.

One of the things that sometimes happens for people on support is that they have a lot of anger, resentment and rebellion because they feel like they're being pushed around, or ordered about, or like they don't have a choice about it.

The key is to remember that it's your choice to be there and have that happen. It's your choice to be on support and have someone tell you what to do. Then the value you get, and what you learn, is huge.

As far as work, you rebel against your own choices: you rebel against what you have chosen because you don't own your choice to be there. It feels like you have no choice, and that's when you go into all your shit. You simply don't own your choice. You get into it and then put a lot of energy into fighting being there - which you think is getting out of it. By resigning you are finally out of it. That's very powerful. The only way you see how to own your choice is to make a totally new one called "resign". Then you feel like you're in control again.

Every support team I went on, I said, "It is my choice to be here. I am here working for me to get more value. I get to have that happen best if you to tell me what to do." That's the bit you miss as if you know it all already. Do you get that?

Participant: ...Yep.

Gregory: We are all always working for ourselves. You resist because you're afraid of being a Moonie, afraid of losing control, but then you lose control to your fear. When you own that you want to be in it for yourself the best way to do that is to get the person who can teach you most. Then follow them, learn from them, and if you're not going to follow and learn and grow, don't ask. Why ask?

There's no way I'm going to go to many people and say, "Tell me how to increase the quality of my personal fulfillment." They don't know. Don't ask if you're not going to do it. That's really insulting. If you're going to ask, at least show enough respect to give it a go.

So what is missing is that you've never owned your choice to be there for yourself. Be absolutely there for yourself, if that is what you want. Be very selfish in that.

Resigning is a really powerful choice for you, and whether it's the only way or the best way isn't the point. The point is you really have done something different.

Participant: ...It gives me opportunity to then make a fresh start.

Gregory: Absolutely. I think you are very clear about what it is required.

One of the things I'm really clear about is that it doesn't work for anyone to work with me who's not committed to me and what I'm doing. It's not just a job. Whether it's for a year or twenty, it's still a life choice, a Path. Working with me, being in my life is being on an ongoing seminar.

For you folk this is a seminar. For me this is how I live my life. Running this seminar is one aspect of my "everyday" life.

You're here to be challenged, coached and confronted and I do that with anyone in my life. People don't stay around me if they don't want that, and if they do they hang out in my life a lot. You know better than anyone what is involved in that commitment to work with me and be in my personal life.

Day 9

"For most people, one of the things in the hard basket is, 'How To Make It Easy!' O.K. Here's one of the keys. Just notice how easy it is for you to make life hard. Life is easy."

LOVE AND VALUE SELF - CRAZINESS - TAKING CONTROL - FANATICS - PAYOFF & PRICE - INTEGRITY - CREATE VALUE - REAL PROSTITUTION - SIGNS - UNCONDITIONAL LOVE - HARD & EASY - COMMITTED COMMITMENT NOT KNOWING - REPULSION - BEING STUCK - REQUESTS - RISK AND SACRIFICE

Participant: ...I'm just noticing my fear of my craziness always shows up when I'm unsure.

Gregory: Yes.

Participant: ...And I'm not totally trusting myself.

Gregory: Yep. But that is when you're crazy, you know?

Participant: ...I'm crazy for not trusting and valuing and loving myself?

Gregory: It's not necessary. You feel terrible when you don't trust and value yourself, and you don't have to do that to yourself, so if you do, you're crazy.

Participant: ...Would that be the same as madness. Just losing it and losing your vision?

Gregory: Yes. I'll tell you something. You'll really like this. When people are really crazy, their doctor or their friends suggest to them that they go to psychiatric hospital. Some do. If they're so crazy that they can't see that they're crazy, they go before a magistrate who commits them to psychiatric hospital. The phrase is, they "get committed".

Participant: ...To their craziness?

Gregory: No no. Because they're crazy what they need is to be committed. When you are crazy, when you feel crazy, get committed to something and end your craziness. When you are not committed you are crazy. You may have heard me say before that while you're not committed you're like a yacht on the ocean without a rudder; the winds and the seas blow you all about. The winds and seas are like your thoughts and feelings. Commitment is the rudder, the tool that lets you use wind and sea so that you are purposefully directed to get where you are going. Without the rudder you get blown about, chaotically out of control.

That is what crazy is like: you're endangered, you're directionless, you're purposeless, you are out of control. You have no choice except to stay on the yacht or drown. Jumping off the yacht and drowning is called suicide. Staying on the yacht is called staying alive - surviving - and apart from that you have no other choices without the rudder of commitment in your life.

That's crazy. That's the ultimate state of crazy and powerless. Commitment is the rudder that you need to change all that and give you power, direction and purpose, control over the elements of wind and water. Wind and water symbolize thoughts and feelings. So once you've got a commitment, you are in charge of your thoughts and feelings, the air and water in you. Thus commitment is the rudder to the yacht of life. Oh God.

(everyone laughs)

Participants: ...(everyone) HALLELUJAH!! Ha. ha.

Gregory: Wow man, that's really profound. Ha, ha.

Participant: ...Open up your wallets for the Lord brothers. Ha. ha.

Gregory: I thought you would like that.

Participant: ...Commitment is the rudder for the right wave.

Gregory: Yeah.

(everyone laughs)

Participant: ...Go for that in the book.

Gregory: I'll put that in the book and then in brackets say that you all laughed mockingly! But really, that's what craziness is like. While you haven't got a clear commitment you do all that crazy shit to yourself, and the minute you get clear about your commitment, it ends.

Participant: ...My fear is that if I am committed I'll be crazy.

Gregory: How does that work for you?

Participant: ...I think it's to do with my masks, by letting go of them I fear I'll go crazy, letting go of all that stuff that I've been hanging on to for so long.

Gregory: One of the things that I see with you is your version of, "Nice masks; I'm not really a Scorpio I'm actually a Libra. I'm not really powerful and dangerous." The fear is, "If I stop that I'll be crazy, and if I make a commitment I don't get to be nice anymore."

We've got a lot of negative pictures about being a fanatic. A fanatic is crazy, out of control.

There are people like the fanatics in Iran, the Irish fanatics, the Arab fanatics, we have Jewish fanatics, American fanatics, religious fanatics and who knows what else, and we sit there saying, "Oh. I'm never going to become one of them." What's true is, everyone of them has an absolute commitment.

We fear that being committed means becoming a fanatic, or obsessed, or ruthless.

Participant: ...That's the only way to keep commitments.

Gregory: Ah ha. So with that belief, that making commitments means you become a fanatic, obsessed, ruthless, crazy man why wouldn't you avoid commitments? Now, given that I have had a lot of acknowledgement today for the degree of my commitment do I fit the picture of a fanatic, obsessed, ruthless crazy man?

Participant: ...Ruthless. but not the rest.

Gregory: What else?

Participants: (various) ...Loving ...Beautiful ...Compassionate ...Passionate ...Sexy ...Enthusiastic ...Giving ...Direct ...Selfish ...Patient ...Supportive ...Animal ...Ruthless

Gregory: Yes, all of those, and I am ruthless, because I committed ten years ago to becoming that in my honesty. That was a part of my commitment. Ruthless is an interesting word because we've got heaps of negatives on it.

Participant: ...Dangerous.

Gregory: Yeah. Dangerous. Now, is there any room for dangerous in all that other stuff?

Participants: ...(everyone) No.

Gregory: Ah ha. I am dangerous. You better watch how dangerous I am when all of this becomes public. People are going to say, "He's really dangerous. He wants people to enjoy sex!"

Participant: ...In the same way Mahatma Gandhi was dangerous, Christ was dangerous.

Gregory: They were dangerous. Anyone who lives with commitment is dangerous one way or another, but I'm safely dangerous. I do not endanger your existence, so I am not a danger, but I am dangerous to the existence of your continued limitations and smallness.

Ruthless is all sorts of words that say the same thing and have different baggage attached. How about dedicated?

Participants: (various) ...Uncompromising ...Purposeful ...Direct ... Visionary ...Focused.

Gregory: Yes to all of those. My son came in with a splinter in his foot and I was ruthless in removing it. I didn't sit there saying, "I'll be nice about this." I got the thing out as fast and gently as I could. That's another way ruthless looks. I knew he was going to scream, and he did. But by my being ruthless in that sense of the word, his pain was diminished. I've been ruthless with a whole bunch of you this week.

Participant: ...Out of compassion.

Gregory: You're afraid of becoming committed in case that means becoming a mad fanatic. You only get to be a mad fanatic if that's your commitment, i.e. you are committed to being a mad fanatic. You can as easily be committed to being a blob for the rest of your life. A totally ineffectual blob. That's also committed.

The question is, what do you want to do? Fanatics of all stripes are very committed and extraordinarily limited in their vision of what's possible. They think that you can make a world at peace by fighting people. They think they can win by killing all those who disagree. To me that's a completely limited version of humanity. The same goes for all the fanatics in Iraq and Israel and America. Some people still think that you get good results by killing other people.

So commit to your value and vision so everyone wins, so that the choices of others are respected, not excluded, as fanatics do. Not keeping your commitment means that you're back in your old commitment of valuelessness and blindness. It comes down to one or the other. This one or that one?

Is your commitment going to be to become a valuable visionary man or woman or to close your eyes and be un-valuable, blind and doing nothing? You don't have any other choices that I see. When you slip into, "I'm no good. I don't know where to go." Just think, "That's my old game and that's not my commitment. My commitment is this..." And get back on track. When you've done that a few times, you'll learn how to stay on track. When you're not doing that you feel crazy and out of control and overwhelmed by fear. That is either no commitment or a commitment to no-thing.

Anyone like to share?

Participant: ...I practiced commitment in being still today and I was really committed to standing still and my body tested me like hell and my ankles were itching and I just said, "Thank you for sharing body. I'm not moving."

Gregory: Very good. How do you feel about that?

Participant: ...Great. I just feel strong.

Gregory: Yeah. In control more? More powerful? More disciplined? More sure?

Participant: ...Yeah.

Gregory: Very good. Whatever part of your life you take control of unstintingly is handled. That's how you experience your integrity; by staying with whatever you choose to do, you have the experience that your body can't change your choices. Circumstances can't change your choices. For me that's key to becoming a spiritual warrior and a Master.

Participant: ...I've moved through a thousand things since yesterday. I haven't thought or pre-planned but just let come out what comes out. In making the decision yesterday to resign, I saw that I have a choice, saw my commitment to myself, that I would give everything up to have me in my life, plus the authority in that for me.

What I also got to see was that doing what I did was a pattern that I have, the pattern of getting to a certain point and then saying, "Right. Quit." This time I've done it in a way so that I can see what it is that I quit from.

I had to get to where I was yesterday to see that I'm committed to myself no matter what you think of me. No matter what judgements you have about me. I know that some people weren't able to see what that choice was about for me. Some people withdrew from me and judged me. Then over the last twelve hours I've had a lot of people come up to me and reach out and say, "Hey. I really get you." They acknowledge me, and my contribution to them.

They were people that I had supported in being here, and I started to see that in the past I didn't think I could contribute or be valuable, and so I separated myself and tried desperately to contribute from the outside, not really being a part of it. Then I thought, if you don't see what I've got to give, well screw you.

I really had to push it that far and let go of it all to know that you did totally support me in having and being my choice, and that you're willing to let me go in order for me to have that. That's opened up a new level of choice for me, and I have totally owned my commitment to myself out of this.

I have put myself through an extraordinary amount of pain. I'm not doing that anymore. I didn't know how to let go. I'll make mistakes. And I'll mess up, but I'll learn from that.

Gregory: Is that it?

Participant: ...And I really want to acknowledge everyone for giving me that space ...I just want to acknowledge to the group it's support, and tolerance of me.

Gregory: Thank you. Anyone else?

Participant: ...I just want to acknowledge to the group it's support, and tolerance of me.

Gregory: What underlies all of those acknowledgements? What's your bottom-line belief about you? They're like the branches. You've got from the leaves back to the branches. What's the underlying trunk of all those beliefs?

You know when you were talking over breakfast this morning about how your father used to beat the dog and you burst into tears? Your father used to beat you as well. Correct? Add two plus two. What's the conclusion you came up with as a child? Your father beat the dog. Your father beat you. Two plus two means you came to the conclusion that...(pause)...Anyone want to tell her. Go.

Participant: ...She's not valuable ...She's a dog.

Gregory: She's a dog. You got that dogs get beaten. You got beaten, therefore you're a dog. All your beliefs stem from, "I don't want people to find out I'm not human. I'm a dog who walks on it's rear paws."

See - the degree of sadness you have talking about the dog being beaten - it wasn't just about the dog being beaten, it was about you being beaten. You let yourself feel it about the dog. You cry for the dog being beaten but you don't cry for yourself being beaten like a dog.

As a kid, you saw that dogs get beaten so you concluded, "I must be a dog because I get beaten." That's how a kid's mind works. You blocked that out. So what I suggest you do is write a letter to your dog. Seriously. Write a letter to your dog and tell it what you saw happening. Tell it how you felt about it. Tell it about your rage about it and your helplessness to stop it happening. Start with what you were telling us and write a full letter until you've got nothing left to say to the dog. Got it?

Participant: ...Yeah.

Gregory: Great. When you've finished the letter, rewrite it word for word except address it to yourself. Write it to you. Post it that way. Do it and if you want to bring it to me and we'll have a look and see whether there's anything missing or incomplete for you.

All the games we develop work while they do. We get the payoff we want and sometimes we pay a high price. And the major payoff is that we survive. The next step is to start growing stronger. I have the experience with the seminars I do that you and other people, “Hide your flame under a bushel.”

Most people have small life flames and they're hidden under bushels. The seminar teaches you how to take the cover off and turn the flame up, safely. You've literally got more fuel. More power. As that happens, you start to see what you've done that either isn't necessary, doesn't work or has too high a price, and because you've got more fuel and more power, you also have more ability to create new games or new ways of being and doing things that have a higher payoff and a lower price.

The more you do this, the more you can. The games you played have worked to a degree, and you're growing out of them. So you get to this point.

One of the things I want to say about your work in advertising is that advertising is like anything else. It can contribute crap or it can contribute value. Most advertising contributes crap, in my judgement. In the same way, most pop music contributes crap. In amongst that crap are some exceptional artists to remind and inspire us.

It's exactly the same with advertising. If you don't want to be in advertising that's fine and simple. But you do want to be in there and you don't think that you can be valuable in it. The issue is, what degree of value are you willing to claim, commit to and go for?

Remember I said I have a picture that Japan could create a National Living Treasure who was a masterful street sweeper, in the same way, you can be a life instructor through advertising, or you can support the status quo and mediocrity.

It comes down to this: the choice in advertising is that you either address people's Higher Selves or you address their lower selves; their Best version and aspirations or their worst motivations and fears.

As you well know the point of advertising is to sell products and ideas and the way to do that is to create a vacuum or a need, then people move into it. Yes? Do you know that?

Participant: ...What do you expect with a breakfast cereal ad I'm working on.

(everyone laughs)

Gregory: It's a really good example of advertising having nothing to do with the product.

Look past the product. A game to play is to cross out the product name and cut out the photo and read what's left. What you read is people's beliefs about people, and you read experiences. It's your choice how you do that and what you change them to. Let me give you an example. McDonald's knew that if they wanted to be successful they had to appeal to families, because ordinary restaurants didn't cater for families. They either catered to teenagers to get together and grab a hamburger, or to people who didn't take children out for meals. You're not very popular if you turn up with four kids at an upmarket restaurant.

They realized there was a huge market that needed to be filled, and they were correct.

Then they proceeded to fill the market. Their advertising was totally aimed at families. Now, they could have approached that from, "If you don't take your kids you're a mean parent. Good parents take their children to McDonald's." That's one way but that would have been the cop out, the safe fear-based negative advertising route. They didn't do that, they said, "Here is an opportunity for families to share a fantastic experience together." Do you see the difference?

Watch a McDonald's ad, what do you see?

Participant: ..."Good time at McDonald's."

Gregory: Who's having a good time?

Participant: ...Families.

Gregory: The families. Now, take away the brand name and every Mcdonald's ad is a visual reinforcement of the belief that families can have a good time together. Is that healing or not?

You better believe it. You get it? See, McDonald's don't sell hamburgers, they sell the idea that families can have a good time together, and because of that they sell billions of hamburgers.

Now, the fact that they've sold billions of hamburgers is a pretty major statement of how much families want to have a good time together. It's not a statement of quality, but it says more about families wanting to have a good time together than about families wanting to eat hamburgers.

A seminar is a space that's created for you to come and be safe to explore and heal and grow. McDonald's is a space that's created for families to practice having a good time together. See?

Your first job is to know what you support growing in the world?

Participant: ...Fabulous.

Gregory: See you didn't know that did you, and you've been a major talent in advertising here in Australia for 20 years?

Participant: ...No I didn't.

Gregory: He's in advertising. She's in advertising. That's why I said I'd be great in advertising. In everything in your life you have a choice: are you going to support the crap or are you going to support the gold? If someone walks up to you and says, "I'm having a real problem," it's your choice whether you sit there and say, "Oh, I bet it's terrible." Or say, "Okay. Do you want to resolve it?"

Participant: ...I'm not sure.

Gregory: Okay. That reflects at least your lack of clarity about what integrity means for you. When you get clear about what you are willing and not willing to do in advertising, and what your value is in advertising, you will create a boss who supports it.

Sometimes the value of a painful experience is simply to find out what you don't want.

You kick your toe on a rock. You get clear that you don't want that, so you don't do it again.

Coco Pops are interesting. I like Coco Pops. I don't eat them often but I like them. I forget about Coco Pops because they don't have a high priority in my life. Your job is to remind me about Coco Pops. Correct?

Participant: ...Yes.

Gregory: If I saw an add about Coco Pops that reminded me how tasty they were and how playful they are then I might buy some again. For me, Coco Pops are playful food. They're fun play food.

Participant: ...They want us to tell you that they're not full of sugar, but they are. (STAMPS HER FEET) So it's a lie.

Gregory: That doesn't work.

Participant: ...They're not good for you.

Gregory: Right. And?

Participant: ...They want us to say that they are. Most cereal brands do.

Gregory: They're pretty sweet. So they want you to bullshit the rest of us?

Participant: ...Yeah.

Gregory: That lacks integrity. If you do it that way you lose integrity. You are then back into mindless, "I'm just following orders Mein Fuhrer."

Participant: ...Yeah.

Gregory: Right. The choice you have is: do you keep integrity or not? If the answer is yes, don't do the ad that way. If that means you get fired, you get fired, you lose your job and you keep your integrity. How far you want to go with that is a whole other ball game. One possibility is that you then go on television and talk about the lack of integrity in advertising. If you want to go for a role in the world that's that big, there it is.

Every talk show in Australia would want to hear someone in the advertising industry say that. And guess what? The public already knows it and they want their suspicions confirmed. By doing that, you support people in not swallowing bullshit.

If you want to, that's how you create a public role, and that's why I said I'm dangerous, because if you do that, you're dangerous. All the bullshitters will say, "Oh she shouldn't have done that." I went to the press about abuses that were going on in psychiatry. You better believe that psychiatry considered me dangerous. So did the government, which ran the psychiatric hospitals. It's the same deal. The question is how high do you want to play it?

The first step is, what comes first? Your pay packet or your integrity? If you are being told to do something that doesn't fit your integrity and you take your shirt off for your pay packet, then that's real prostitution.

That is what prostitution means. I've had so-called prostitutes do the seminar who weren't "prostitutes". They were women who sold a service for money out of very free choice and totally loved it. They loved their job. They're not prostitutes. Most prostitutes have nothing to do with sex, they wear ties and power suits and turn up for work in offices. And some of those are women, some are men.

Selling out your principles for a pay packet; that's prostitution, and then you live your life like a dog.

The truth is you're not a dog but you didn't know that when you were a kid. You thought you were just a dog that looked different, you've set up a lot of your life to be a dog's life.

Look at what you go through and put up with at work. That's what I call a dog's life. Going through that crap is called a dog's life. Human beings deserve better than that. So do dogs by the way.

If you resign from that place, your energy and self respect will go through the ceiling. Simply sit down and say some version of, "The way you want me to do this ad lacks integrity for me, it's not true and I'm not selling my integrity for a pay packet. Either we do this ad with integrity or I leave."

You then give your boss the opportunity to regain integrity, and you see whether he is willing to or not. If he says, "Wow, I see your point," then you have an opening to create an ad with integrity. If he says, "How dare you?" you'll see that people let you know where they're at by their actions. I keep saying it.

It's no good wondering if he really wants integrity. Find out! If he says, "No we're not doing it. How dare you?" Great. He is demonstrating that he is not willing to have integrity as you define it.

Participant: ...I don't know why he hired us.

Gregory: Well he might have hired you to get his integrity back.

Participant: ...It's the men there that are fucking it up.

Gregory: And the women there, including you two.

Participant: ...Well, no.

Gregory: Well, yes.

Participant: ...They buy into the game and we have to go along.

Gregory: No. No no no. They buy into the game and so do you.

Participant: ...Yeah but they do it first.

Gregory: You still buy the game. What you are saying is a nice justification for your victimhood, to not take responsibility for your choices ...it's the fault of those bad, bad men!

Participant: ...Yeah.

Gregory: Really, notice that you still buy the game and then play victim to the men, like it is their fault and you are of course innocent. Then you get to be powerless and resentful of them since they are "doing it to you". Thus you also get to play poor powerless little victim woman as well. The beaten dog. Boo hoo. All to avoid the fact that you are choosing to sell out on your principles!

Participant: ...In one meeting he said that the whole thing was crap, then after the meeting he said to us, "What you've got to do is simple."

Gregory: Follow orders and deliver crap.

Participant: ...That's right.

Gregory: Look at the difference between that and the ad Joe did for McDonald's. What was it?

Participant: ..."Before it's cooked the meat is grilled."

Gregory: Yes. The copy went on to talk about the incredible quality of the meat and the meat inspection, they literally "grilled" the meat: "Are you good meat? Are you good meat?" The meat was grilled before it was cooked. What was the fish one?

Participant: ..."Real fish, no catches."

Gregory: Yes, great. See, get the difference? Apart from the humor in it, the difference is that it's saying something that is uplifting.

But the point I want to make is, that he created a space to do uplifting ads. You haven't mastered that yet. You blame it on the boss and the system and the sugar and the Coco Pops and on being a victimized powerless female. Boo hoo.

Participant: ...How can we? They say, "Coco Pops sales are going down." Then they go and do market research. Women say, "I don't want to give it to my kids. It's got too much sugar."

Gregory: How did the sugar industry deal with that? They ran an ad squeezing sugar from a sugar cane saying: "Sugar, a natural product." Which is true.

Have new clients. You're giving it away to, "It's the boss. It's the client. It's the public's beliefs. It's this or that or the other." The truth is you haven't learnt how to deliver quality ads that fit your value and integrity. Once you do then it will shift.

Participant: ...But it's the whole industry.

Gregory: Pick any industry and you can talk about lack of integrity. It's not the industry. Sure the industry has it's own peculiarities and idiosyncrasies, but that still misses it. Everywhere in the world, in any area, in any industry, you have a range, a spectrum from absolute garbage through to excellence.

You're not acknowledging that you haven't yet learned or committed to be at the excellent end. That's the truth. Then you find reasons like the boss, the industry, the this, the that. That doesn't change it. As well you keep denying that Joe works in the same industry and creates high quality ads, time and time again. AND wins advertising industry awards almost every year. It's you being a victim to it all.

Participant: ...We have in the past created ads that have integrity and are brilliant. The feedback we've got is that we've got one of the best portfolios in Sydney, and we're only 24!

Gregory: Great. One of the things I went to the papers about with psychiatry was that a doctor ordered shock treatment for a patient and none of the nurses agreed that that patient should have shock treatment. Another doctor was called in who agreed with the original doctor, not from a treatment point of view but to "stick up for the doctors."

Yet another doctor was brought in when the nurses still objected so there were three doctors involved. Another charge nurse and I demanded that an outside consultant be brought in, to end the game, we thought. The outside consultant was finally brought in and he said, "This is outrageous. There is no basis for shock treatment for this patient." He didn't have anything to protect, but they still wouldn't reverse the decision. At that point, the nurses had two choices, they tended their resignations in protest or they backed off and lost integrity.

Participant: ...Were you one of them?

Gregory: Yes. Seven Charge Nurses, some of them who had a twenty year career at stake, who had literally hundreds of thousands of dollars worth of superannuation benefits at stake five years down the line, tended their resignations in protest with a statement that said, if the resignations were accepted, they were then freed from their agreement to not talk to the press.

Public servants have to sign an agreement that says they won't talk to the press. I mean, when I left and finally went to the media, I had the C.I.B. - Criminal Investigations Bureau, like the FBI - ringing me everyday for months "inviting" me to go down to headquarters to be interviewed. I declined, on legal advice. At any time they could have come and arrested me for breaking that agreement. I was also warned by a journalist that my phone had been bugged, as had his, and that warning came from the editor of a major newspaper.

Participant: ...But you'd resigned.

Gregory: Oh, no, I'd left the hospital, I hadn't yet resigned. I broke the agreement. The point is that you get your integrity by putting your butt on the line and being willing to lose what you've been holding on to. It's the same as, "What is your price to take your shirt off, to sell out on yourself?" And the irony of it is that, to the best of my knowledge, at least five of those charge nurses subsequently resigned anyway and all went on to bigger and better things.

Participant: ...Emptied the cup.

Gregory: They emptied the cup, risked losing it all, and once they grew their integrity, they grew bigger than their current job, so they had to do something bigger.

That's why there are so many ulcers, breakdowns, drug and alcohol abuse and heart attacks in the work force. People sell out and pay the price.

Get clear about what you want and keep doing it until you get it. What I've seen people do time and time again is end up like the little guy in the corner of the dead end alley in the cartoon by R. Cobb called "Schizophrenia." Above him is a sign that says, "No loitering." The door's got a sign that says, "No entry" and the alley's got a sign saying, "One way, that way." He believes the signs and he's trapped. All he has to do is get clear about what he really wants to do and walk out and do it. To do that he has to ignore all the signs telling him what he can and can't, must and mustn't do.

Who's ever said, "I'm going to do this," and people say, "Oh you can't do that." They're holding signs up, but it's up to you whether you believe the sign or you say, "I'm not following the sign." It's another version of, "nothing is as it seems," from Karate Kid. It seems like he's screwed and like he can't win, yet he ignores all those signs and goes on to win.

The joke of that cartoon (and I got it years after I first saw it) is that what ever he does he's ignoring one sign. The sign he's ignoring at that moment is, "No loitering." So he might as well ignore the "One Way" sign and leave the alley, or ignore them all. Or he can just get clear about what he wants and go for it, regardless of limiting signs.

What you all do, until you don't, is you say, "Oh, I'd really like that," then you get a message that says you can't have it or someone says, "No," so you stop. Give up. The guy at the Zen Monastery didn't buy the sign. The sign was "Piss off" but he thought, "Well that's an interesting sign but I'm not doing it." He kept doing something else because he was clear he was going to get there and he got there.

Participant: ...I don't understand that he was killing himself to do it.

Gregory: He wasn't. The analogy is that sometimes to get what you want means sacrificing something else that you want less. That was the message for me. He wasn't killing himself. In terms of Zen Buddhism, the story of Buddha's enlightenment was that he was so desperate to get his Self-enlightenment that he sat under a Bodhi tree and said, "I am not going to move until I am enlightened, and if that means I starve to death, then I starve to death." In other words he was willing to risk everything to have himSelf, he was willing to let go of him-self to get his-Self, and he didn't die.

I say that there is no such thing as a real "no". No is a sign, just another sign, and the sign is saying, "Pause and show me that you've earned it." Or, "Pause and show me your worth in this."

Participant: ...How important it is.

Gregory: Or how important it is to you. Exactly. When someone says "no" to me or when it seems like I can't have what I want that gives me a chance to check how much I really want it. Sometimes I get a "no" in the form of an obstruction or, "It seems like I can't have it," or some other sign appears.

I talk about flag posts, or barriers or blocks that come up in the process of creating your script, your vision. They equal signs, like, "You can't have it. No. It's not possible." Or, "I can't do it until they say I can." Stuff like that. That simply then gives me room to think, "Do I really want it?" If the answer is "no" I might leave it at that: "Fine, thank you." If the answer is, "Yes I still want it," then the next question is, "What do I have to do or learn to get past that sign saying No?" The "signs" are your social and family rules and conditioning that you are breaking out of in order to expand and grow.

So it's like, someone comes up to Mike and says, "I want a job in the cleaning industry. Will you give me a job with your company?" His immediate response might be, "No," because he doesn't need someone, or he doesn't have the money to pay them, or he doesn't have the work. If that person says, "Oh I can't have a job," he's giving his power away to Mike in that, and the truth is, he doesn't want it that much. It's not that important.

But if he then says, "Why not?" and Mike says, "Well I don't have enough money to pay you," and he then says, "I won't take wages," or, "Can you pay me enough for food and lodging?" Mike will immediately say, "Wow, this kid is really serious about this." Won't you?

Participant: ...Yes.

Gregory: Then you say, "Okay, but there really isn't any extra work for you." And the kid says, "I'll do some of your work and hang out with you and make life easier for you." By now he's really got Mike's attention.

Participant: ...I got a job that way last year.

Gregory: Wonderful! It's about getting clear about what you want. If you want it enough, you will just keep upping the offer. Life is a continual trading process that we lie about to ourselves. The truth is if you keep giving and giving and don't get something back, you'll stop giving. When you give you want something back. If you don't get it you eventually bugger off. It's a hell of a lot easier if you get clear about what's given.

Participant: ...What about unconditional giving?

Gregory: Unconditional giving exists. People come on seminar support and their choice is that they'll do whatever is required. That fits a picture of unconditional giving, but they get something back: they get the pleasure of support, they do the seminar again, they get a lot of coaching and learning and new experiences through giving unconditionally. Unconditional love doesn't mean you don't get anything back. When you're willing to love or give unconditionally, guess what you get back?

Participant: ...Unconditional love or giving.

Gregory: Of course. We bullshit ourselves by not acknowledging that we want something in return. When you're willing to say up front, "I really want this with or from you, and I'm willing to offer whatever makes that work." You may come up to me and say, "I really want to spend the day at the beach with you. Tell me what you would like to have that work for you." I might say, "Well I'd like you to bring an umbrella and some suntan lotion, give me a one hour massage and bring a lovely lunch. That would really work for me." So you know what you're getting. You're getting to have the day with me which is what you wanted and I'm getting to have what I want to make it work for both of us. If I didn't like you and I went to the beach to get those things, then I'm taking my shirt off.

But if I didn't like you, you're not likely to ask anyway.

It's a paradox. Sometimes I do everything I know to do and I don't get the result I want, so there's several possibilities. The first possibility is that the Universe is telling me I'm bullshitting myself about what I really want. Second possibility is simply that I haven't yet learnt what I have to do to get the result. The third one is that the result isn't as important as I thought it was. It could be any or all of those.

I find out by doing everything I know to get what I want and when I run out of things and haven't got the result, then I see where I am with it. But what we usually do, and what I see you all doing in different ways is risk one thing and then run away, when you've actually got 20 things that you could risk.

That's also how you get to empty the cup. For example, if I said to myself, "I'd love to spend the day with her at the beach. She's good fun, great company, I really enjoy her." Then I walk up and say, "Would you like to spend the day at the beach with me?" and I'm already scared that she'll say no, and that I'll feel rejected. So I'll ask her as if it doesn't really matter to me that much to delude myself, so that if she says no I won't feel too hurt.

I cut off the importance to minimize the pain of rejection: put on my "cool act". I cool my feelings, I cool my desire for this experience. I say, "Do you want to go to the beach today,' and she says, "No." I think, "Phew. I'm glad I didn't put it out strongly because then I'd feel really hurt." It's back to front. Now, what I do through that is keep my current cup full of all my fears and holdbacks. Let's play this out. Will you play this with me? Yes? Okay.

I want you to come to the beach with me next Tuesday.

Participant: ...No.

Gregory: Okay. I really really want you to come to the beach with me Tuesday.

Tuesday's the only day I've got off and I want to spend it with you. What can I do for you to have that work for you. Just tell me whatever it is you need to have it work for you to come to the beach with me on Tuesday and I will do it. I'm jumping right ahead. Get it? Tell me.

Participant: ...Well I've got a commitment to go and help a friend move some stuff into their apartment so if you were willing to come along and help me with that so that we could get that out of the way.

Gregory: Absolutely.

Participant: ...If we can do that in time and there's still time to go to the beach, then I'll definitely go to the beach.

Gregory: Right. So how about if Tuesday morning you and I go there and I bring a gang of people?

Participant: ...Yeah that would work if we get it done.

Gregory: Yes. We can get it done really fast and you'll be there helping. Okay. Is there anything else that you require to have it work for you going to the beach? Anything else you would like in return?

Participant: ...The head boggles.

Gregory: Name your price. I'll do it. I really want you at the beach on Tuesday. Whatever you require.

Participant: ...Well, hire a limo and pick me up.

Gregory: Fine. That's handled.

Participant: ...I feel like really testing this to get you to a point where you get to say, "Ohh, I didn't really want to go to the beach with you that much."

Gregory: Right. But we're playing this game as if I'm absolutely clear about it. This game is a version of, "I'm going to become a Zen Monk."

"Bugger off."

"I'm going to become a Zen Monk."

"Piss off."

Participant: ...Okay. So I want you to hire a limo and come and pick me up and I want to go to a beach of my choice that's really secluded and I want you to organize to bring a picnic.

Gregory: What would you like to eat?

Participant: ...Yeah. I've got it. I'm there.

Gregory: Okay. So tell me some more things you'd like. See she's there. I've got what I want. Now, this is where I go into total indulgence. What else would you like?

Participant: ...What I'd like at the picnic?

Gregory: Lobsters, ham, caviar?

Participant: ...Yeah. Seafood and wine. And bread and dip. And I'd like a mattress.

Gregory: Right. Bring a mattress. Got it. What else would you like? See now instead of her feeling like she's got to get things from me, I'm making other suggestions. Do you feel abundant right now.

Participant: ...Yeah. I feel like royalty!

Gregory: Okay. Would you like music and a massage while we're at the beach?

Participant: ...Sure.

Gregory: So now I'm thinking of all the things I might like that she might like. Now. instead of leaving it there, what kind of music do you like?

Participant: ...Just some really mellow relaxing music.

Gregory: Great. Okay, see you Tuesday morning.

Participant: ...Okay.

Gregory: Now. I've got a few things to handle.

Participant: ...Get your limo booked.

Gregory: I've got to get a limo. I've got to get a gang of people together. Mike will you come and help me move furniture on Tuesday morning and tell me what you would like in return from that from me?

Participant: ...A day off.

Gregory: You got it. Okay, how about you?

Participant: ...Just a hug. Ten minutes.

Gregory: Okay. Would you like one for an hour with a back rub?

Participant: ...Sure!

Gregory: She's into abundance. See, it's going to take about 15 minutes to get all of you along to the apartment on Tuesday morning. Then I ring the caterer and I say, "Friend the caterer, will you get together a picnic basket that's this this this and this and send me a bill?"

Ring the limousine person and say, "Limousine person. Pick us up at such and such a time and bring a mattress." That's how you get what you want. We have a fear that getting what we want means someone misses out or you're being selfish or you're being controlling. Selfish in the bad sense of the word. Did any of that appear? No. Is everyone happy?

Participants: ...(everyone) Yeah.

Gregory: You better believe it. Do I make everyone win?

Participants: ...(everyone) Yeah.

Gregory: Do I have a commitment to action so that others win?

Participants: ...(everyone) Yes.

Gregory: In other words, I create the space for you to win with me. That's important. How you get to create the space for you to win in your life is by making sure that everyone else is winning.

For me it's this simple: I will have anything I truly want and act according to that. If I say, "I truly want that, I will do everything I know to get it 100%." If at that point I don't get it then I know that either I didn't want it or I haven't yet learned how to have it. Either way it's fine because then I do something else, but I'm complete with the experience. It's very Simple.

Now apply that to all of your relationships and how you interact in them.

Participant: ...If you haven't learnt what it takes to get it yet, then for me, instead of resigning at that point, I can go out and learn whatever it takes to get it.

Gregory: Exactly. What happens at that point of emptiness is that I know whether it was my real and deepest choice or whether it's simply that I don't know how to have it. I can't explain that, it's just what happens.

There's a point of knowledge that occurs then, and if you back off before you reach that point, then you don't KNOW, you just think. You produce lots of thoughts, reasons, justifications, excuses and stories, but you don't connect with your knowledge about it.

By going for it 100% I get there. Emptying the cup means I get all the stuff out of the way to get to my knowledge about it. It was always there, I just blocked it or muddied the waters. I get to my knowledge by living at 100%. When I am in confusion, I know it's because I haven't gone 100%. Go for everything 100%, then it gets real simple.

Participant: ...Sometimes I get what I want, then pretend that I've got something else. I'm just relating this back to my relationships.

Gregory: There are many angles, and many things to learn, many ways to look at it.

There are many different ways to look at a tree. You can dig a hole and look up. You can climb up through it, and the tree is the tree is the tree is the tree.

The paradox is, it can seem very complex and it can become very complex but fundamentally it's incredibly simple. It's called love and value yourself. Acknowledge yourself and go for it. The rest falls into place if you're doing that. A lot of the time people use the complexity to avoid doing that because it's safer to stay in confusion and inaction. You stay powerless because at least that feels safe, at least you know that feeling and it is familiar.

Let me just give you an example of another way I've handled it - same principle but another story. When I did Feast For Famine one of the first things I realized was; I don't know how the hell to do this. I don't have many of the many skills that I need to create this project.

So what I would do is pick up the phone and ring a journalist or I'd ring a T.V. producer or I'd ring a bishop or a company director and I would say, "This is what I'm doing and I don't know how to get there. I'm going to do it, do you want to be involved?" One friend put me on to the Marketing Manager at Sanitarium Health Foods because Sanitarium is owned and run by the Seventh Day Adventist Church; they're very committed to social issues. I rang and I said my thing, and the guy said, "Oh great. What you need to do then is put it all on paper in this form." I said, "I don't know what that means. I just don't know what you're talking about." And there was silence for a good half a minute, which is a long time on the phone.

Then he said, "That's fantastic." I said, "What?" He said, "Just that you admitted that you didn't know. I'm really impressed. You could not believe the number of people I talk to who won't admit that they don't know."

This guy, a marketing manager of Sanitarium who is a busy man, spent ages on the phone with me explaining the steps I had to take, why I had to take them, and how they affected everything else. He finished up by saying, "If you have anymore problems, ring me anytime." I was in total confusion, and ignorance, but I knew where I was going. So I simply stayed with, "This is where I'm going and I don't know how to get there. I don't know what you're talking about. I don't know what to do next."

It's very simple because I knew where I was going, I knew what I was going to do but I didn't know how to do it, so I just kept trying everything. Sometimes I'd ring people up and they weren't interested, or I wouldn't get any support or assistance or coaching or anything. So I'd think, "Fine. That's not where it is." Keep doing it. Keep doing it. Keep doing it. Be willing to make mistakes, to not know. And it happened. I got there, with the help of a lot of people, we created the project. I did over 40 interviews, we created a TV ad and had it shown over 60 times on national network TV for free, and so on. It all happened. My son Luke starred in the TV ad and was brilliant!

So here is a mantra I created about mistakes and learning ...

Mistakes are Nature's way ...of letting you know ...what you need to learn ...in order to get where you are going.

Participant: ...What is really standing out for me is to just stay with your commitment. If you really want it, nothing will stop you, if you want it you'll do it.

Gregory: In life we put things in a hard basket or an easy basket. If you want to fast track your life, take on doing the hard things, the challenging things. Go for it, but don't make it hard doing that.

Any choice you don't own is hard. If you don't want to chop wood and someone says you've got to chop the wood, it's going to be a hard job. But if you say, "Gee, I think I'll go and chop some wood," then it's an easy job. You get it?

Have you ever been in a work situation where one person totally loves what they're doing and the other one makes it hell? They're doing the same job! It has nothing to do with what they're doing, it's how they approach what they're doing. Take things out of the hard basket and say, "I'm going to deal with some of the hard things and I'm going to enjoy it, I'm going to get excited with the challenge, I'm going to go for it." Then it's not nearly as hard to deal with the hard things. It might even be real fun!

For most people, one of the things in the hard basket is, "How To Make It Easy"!!! Okay. Here's one of the keys. Just notice how easy it is for you to make life hard. Life is easy. Whatever you commit to is easy; the minute you commit to it 100% it becomes easy. You're committed to having it hard, so that's easy too. Here's the thing: when you experience it being hard, stop and say, "Gee it's easy to have it this hard." That's the breakout realization. When I had very little money and wanted it I would walk around saying, "I'm rich in poverty. I have an abundance of poverty. I have a wealth of poverty." Then I would see how I directed my wealth and richness towards lack, and so I was richly lacking!

Participant: ...Like, I really trust myself not to trust myself.

Gregory: Yes, totally. Totally. I have a journalist friend who constantly breaks agreements. I totally trust that he'll break agreements, and I deal with him accordingly, which means I never ever ever ever set up anything important with him. I know that I'll see him when I see him, and when I do, we have fun. He's totally reliable in his unreliability. In fact, I said to him, "Please don't keep a commitment with me because then I won't be able to trust the fact that you break them."

(everyone laughs)

Gregory: See, some people always keep their commitments with me, I trust that they'll keep their commitments. Their commitment is to keep their commitments. He always breaks his commitments. So his commitment is to break commitments. He's very committed. So I said, "Don't break your commitment to break commitments by keeping them."

It freaked him out I might add. It was very funny. We have lots of discussions about commitments. He sent me a 25 page closely typed thesis on commitments. And I read the first paragraph and threw it away. I just knew what it was going to be.

He rang me up about a week later and he said, "Did you get it?" I said, "Yeah." He asked, "What did you think?" I said, "About what?" He said, "What I wrote." I said, "It was long." He said, "But what did you think?" I said, "It must have taken a lot of time." He said, "What else did you think?" I said, "I didn't think anything else." He said, "DIDN'T YOU READ IT?" I said, "Actually no. I threw it away." He flipped out. What was clear to me in that first paragraph was that he had written an essay to justify his breaking of commitments. Thanks but no thanks.

When I made the commitment to become an instructor of the seminar, I knew that I didn't know what it would take. I had to confront my fear that it might take 20 years, that I may have to be doing that commitment for 20 years. I had to ask myself "Now, is it worth making? Do I still want to make it?"

That's another way to get clear about commitment. Make up the worst version you can imagine of what it might take and then see if you still want it. All the things I was afraid that commitment might involve I visualized to see whether I would still want to do it. "This might take 20 years. Do I still want to do it? Yes. It might be incredibly painful and I might be broke for 20 years. Do you still want to do it? Yes." I went through everything and every time I got a "yes".

Then I made the commitment. It took 20 months, and if I hadn't made the commitment that fully, it would have taken 20 years, except I wouldn't have got there because I didn't have the commitment. People sit around in their lives saying, "I want to stand up. I really want to stand up. I've been wanting to stand up for years. And I've been analyzing it and owning my choices. God, I want to stand up. You can't imagine how important it is to me. (Gregory pretends to cry) I get really excited about standing up. You know? I just get… "(Gregory dramatically cries and moans some more)

Participant: …Get off your butt.

Gregory: "I just feel really silly because …" (he cries more)' You get it?

(everyone laughs)

Gregory: I'd be a great actor. I can cry easily.

Participant: …You are.

Participant: …When I'm in a particular situation, say in a relationship a flash of what I've got to do to complete this relationship or whatever occurs to me and it freaks me out because it looks too hard, so then I just totally block it out and forget that it exists, and go around asking people, "What will I do? What will I do?"

Gregory: The payoff is you stay incomplete and therefore keep your power down, and keep yourself ineffective, so no one can expect anything of you, and yet you appear to be wanting a resolution.

The other thing that I just want to add is that I spent many years doing many things that weren't IT, were not what I was looking for or wanting. There is a Zen koan for enlightenment, which is to say to everything you see, "That is not It." When you run out of things, you get It. Again, it's emptying the cup, in order to fill it.

If I'd known that the end point was called becoming a Seminar Instructor, then I could have said, "this is necessary to get there, all of it is necessary." Every moment of your life is the best choice for you in the entire world. The only other possibility is that it's wasted.

I choose to believe that it's the best choice, that every moment is your best choice and you don't always know where it's leading. You don't always know what the value is.

So, I went and did all these other things, one, to find out what wasn't it, and two, to give me the preparation and foundation that I needed to get here, except I didn't know where it was I was getting to or that I was doing that. My Purpose was to prepare for my Purpose when it arrived! One result of all that is I can't imagine a situation in our society that I can't walk into and relate to.

I have had a Jesuit priest come and do the seminar, and a minister. I haven't been a priest or a minister but I had a religious background, went on retreats and had uncles in religious orders. An agnostic comes in and I can relate to that because I totally rejected my religious background at one point in my life. Someone comes in with an unusual religion, I relate to that because I really got into Buddhism, not to mention psychiatry! Someone comes in who's a prostitute and I worked in Sydney's Red Light District with prostitutes, and I've prostituted myself in the sense that we talked about work earlier. Someone walks in who plays at high influential levels of society - I've done that too. Someone walks in who's a millionaire and I've mixed with them and am becoming one. Someone walks in who's been broke. I've been there.

Someone acknowledged me the other day for having an extraordinarily broad understanding of human beings. What's also there to be acknowledged is that I've had an extraordinarily broad experience of where human beings are and what they do. And if you want it too, go do it too.

Participant: ...What about when someone like my father whom I have a great sense of obligation to, asks me something and I say no and then he starts throwing all this guilt at me and says, "Go to hell," or that I ask him and he says yes but he really means no.

Gregory: The problem with that is that I'm not you and I don't know your father. So in that sense I can't give you a formula.

I can't give you a formula so apply the principles. I can give you the principles and you've got to find out how to apply them. It may be that you simply haven't learnt how to communicate with your father.

So you need more communication skills. It may be that you haven't risked enough with him to reach him. It may be that yours and his best choice is to not communicate.

There are a million possibilities. Let me give you an example. My father did the Turning Fear Into Power seminar two years ago with me running it, and I really wanted him to do The Living Game Seminar too. I really wanted him to do it. I did everything I could to communicate that to him. Then there was nothing else to say about it, so I didn't talk about it for a year. Then I saw that there was one thing I hadn't done to reach him and that was to beg him to do it, so I wrote him a letter and I said, "The truth is, whether you get anything out of it or not, I want you to do it, and I believe you'll get something out of it." That was also one of my truths that I hadn't acknowledged.

In posting the letter to him, I got to complete the whole issue for myself, because it had been the last drop in my cup to empty out. What I saw was, "If he does it that's perfect and if he doesn't it's also perfect, because that will show me that he really isn't meant to do it; it's not his best choice. I don't understand that, but I know it."

If my folks said yes and I knew they meant no, I'd say, "I think you're being polite about this, and I don't think that you really want to. So I will let it go. Thank you." If you feel your father is saying "yes" and meaning "no" and you let him do it, then you're losing integrity with your perceptions.

Participant: ...There's one thing I would like to acknowledge, that I am sometimes repulsive. I really got that it must be something incredible to be living with me and to see me six days out of seven each week.

Gregory: Interesting the word repulsive. It means to repulse, to push away. Most people are repulsive a lot. The opposite of repulsive is attracting, welcoming or embracing or open.

Sometimes I repulse people and things. I just don't have a judgement about it. It's fine with me to repulse things. I'm totally repulsive towards mosquitos.

(everyone laughs)

I am! I repulse them with all my energy. So I am repulsive sometimes. Actually it's not accurate to say, "I am repulsive." What is more accurate is, "I do repulsion." That's my action. The truth is, I am open, including I am open to repulsion.

Participant: ...I have created this enormous tangled web of commitments and communications with people. How do you stop yourself from being swallowed up from not allowing enough time for yourself? It occurred to me that you have to be incredibly creative to keep control of what you're doing so that you do allow yourself time when you need it.

Then I realized, I've become a lot clearer about where I fit in and what my role is. All through my life I've been trying different things and setting myself very high standards; I would like to be good at this and I'd like to be good at that, then at this seminar and at the last seminar I went to last year, I became very much aware of being slightly envious of people who have talents.

Now I'm realizing that where I fit in is to be able to draw those talents together into a network with intention. I guess selfishly what it's doing is bringing all those people into my life to teach me all those very exact things. But I'm really feeling very strongly committed to integrating and networking. You know what I mean?

Gregory: Come back to the start which is you freaking out a bit. You saw me creating an incredibly complex web or network of commitments, and to you it seems that that's going to fill my time and energy, and that it's overwhelming.

I say it's the opposite. The clearer I am about my commitments the more time I have and the more space I have and the easier it becomes because the bullshit disappears. I'll give you an example. When I play this out I want some of you to agree and some to disagree. I want you to put out opposing and differing opinions.

Let's say that I think I want to get to the corner of the room. I think I do but I'm not committed to it. It seems to me like it could be nice. This is a demonstration of how we usually run our life so you have no time, no space, and are entangled.

Okay, so I sit here and I say, "Oh gee folks, I've been thinking about something. I think I want to get over to the corner of the room. What do you reckon I should do?"

Participant: ...No. No.

Gregory: No?

Participant: ...I think it's a good idea. I think it would be great to do that. Which comer do you want to go to?

Participant: ...Are you sure you want to go to that comer?

Gregory: No. I think I want to go to that one but I'm not sure about that one or that one.

Participant: ...Go to that one.

Gregory: Why?

Participant: ...Because that corner's got more light.

Participants: ...No, no, no, no, no .

Participant: ...I think you've got much more of view.

Participant: ...Why don't you stay where you are?

Gregory: I'm not sure. That's a good point. Why not stay here? I mean, this is okay but I thought it might be better over there. Why's it better over there?

Participant: ...It's just nicer energy over there.

Participant: ...I saw somebody do it once and they went to that comer and it was great for them

Gregory: Was it? Oh great.

Participant: ...If you'd love all the light to shine on you and behind you, you'd be able to see.

Participant: ...Yeah. You're better off under the light.

Gregory: Yeah. I thought that corner.

Participant: ...So why do you have to go?

Gregory: Well I'm not sure. That's the problem. I thought that might be better.

Participant: ...It's too breezy over there. Very cold.

Gregory: Right. You didn't think of that. The energy might be better but he pointed out that it will be too breezy.

Participant: ...Well, close the frigging door.

(everyone laughs)

Participant: ...I just want to let you know that I'll support you in any decision you make except I would go to the other comer.

Gregory: To that corner? You've changed corners?

Participant: ...Yeah I have now.

Participant: ...I think you should stay where you are.

Participant: ...If you go there I won't talk to you again.

(everyone laughs)

Gregory: Okay.

Participant: ...Why don't you go outside and sit on the verandah?

Gregory: Well look, I think what I'll do is, I think I'll take a risk.

(everyone laughs)

Gregory: I think I'll take a risk and I'll go there. So how do you reckon I ought to get there?

Participant: ...Just do it if you're going to bloody do it.

Participant: ...Around the back way. There's so many people here.

Gregory: Go around the back and come around? Yeah. That sounds good.

Participant: ...Do forward rolls.

Participant: ...I don't reckon you should go. I reckon you should stay there.

Gregory: A forward roll. I might hurt some people.

Participant: ...We'll move out the way.

Participant: ...Do you really want to get there?

Gregory: Well I'm not sure.

Participant: ...Then why don't you stay there?

Gregory: I think I'll go a bit there.

Participant: ...Yeah. Go halfway and see what it's like.

Participant: ...Not that way.

Participants: ...NO. NO. NO. NO. NO. NO.

Participant: ...YEAH. KEEP GOING. KEEP GOING.

Participant: ...Gregory! WRONG WAY! WRONG WAY! (everyone SCREAMING all sorts of things)

Gregory: (moves to a corner) Not that good you know.

(everyone laughs)

Gregory: I wonder if I should go back.

(everyone laughs)

Gregory: Get the point? See yourselves in your lives?

Participants: ...Yeah. Yikes!

Gregory: Okay. That's the most painful way to do it. Now for a more effective way to play it.

I think I want to go to the corner. Has anyone been there, to the corner?

Participant: ...Yeah, I've been there.

Gregory: What's it like for you?

Participant: ...Oh, sensational.

Gregory: How did you get there?

Participant: ...I walked there and sat in the chair.

Gregory: You walked straight over and tried it?

Participant: ...Yeah. That's my corner.

Gregory: Okay. That sounds good. I'll try that. What?

Participant: ...I got there and I hated it. It took me a long time and all I wanted to do was turn around and come back.

Gregory: Right. Okay. So what I know now is that some people enjoy the corner, some don't. I can think for myself, I can go into doubt and confusion and try and work it out or I can find out for me. So I get up and I walk to the corner. (walking) When I get there I'll either think it's fantastic, think it's terrible or think it's okay. Then I have another choice. I'll do that. (walks to the other corner) Well it's different. I think I enjoy sitting down over there more. It's different. It's interesting. There are things about it I really like and things about it that I don't like. I could change them if I wanted, but I think I'll go back where I was. No, I know what I'll do. I'll try this corner. (walks to another corner) Yep, that's different. Yep, that's okay. I like that. It would suit me fine, I could get you all to turn around and I'd sit in this chair.

Okay. So now I have three choices, but which one suits me best? I think I'll go back there.

Participant: ...You didn't try one corner.

Gregory: I can already see that I don't want to sit over there. There isn't a comfortable chair for me. I already know I don't want to sit there.

Participant: ...What if you bring that chair over?

Gregory: I'm still sitting in this chair so I may as well stay here.

Participant: ...We'll carry it for you.

Gregory: No point. No advantage. See the difference? Right.

The next level of getting what I want is that I don't even tell you what I'm going to do.

I don't ask you what I think about it. I simply think, "Gee, I wonder what that corner is like?" (Gregory walks over to a corner) You already know what I'm doing.

(everyone applauds)

Gregory: Did I have to say anything? Did I need to waste so much time in mental loops and discussions?

Participant: ...No.

Gregory: You already know, actions speak louder than words.

Participant: ...That's the thing about not asking people questions. If I've got a question, don't run around asking other people to solve it.

Gregory: Or, ask someone who actually knows. That's the important thing.

If you know that you know just do it. If you don't know or you're not sure, find someone who's been there, as I did with the corners. I seek teachers, instructors, coaches. That's getting valuable advice, but most of you folk haven't been to visit and explore the corners, so what's the point of even talking to you about it?

What a wank. I haven't been there. You haven't been there. So we all sit around wondering and discussing what it would be like if we went there! It's called "uncommitted opinion". Everyone has opinions about everything. Give me your opinion about Cane Toads.

Participant: ...They're ugly.

Participant: ...They sting I think.

Gregory: Right. Give me your opinion about Space Exploration. Should we keep going or not?

Participant: ...Oh definitely

Participant: ...That's a worthwhile thing

Gregory: See? See, I could sit here for three weeks and she'll have an opinion on everything. So will all of you. So what?

If you want to know about how to do stuff in your life, you get a committed opinion. That is, you hear from someone who's done it. That's smart by the way. The point is, I just want to find out. It doesn't matter whether it's good or bad, better or worse, I want to know what the experience is, then I have a choice.

Participant: ...When I was traveling, hundreds of people said Paris was revolting and that it wasn't as wonderful as everyone said, etc. I just said, "I don't give a shit what it's like. I want to go and find out for myself."

Some people go there with expectations and are disappointed but I had no expectation. I just knew that's where I want to go. Then you can make your own decision. I might have loved Paris or I might have absolutely hated it.

Gregory: That's right. Anyone else?

Participant: ...I think I'm totally schizoid now.

Gregory: What do you call totally schizoid?

Participant: ...Well I'm the guy in the comer of the Cobb drawing with a clear view of myself.

I'm taking those signs and I'm head-wanking like anything, trying to get to my heart and to my total truth. I enjoy my work in advertising, it's exciting and challenging, and I get to feel schizoid.

Gregory: Okay. Instead of talking about it, act it out. Let's say this room represents the world and every possibility in it. So you're saying that where you are in the world is exciting and challenging and you feel schizoid. The payoff is called exciting and challenging and the price is called, "I think I'm crazy."

Participant: ...Right.

Gregory: So pick a new spot to sit in the room. Pick a different place to live in the world. A different way. Go on.

(participant moves to another spot in the room)

Gregory: How's that? Better? Sure? Yes or no?

Participant: ...Yes.

Gregory: Right. Is there anywhere else in the room that might be better, that you might enjoy more?

(pause)

Gregory: The answer is yes, no or I don't know.

Participant: ...No.

Gregory: There's nowhere in the room that's going to be better than that?

Participant: ...Oh, see this is where...

Gregory: No. You're not answering my question. Is there anywhere in the room that might be better than there? Yes, no or I don't know.

Participant: ...I don't know.

Gregory: Okay. How are you going to find out if that's the best place in the room to sit?

Participant: ...Try other parts of the room.

Gregory: Go on then.

(participant moves to another part of the room)

Gregory: Is that better? Yes or no?

Participant: ...No.

Gregory: No. Try somewhere else. We saw how he did this for six years right. Is that better?

Participant: ...This is excellent because I'm connecting my truth.

Gregory: I don't want to hear Why. Just, is it better sitting there than in the centre?

Participant: ...No.

Gregory: No. Okay. Now one thing I want to point out. One of the signs that's ruling you says you can only sit where no-one else is sitting.

Is there any spot in the room that someone else has got that might be better? Any spot?

Participant: ...It's interesting.

Gregory: I'm not interested whether it's interesting. Is there or isn't there? See, he wants to sit and talk. He keeps postponing it. Is there anywhere else that might be better?

Participant: ...I suppose it's in your chair.

Gregory: Okay. Great. I'm really delighted you said that. The place that might be better is in my chair. What are you going to do about it? Keep it simple. Do you want to sit here and try it?

Participant: ...I don't feel qualified.

Gregory: Ah ha. I didn't ask you if you felt qualified. I said, do you want to sit here and try it? See that's another sign. "I've got to have the right qualifications." Do you want to sit here and try it? Yes or no? This isn't a difficult question. Do you or don't you want to sit here and try it?

Participant: ...It's funny how I...

Gregory: I don't care whether it's funny or not.

Participant: ...I'm like that.

Participant: ...Yeah. So am I.

Gregory: Do you see yourselves? He's trapped because he's got 1,000 signs saying, "Yes? But? If? Then? What? Can? Qualified? Wank. Wanko Wank."

(everyone laughs hysterically)

Gregory: Listen. There's a level where the Universe only ever asks you Yes and No questions. Do you want to sit here and try it or don't you?

Participant: ...Yes.

Gregory: Great. Powerful. That's taken you to the next step. How do you get anything in life?

Participant: ...But ...

Gregory: Not but.

Participant: ...He's wanking.

Participant: ...Sperm.

(everyone laughs)

Gregory: Their laughter is at themselves by the way. You're showing them how it looks when they do it. That's why they're cracking up. They're laughing with you not at you. Since you've said that you want to sit here, how do you get to do that?

Participant: ...Learn how to do it.

Gregory: How? You only learn how to do it by doing it. So how do you do it? Keep it simple. You're sitting there, I'm sitting here. You want to sit here for a while and try it.

Participant: ...Pull you off the chair.

Gregory: That's one way. That's what you're afraid of. That's one way you can try it. You can have a fight with me. Do you like having fights?

Participant: ...Certainly don't.

Gregory: Right. So what's another way?

Participant: ...Ask you.

Gregory: GOOD. Great!

(everyone applauds)

Gregory: Major milestone. Got it? Do it.

Participant: ...Gregory, I'd like to try sitting in your seat.

Gregory: Thank you for sharing.

(everyone laughs)

Participant: ...Gregory, I'd like to sit in your seat.

Gregory: Again, thank you for sharing.

Participant: ...Oh God I'm hopeless.

(everyone laughs)

Gregory: Notice the sign that just popped up that said, “Uh uh. I can't do it. Give up. I'm screwed.” You want to sit here in my chair? You know how you do that is to ask. So ask.

Participant: ...Gregory?

Gregory: Yes?

Participant: ...Can I sit in your seat?

Gregory: What did he do?

Participant: ...He asked.

Gregory: He asked. Hear the difference between, "Can I sit in your seat?" and "I would like to sit in your seat."?

Participants: ...(everyone) Yeah.

Participant: ...Gregory, I want to understand this difference fully.

Gregory: Remember the other night when someone said, "You're welcome to join in for dinner." My internal response was, "Thank you for sharing." Then she said, "I would like you to sit in for dinner," which is asking. It's a lot closer. It's still a little bit of a gap because she didn't say, "Will you sit in for dinner?"

So, "I would like you to sit in for dinner," is a much more powerful degree of asking than, "You can." It still didn't get to asking, "Will you sit in for dinner?" So you've asked me. Ask me again.

Participant: ...I have to tell you that my mind is spaced out.

Gregory: It's alright. I'm pleased to hear it. It's called emptying the cup. Your mind isn't spaced out, your bullshit is getting spaced out. That's where it belongs. All your old limiting signs and patterns of NOT getting what you want are disintegrating as you learn how TO get what you want! Okay. Ask me again.

Participant: ...Gregory, can I sit in your seat?

Gregory: No.

Participant: ...What can I do for you so that I can sit in your seat?

Gregory: Isn't that wonderful? He has taken the next step, which is to ensure that I win too. Okay, I'll let you sit here if you give me a big hug after you do it. You willing to do that?

Participant: ...Most certainly am.

Gregory: Okay. One more thing. How long are you asking to sit in my chair for? See, I'm not silly. At this point, he might sit in this seat for the next year.

Participant: ...Just to experience the fear.

Gregory: How long is that going to take?

Participant: ...Probably ten or twenty seconds.

Gregory: Make up your mind.

Participant: ...I'll have to sit in it to know.

Gregory: Yeah. So at this point, how long are we negotiating for?

Participant: ...Twenty seconds.

Gregory: Okay. Would you like a minute in return for a hug?

Participant: ...Okay.

Gregory: It's a deal. Where's the stop watch? Can you time it from when his bum hits the seat? And your agreement is that when she says, "Time," you stand up. No matter what. Yes or no?

Participant: ...Yes. I'll sit there for 60 seconds.

Gregory: When she says, "Time," whatever you think or feel, you will stand up and give me my seat back. Correct? If you have a heart attack at fifty-eight seconds, you will fall off the chair at sixty seconds, and keep your agreement. Do you agree with that?

(pause)

Gregory: Where's your head gone?

Participant: ...My head feels I'm being tricked somewhere.

Gregory: No. You're not being tricked. I'm offering this seat for a minute which is three times more than you asked for. How can I be tricking you? I just want to know that we both understand what the deal is here.

Participant: ...Right. I certainly will give it up.

Gregory: Great. Just notice that. When people start insisting on clarity, the response is often, "Whoa, I'm being tricked here." He's already forgotten that I'm giving him three times more than he asked for and wanted at the same price; a hug.

People who trick you don't give you more than you asked for unless they're very, very tricky!

It's not about tricking you, it's about you and me being totally clear about our agreement so we both get what we want. At the end of our experience here we will both be satisfied, and grow our trust in the other.

If you stay 62 seconds on this chair, you're probably never going to get it from me again. I want to see that you keep your agreements. So, sixty seconds on the chair in return for a hug. Any questions? This is the next important step. Make sure that there aren't any questions left. In other words by saying, "Any questions?" I ensure that he gets totally clear and I get to see that we are both in total agreement. So any questions at all?

Participant: ...The question is whether I'll still feel fearful after 60 seconds.

Gregory: It's impossible to know that before you do it.

Participant: ...That's why my head is so schizoid; I keep intellectualizing what may happen.

Gregory: That's what your head does with commitments, and with stepping into new places. Your head goes bananas, so does mine at times. Your head's job is to keep you where you were. Boring. Every time you take a risk, every time you step out of your usual comfort zone your head will go bananas for a while, until finally it gives up, and learns that change and newness is safe and okay. Instead of saying you go schizoid, change the words and say, "My head is producing hundreds of signs." When you say, "My head's going schizoid," it's saying, "Do I do it? What about this and that?" You don't know, it might be scary. You might give up. You mightn't want to get it." etc. etc.

That's all true. All of the above is true - it might happen.

Participant: ...Exactly.

Gregory: And it comes back to; do you want to sit there and listen to the signs or do you want to go for it?

Participant: ...In this game I want to go for it. In real life I don't.

Gregory: I'll tell you a horrible secret. This is the worst secret of the seminar, and I've withheld it.

I acknowledge that I've done that and I feel really ashamed for doing it. Ready for my horrible secret? OK.

This IS real life! This seminar IS real life! You're really alive. I'm really alive. They're really alive. This is real life.

Furthermore breaking habits from your old life here in the seminar breaks them in your new life after the seminar because this IS REAL LIFE!!!

Participant: ...Right.

Gregory: Now, after all that interesting discussion, back to the point. Do you want to sit in the chair or not on the basis of our agreement?

Participant: ...Yes.

Gregory: Great. (Gregory leaves his chair and the participant sits in it)

Participant: ...So people, what would you like to know?

(everyone laughs)

Participant: ...Bless me. How naughty!

Gregory: You think sitting in the chair also means you have to be the instructor like me.

Participant: ...Yes. I wasn't sure.

Gregory: Are you listening for her to say time's up? Stay conscious of that. You've got an agreement to keep. While you talk keep one ear posted on the time, otherwise you'll blow it.

Participant: ...Right.

Participant: ...Time.

(participant rises from Gregory's chair)

Participant: ...We haven't had the hug yet.

(they hug)

Gregory: Very good. Agreement completed. Okay. Now, first, how did you feel sitting there?

Participant: ...I felt much more relaxed than I thought. I thought I'd feel a bit fearful.

Gregory: Yep. So you felt some fear, some ease. Did you enjoy it?

Participant: ...As an experience, yes.

Gregory: So there were some enjoyable things about it, some not so enjoyable things about it. That's how new experiences are, then you learn how to make them more enjoyable. The point is you did it. Now, do you want to be sitting there? Does it feel different sitting there now? Because you look different sitting there now.

Participant: ...Yes.

Gregory: Great. Why? Because you've tried something new. In trying other experiences you get more of yourself. Your earlier statement was that you want more of yourself: do it by having more experiences of yourself, and you get more experiences of yourself by doing more things.

Participant: ...I have had so many experiences.

Gregory: And so many that you haven't had.

Participant: ...Yes.

Gregory: So go and have them, have the experiences you haven't had. Start collecting new experiences. You just discovered how to do that, you just did so keep doing it.

Each time, it becomes more easy and more automatic until you don't even have to think about it, you just do it. You've mastered not getting results. Correct?

You've mastered it by practicing it a lot. If you want to master getting results, keep doing what you just did until it becomes easy and automatic, then you just automatically get results. It takes time, and it takes commitment, and it takes some courage, then you get the rewards.

Thank you.

(everyone applauds)

Gregory: I gather that you all saw yourselves in that.

Participants: ...(everyone) Yeah.

Gregory: It's painful isn't it? Isn't it sad? Isn't it unnecessary?

Participants: (various) ...Yeah ...And it's boring too ...Complicated ... Stuck ...It's so obvious in stepping out of it and looking at it.

Gregory: That's right. Just do it. Keep asking. Keep finding out what others want to have it work for everyone, then do what you agree to 100%. Yes? This applies in sex, in love, in work, everywhere.

Incidentally, you just discovered something: how to get the result. The word "discover" is literally to dis-cover, to uncover. That implies that you already had it, you already knew, it was just covered.

I believe that you already have everything that you will ever have; all the value, talents, abilities, love, power and so on. Life is a process of dis-covering what you have and Who you are, and of learning to use and apply that.

The only question that you ever have to ask yourself is, "What am I going to settle for?" or, "Am I going to settle for this?" or, "What do I really want?" or, "What am I really willing to go for?"

What is the level you set that people have to earn you? To earn the right to be with you?

The movie theatre manager sits inside the movie house and he says, "What I require for you to show me that you really want to see this movie is $9.50. If it's not worth it to you, don't come in." Then you have a clear choice. What is it that lets you know that people are entitled to your time and presence? Or do you play a game that anyone can have you on any terms? That's what it comes down to.

What are you worth?

Participant: ...I haven't paid much attention to that.

Gregory: Yeah. If there's someone in your life that in one way or another isn't showing respect and honor and valuing you, it's your choice whether you devalue yourself to their level or whether you own your value and tell them to piss off or up their game around you.

Participant: ...Some of my relationships I'm clear about, the ground rules are set, and with others I'm not. I guess I'll find out as I go along. Once I start making some particular relationships, I'll learn how to do it.

Gregory: Your old game is to not offer anything but to say, "What do you want?" You're not saying, "I will do what you want." You're saying, "What will you want?" In different words it's called walk in sucker.

For example, "I really want to be in your life. What do you want from me?" It could be anything. It could be, "I want you to give me oranges. I want you to say good morning in the morning." Anything.

Participant: ...Buy me a cup of coffee in the morning

Participant: ...And then breakfast and feed me. And come to my place and see my place.

Gregory: Here comes the sting. I'll think about that. I'll let you know what I'm willing to do. Let's play that again. I'd really like to be in your life. What do you want me to do?

Participant: ...Buy me breakfast, lunch and dinner. And fish.

Gregory: Ah ha. What else do you want?

Participant: ...That's it.

Gregory: Okay. I'll think about it and I'll let you know what I'll give you when I'm ready.

See the power game in that conversation?

He's waiting for me now.

Participant: ...If I value myself enough I can say to you, "I want to be in your life and I'll do whatever that takes and I'll give you my company and me and what I know."

Gregory: That may be it, or it may be you say, "I want to be in your life and I'm not offering anything." Great. But don't get pissed off if I don't spend a hell of a lot of time with you!

Everything has a price. You don't get to climb to the top of Mt. Everest by having it easy. There is a price to pay and there is a risk to take. That's life. It's called, you risk your life and you sweat and struggle and strain and be in extreme physical agony for about a week. If you don't want to go through that effort, don't climb Mt. Everest. No-one says you've got to.

But if you want the reward of climbing Mt. Everest, that's the price. That's Nature's way of testing you. We are all tested, you earn the right to the treasures of life. Nature doesn't cast it's pearls in front of swine. Nature says, "You want pearls, show me that you'll use them and appreciate them. You have to do what that takes." Of course it also seems that nature gives us a few pearls to kick off the game, then leaves it to us to collect more!

Words are important. The difference between saying, "I'd like to sit in your chair," and, "Can I sit in your chair?" is huge.

Get the form of the words correct, in other words, learn to communicate what you actually mean, clearly. If you're just saying the right words and there's nothing backing it up, why bother?

Some more on our conditioning, our programming, on the signs we learn: how they train elephants to not run rampage is that when elephants are little, they chain their leg to a huge log. The elephant tugs for years until it finally learns, "I can't move the log. Whenever there's a chain on my leg, I can't go anywhere." Then as the elephant grows bigger they make the log smaller. By the time the elephant has grown up the log is a peg hammered in the ground.

At the circus you can see them put a chain on a five ton elephant and bang a peg in the ground and it doesn't go anywhere because it knows it can't. It has a huge sign that says, "You can't move when you've got a chain on your leg." It believes the sign and therefore doesn't even give it a pull. Now, my job is to come along and I say, "Hey, you can pull it out." You say, "No, I can't. I definitely can't," and I say, "Yes you can. Watch." And I pull it out.

But I can't make you walk. I can show you that the peg can be pulled out. I can show you that you can pull it out. I can show you how I pull it out. Do you know what happens with one of those elephants if you walk up and pull the peg out? Nothing. Because it already knows it can't move with the chain on its leg. That's why every time you say "can't", you're just reading an old sign. "No I can't. Sorry I can't. I'd love to, I can't. I can't."

So my job is to be there and tell you that you can, to show you all that and at some point I have to be willing to acknowledge you're going to get it or you don't want to get it, and accept your choices about it.

Day 10

"There is no such thing as 'the real world'. There are billions of real worlds and everyone creates one. Who's to say whether it's the real world to live in Buckingham Palace or a slum in Calcutta?"

FANTASIES - STEPPING OUT - PROSPERITY - ABUNDANCE - YOUR SPACE - BOUNDARIES - CREATING YOUR WORLD - MEDIA MADNESS - BE WHERE YOU ARE - ENJOY NOW - FANTASY

Gregory: Someone once said to me, jokingly, "When you're about sixty or seventy years old you'll do the seminar where everyone walks in on Friday, you're introduced, you sit up the front, you make eye contact with each one, everyone gets it and you all go home?" I said, "Yeah. That's a possibility: but I don't know how to do that yet. So I do it this way."

Have you ever heard of the idea that everything that ever happens is happening at once? That there's actually no such thing as time, it's another sign we believe. I'd heard that concept and I thought, "Oh that's real space cadet crap."

I was shut off to the idea, and I was doing a visualization on healing the child that I was, my child within, the child I had been.

What I visualized was that I was in the air looking down at the ten-year-old that I was back then, in the backyard where I used to live. I saw it all really clearly and I just kind of floated above him and spoke to him. It was at a time in my childhood when I was feeling incredibly distraught. My pet parrot had died, and I was really in deep, deep, despair and abandonment.

What I the adult, in my mind's eye, said to the 10 year old me who I was picturing in my visualization, was something to the effect of, "Hey, it's okay. I know you're hurting. It's okay. And you made it because I'm here.

I made it. I grew up. I survived this hurt. I'm doing fine. So let yourself know it's okay."

The minute I said the words, something flipped, and I remembered that when I was that child, a voice in the sky actually spoke to me and said those words. At the time I thought it was God.

"It's okay. You grew up and I'm with you and I'll never abandon you and I won't forget you," When I really was ten, I really heard that said, by a voice from the sky!!

I looked up to see who said it, and there was no-one there. I totally forgot that happened until I did the visualization and said it and I thought somehow all of that is happening now. Richard Bach talked about it in A Bridge Across Forever.

Participant: ...He did it in his sleep.

Gregory: He did it in his dreams or in his sleep, and I'd done things like he describes but what was so shocking was that I did it awake.

Because I couldn't say, "Oh, it was a dream," I couldn't push it away. There was nowhere to hide from the fact. It was amazing.

***

Gregory: Change takes time. It has to take a given period of time. You can change anything quickly or slowly and you can master anything quickly or slowly. Let's say you present yourself with an issue or a problem that is big. (Gregory uses his hands to demonstrate) You can let it sit there that big forever and never change it, theoretically. It may be that you take it on but you don't get it so you make it even bigger to see it all. Or you create the same thing again and again and again and again until you get it. If you don't deal with it, it won't go away. Because that's the next thing to do.

Three years ago I got really clear that what was on the horizon was to start doing a lot of media work. It didn't have my attention much. I wrote a script about how doing media would be for me, then let it go. A couple of days after I get back to Sydney next week, I'm being interviewed on national TV, which means that I have moved from that spot to the horizon in three years.

There's a paradox in this. Things take the time they take, and it's your choice. Some people choose to spend ten years handling an issue. Someone else says, "Oh, I handled that in an hour." It's a little like the demonstration I did of getting to the corner. Sometimes you take a long time to get to the corner, and it doesn't have to take a long time. It always takes some time but it might be five seconds. Or I could sit here for three years. Whatever time it takes, at any given time, trust the timing!

Participant: ...I've been feeling really stuck with all of this. I sit here, I don't know how long have we been here?

(everyone laughs)

I feel like I'm full of rubbish. I keep saying to people, "Oh I'm going to do music," and they believe me and I'm not actually.

Gregory: Okay, so it's exactly the same issue as telling people to piss off. Tell music to piss off. You're not doing music. So tell the truth about it. Turn it around to, "In the past I was a world famous musician, and in the future it is my intention to do music and I'm choosing not to now." That states your actions. So take responsibility for your actual choice. Notice the connection between action and actual. What your ACTions are is what you're ACTually doing, where you're ACTually at.

So your actual truth is that you're not doing music and you have the intention to, sometime. You have the judgement that you can, therefore you should, and the truth is you can and you might. Stop saying it until you do it, and then you don't have to say, "I will." Instead you say, "I am."

Participant: ...The only way I relate the idea of a "fantasy" is when I listened to fairy stories. Up to about three or four months ago I'd never even realized you can have fantasies related to sex.

Gregory: Children's stories do exactly for children what sex fantasies do for adults, which is that they give them a safe, playful way to feel scared, angry, left behind, abandoned, excited. That's why there's all those fairy stories.

It's funny to think of taking the violence and fear out of fairy stories. Kids won't be interested.

They read them in order to safely feel their violence and fear and to reassure themselves it will turn out alright in the end. So sex fantasies are just adult's fairy stories.

***

Gregory: Next thing to do is to look at and share what fantasies you have that you would like to act out. You may have already done it and you may have not done it.

This is a very special opportunity for you to give yourself that. Don't go and assume, "Therefore I must do it if I share it." It's simply sharing where you are now, what fantasies you've got that you might like to do and any you're scared of doing. Yes?

Participant: ...My fantasy I haven't acted out is being smothered by six or eight women with good tits all over my face.

Gregory: How do you get 12 boobs on your face?

Participant: ...I don't care!

(everyone laughs)

Gregory: Okay. Does your fantasy include a breathing tube?

Participant: ...Snorkel. I just want to be smothered by tits all over me.

Gregory: Smothered in tits? Fantastic. Okay. Are you willing to do it?

Participant: ...Oh, absolutely.

Gregory: Great. Yes?

Participant: ...I want to beat somebody up and I want to be beaten up.

Gregory: Right. What does beaten up or beating someone up look like? Take one at a time. What does that look like?

Participant: ...Being beaten up and not being able to do anything about it. Being tied up.

Gregory: Tied up. By a man or woman? One of each? Many? Mixture? Some men, some women?

Participant: ...A man and a woman. Or we could have a few men and a few women.

Gregory: Right. Stay with getting beaten up. So you want this man and woman to tie you up and beat you up. Do you want them to be anyone in particular or to be strangers who've abducted you or your parents or to just be friends who go berserk? How did they get to be doing this thing?

(pause)

Gregory: What comes into your mind?

Participant: ...Strangers.

Gregory: Right. They're strangers. What did they do? Did they break into your apartment? Did they abduct you on the street and throw you in the back of a car?

Participant: ...They got me on the street.

Gregory: Whose place are you at? Theirs? A hotel?

Participant: ...In the cellar of a dungeon.

Gregory: Fantastic. See how you get clear about it. Okay. So two total strangers, a man and a woman, have come along, they've grabbed you on the street and they've dragged you off?

What did they do? Just pick you up and carry you off and throw you in a truck? A car?

Participant: ...They dragged me off and I was resisting.

Gregory: They dragged you off. You were screaming and resisting. Down the cellar. Tie you up. Do they strip you first? Strip you later? Leave clothes on?

Participant: ...They strip me while they're doing it.

Gregory: Right. So they're holding you down and tying you up and stripping you?

They've got you naked. They've got you tied up. You're in the cellar. There are others waiting there. What do they actually do that you call beating up? Are you on your back or your front? Are you squirming around?

Participant: ...I'm on my back and they're whipping me with a belt and slapping my face.

Gregory: All of them or are some watching?

Participant: ...Some are watching and laughing.

Gregory: Right. So they're laughing. Are they making any comments?

Participant: ...They're laughing and they're calling me a tart and a slut.

Gregory: Great. Mocking you and putting you down? So they slap you around the face, they hit you with belts, then what happens? Does it get sexual?

Participant: ...I'm trying to decide.

Gregory: No, there's nothing to decide. Just watch the movie that's in your head.

Participant: ...Okay. It gets sexual.

Gregory: Great. See she's already got the movie in her head hasn't she? Every time I ask her a question she knows in exact detail. How does it get sexual? What do they do? Watch the movie and describe it.

Participant: ...I get raped by a man.

Gregory: Right. Any details about that?

Participant: ...No.

Gregory: Does he just grab you and stick it in?

Participant: ...Yeah.

Gregory: Are the others holding you down during this?

Participant: ...Yeah. They're still calling me names and hitting me around.

Gregory: While the man's raping you?

Participant: ...Yes.

Gregory: What happens then?

Participant: ...I get really angry. I'm really angry already. I get to the point where I'm so angry that...

Gregory: You break your bonds and put on your Super Woman's cape.

(everyone laughs)

Participant: ...I get so angry that they really stop when I get angry enough.

Gregory: Right. And what do they do?

Participant: ...They bow down.

Gregory: They bow down? Very good. Then what happens? Now that he's your slave you say, "Will you rape me?"

(everyone laughs)

Participant: ...I make them untie me and they make me a Queen.

Gregory: Right. How do they make you a Queen?

Participant: ...No, they bow down and they untie me, and I walk out.

Gregory: Right. Who gets a sense of a past life experience?

Participant: ...Yeah.

Gregory: Very good. Do you want to play it out?

Participant: ...Why not?

Gregory: Do you want to play it out?

Participant: ...Ah. Yes.

Gregory: Okay. Anyone else? Yes?

Participant: ...I've got a fantasy that I'm standing in the red light district really tarted up. Two women come up to me and gain my trust and then they propose going and doing a modeling job with them. I go off with them and then we're walking down this lane and all of a sudden they handcuff me to their wrists and to their legs, saying to me, "It's safe. You'll be alright."

Gregory: It's a modeling job for a handcuff advertisement?

(everyone laughs)

Participant: ...Then we get to this really yucky door and we walk down stairs to this bar. I'm sitting on this round bar seat and the handcuffs are gone. I'm sitting on this bar seat and this really good barman on the other side gives me a drink and it's like black coconut. They keep on getting my trust.

Then it changes and there's two little places for my feet to rest, spread apart. He gives me this drink and then they handcuff me and my feet get cuffed again.

Then this really weird guy comes out and checks me out and says, "Oh this is a nice specimen." He calls these other two guys and they come up with hospital gowns on and I can see their bums. He says, "Inject enough to enjoy it but not enough to put her out." I'm being drugged, and I'm totally a victim to it all.

They push this chair into the bar and there's someone's head there and he starts eating me out. Then there's a whole group of men coming in. There's one guy ordering it all to happen, and this one guy is saying, "You'll be right. You're okay. You're going to enjoy it and you're going to have a good time," and all these people are sitting around laughing. It is almost like an initiation.

I'm really freaking out about it all and they pick me up and carry me, really strong biker men, and they throw me down on the pool table and one guy's at the front and he's sticking his dick in my mouth making me suck him off and another two are biting my tits and other guys are wanking on top of me and then a section of the pool table comes out and ...

Gregory: This is just off the top of her head folks. She hasn't really thought about this much.

(everyone laughs)

Participant: ...Then one of the big bikers comes in and he's really yuck and just starts really thrusting and then gets a pool ball and rolls it into me.

Gregory: Very good. Is that before, after or during his dick's thrusting?

Participant: ...That's after. And then they get my legs and put them on a broom stick and string it up. Like a wedge. Wedge my legs up, then that's it.

Gregory: Right. That's it?

Participant: …They leave me there.

Gregory: You're left there? Sounds like an average evening in your nice little town. So do you want to act it out or some version of it?

Participant: …Not now.

Gregory: Okay. Very good. Just out of interest for everyone, what feels scary about acting it out?

Participant: …My picture of doing that to somebody would just be that they'd be absolute shit.

Gregory: If you did it to someone?

Participant: …Yeah. If I could bring myself to actually do that to someone, be motivated to do that to someone, I wouldn't be able to see them as a human being.

Gregory: Right. So is the fear that if you act that out you will find that people really treat you like absolute shit? Or you will have a full experience of you as a big shit?

Participant: …Yeah. Yeah. I'll really get to see how valueless I am.

Gregory: Okay. The truth is that part of you already thinks you are worth shit, and that part forces you to do all sorts of things so you'll never find that out. You live in fear of the possibility that you're really a shit, or you're full of shit, or you've got no value. When you are ready to act the fantasy out, by fully experiencing that part you, then you get to release it and have the rest of you come back. Do you follow that?

Participant: …Yeah. This little voice just said, "Do it. You really do want to act it out."

Gregory: You're already in the place you fear. You're already afraid that you're worth shit, so the worse that's going to happen is you're going to know you are.

Even if you are worth shit then you can do something about it. But at this point you're just afraid you are, and your fear stops you doing anything about it. It's fine if you don't act it out, I just want you to be clear about it.

Participant: ...I agree with all that, and it's a real turn on for me as a fantasy. I get off on it a lot, and have gone into so much detail it's just like a movie. To actually ask someone here to rape me would just be a bit much I think.

Gregory: Mmm. Fine. For me, this has been the value in acting out fantasies: I was sharing this morning that I used to regularly have the fantasy of been a big Eastern potentate lying back on this couch covered in silks and furs and totally attended by about 20 nubile women who are at my absolute beck and call. Anything. I owned them, literally. Again I get a past life thing with this, I used to have this fantasy when I was a kid!

(everyone laughs)

Gregory: True. It wasn't sexual then it was just the picture. As I got sexual the picture got more sexual. I had a fantasy and I really wanted it and I was terrified of creating it. Actually terrified that I would enslave women.

What I did several times was attract women into my life who really wanted to be my slave.

Like, "Own me, beat me up, use me," the works. I just split, and just cut them off. Then I was ready to act out the fantasy, and I did. I loved it, and I got to see that as a game it's fantastic and the truth is I don't want to enslave anyone.

What changed after that was I started creating, overnight, an enormous amount of support from other people. I used to resist support or keep support away, for fear that people are so stupid that they'll come in and I'll enslave them, that it will be effortless and then I'll hate myself. So I kept people away to protect them from me. Once I'd played it out, I saw that the real real truth is, it's a lovely game to play and I don't want to do it in real life. I just don't want to do it. Not interested. And therefore people flooded into my life in a supportive way. You get that?

Participant: ...Yep.

Gregory: Your version of that is that when you do let yourself have the fantasy and risk experiencing that you are a total shit, I say what you'll get is the experience that some of you is very shitty and you're not a total shit. Out of that you get to let in your value. It's another version of emptying the cup. There's a high chance that you'll enjoy the game, then you can get to act the game, play the rape fantasy game, without ever having to create an actual rape in order to have that experience and with knowing the truth that you're not a shit, and you are not dehumanized. So, let us know when you're ready.

Participant: ...I'd like to do a version of it and not actually have penetration... just held down and restrained and that sort of stuff.

Gregory: What would look safe for that? Would it include one of them sticking their dick in your mouth or would it include still having your tits bitten or dicks rubbed against you or play with dicks or whatever?

Participant: ...I think being wanked on... if they could get themselves to come, and having my tits bitten.

Gregory: Yep. Fingers in? By the way, anyone who plays out a fantasy gets to choose who plays what roles. Also, get the detail as accurate as you can and stick to it when you play it out.

It's okay to have the fantasy but not to actually do it. So you want to do a modified version.

Anyone else? Yes?

Participant: ...I want to have my hands tied behind my back and be locked in a cupboard unable to get out. Then I want to come out and I want to bully someone.

Gregory: With your hands tied behind your back?

Participant: ...No.

Gregory: A man? A woman?

Participant: ...A man. And then I want to beat him up, and I want to shift from being aggressive to being controlled and treated like a dog.

Gregory: Yes?

Participant: ...I'm not sure if this is going to be possible to act out but I have a fantasy of killing another human being.

Gregory: Become a mercenary so it's easy to act out.

Participant: ...Yeah. It's not what I want to do, and I'm not sure what to substitute so that it gets as close as possible without actually doing it.

Gregory: Is it stabbing?

Participant: ...It's tearing their heart out with my teeth.

Gregory: So, look at ways to make it up.

Participant: ...One thing I thought of was getting stuck into my punching bag.

Gregory: No. That doesn't work. It's a shame we didn't have some warning, we could have brought a sheep's heart, that's a good way to do it. I've actually got steak in the fridge. Maybe actually get meat in your mouth and pick someone to attack and throw down, tear their shirt open and just rip and tear with your eyes shut. Have them screaming.

Participant: ...They could have the steak under their shirt or something.

Gregory: Maybe even people in the background yelling, "MY GOD! HE'S TEARING HER HEART OUT! OH GOD!" or whatever fits the fantasy. Anyone else?

Participant: ...I have a fantasy to tie up, beat up and rape a woman, then kill her.

Gregory: Right. Great. How do you want to kill her?

Participant: ...With a knife and cut her up.

Participant: ...(several people) Oh God. Ohh.

Gregory: Listen. Before you go into, "Oh no," just notice the courage and risk it takes to share that. A lot of what I call core fantasies are past life experiences that you didn't get to own and complete. In this life you can complete it and let it go by acting it out in fantasy. I think that that's a past life you had.

Participant: ...I don't get that. Being given time to complete, or given the opportunity.

Gregory: Well let's say he actually did that in a past life. Let's say he was a paid torturer during the Inquisition. Witches would be arrested and brought in. The witches who admitted that they worked for the Devil were the lucky ones. They got burnt at the stake.

That was considered an honorable death for a witch. The unlucky ones were handed over to the torturers, maybe him, and they would tie them up, torture them, rape them, and then kill them in a mutilating way, believing that the witches were the Devil's servant.

One of the more humiliating and dehumanizing ways to kill witches was to shove a spear or a stake up inside their pussy. Caligula had another cute one. He used to hold people down and stick a spear, a lance, up their butt and had it pushed right through until it came out near their neck. If they were still alive they then got publicly put up on stakes, spitted. It became a regular punishment for Roman soldiers.

So it's like, if he did that in a past life and let's say he did, that stays as a psychic wound in his Oversoul, to be completed and healed, by being brought to awareness and released. At the moment it is like a wound that needs to be lanced in order to heal.

It remains a wound in his Oversoul or in his psychic being. To act it out and see that it really was his choice, and that back then he was playing out a part, he gets to complete the experience. Carrying that old experience, or the memory of it, is also a source of a lot of fear: if he could do it then, and lets go and loses control now, he might do it again. Therefore he must keep a tight rein on himself, keep woman at a distance for their own safety, and not relax or trust himself.

By acting it out, he releases the old memory and it's power over him. He also learns that he is now in control of the choice to do or not to do it again. In that is incredible relief and freedom.

My experience with fantasies is that at first core fantasies have a huge charge to them, and as you play them out, the charge diminishes and you get to a point where either it doesn't have any attraction anymore or you keep doing it for the sheer fun and pleasure of it.

Participant: ...Can you re-explain the reason for acting out a particular fantasy.

Gregory: Right. I'll do it by looking at what happens for children. Children get scared.

Children get sad and sometimes don't connect with it. Any good children's story has loss, sadness, anger, danger, fear and a happy ending. At least. In reading the story, the child has permission to feel those feelings safely, and in doing so to experience them and release them to some degree. As adults when we have fantasies we've learnt to hold them inside. By putting them out there, acting them out, you get to actually "have it" as a measurable, tangible thing.

If you have a picture that says you can't ask the boss for a day off, then you can't. You walk around with a fantasy saying, "The boss will bite my head off." At some point you may decide to go and ask the other bosses or practice with someone. You come to me and you say, "Gregory I'm really scared that if I ask my boss this, he'll bite my head off," so we practice it. Say to me, "Can I have a day off?"

Participant: ...Can I have a day off?

Gregory: No. Get screwed ...What happened?

Participant: ...I didn't like it.

Gregory: Yeah. But did it destroy you? No. So you do not like it AND it is safe to do.

What happens if he now says, "No, get screwed."? You're used to it. It's not going to destroy you. My experience is that there's great value in acting it out. By acting it out in a safe place, you can actually acknowledge the feelings you're going through instead of suppressing and getting angry about them or afraid of them.

Participant: ...I get this fantasy which is incomplete. It's like a past life that didn't work.

I'm sitting in a pub in London and it seems to be about 1800 and this woman comes in and we start talking and she says to me, "Let's go to another club." I get into a coach with her and we go underneath a house. There's some other people there all dressed in leather gear with boobs hanging out and a few whips.

I start to freak out a bit but she pushes me in and they lock the door and there's three naked women in a circle and I'm really sort of frozen up in fear. And they start to tease me just to abuse me. Call me names and I collapse on the floor and they tie me up and they tease me even more. When I wake up I'm naked and they tease me even more and after a while one of them sits on top of me and something comes up my butt and I look down and there's a guy screwing me up the butt with a table leg. It just makes me black out. That's all I get of it. I had that dream when I was about fifteen. The same club. The same feeling. A real fear. I don't know whether I want to act it out but it is a fantasy. It's become a fantasy.

Gregory: Okay.

Participant: ...I've got one where there's been some tragedy. I escape. I'm in a boat with either my mother, daughter or wife and we go to one island and they rape her. They rape and torture her.

Then I escape from that without having seen them do the horrible things and then go to another island where there's another tribe of men and women and they all take me to be sacrificed and the men laugh as the women go animal over me. Clawing me, fucking me, sucking me, a combination of pleasure and pain.

Participant: ...Mine's just really soft where it's all women and I am touched and massaged without my permission. I am touched safely and I don't get hurt or damaged at all, just with pleasure, safely.

Gregory: When you say touched and stuff, is that including sexually?

Participant: ...Sexually touched, my pussy and so on, and not actually bonking at this stage. Then after that I will rerun the same fantasy with men. That's also something I want to get to, to have a sexual experience with a woman.

Gregory: Okay. Anyone else?

Participant: ...I don't think I've got any fantasies.

Gregory: Have you ever imagined going to bed with someone?

Participant: ...Yes.

Gregory: That's a fantasy. Have you ever met a man and thought what it might be like to go to bed with him?

Participant: ...Yeah.

Gregory: That's a fantasy. Have you ever thought what it might be like to go to bed with two men?

Participant: ...No.

Gregory: No. With a woman?

Participant: ...Yes.

Gregory: That's a fantasy. Anything you imagine is a fantasy. Some of them you've acted out and some of them you haven't. So you've had fantasies. Anyone else?

Participant: ...One of myself with two women.

Gregory: Right. What do you all do?

Participant: ...That's about as far as I got.

Gregory: What do you think you might do? You've got the initial idea for a movie; the script writer's walked up and said, "Hey, I've got an idea. Let's do a movie about a man with two women..." What are they going to do together? Cook food? Talk? Have sex? That's how you can generate fantasies by the way. Imagine that you're writing a movie script. What would you do with these people?

Participant: ...No, we're not going to cook!

(everyone laughs)

Gregory: Okay. So what are you all going to do?

Participant: ...They bring me to a state of sexual arousal, then maintain the feeling for as long as possible.

Gregory: Make it up. How would you like them to arouse you? Do you want them to read you beautiful poetry? Play with your dick? Eat you? Kiss you all over?

Participant: ...Touching.

Gregory: And do they maintain that state by continuing to touch you or bonking you or eating you or...

Participant: ...Maintain the state by touching.

Gregory: Do they all touch your toes, your left elbow? You're being coy. Do they continue until you have an orgasm? Does that mean that they're going to end up wanking you or does it mean just before you have an orgasm, one of them jumps on you or they both jump on you or you jump on them or…

Participant: …One of them jumps on me. It's a matter of the timing.

Gregory: So if you want the time in place as you get aroused you can say to them, "Jump on me now. Here I go." Okay. Great. Would you like to act it out?

(pause)

(everyone laughs)

Participant: …One fantasy for me is to be totally dominated sexually and tied up.

Gregory: Right. I think you have a lot of volunteers.

Participant: …A similar fantasy. It's not something I've really thought about a lot but…

Gregory: Don't justify. That's the bullshit. Come on, what's the fantasy?

Participant: …Two women. Two or three women. I let them have the oil, giving each other massages.

Oiled up or soaped or something. So they're slippery. And myself. I'd be included in this too, having a massage. And they'd massage each other with their breasts, mainly with their breasts. And then massage me and get me aroused then I have intercourse with one or both of them.

Gregory: Great. Do you want to act it out?

Participant: …I would.

Gregory: Great. Very good. Anyone else? Yeah?

Participant: …One of my terrors is…

Gregory: I don't want to know what your terrors are. I want to know what your fantasy is.

Participant: ...A homosexual experience.

Gregory: Right. What's that like? A man comes up and shakes hands and walks away?

(everyone laughs)

Gregory: That's a homosexual experience!

(everyone laughs hysterically)

Gregory: It is. If a man shakes his hand it's a homosexual experience. He just had an experience with someone of the same sex. That's what homosexual means. Same sex.

Participant: ...Not just an experience. A sexual experience. Being tied up and attacked or raped by a homosexual.

Gregory: By another man. Raped anally. Do you want to act it out?

Participant: ...Not totally. No.

Gregory: Right. Okay. How much do you want to act out?

Participant: ...All except for the last part.

Gregory: One of the possibilities between that and the full thing is to have a small version of it. Instead of getting a dick rammed up your bum, get something small. It could be a finger stuck up your bum.

I'll tell you a funny little sex story. A few years ago a mate of mine who was a total maniac had a huge fake dildo. It strapped on and it was hollow, so you put your dick in it, it was big enough to put your dick inside.

There was a hollow space to put your dick in and there was a hole down through it to pee through. So he put it on and we went to a pub in Paddington. I didn't know he owned this thing, let alone that he was wearing it.

He said to me, "I'm going to have a piss. Come and have a piss with me." I said, "What?" He said, "Just come and have a piss with me." So we went in, and he pulled it out, and held it right out in front of himself. It looked totally real.

(everyone laughs)

Gregory: He's standing there having a piss and the toilet was really busy. Like, it was one of those little pubs with little toilets. And all these guys were just bug eyed, and then he said, "Oh Jesus it hurts."

(everyone falls into hysterics)

Gregory: By now there's like thirty men in the toilet totally agape, and when he finished peeing he walked to the side of the urinal and banged this 24 inch (61cm) monster against the wall, to get the drops off the end!

(people shrieking with laughter)

Gregory: After banging it about four times he stuffed it back down his pants, did his fly up and walked out. The next time he went to the toilet, every man in the pub including the barman went to the toilet. Very funny man.

Participant: ...They sold hundreds of triple scotches that night.

Gregory: I had this vision of 140 men going home that night weeping with envy. Fantastic. He's a maniac. He's a crazy man.

It's easy to step outside of the everyday. I had a mate, a nurse, who had one of those Mickey Mouse watches from Disneyland. He went off to a general hospital for three months on transfer and he was assigned to the operating theaters. General nurses are such dedicated Florence Nightingales, that during an operation if it's their meal break, they don't go. They don't even get a replacement to have a meal break. They just stay there and slave away. That's not Bob's style at all.

Well they're in the middle of this intense operation with all these surgeons and nurses, and Bob just said, "Mickey Mouse says it's time for lunch," and started walking out. The head surgeon dropped his scalpel and said, "WHAT?" Bob walked up to him, put his Disneyland watch in his face and said, "See, Mickey Mouse says it's time for lunch," and the guy cracked up, and Bob walked out. He's a maniac.

He was really good at reading people's signs and pressing their buttons. They hated him in General Hospital. The Head Sister of the first ward he worked in said, "Mr. Zaab, I want you to take the blood pressure on bed 23." He went and said to the patient in bed 23, "Mr. Jones, do you want to play a joke with me?" Mr. Jones wasn't very sick and he said, "Sure."

He got Mr. Jones out of bed and sat him on a wheel chair, then stripped the bed and put the blood pressure cuff across the mattress, and sat there talking to Mr. Jones. Twenty minutes later he heard the head sister coming up the hall calling, "Mr. Zarb, where are you?" He threw himself on the floor and burst into tears. She walked in and she said, "What's wrong? What's wrong?"

He said, "I'm sorry sister. I'm a total failure as a nurse. I've been trying for half an hour to take the blood pressure of bed 23 and I don't know how to do it."

(everyone laughs)

He had long hair and the same sister told him to go and get a hair cut. So he came back the next day and she exploded and said, "I told you yesterday to get a haircut." He held up one strand of hair and said, "I did. This one."

(everyone laughs)

***

Participant: ...Oh God. my whole body feels like exploding. It's an absolutely fantastic feeling. I've never had this feeling before.

Gregory: It's called sailing without a boat.

Participant: ...I'd just like to say I feel very safe. Yesterday I faced probably one of the greatest fears that I had. The one about being with men. Letting myself go. I enjoyed it. I felt very vulnerable in the beginning of the process and then very safe at the end of it.

Gregory: Exactly. Exactly. Now when people come up and start telling you what to do in your life, you can say, "What do you know? I sucked cock."

(everyone laughs)

Participant: ...Gregory, with regards to commitment, what happens when you have two commitments in your life and they tend to overlap to a degree.

Gregory: If you have conflicting commitments, you sort out the mess and stop making conflicting commitments. If you have to break one or the other, choose which one to break, then go and acknowledge that with the person you've broken it with, "I am breaking this commitment. I screwed up making a commitment with you, and I'm committing to keep further commitments. What do I need to do to make that work for you?" Then learn the lesson and don't make conflicting commitments.

Participant: ...My experience was that in coming up to do this seminar, my wife and I had conflicting commitments. One commitment was to come here and the other commitment was our child. We looked at the possibilities and the alternative solutions weren't options.

Gregory: So she broke her commitment. That's right.

Participant: ...And you say that's okay?

Gregory: No I didn't say it's O.K. Because you're involved, you can both see how you set it up to break your commitments. You set up conflicting commitments and you didn't have to. You could have found a way to keep both commitments. Sometimes you can't find a way. If I make a commitment to walk over to you right now and I make a commitment to walk over there to her right now, I have to break a commitment at this point in my life.

So I must then break one, acknowledge and take responsibility for it and not do that again. The truth is, your wife chose to not be here, and to use the commitment to your daughter as the reason, by not finding another way to handle the daughter. So that's the bottom-line. She didn't want to be here, and that wasn't exactly news for her.

That's an interesting story and the bottom-line is she broke her commitment. She didn't find another way to handle it so it would all work.

Get creative. It's not that she's wrong making that choice, but if she goes into, "I couldn't do the Sex and Relationships Seminar because of the kid," then she's going to blame and resent the kid. If she is willing to own her choice, then she'll say, "I used the kid as my way of not doing the Sex and Relationships Seminar because I wasn't ready."

We often think, "I can have this OR this." I say, you can have this AND this if you're willing to be creative. The saying, "You can't have your cake and eat it" is the perfect example. Bullshit. Go and buy two cakes. Sit one there and eat the other one. In fact in recent seminars I've been recommending that people actually do that, to have the experience that what they've learned is bullshit.

Participant: ...I eat both cakes.

Gregory: ...Okay. So buy three. Buy more cakes than you need or can possibly eat. Sit them on the table and eat your head off and then look around and say, "I can't eat anymore and I've still got cake." It's a totally powerful process in abundance and prosperity.

I recommend that you actually do that as a process at home. It will change your life.

It will change your prosperity. And it will change your approach to things. The way you and and your wife approach it is, "We can do the Sex and Relationships Seminar or look after the kid." What you need to start to learn to do is say, "I want that and that, so how do I find the solution that gives me all of it?"

That's why people collapse when they don't get what they want. They think, "I can't have it, poor me." Instead say, "Okay. I can have it and I'm not getting it this way."

She'd withdrawn and re-enrolled and withdrawn and re-enrolled with this seminar half a dozen times. Literally until the day before, it was touch and go. The powerful thing is just to own it. "I broke my commitment." The reason why is irrelevant, ultimately. It's interesting but irrelevant.

Participant: ...Gregory I just want to share with everybody that I feel today the most peaceful and relaxed that I can ever, ever remember.

Gregory: Fantastic.

Participant: ...I feel like I've got a lot of people behind me now.

Gregory: You have. Look around.

(everyone laughs)

Participants: ...(everyone) Hi!

Participant: ...I feel quite incomplete about last night.

Gregory: What about last night?

Participant: ...Just the fact that I wanted to complete that thing with myself and I feel quite ill today. And then I thought, "Oh this isn't how I wanted to end up on the Sex Seminar."

Gregory: It's a great way to end The Sex and Relationships Seminar.

Participant: ...Is it?

Gregory: Sure. Yes you feel ill and you feel incomplete about it, but one way of looking at your Sex and Relationships Seminar is that you needed to be here for eight or nine days to feel safe enough with yourself to let this come to the surface. Out of that you'll complete it. Do you know what I mean?

Participant: ...Yeah.

Gregory: So it's actually possible to be here, feel sick and incomplete and also delighted about it.

I can remember as a kid we lived in the countryside and there were bush rats. I remember once a terrible smell somewhere under the house, we knew that something was dead, but we didn't know where it was. We went looking for it, and my Dad and I found it and it stank and it was disgusting. I thought, "Ooh yuk, I don't want to smell it or look at it or touch it." Yet it was a relief because we knew we could do something about it then. That's the place: to have both. When you let yourself have both of those, that's where you get to be complete for now.

Participant: ...Yep. All I knew was that in your questionnaire where it asked, "Have you got any traumatic sexual experiences to heal?" I answered, "Oh there's some past life stuff there and I know it was traumatic but I don't know what it was."

Gregory: Yeah. Where the others are at now is that they knew there was a dead rat and where it was, and last night they chucked it out. You're a step behind: last night you found it but you haven't chucked it out yet.

It's not worse, it's just where you are with that issue. You can be complete about that for now. Give yourself a pat on the back. Very good. Yeah?

Participant: ...I've got a lot of contrasting things going on in my mind.

Gregory: Of course.

Participant: ...I am a bit worried about when I get back to the real world.

Gregory: You're in the real world.

Participant: ...I know but I've unfortunately made this into a little world of my own.

Gregory: So make a little world of your own when you get back home. Look at how I do that in my life.

Actually do it this time. You can create a little world in your mind and retreat into it or you can create your own little world in the world and live in it; know that that's the real world. Those of you who've been down to my seminar centre know that I live in the real world very fully and I create my own world very fully.

It is my choice that my world is filled with people who are living their life and committed to doing their life through doing things like seminars, and there are a few other people in my life who haven't done seminars and they're committed to living their life to the full in other ways.

I fill my world with people who are committed to living their lives as creators. I'm not interested in playing with the others, the victims. I did that for about thirty years and it's dead boring. Yet I definitely live in the real world. The point is to consciously surround yourself with people who fit your value system, who you enjoy being with. The problem you are identifying is that you still see your ideal as unreal, so that living your ideal also appears to be unreal. Your vision of life as shit is still real, so you keep it that way. In the process you get to feel like shit and you get to create more shitiness in the world. Committing to living your vision is not creating "your own little world", it's creating your own big game to play in. I used to live in a real game called the Rescuer and Victim Game. Now I live in the real game called the Being Alive with Other Creatives Game.

Participant: ...I believe I have the same problem.

Gregory: What same problem? I just identified how to end the problem. We don't have the same problem, though we used to.

I get bored with you at times. Sometimes whatever I say you say, "Yes," and then tell me something else that's terrible. In other words you put a lot of energy into what doesn't work, into your fear, instead of putting that amount of energy into doing something about it.

Sometimes you do something about it. Yes? You need to get clear about how you want to have it and then find out how to create that, instead of yo-yoing between how you want it and the old safe shitty place you hang onto. It's that simple.

There is no such thing as "the real world". There are billions of real worlds and everyone creates one. Who's to say whether it's the real world to live in Buckingham Palace or a slum in Calcutta? They're both real worlds. Or to sit here in a seminar. They're all the real world. The name of the game is to choose which one of the games you want to live? That's it. It's that simple.

Participant: ...Part of me is saying that I don't want to leave this space, because it's so safe and nurturing. There's another part of me that's saying, "Right. It's finished. Done. Let's get out there and do it."

Gregory: Who created this space for you?

Participant: ...I did.

Gregory: So take it with you, and then take responsibility for who enters your space. That's what it comes down to. By doing this seminar, you have shown yourself the space you can create for yourself, and you can take it with you. You are responsible for who you let into your space. If you let people crap in your space, don't say, "God I wish I was back on the seminar where I could have it good." Say, "I didn't let people do this on the seminar in my space, so why let it happen now?" Say to the person, "Clean your crap up and go."

That's the thing. It's not something different to your life. You're here. You're alive. So this is your life and this is what you're doing in your life. You've shown yourself what you like to do in your life and how you want to be in your life, so when you go into other areas of your life, it's still your life whether you're sitting in a seminar or sitting in a restaurant; you can always be this version of you, and practice your ability to do that.

Participant: ...Just do it.

Gregory: It's up to you whether or not you treat other people differently to these people. Right? I can be as open with you as with a waiter in a restaurant. It's my choice. There are many signs that say I can't, but I'm not interested in them. The question is, do I want to? Do you?

Most people are going to ask, "What did you do on the seminar?" Then they're going to go and gossip about it, and it becomes distorted, twisted and bent. Most people will ask with absolutely no interest in the seminar - they want a quick naughty hit.

I support you in not encouraging that. As you well know, people do some very strange things around sex and sexuality. Let's say four of you talked about the process you did yesterday, I guarantee that within a month thousands of people will know about it, if not hundreds of thousands.

I would probably have reporters kicking the front door down, and be spread in the papers as, "Weird Sex Guru in Country Orgy Scenes." It's not my intention to hide anything, it's my intention to be consciously in charge of how and when I declare myself to the world about what I know about sex, and what I do with what I know about sex.

That's true for me and to some degree that's also true for you. It's equally true that you could go talking about it and you'll have reporters at your door saying, "Is it true that you were in an orgy with naked men and women the other day?" That's a possibility. That's not the process, but they will hear it that way. I'm acknowledging a possibility that I'm clear I don't choose to create.

One way to not get my head bitten off is not to put my head in the lion's mouth. At some point when I am ready, I will fully declare myself, where, when, with whom and how I choose.

A lot of you talked to me about this Sex and Relationships Seminar. Did I tell you what happens on it?

Participants: ...(everyone) No.

Gregory: You all came and did this seminar without knowing much about it at all.

All you had to go on was my word and your trust. You don't need to tell anyone about this seminar. You don't need to sort out the genuine enquiries from the titillating enquiries. Whoever asks you about it will sort that out.

You have a choice about what you share with whom. I share a lot of stuff in The Living Game Seminar that I don't share with people generally. I've shared a hell of a lot more this seminar that I don't share on that seminar. That's my choice.

This is a reactive subject. People have got a lot of issues. You have taken the risk to clear a lot of those issues, and it's fine to give yourself a margin of safety in the way you deal with people about it. Go out and share to the degree that you feel totally safe about sharing. Maybe if people say, “Oh, I hear you did The Sex and Relationships Seminar. How was it?” and you say, “Fantastic.” Then let's say they ask, “What happened?” and you can say, “It's all confidential and all I'm going to say about it is that it was fantastic, and if you want some great value go and do it.”

Leave it at that. That's fine. Or you may want to sit down and share some of the realizations you got, the things you moved, the breakthroughs you had.

The value is in your experience not in how you got it. Above and beyond saying, “On The Sex and Relationships Seminar I got this experience…” it may have been you got it by going in there today and washing the dishes and had a realization. That's not the point.

Participant: …While this has been a Sex Seminar and we've dealt with a lot of sexual issues, nearly all of what we've talked about is applicable to life in general. So you can talk about it in those terms. Like, for instance, commitment.

Gregory: Yeah. That's why I call it The Sex AND Relationship Seminar …it's your relationship with you, then with others and your world. How you do your sexuality affects all of your life, and when you deal with your sexual issues that clears those issues throughout your whole life. You can't separate them!

Participant: …Just one of the major things I've got is about going for what I want, for my truth.

Commitment and all of that is scary for me. And I really know that when I do that and practice it the easier it will get. And I'm willing to go for it.

Gregory: Okay. So that links into the next thing which is - what next? That's scary for you. He's concerned that he's got to go back into the rest of the world. So the next thing to look at and handle is, what are you going to create to support yourselves in continuing this space in your life? What do you want to create?

Participant: ...I realized why I'm here. I saw why I created my experience of my parents and my past and that is to reach out to people and to touch people on a world level.

Gregory: Yep. So what are you waiting for?

By the way, enrolling people in seminars only works when you're being totally selfish.

What that means to me is that I tell people about seminars because I want more people to play this game of life with fully. One of the reasons that I kept myself struggling with money was to get to a point where I was 100% clear that I wasn't doing this for the money. You'd have to be an idiot to be doing this for the money the way I've done it.

What I saw was that I may never get a lot of money out of this; so do I want to keep doing it? The answer was a 100% Yes. Then it was safe to make money and get paid appropriately and abundantly for the value I add to people's lives. So I do this because I want to share what I've learned. Being Instructor in your life looks like you sharing with others what you've learned.

The opportunity for you, the payoff for you, is like the payoff for me, which is I get a lot more creative and enthusiastic people to play with. That's what enrollment is for me. See, my job isn't to get people into seminars, that's not enrollment for me, that's sales. My job is to let people know it's available if they want it. You get the difference?

So I just let everyone know it's available. That's why I'm doing media. Because I believe that there's lots more people out there waiting to hear that it's available, and it's fine with me if they do it or they don't. My job isn't to put bums on seats, it's to let them know that there's seats there, so to speak. So do your version of that. Tell, don't sell.

Participant: ...I keep getting this sense of, I didn't make it. I'm not good enough. I think, I don't stay with my truth and when I don't stay with my truth I go into, "I'm not good enough. I didn't make it. I didn't get it." Damn.

Gregory: Beating yourself up for it doesn't help. What works is to say, "Ah ha, that's where I am and that's where I'm not. This is where I am now, what's the next step?"

Participant: ...So it's an acknowledgement of where I am in it.

Gregory: Yes. You're one of the people who came very close and you didn't complete everything you came here for. Yet. What you know is that you've come a hell of a long way and there's something left to learn that you want to master. The truth is that when you don't complete something or you give up on yourself you feel ratshit. When you're sick of feeling ratshit, that will motivate you to stop giving up and keep completing.

Participant: ...Yeah. Thank you.

Gregory: That's the payoff. It's not that you're wrong for not doing it. If I thought that you or anyone else was wrong for not doing it, I couldn't have sat here giving this seminar. That's not where it's at. The value for me is for you to say, "This is where I am," and not con myself about where I am. I love you for where you are not for where you're not and not for where you can be. Put simply, "Yep, she's real close and she's not there. And I love her."

Participant: ...Yes. I love me for where I am and for where I'm going.

Gregory: That's true for everyone. That's how you get to be where you are. One of the ways you get to be where you are is to be honest about where you're not. Value yourself for who you are and what you have achieved and then make a choice about what you haven't. "Do I want to do that or not?" If yes, then find out how. For example, years ago I got to see that I took my shirt off for social contact with people. That gave me a new choice.

You got to about 98% of what you set out to create. That is rather brilliant and the remaining 2% will come. Well done!

We're going to do a completion process and I'll explain it in a minute. Then what's there to do is pack your stuff, clean up and go home safely.

Okay. Fantastic. Let's do that. And before you do, I would like to make a group acknowledgement of thanking you all for being here and acknowledge every one of you, I know what it took for you to get here, and that is called courage. I acknowledge you all for being here doing your 100% for these ten days. I acknowledge you for honoring me, and you, in that, and for our creating the opportunity for me to have the most amazing ten days of my life. Unquestionably and unconditionally. And for me getting a whole new load of evidence and reinforcement about why I'm doing what I'm doing. To put that simply, thank you for inspiring me yet again.

Participant: ...Your commitment is incredible.

Gregory: Thank you.

Participant: ...And thank you for creating this amazing space for all of us.

Gregory: My pleasure.

The Seminar ends

Glossary

Acknowledge: is to state what is so, what is real, actual and true, to name. We are taught to NOT acknowledge ourselves and each other for Who we are, only for what we DO. True acknowledgement is without judgement of positive or negatives, but of what just IS.

Blank: see 'going blank'

Bonk: n. the act of sex v. to have sex with another person

Catharsis: n. The process of releasing, and thereby providing relief from, strong or repressed emotions.

Commit: Commitment: To commit to an outcome, to truly commit, leaves no room to NOT do the commitment. Excuses and reasons for not completing a commitment are covering up the fact that the commitment has NOT been kept, but has been broken. Excuses and reasons all say "I do not have the power to fulfill my word. Circumstances 'out there' have more power than I do." To truly commit is to say "I will ...(no matter what it takes...)" then doing it, no matter what it takes. (I am not advising law-breaking, by the way.) To complete thus creates Will-Power, the power of your Will to create desired results and outcomes.

Cot: in the USA is a baby's crib.

Create: (a) v. Bring (something) into existence: "he created a lake"; "jobs were created".

v. Cause (something) to happen as a result of one's actions.

A core idea of the seminar is that we create the whole of our lives either consciously (with awareness) or unconsciously (from either past-life or this life hidden choices and patterns). If and when we take responsibility for what we have created then we can change it i.e. create something else.

Crook: sick, wrong, bad, poorly, ineffective.

Date: dating has different cultural meaning in Australia than it does in America, where it implies a serious relationship approaching possible marriage. In Oz it is rarely used and when it is means you are in some relationship now together with no implication into the future. So, a coffee date or a dinner date.

Disappear: when you fully acknowledge something in your life and take full responsibility for having somehow attracted it or created it you then have a new choice about it, which may be to make it disappear. This also requires seeing the value of why you attracted it, or created it. While you do NOT take responsibility for creating it then you are saying you have no power in the matter, that it "happened" to you, and so you are stuck with it. As well when you master a challenge, it disappears. Once you master the challenge of riding a bike, the riding is easy. The challenge has disappeared.

Dross: n. Something regarded as worthless; rubbish.

Follower-ship: while we hear a lot about leader-ship little is said about follower-ship in our dominant and dominating control culture. A leader can only be as good a leader as his or her team are good followers. The art and mastery of followership requires that the followers, team members, are taking full responsibility for their role and for their choice to create and support the leader to be the best possible. It means putting ego aside for the best outcome to be created.

Get: to understand, to comprehend.

Going blank: when a person 'disappears' on themselves, or an issue, or moment in time. This will occur when they enter into an area of their own unconsciousness. So in the seminar if Gregory addresses a certain issue and that issue was big and painful for a participant, they might 'check out' and just not hear or take in what is being said. They go 'blank'.

Guru: there are three types of Guru. (a) it is a common term in Asia and India for any teacher of any subject. (b) Many Western gurus take a position that says that they have your answers. (c) Gregory's type of guru is one who tells people G, U - R - U (Gee, you are you.) as a teacher.

Masks: (also see the Self): In Gregory's seminars he uses a model to explain how we got to be who we are now. Our Self - which is perfect - got the message that we had to be a certain way to be loved and valued as we grew up. That then became a performance of who we were, hiding Who we Are! We presented ourselves in a certain way to get love and that became our front mask. That also created a second hidden mask of what we were scared others would see about us because we learned that those parts of us were negatively judged and so resulted in a loss of love and approval. Our mask becomes our "person-ality", a weak version of the totality of our Being.

Own: is to take responsibility for whatever we create, whatever occurs in our lives.

Past life, reincarnation: Billions of human beings believe that we have many lives whereas some believe we have only one. For many Westerners the idea that we have many lives makes more sense and answers many questions that a one-life belief does not.

Primal (see Catharsis): is a process of learning to release, through sound and movement, deeply buried hurts, pains and fears from childhood that at the time were too big to feel or too dangerous or unacceptable to express. So they remain buried and have a great affect on our lives, until they are released. They hold enormous energy and it takes an equal amount of energy to keep them repressed. Once felt (old sadness cried out, old anger yelled out etc.) they disappear, leaving new space and energy for new emotional choices instead of being stuck in old emotional patterns and reactions.

Process: (a) a process (noun) is a discreet series of steps designed to get a given result. e.g. there is a clear process of mixing sand, gravel, cement and water to make concrete. Equally there are steps (processes) to improve communications, to heal old emotional hurts and wounds, to create new results, and many more. (b) To process (verb) is to digest, assimilate, sort through new information, realizations, ideas, awakenings and more.

Reincarnation: see 'Past Life'

Script, scripted: In seminars I invite people to play with the idea that their life is like a movie that they (or their Higher Self) scripted for them, and then to write new scripts. As a result people move out of old limiting boxes and create the lives they dream.

Self: Who we Truly Are, the Soul, Spirit, the Is, the Being, the Creator, the God(ess) within. Our true Self is who we really are and who we were (let's say) at birth, before we were shaped, moulded, limited, wounded etc. My "Self" is the me who knows the plan and has chosen the best Path for my life. My Self has chosen the perfect moment, family and circumstances to start this life in order to have the story, the script, that it/I need to have the lessons and experiences for my Spirit to grow, learn and expand through this life. It is also called the Soul, the 'Is'. When we limit our Self (with masks) we get to present a small version of ourselves, the self, or ego, the parts of us that we identify as being ourself.

The Living Game Seminar: a three day seminar taught by Gregory in many countries to thousands of people in groups up to 20 people over the past 28 years. Participants have a profound experience of their own value, beauty, potential and power to create their dreams and visions, and then they do. The seminar gives people new choices in life and new techniques and methods to make those new choices actually happen. People experience previously impossible results with health, family and other personal relationships, releasing their creativity, aliveness and more.

Twigged: to realize, to have an insight or a recalled memory of something.

Value: Gregory's starting point is that we are all valuable, that we all seek to grow and accumulate value, and to dis-cover and un-cover our inherent value and beauty as fully formed and expressed humans Being. We are all Living Human Treasures and we have been taught and conditioned to hide our inner value: taught that we must get and buy value from outside of ourselves, and to identify our value through possessions etc. to fill the emptiness.

Acknowledgements

This book could never have been born without the investment of time, money, skills, resources, love, encouragement and support of many, many people.

That includes all of those 40 people on the seminar herein, and the tens of thousands before and after them who have attended my seminars and talks and who continue to spread the word that they gained great value with me, thus encouraging others to attend to grow their value in their lives.

When I think about who to acknowledge, and where to begin, I must start with a loving smile toward my family: my parents, Stella and Charlie, and my brothers Kevin, Garry and Jeff. I thank you all for all the love and support you have offered me through the years, especially when I challenged you in some way! Then to our greatly extended family of Irish Australians with about 40 uncles and aunties and many, many cousins, all of whom maintained strong bonds, and all of whom were my early fertile ground for growing and building loving relationships. Every one of them was, and is, special to me.

So very many people have had such important places and roles in my life, both positive and negative, to give me the gifts, lessons and challenges I needed to get here, and to become who I am. I love every one of them including the bastards among them, and there were a few, all my necessary teachers.

The past 12 years I have been something of a hermit, supported by the gifts and love of friends who knew me and believed in my Quest and Vision which is now, with this book, re-entering the world with me.

Of those many people I must first and foremost thank my beloved son, Luke Seer, who never for a moment wavered in his love for me and sharing with me, and who has in all ways been the most amazing son and friend any man could ever ask for or imagine, and who has inspired and taught many others as well as me since his birth. It was Luke who who created the wonderful Yin/Yang symbol on the cover of this book. It is my ultimate symbol for healthy inner and outer relationship.

As well my Aussie friend of nearly three decades, Domenic Lattari, who was a participant on the seminar of this book, and who has been a stalwart friend throughout these past many years, and who designed this book. Dom built my website with his wife and my friend Karen Lattari. They are soul mates who met and came together in my home in Colorado and I never let them forget it!

Karen Jokela has been my first and greatest friend and cheerleader in America, 'seeing' me and my vision from the start, and backing that up in every way she could. She is a true visionary and urban shaman in her own right, and one with a high mystic Spirit indeed.

At a critical time of development of this book appeared the wonderful Katrina Pratt to be my personal assistant, life apprentice and loving friend. Kat has done an enormous amount of work helping us to develop this book, adding great value along the way, including writing the Foreword.

My deep appreciation goes to my guardian angel, Pam Schilhab and her daughter Kristen Kauffman, who keep my affairs in order for me, freeing me for my gypsy lifestyle. They are two beautiful quality women and pillars of strength for me.

I must make special mention of Mike and Karen Rudat who have become trusted friends, being there in so many ways to support me to unreasonable degrees at all times, and who have applied my teachings to their lives with great mutual enhancement, and who proclaim that to all who will listen!

Thank you.

There are so many people who directly made my path, and this book, possible over these past few years. I thank you from the bottom of my heart.

I owe so much to all of these friends, and to the many others over the years I have not included. My life is so much a better, richer and more fulfilling place to be because they share it with me. I am honored to be able to give them this public acknowledgement, which they all so richly deserve, as good, good, good high quality, idealistic people, doing their best and highest lives for the good of all. These people are all an inspiration and a bulwark for me. Thank you.

I also acknowledge and thank all of the women who have passed through my life, or who are still in it, who have been friends, lovers, or adversaries. Each and every one of you has taught me, and reflected aspects of my inner female, guiding me to uncover and discover the Divine Feminine within me to balance the Sacred Masculine, as so perfectly captured by my son Luke's Yin/Yang symbol.

Hall of Fame (in first name alphabetical order)

Ali Everett
Asha Kirana
Bob Braudis
Bobby Richards
Bobby Wood
Bud Wilson
Glenda Walden
Holland Franklin
Ian Graham
Janice Hall
John Van Ness
Lauren Rae Champa
Marie Burrows
Maura Hoffman
Paul Johnson
Rennie Davis
Robbie Goodwin
Rob Wyatt
Susan Wheeler
Trevor Hart
Wil Higley

Thank you all.

Gregory Charles, San Diego, 2011

About Gregory Charles

Gregory Charles is a true Master. He will open and enlighten you to who you are, to your best version and expression of you, to have the best life you can have.

Being with him is an experience in powerful humanity: laughter, integrity, commitment, compassion and so much more that has uplifted the lives of some 50,000 people around the world who have attended his seminars, talks and lectures.

Over the past 35 years of world travel, study, research, exploration, and living his life to the full, he has astonished social and business leaders, academics, professionals, and others in a dozen countries with his wisdom and knowledge, simplicity, genius, clarity, humanity and availability. Gregory has met heads of State, been hugged by the Dalai Lama and had his hand kissed by a Pope. His work has been publicly endorsed by members of The Royal Colleges of Physicians, and Surgeons.

Traveling, living and studying in many countries he has merged the best of the knowledge of the East and West - of traditional and alternate approaches - to everyday realities to have Life be all it can be.

He has created a body of knowledge that teaches people how to themselves become Masters by learning to master more and more aspects of their own lives.

Gregory's wisdom has helped heal and enhance tens of thousands of lives in all arenas - love and relationships, business, family, finances, sexuality, health and wellbeing - to increase overall quality of life and spiritual meaning, direction and purpose.

He teaches people how to access, define and create their highest best versions of themselves and the lives that they want, over and over and over again. This understanding of life is for everyone who wants more quality, and is committed to being the best human being they can be. People attending his seminars, talks and lectures have represented every religion, 36 nationalities, all political stripes, ages, backgrounds and occupations. .

This has led to him being interviewed on national TV, radio and print media, in Australia, New Zealand, America and the UK, and having articles he has written published in them. He has appeared on 'Good Morning America' and MTV with Carmen Electra.

Gregory has also been a Visiting International Lecturer at UC Boulder, The London School of Economics, Henley-on-Thames Business School and was a Consultant Faculty Member at UCLA teaching alternate healing.

We live in an age of almost incomprehensible change and equally we are striving to adapt and grow to integrate all of this change. Gregory teaches us new ways to adapt, to handle the change, to embrace our growth with passion and excitement and to flow easily with ourselves in our ever-transforming lives.

For great free content from Gregory Charles:

www.TheAussieRelationshipGuru.com

Free video at:

www.youtube.com/user/gregoryaussie

REAL AMERICA SERIES (10)

AMERICAN CULTURE SERIES (6)

COMMITMENT SERIES (4)

More coming!

Published by Look At It LLC.

www.ingramcontent.com/pod-product-compliance
Lightning Source LLC
Chambersburg PA
CBHW072009270326
41928CB00009B/1596

* 9 7 8 0 9 8 4 9 4 0 1 0 3 *